THE BOMBER OFFENSIVE

THE Bomber Offensive

Anthony Verrier

THE MACMILLAN COMPANY

940.544
√

Library of Congress Catalog Card Number: 76-75410

FIRST AMERICAN EDITION 1969

First published in Great Britain in 1968 by B. T. Batsford Ltd., London.

The Macmillan Company

Printed in the United States of America

Contents

Part III

THE YEAR OF STRUGGLE 1943

Part IV

THE YEARS OF SUCCESS 1944–1945

The Illustrations

The Maps

Acknowledgments

Any list of acknowledgements is either invidious or inadequate. So many people have helped me in so many different ways with this history that to specify the nature and extent of each contribution would much weary the reader. It seemed best therefore simply to list those to whom I have written, or interviewed, or turned to for help or relied on as one source of information. I am conscious that there may be omissions, but whether that be the case or not, I am grateful beyond measure to all who have helped me in a task where reliance on official records is not always possible. Finally, I must express particular thanks to Mrs Caroline Cox and Mrs Rose Quint, who have tackled a complex manuscript with unfailing efficiency and good humour, and to Mr David Merryweather, who has so skilfully drawn the maps and diagrams. I should like to add my grateful thanks to the staff of the Royal United Service Institution for their help and co-operation at all times.

My thanks are due also to the following:
Air-Vice Marshal E. B. Addison, Mrs J. Andrew, the late Rt. Hon. Lord Attlee, Air Marshal Sir John Baldwin, D. J. Beere, Flight Lieutenant F. J. Belfitt, Air Vice-Marshal D. C. T. Bennett, Lord Boothby, Air Chief Marshal Sir Norman Bottomley, Wing Commander R. L. Bowes, Air Vice-Marshal S. O. Bufton, Lord Butler, Air Vice-Marshal A. J. Capel, Group Captain Leonard Cheshire, J. T. Chrystal, Air Chief Marshal the Hon. Sir Ralph Cochrane, Captain W. G. Cole, R. Collison, Dr David Cooke, Group Captain S. P. Coulson, Air Commodore J. Davis, Sir Maurice Dean, Marshal of the Royal Air Force Sir William Dickson, Wing Commander D. F. Dixon, J. A. Dixon, Mrs Violet Dorehill, Lord Douglas of Kirtleside, Sir James Dunnett, General Ira C. Eaker, John Ehrman, Air Chief Marshal Sir Charles Elworthy, David Farrer, Dr Noble Frankland, Roger Fulford, Mrs E. Gaythorpe, Air Chief Marshal Sir John Grandy, Squadron Leader W. G. Green, L. H. Gregson, Vice Admiral Sir Peter Gretton, Group Captain R. G. Harman, Marshal of the Royal Air Force Sir Arthur Harris, Air Vice Marshal R. Harrison, M. W. Hartford, A. E. Heron, R. M. Hilliard, Adrian Hore, H. H. Houghton, Professor Michael Howard, Commandant Itart-Longueville, David Irving, Air Chief Marshal Sir Ronald Ivelaw-Chapmen, L. A. Jacketts, D. A. Jackson, Major General W. G. F. Jack-

son, Squadron Leader P. Jacobs, Professor R. V. Jones, F. George Kay, Air Chief Marshal Sir Wallace Kyle, Flight Lieutenant J. S. La Planche, Major P. Le Clus, Roger A. Leonard, Flight Lieutenant D. P. McElligott, the late Captain I. A. P. Macintyre, Lieutenant Colonel Jan Markowski, Air Vice-Marshal H. B. Martin, Rt. Hon. Reginald Maudling, E. Y. Oliver, L. Overton, Kenneth Pagett, Flight Sergeant M. D. J. Parkinson, Air Chief Marshal Sir Richard Peirse, Lord Portal of Hungerford, Eric T. Rawlins, Wing Commander W. D. Rooney, Captain S. W. Roskill, Dr A. P. Rowe, Air Marshal Sir Robert Saundby, Wing Commander C. W. Scott, Group Captain L. C. Slee, Marshal of the Royal Air Force Sir John Slessor, General Carl A. Spaatz, C. P. Stacey, R. A. Stamp, W. J. Taunton, the late Marshal of the Royal Air Force Lord Tedder, Wing Commander R. W. Turner, Air Chief Marshal Sir Augustus Walker, Air Commodore J. Wallace, Squadron Leader J. W. Ward, J. P. Wynton.

The Author and Publishers would like to thank Her Majesty's Stationery Office for permission to quote freely, and to include the Appendices on pages 326–42, from the Official History of the *Strategic Air Offensive Against Germany 1939–1945.* Acknowledgement is also due to the following authors, agents and publishers for permission to quote from the books listed: Andrew Boyle, *Trenchard*, William Collins Sons & Co Ltd; Ronald W. Clark, *Tizard*, Rupert Crew Ltd; W. E. Craven and J. L. Cate, *The Army Air Forces in World War II*, University of Chicago Press; David Divine, *The Broken Wing*, Hutchinson Publishing Group Ltd; Noble Frankland, *Bombing Offensive Against Germany*, Faber & Faber Ltd; Guy Gibson, *Enemy Coast Ahead*, David Higham Associates, Ltd; R. R. Greenfield, *Command Decisions*, Harcourt, Brace & World Inc.; Sir Arthur Harris, *Bomber Offensive*, David Higham Associates, Ltd; John Herington, *Air War Against Germany and Italy 1939–43*, Australian War Memorial; Denis Richards, *Royal Air Force 1939–45*, HMSO; S. W. Sears and M. W. McFarland, *Air War Against Hitler's Germany*, American Heritage Publishing Co. Inc.; William L. Shirer, *The Rise and Fall of the Third Reich*, Martin Secker & Warburg Ltd.

The author and publishers also wish to thank the following for permission to reproduce the illustrations in this book: Associated Press for figs. 19, 20, 34 and 44; Bildarchiv Knorr and Hirth for fig. 2; *Flight* for fig. 1; Imperial War Museum for figs. 3–18, 21–23, 25–27, 31, 37, 38–41, 43, 45 and 51; Planet News for fig. 30; Süddeutscher Verlag, Munich for figs. 32, 33, 35, 48 and 50; Verlag Ullstein, Berlin for figs. 36, 42, 49, 52 and 53; US Air Force for figs. 29, 46, 47; US Army Photo for figs. 24 and 28.

The maps on the endpapers and on pages 84, 259 and 268 are, with the permission of HM Stationery Office, based on material in the British Official History; those on pages 178 and 268 are adapted from material in the German and American Official Histories.

Preface

The book which follows is an account of what happened over Germany between 1939 and 1945. It is one writer's account, although he has been supported and sustained by many former participants in, or observers of, this longest of campaigns in modern war. But being personal and unofficial, the account will unavoidably be received subjectively by the reader, however great has been the effort to be objective in seeking facts, telling the tale and drawing conclusions. If the Official History of the offensive—a very Clarendon among narratives—could not escape the most pungent attacks of its critics when published in 1961, it is hardly likely that what I have set down will, in some at least of its episodes and analysis, pass unchallenged. I hope therefore that readers will reflect on the reasons for writing this book and the conditions under which it has been undertaken.

The reasons are, I hope, made plain in the Introduction and the underlying structure of both the analytical and narrative passages which govern much of this detailed history. The air offensive conducted against Germany for four years and seven months, night and day, with clear success sometimes, with dogged resolution always, is more relevant to contemporary strategic issues than the analyst of purely nuclear matters would believe. The control of the offensive—and, as sometimes happened, the lack of well-defined control—are relevant to any consideration of the conduct of strategy today. The only person likely to disagree is he who believes that war is safest in the hands of Generals—or Air Marshals. It is not for such a person, if any now exist in the Western world, that this book is intended.

Some words on the manner in which I have worked are, however, exclusive to a preface. The book is not only unofficial, it is more limited in research and hence scale than a definitive study can dare to be. It was

originally hoped to produce a work not dissimilar in concept and scale
to Mr Robert Rhodes James' *Gallipoli*; and I may add, personally, that,
although such a work would certainly have fallen far short of that magis-
terial piece of history, the opportunity to write in comparable detail of
a campaign infinitely more prolonged but, in some curious ways, not
unlike that Eastern adventure, was not happily or easily cast aside. But,
in fact, British history can only be written on the *Gallipoli* scale if the
authors are official or the period sufficiently remote to enable those living
to feel comfortably irresponsible about it. In short the 'thirty-year rule'
and the habit which British Ministers of the Crown have of regarding
State papers as their private preserve are an effective bar to the unofficial
seeker after definitive truth about recent events.

This we may know. But there are some other factors which apply to
anyone who writes about the strategic air offensive—arguably Britain's
last throw as a major, and independent military power—even though the
political premises which underpinned the aerial battle against Germany
still obtain with the role of Strike Command today, facing a rather more
formidable opponent. The first of these factors is that the Official History of
the offensive was published a mere six years ago. This is a work massive in
scale, unrivalled in documentation, brilliant in analysis of operational
problems, sympathetic in narration of operations as such—but hesitant and
uncertain in its conclusions about whether the campaign was an outright
British victory, a major contribution to allied victory, or a relatively
unsuccessful display of brute force, only redeemed in the last nine months
of the war by striking power which was of unprecedented weight, accuracy
and destructiveness.

No true student of the offensive can fail to understand Sir Charles
Webster's and Dr Noble Frankland's doubts. They were charged to
record for posterity and for the enlightenment of future generations of
strategists a campaign as bloody as any in all history, which was dominated
in those who directed the offensive part by a profound belief in the supremacy of air power, plus a complementary unwillingness to consider
whether those conducting and forming the defence might not prove to be
exceptionally resourceful and brave—as, in a shameful cause, Germans at
all levels found themselves to be. Here, in short, was a mystery—why
did the Royal Air Force and the United States Army Air Forces fail to
'knock Germany out of the War'? In these words, attributed to Sir Arthur
Harris,[1] is summed up the belief that air power dominated all modern war,
wherever and however conducted. The history of the strategic air offensive, based on 12 years' research, a rare combination of talent and a deep

native desire to honour those who died, revealed, if unintentionally, that air power did not so dominate.

In one sense, therefore, Webster and Frankland is true history. Turn the pages and the 'business of war' is seen as what we know it to be—muddle, contradiction, inter-Service and personal rivalries inflamed rather than softened by issues of victory or defeat, the energetic effort to impose order on conflict vying with ignorance or faulty analysis of the enemy's plans and power. But in another sense Webster and Frankland give us only half the story. Despite the sheer quantity of sources cited or noted, all too often an interesting track towards the truth fades out in a thicket of non-committal text, with no guide to why, say, long-range escorts were not planned for Bomber Command, or why intelligence from agents in Germany was so consistently poor. I cannot claim to have solved these secondary mysteries, but at least the following pages may throw an odd shaft of light or two on their nature and relevance to the history of air power in the age of the manned, subsonic aircraft.

Webster and Frankland are also discreet—and doubtless so from inhibitions laid down by higher authority—about several major issues which affected the conduct of the offensive. Chief of these was quite simply Anglo-American relations, that hardy perennial of international necessities and rivalries. Virtually nothing is said about a relationship which was —and is—as much concerned with Humpty Dumpty's 'It's a question of who's master . . .', as it is with a common front against foes. Perspective would have been introduced into the history of what, after the 1943 Casablanca Conference, was formally known as the 'Combined Bomber Offensive', if the British authors had dealt openly with one issue typified by what General Arnold wrote to General Spaatz in 1944, apropos of the latter's relations with General Eisenhower: 'I want him to recognise you as the top airmen in all Europe.'[2]

Of this more later, but it must be said that we have to turn to the history of the USAAF in World War Two by W. E. Craven and J. L. Cate for a candid account of what took place in the corridors of air power, whether in Washington or Whitehall. These American scholars display none of the doubts afflicting Webster and Frankland; they see no need to disguise the unequal relationship between an expanding and a declining power. They are courteous about it, but the necessity of considering the bombing of Germany as much as a matter of compromise between unequal allies as of the application of available and economic force is never in doubt.

By contrast, Webster and Frankland minimise the importance of several strategic factors deriving from the capacity of the American military

arsenal to meet challenges from the enemy which were as much physical
as conceptual. For example, it is not until page 135 of Volume III that we
read: 'It is, indeed, difficult to see how night air superiority could ever
have been gained if day air superiority had not first been achieved.' Day
air superiority came when the USAAF Fortresses and Liberators were
escorted by the Mustang fighter; the latter's success as a long-range escort
was based on technological skill and industrial resources, not on strategic
insight.

It follows therefore that Webster and Frankland eventually arouse in
the reader a sense of paradox. An extreme example of scholarship devoted
to the sifting of evidence still leaves one wondering what personal, let
alone historical, factors governed the strategic air offensive. Although Sir
Arthur Harris, from a sort of elemental tenacity of purpose and simplicity
of conviction, does emerge to arouse positive, if not invariably commen-
datory reactions, his superiors and subordinates remain grey and colour-
less. In particular, the verbal strife—for it was no less—between the
Commander-in-Chief Bomber Command and the Chief of the Air Staff
is quoted or cited, dealt with fastidiously and euphemistically, but never
subject to scrutiny. For the short point is that Harris ignored Portal's
pleas to consider whether flexibility might not be introduced into the
offensive once command of the air was won; when orders replaced
requests, Harris ignored those too. Harris may have been right to act as
he did; what is significant—and relevant to contemporary issues—is that
he was allowed so free a hand to execute a strategy he alone at the level
of high command believed in with total and undeviating fervour.

Ironically, one result of this undue discretion has been to present a
distorted picture of the Commander-in-Chief. He was neither the ogre—
'Butcher' Harris—nor the oracle—'Bomber' Harris—that popular
account has portrayed. Here, let us simply say that he was a Commander
who caught Churchill's fancy in 1942 when defeat was a more distinct
possibility for the British Empire than it was in 1940 for Britain alone.
But he was also a Commander whose fight for his Service and whose
conviction that killing German civilians would win the war lost him
favour and support in high places once victory seemed assured by more
conventional methods. He was less fortunate than Haig, who in many
ways he so strongly resembles, in being overtaken by events, by a combination of factors resulting in the unconditional surrender of Hitler's
armies, a situation in which Bomber Command seemed to be of rather
less account than the allied armies, competing for the division of Germany.
Shortly after came Hiroshima and Nagasaki, and Sir Arthur Harris and

the 55,000 British and Commonwealth airmen, most of whom died under his command, passed into a strategic limbo—or so it seemed at the time. Only now perhaps can we put this singular commander into some sort of strategic perspective.

And it is at this point that I must mention the variety of methods used in the attempt to treat of the strategic air offensive as the personal, heroic and terrible business that it was. Despite the inhibitions which have just been described, Webster and Frankland remain indispensable to any who come after them, as, with their grasp of strategic fundamentals, do Craven and Cate. Material kindly placed at my disposal by Mr L. A. Jacketts and his Staff of the Air Historical Branch has often provided corroboration of suppositions if rarely confirmation of suspicions. All too often the missing link lay hidden. But it is essential to give one instance here, at the Prefatory stage, of how what is officially presented to the public gaze differs from what lies secreted in official archives.

Perhaps unwittingly, official accounts of the offensive tend to describe the period from the outbreak of war until Harris' arrival at Bomber Command in February 1942 as one where crews deluded themselves they were finding and hitting their designated targets, when in fact they were not. Hence, via intelligence summaries, a similar delusion prevailed in the War Cabinet. The truth, however, as revealed by a study of what aircrews actually put in their reports, is that they knew quite well how infrequently their sorties succeeded. That misleading accounts of the offensive in those years were sent to the Air Staff and thence to the Cabinet reflects on the natural if dangerous wish of intelligence officers and commanders to look on the bright side, or devise one. But the crews were as little deluded in 1939, 1940 and 1941 as they were in more successful days thereafter.

This discovery about what air crews knew to be happening—or rather, not happening—affords a clue to the indifferent quality and indeed paucity of personal published accounts. The offensive to those fighting in it was nothing much to write home about. It has no Richard Hillary, certainly no Cecil Lewis or St Exupery. Mr H. E. Bates, transmogrified in war-time as 'Flying Officer X', did his considerable best to convey the atmosphere of operational flying, but, to this groundling at least, the stories bear little relation to the ineffable monotony shot with fear, fatigue, determination and—very occasionally—professional interest, which comprised the fighting over Germany.

And although Dr Frankland, responsible for the narrative parts of the Official History, was a navigator with a full tour of 30 operations to his credit, he was prevented by lack of space from doing more than allude to outstanding feats or conveying in its briefest form the challenge to courage and discipline entailed in flying over the armed anti-bomber camp that occupied Europe was in those years. Naturally, other publications of an analytical nature—few enough in all consequence—concentrate on the nature, not the execution of the offensive. The 'Grand Strategy' volumes so far published in the *History of the Second World War* treat the offensive perfunctorily, but in this they only reflect a similar treatment by the Supreme Command. The sacrifice of these thousands of young men has therefore received little written recognition. Just as so many of them have 'no known grave', few are more than a memory.

The least of my claims is that I have been able to remedy this deficiency. But just as the many interviews with commanders and their like afforded essential insight into some dark corners of the offensive, so the dozens of occasions on which civilians in the forties and fifties returned to their young manhood and recalled their part in the bombing of Germany have provided the foundation for narrating it. What emerged for me in the course of these talks was example upon example of Stevenson's 'dour, cauld, deidly courage'. If, unlike Stephen Spender's heroes the crews of Bomber Command did not leave 'the vivid air signed with their honour',[3] they left their bodies in a land where recourse to war should, at last, be seen as utterly fruitless. Let that lesson be their epitaph.

Introduction

The Bomber Offensive was neither a victory nor a defeat. Its essential modernity is just that it lacks a decisive form; no second Creasey is likely to chronicle a battle whose contribution to the final defeat of Germany lay as much in the fact that it was waged at all in the face of mounting odds, as in the manner in which those odds were, finally, surmounted. Total war does not produce total decisions. Even in the distant years of World War Two, when unprecedented destruction and suffering was meted out and received, the 'Thunderclap' theory of strategy (to borrow one of the planners' less obviously inapposite code names) was constantly falsified by actual events.

Yet 'a contribution to victory' is, to the strategic purist, a damning phrase. 'Victory, speedy and complete'[1] was promised by Sir Arthur Harris when he urged upon Churchill in mid-1942 the concentration of bombing operations against great German towns—an end to dissipation of resources in support of the U-boat campaign and that conducted by the Army in North Africa, above all a quietus to the debate about which German targets offered the best returns. Although the core of Harris' belief was empiric rather than analytical, being governed by experience that the strategically feasible was dependent on the operationally possible, his advocacy has come to be taken as the most positive expression of belief in air power.

Smuts, Trenchard, Mitchell and Douhet were its protagonists in the breathing space between the world wars; since the latter's end, the doctrine of air power as the arbiter of grand strategy has hardly lacked champions; the nuclear bomb may appear to have relegated the lumbering Lancaster and all that it evokes to the scrap heap, but the notion that air power remains novel and dwarfs all other strategies is largely responsible for the size of defence budgets and the shape of defence policy in Britain, the

United States, the Soviet Union and France. Events may again negative the value of the notion, but, as of now, it still flourishes.

Why? This Introduction is concerned with seeking an answer to that question, because, unless we understand its controversial nature, it will be possible neither to appreciate the course of the strategic air offensive nor the courage with which those who waged it went to their deaths. Equally, the relevance of bombing operations between 1939 and 1945 to those contemplated and executed since then can only be appreciated by recognising the intense convictions sustaining the proponents of air power. The aerial offensive against the Viet Cong and North Viet Nam is believed in utterly—or repudiated utterly. The very nature of an independent air offensive makes for partisanship and public debate.

The short answer to the question is that the twentieth-century version of total and global war has led to a search for deterrents to it, but one on the whole conducted by men whose capacity for taking a political or strategic argument to its logical conclusions has been rather less than their wish to preserve the fabric of national armed forces and, above all other considerations, retain separate and, so far as it is administratively and operationally possible, independent services for the planning and the prosecution of campaigns by sea, land or air.

This central issue of control, or, more narrowly, of preservation, either transcending or absorbing what should properly take priority in national defence policy—moral considerations, however tender and likely to be nipped by the frost of war, or strategic requirements, however much the creatures of tradition rather than the offshoots of rational analysis, or even what the budget will stand—is peculiarly relevant to our understanding of Bomber Command and the battle it fought. It is sometimes supposed that, because Lord Trenchard was ordered in 1917 to create an 'independent' force to bomb Germany in retaliation for the raids of the German Gothas on Liverpool Street Station and like places, he was dragged unwillingly from his duties of supporting Haig's armies, or at any rate his artillery. The substance of this belief is therefore that the Royal Air Force in its offensive role was the brainchild of a coalition government determined to answer public disquiet at the immunity the Gothas enjoyed and the terror they wrought with a punitive force designed to repay in kind. Hence the Smuts Report.[2]

Dr Frankland, in the Lees Knowles lectures for 1963, writes: 'Smuts was an advocate of strategic bombing even before much possibility of carrying it out existed. He believed that the direct bombing of populous cities would become a principal means of waging and winning wars.

He even thought that this might render military and naval activities "secondary and subordinate".'[3] Smuts wrote further in his report: 'An air service ... can be used as an independent means of war operations. Nobody that witnessed the attack on London on 16 July could have any doubt on that point.'[4]

The evidence however for not ascribing too much to Smuts is that Trenchard and most of his brother officers of the Royal Flying Corps had contemplated both an independent flying service and a different, an exclusive strategy to justify it from the early days of the war, although to their undying credit they put their duty of support to the Army before all other aspirations, and, characteristically, hoped for events to provide a means of achieving freedom rather than worked out a theory of air bombardment for themselves. The evidence also shows that their thoughts ran in this sequence and not, as they logically should have done, the other way about; that despite Trenchard's considerable loyalty to Haig and his practical appreciation of the many difficulties he faced—not all of which were purely military—the collective reaction of the Air Board, of which Trenchard was a member, to the Smuts Report was to urge—and to lobby for—a new freedom to make strategy, not simply greater influence in its execution.

In short, although the RFC, looking down on the battle, both pitied the infantry dying on the wire and earnestly believed that there was a way round, or rather over, this impasse, the motive that sustained its commander was not excitement at discovering a new strategy but the ambition to form a new Service for its execution.

On 1 April 1915 the Royal Air Force was established; following on the intermittent 'strategic' raids of 1917, a few short weeks were spent by the 'independent air force', as it was officially called, in bombing German targets, military or industrial targets, although to the War Cabinet they were simply targets in Germany and hence likely to contain Germans, of the civilian variety. Then came peace—and the struggle for the survival of the RAF as a separate, an independent service. As Dr Frankland says of Trenchard:

> Freed from the requirement of loyalty to Haig and the object of a military break-through from the trenches, this remarkable man, who had previously thought of air power as an integral part of the army, now devoted his fiery nature to the establishment of it as an independent service. His life's work became, in fact, the preservation of the Royal Air Force through thick and thin. His case turned upon the theory of a strategic air offensive, for without it there was no convincing case for the preservation of a separate air service, just as without it there would have been no case for its creation. For ten

years Trenchard was Chief of the Air Staff and for another ten years his influence was a prime factor in the making of Air Staff policy.

The theory which Trenchard fortified was this: the heart of air power lay in strategic bombing of an independent character. Operations in direct support of the army and navy, however necessary they might be from time to time, were subsidiary and diversionary. Fighter defence against enemy bombing was fruitless, and had to be catered for mainly as a sop to politicians and other civilians. This theory had certain defects, but it had one crowning merit. It kept the Royal Air Force in being when nearly every other circumstance favoured its disbandment.[5]

To point the finger at what was, by any interpretation of that imprecise adjective, a remarkable man, would be inaccurate and unfair. Trenchard, by background, temperament and experience, was not singular as a commander in his passion for 'independence'; he only carried a national military characteristic to an uncommon degree, and he might also have claimed with justice that not only had he for three years of total war subordinated his ambitions to that of Haig's strategy, but had even, shy of the written word though he was, gone so far as to say:

> The aeroplane is a weapon which has no other exact counterpart any more than a submarine, a cruiser, a destroyer, a gun, a tank or a horse. It has its own definite limitations and powers, but the principles which guide it in warfare . . . are those which guide all other aims in all other elements of warfare, and the most important of these is the will and the power to attack the enemy, to force him to fight and to defeat him.[6]

Prophetic words! But in 1917, when they were written, the Germans had bombed London, and by the twenties Trenchard had become the champion of air power in absolute, not relative terms. Despite the absence of doctrine or debate—editions of Douhet were rather hard to come by at the RAF Staff College between the wars[7]—independence became synonymous with a strategic air offensive. Although the opportunity to practise independence between the wars was confined to the so-called 'air policing' operations on the North-West Frontier of India, in Transjordan, the Western Aden Protectorate and Iraq—where, taking a long-term view, they must be judged a failure—RAF officers were explicitly taught that the raison d'être of an air Service was its independence. Officers who took a personally independent line, by arguing that land-air warfare was at least as worthy of consideration as a strategic air offensive, were not looked on with much favour.[8]

The concept of air force independence, and of making it synonymous with the execution of 'strategic' operations—relegating 'tactical' operations to the level where the Services perforce are dependent on each other

—is an aspect of British defence policy which has received scant mention in official texts. Only the more radical commentators have chosen to point out that the largest scale of operations should, in reason, receive the greatest amount of concerted effort, whereas those on a smaller scale may with equal reason be accorded a degree of independence. It may be added here that confusion over the correct meanings of strategic and tactical does not ease the task of those who study the bombing of Germany. Phrases like 'area bombing', 'selective attack' and 'precision bombing' were also used in official directives and the like with a comparable lack of regard for clarity and consistency of definition.

One unfortunate result of this lack of clarity and exposition has been to get matters out of perspective. Much ink was spilt by reviewers of the Official History on the secondary issue of how the strategic offensive should have been conducted; less space was devoted to why it was devised in the first place. Debate on whether factories were more important targets than the centres of towns, or vice versa, is clearly a necessary part of any consideration of the offensive as such. But setting aside operational factors, this kind of choice remains subordinate to the issue of control, namely to the choice between strategies. However strongly Harris and Portal disagreed, or however frequently other senior RAF officers proposed alternatives to or variations on the Commander-in-Chief's simple strategic theme, RAF ranks invariably closed in support of 'independence' and hence the Harris thesis, when outsiders tried to capitalise on these internal differences. It is this factor in the Battle of Germany which has been disregarded.

To emphasise Service loyalty as the basis for the collective belief in an independent strategy must not be taken as an assertion that the RAF in general and Bomber Command in particular got all that it asked for from the War Cabinet. The latter was more than willing to regard Bomber Command operations as a morale raiser for the British people (to put the lowest political case for the offensive) and, just occasionally, to speculate on whether it might not be the war winner and alternative to the invasion of Europe by a costly land campaign that Harris claimed. But Harris never got the 4,000 Bomber Command front-line aircraft he wanted[9]; the notion that the strategic air offensive could achieve the reconquest and not merely the razing of Germany was not often or seriously entertained by the Churchill Government; the notion never affected the deliberations of President Roosevelt's Administration, doubtless because the American strategic imperative of 'Germany first' precluded simple assumptions about how that prime objective could be achieved.

It is important to understand that in terms of grand, global, Anglo-American strategy Germany did remain 'first'. The effect of this choice of a priority did not, however, accord an undue place to the bombing of Germany at the level where Roosevelt and Churchill deliberated or were advised. Although in 1944 Harris successfully disobeyed orders issued under the aegis of the Supreme Allied Commander, General Eisenhower, to increase the number of raids on oil and communications targets, and was certainly able in terms of sorties and tonnages to bomb the targets he believed consonant with the 'Thunderclap' strategy, the overall allied policy of fighting Germany primarily on the ground was unaffected. Except for the three months immediately preceding the mounting of 'Overlord', when targets in France and the Low Countries were heavily attacked, Harris was left pretty much to go his own way. This situation reveals less about Harris' belief in independence than it does about the nature of British defence policy between the wars and the tacit American assumption during World War Two that, if nececessary, The White House could always call the strategic tune.

The truth of the matter lies between the extremes of absolute independence to devise strategy and be provided with the means to execute it and the complete subjection to a combined offensive, involving all Services and aims and the equitable distribution of industrial resources and of manpower. Bomber Command certainly achieved relative independence from higher civilian or military authority. This relative independence was between 1918 and 1945 a substantial thing, as indeed it is today. But what did it amount to in practice? Between the wars Trenchard and his disciples were left free to argue the case for an offensive which was 'strategic' both because it was to be independently framed and executed and, to use the word in its more normal sense, was to be directed at the vital rather than the peripheral parts of an enemy's war-making capacity. First Sea Lords and Chiefs of the Imperial General Staff were comparably free, it is true, but the singularity of the RAF's position was just that history was not lying in wait to discredit or invalidate service claims for special consideration. The Navy had Jutland and inadequate defence against the U-boat to live down; the Army was scarred by the memories of stalemate and attrition in the Flanders mud. The Royal Flying Corps, however, had no record of failure.

Thus in so far as the RAF bothered to frame doctrine explaining or justifying an offensive couched in the language of the Smuts Report, it relied heavily on novelty. 'The difference between Army and Air is that between earth and air, no less', wrote T. E. Lawrence in 1925, when longing to return to the RAF.[10] It is not necessary here to explore the way in which the novelty or supposed 'freedom' of the air was, and is, handled by writers and artists; in the mundane fields of defence policy the idea that a new dimension had been introduced into strategy was held by its proponents to be sufficient justification for the RAF being given a prime role, indeed of superseding the Navy and Army in such matters as the defence of Singapore and the maintenance of internal security on the North-West Frontier and the Middle East.[11]

By 1928 Trenchard had forgotten or foresworn his wartime observations to Haig. He was encouraging his disciples, young men like Portal, Harris, Slessor, Saundby and Tedder, who had looked down on armies locked in a death grapple, to agree with him that:

> The aim of the Air Force is to break down the enemy's means of resistance by attacks on objectives selected as most likely to achieve this end.... It is not necessary for an air force, in order to defeat the enemy nation, to defeat its armed forces first. . . . Is an air offensive of this kind contrary to international law or the dictates of humanity? . . . It is an entirely different matter [from the indiscriminate bombing of a city for the sole purpose of terrorising the civilian population] to terrorise munition workers, men and women, into absenting themselves from work . . . through fear of air attack upon the factory . . . such destruction . . . is 'imperatively demanded by the necessities of war' . . . is this object one which will lead to victory, and a correct employment of air power? . . . This form of warfare is inevitable.[12]

There, in essence, is the doctrine of air power, as established for the RAF in its offensive role. The very core of the belief is that 'it is not necessary for an air force, in order to defeat the enemy nation, to defeat its armed forces first'. This claim, which we may think extravagant or natural according to our views about the history of strategy, was, it must be emphasised, welcome to British governments of the thirties, however much opposed by the other two Services when it appeared to encroach on particular prerogatives of command or function. For centuries Britain had striven or had seemed to strive to maintain the balance of power in Europe. However, given imperial proclivities, an ostensibly voluntary tradition of recruitment to the armed forces, and an industrial sector less adept at devising and perfecting weapons of war than its foreign rivals, British governments had grown increasingly sceptical of their country's ability to maintain this balance.

Since 1918 scepticism had been strongly reinforced by the sentiment that never again would British armies be bled white on a European field. The margin between stalemate and defeat had been very narrow in 1917— as it was to be in 1940 and 1942. A solution to this political and strategic dilemma was badly wanted. Trenchard offered to provide it. Although we shall see that the accord between Downing Street and Trenchard did not result in the actual establishment in effective terms of the deterrent and offensive forces the RAF wanted (whereas, by contrast, the US Army Air Force had a four-engined bomber equipped with an advanced type of bomb sight operationally flying by 1937),[13] the idea that there was a solution to a national dilemma remained a comfort to Cabinets and a stimulus to the RAF.

No cool and critical analysis was, however, offered from an intellectually and strategically independent source, to subject the new doctrine to close examination and, maybe, to point out that it required translation into forces if it was to deter potential enemies and encourage Britain's friends. Indeed, it is permissible to argue that lack of independent analysis and lack of cutting edge in Bomber Command in 1939 are directly related. The genius of Liddell Hart and the eloquence of General Fuller were concentrated on the adaptation of new methods of warfare to the classical principles of strategy. In this monumental task the Trenchard doctrine was thought fit only for a disarmament conference; co-operation between Army and Air Force certainly formed part of the credo of all military radicals in the thirties, whether they were serving or civilian. But despite this advocacy, the work of the School of Land–Air Warfare and some practical demonstrations in China and Spain of effective co-operation between commanders of ground and air forces, the collective RAF reaction to these truly novel developments involving the two Services was to regard them as an irritating distraction from the real business of air power.[14] The passage of 30 years has not gravely impaired this belief.

Before 1939 Bomber Command was therefore in a position of some peril. Unless that fact is realised, the Command's tribulations between the outbreak of war and the launching of Overlord cannot be understood. It was expected to achieve what British armies, supported by a reluctant America and a tottering France, had achieved in 1918. But assumption of strategic domination—and independence—was not backed by the kind of aircraft, bombs, or target locating and destroying devices which would be required to match performance to desire. Nor, granted the optimistic assumption that a rain of bombs was bound to cause havoc, would indeed 'win the War', was much thought given to defending a bombing force from enemy fighters and anti-aircraft fire. An absolute strategy apparently disposed of the need to maintain a balanced force of offensive and escorting aircraft.

Moreover, there was a particular logical fallacy in the Trenchard doctrine, which Dr Frankland exposes thus: 'The hope now existed that the German bombers would not get through but it did not kill the belief that the British would.'[15] In this fallacy lay the real dilemma of Britain in the thirties—and it is a dilemma which exists today. A defensively minded power which still retains many strategic commitments seeks to deter war, not to fight it. Deterrence is less of a drain on the national economy than a cap à pie defence policy which can be put to the proof. 'The morale factor in war is to the strategic as 20:1',[16] wrote Trenchard in a passage whose arguments sought to elevate the former to a plane where effectiveness and economy can be combined. This was an argument very attractive to British governments, which hoped that the 'morale' effect of a heavy bomber force on Hitler would be to deter him. Yet a policy which is cheaper than deterrence in fact is aggression, because a single smashing blow followed by surrender makes little demand on the industrial or manpower resources of the state which wields it.

It was the belief that Germany's strategy would take this form which troubled the minds of those responsible for British defence policy before 1939. Alas, it did not trouble them enough. Inertia and incompetence may be the explanation for allowing logical fallacies to flourish, but, although hindsight can fairly assess why and how a thing happened, it is difficult to prove that the actual capacities of one government are different from another. The British tradition of allowing the Services much freedom to frame strategy in return for final subjection to political authority is a more plausible explanation. The virtual lack of any analytical or critical apparatus is the most convincing explanation, with which should certainly be coupled the sheer lack of information about Hitler's strategy, the state of his armed forces, war economy or the attitude of the German people to bombing others—or being bombed themselves.

The situation deteriorated in this regard as war approached and men in responsible positions in Britain sought a refuge from painful decisions. Lack of resources could be advanced as another explanation, but there was no lack of aircraft in the RAF before 1939; they simply happened to be the wrong aircraft—except, of course, for those committed to defending the United Kingdom. And it is here that we come to the answer to the conundrum and to a fact about British policy in the thirties which has been insufficiently considered, but which is truly related to national defence and yet is directly relevant to the strategic air offensive. When Hitler's ambitions did at last become clear, and were seen as insatiable, resources were mobilised to use the RAF in a classical, not a revolutionary way, although it meant abandoning for an indefinite period the development of an

effective air striking force. Although the specifications for three new
heavy bombers had been written by 1936, none of them was flying operationally until 1941.

Fighter Command, however, was re-equipped with the Hurricane and
the Spitfire, with results we all know. The defeat of the Luftwaffe in
1940 was, among other things, a victory for the proper ordering of
strategic priorities. Mr Baldwin had said in 1932 that the bomber would
always get through.[17] At the eleventh hour a British government, two
unusually gifted aircraft designers, a few very pertinacious scientists and
Fighter Command decided to disprove the truth of this assertion; that
they therefore set out to disprove the essence of Trenchard's argument should also be remembered. The story of the offensive is, in a
sense, that of Bomber Command's attempt to ignore the strategic lesson
of 1940.

The method chosen was to inflict as much damage as possible on
German towns, to propagandise the fact to an embattled British people,
and to hope that the results would justify the losses suffered and meet the
criticisms, especially from the Admiralty, that air power might be used
in a more flexible way and one which contributed directly to Britain's
survival as a free and fighting nation. In this strategy, as much political
as military, Sir Arthur Harris achieved a success denied to his predecessor
or to other Commanders-in-Chief less outspoken or more distant from
Mr Churchill's midnight colloquies.[18] Only a commander of quite
extraordinary determination, operating in a situation where the Royal
Navy and the Army were engaged in a series of desperate defensive or
relieving operations, that were widely believed to be unsuccessful rather
than otherwise, could have got away with the argument put to Churchill:
namely that the way to disprove, almost to ignore, what had happened over
Britain in 1940, was to batter away at the largest targets, with the largest
possible number of aircraft, on any night when conditions of weather
and visibility did not make operations obviously self-defeating.

Churchill may have admired Harris for his courage when the outlook
for Britain was grim; there is little doubt that, although the British people
were not quite as bellicose about the Germans as popular report suggested
(the Blitz had brought feelings both of fear and revenge), the sight of
Bomber Command setting out stoically night after night kept national
morale steady and may even have saved Churchill's government in 1942.
But, equally, the record shows that the Prime Minister had seen too many
wars and had pondered strategic truths too deeply to believe that Harris
and Bomber Command were war winners.[19] It is also the case however

that the strategic air offensive in terms of bombing German cities was felt rather than understood to be the only one possible, unless a different, a subordinate role for Bomber Command was to be adopted. That choice was ruled out by habit, by Bomber Command's political value, and by the fact that a role in support of the Navy and Army required a force which could bomb certain selected targets with considerable accuracy and could be escorted while doing so.

Bomber Command never did achieve such a capability, although it acquired much of the apparatus for it. It has been said, I think unjustly, that Harris was determined that his command should not acquire the power to switch from a strategy of terror to one of interdiction, in the interruption of vital supplies or the disruption of essential routes, or to close support of naval and ground forces. What appears as a far more convincing explanation of the situation confronting Harris in 1944, when he found that even terror bombing was becoming appallingly expensive and could not indefinitely be sustained, is that he became determined that any improvements in capability should not be devoted to bombing new types of target or to bombing them more accurately. No, these improvements should be utilised in order to recommence the offensive with the original objectives once the USAAF had secured command of the air for him.

The essential requirement for that command was escorting fighters. The US 8th Air Force in Britain, commanded by General Eaker, not only had an escort fighter component, commanded by the energetic General Kepner, but by 1944 had the right aircraft to protect the Fortress and Liberator. It is one of the ironies of the strategic air offensive that this escort aircraft—the Mustang—was provided with its long-range capability through the experiments of British technicians three years after the outbreak of war and well before Harris demanded, but unsuccessfully, that Bomber Command be provided with escorts also.[20]

In the light of these factors, and of the fact that the formally designated role of Bomber Command on the outbreak of war was to bomb industrial targets and to do so in formation by day, whereas throughout most of the war and for most of the time its aircraft operated at night against cities, how should we summarise, and at this point only, the contribution to final victory which Harris and his men undoubtedly made? Secondly, accepting that the basic strategy was the fruit of political indifference to defence policy and of the service lobbying which was thereby permitted, and that therefore fundamental changes in wartime were ruled out, could any substantial modification of terror bombing have taken place?

The contribution must be analysed and narrated in detail. In summary and chronologically it amounted to this:

1 Defending Britain against the threat of invasion in 1940, by attacks on 'Sealion' forces (1940)
2. Sustaining the morale of the British government and the British people (1940–45)
3. Fighting a battle of attrition, and particularly when the USAAF had suffered defeat in daylight operations (1942–43)
4. Causing a measure of damage to the German war economy, specifically in regard to new U-boat fabrication (1943)
5. Destroying flying-bomb sites (1944)
6. Causing severe damage to and in some cases virtual destruction of oil installations and similar interdiction targets (1944–45).

What the bombing of Germany did *not* do was to defeat the German Air Force, utterly destroy German industry or affect the morale of the German people—although Messrs Craven and Cate believe it extinguished their willingness to endure the same experience again. Thus all the strategic novelty claimed for air power was rendered null and void. But what the bombing of Germany *did* do was to prove that air power had a decisive, if not the decisive, part to play in modern war. Contributions 1, 3 and 4 have not been sufficiently recognised, but they were arguably decisive at two particular stages of the war, when the threat of absolute disaster had been averted but the issue of victory or compromise was still in the balance. Moreover, the resolution and courage with which Bomber Command fought the Battle of Berlin in the winter of 1943–44, while the 8th Air Force was preparing a decisive strike against the German fighter forces, was a contribution to victory despite being a grievous defeat at the time.

Above all, the bombing of Germany forced Hitler on to the defensive, by robbing his armies of air cover in order that the Reich might be preserved. The effect of this switch from offence to defence most obviously benefited the Russian armies, but the effects were felt everywhere and on all the fronts forming the ring which gradually closed round Germany. Yet this contribution to victory was not the objective which Bomber Command set itself, nor was it an achievement by which Harris set much store. It was indeed the kind of contribution which strengthens the hand of those who say that Bomber Command could have been more effective if it had formed part of a combined offensive strategy, designed to strike at more vital parts of the enemy than the defensive capacities of his night fighter force.

We have seen that for Bomber Command to have been more effective in this sense would have required a situation between the wars which just did not obtain. A command which entered the war with bombers unable to defend themselves by day, whose target locating and destroying devices were either non-existent or grossly inferior to their enemy's, with bombs that frequently failed to explode, whose crews lacked the protection of de-icing equipment, oxygen and self-sealing petrol tanks, and with aircraft for the support of ground operations wholly vulnerable at all points—such a command was simply not going to participate in striking and concerted successes or war-winning combined operations. A command whose bombers lacked escorts was not going to participate in much more than a battle to survive. The question therefore is not: could Bomber Command have concentrated its resources on repeatedly attacking certain targets which were demonstrably vital to the German war economy? The question is not: could more attacks of a demonstrably selective and precise nature have taken place? Such attacks of this kind— and, in sum they were many and costly—demonstrated what Bomber Command could sometimes do, but there is no evidence that such demonstrations affected the course of the war. Even the attack on the Mohne and Eider dams, rightly described as one of the greatest feats of precision bombing, was more of a propaganda than a strategic success, and it was achieved at crippling cost.[21]

The question is rather: could the strategy of Bomber Command have been modified? Could Bomber Command have devoted more resources to the anti-U-boat campaign and those waged in North Africa? The answer is that of course the strategy could have been so modified. To pose the question is only to make again the point that nothing but habit and convenience prevented Bomber Command from being used in this more flexible way. To say this is not to deny the great support which Bomber Command gave to the anti-U-boat and North African campaigns. Bomber and Coastal Command aircraft between them sank more U-boats than the Royal Navy, a fact which airmen like to recall. Mining operations accounted for the bulk of German coastal shipping which ventured from port. Rommel's supply lines were cut effectively enough to halt him in front of Alam Halfa before the Eighth Army had been taught by Montgomery how to defeat him.

Sir Arthur Harris would indeed call this contribution a great sacrifice. His front line strength as 1943 dawned was actually less than when he assumed command, despite the mobilisation of British labour so largely on aircraft production. The explanation for this situation is that squadrons

already in the Command and those formed to strengthen it were despatched to bomb U-boats and Rommel's supply lines. They left or did
not join Bomber Command in the year which not only saw the first
effective British demonstrations of attacks on cities—starting with Lübeck
in March, when that ancient wooden port was reduced to ashes—but
also what the official history calls 'a remarkable precision attack on the
Renault factory near Paris'[22] in the same month.

We can now see that the Renault attack did not presage a strategic
revolution—although it was prevented from doing so by the locust years,
not by any fault in the theory of using bombers as opportunity offered.
But a year which saw this degree of development in precision bombing,
in target locating and destroying techniques, in improved bombs and the
arrival of aircraft to carry them, also witnessed the arrival in Britain of the
Fortress and Liberator, forerunners of what was intended to be and became
a larger force than Bomber Command was ever able to create, although
one whose aircraft were markedly inferior to the British in bomb load.
It is arguable therefore that the right use of Bomber Command in the
decisive year of 1942 would have been to leave a small element to maintain a purely holding operation against Germany, while most of the
resources, comprising the new-found skills, techniques, weapons, aircraft
and devices, were concentrated on two other fronts, the Atlantic and
Mediterrannean, where, moreover, German fighters were either few or
relatively ineffectual.

But if that strategy had been followed, would Bomber Command have
made the contribution to victory which has just been summarised?

The questions, although real enough and necessary in any consideration
of grand strategy or in deciding what relevance World War Two has
to contemporary issues, are academic so far as the Battle of Germany is
concerned. They have been put here in order to make the point that
improvements in capability and technique could arguably have been
more usefully applied to the support of maritime and land operations than
to strengthening an offensive which, of its conception and execution, was
a blunt instrument. Yet Harris wanted more accurate bombing and a
lower loss rate in order to retain the justification for an offensive against
German cities, not for attacking selected industrial plants or interdiction
targets; he wanted escorts—and eventually pleaded for them—in order
to keep his offensive going at all, not so that it would change its nature.
The arguments in 1943 and 1944 between Air Vice-Marshals Cochrane
and Bennett, commanding 5 and 8 (Pathfinder) Groups respectively,
about which target-marking and bomber-stream controlling techniques

were more likely to produce results, arose from differences of opinion about the conduct, not the nature, of their chief's strategy.

Although therefore Navy and Army spokesmen had a good case when they declared that the primary function of the RAF's strike element should be to support holding or offensive operations against the enemy's naval and military forces, their arguments were vitiated in practice by the fact that Bomber Command needed all the help it could get just in order to remain in the line of battle. In terms of capability rather than political preference Harris correctly interpreted the diversion of his squadrons to North Africa and the Atlantic as wholly injurious to Bomber Command. With comparable shrewdness Harris realised that the arrival of the USAAF in Britain, coupled with the build-up of the 15th Air Force in the Mediterranean, threatened his position as the arbiter of the 'Thunderclap' strategy, and might well reduce him merely to being the executant of one of attrition.

Whether one accepts or rejects Harris' basic strategic beliefs, it must be said that he was far more clear in his mind about the availability of material to prosecute offensives or defend vital interests than most of his contemporaries. (Obviously he had a far more accurate picture of this situation than those of his subordinates who agreed with sailors and soldiers that a more flexible use of air power was both necessary and possible.) So far as Bomber Command was concerned, its offensive against Germany demanded everything that could be spared; this demand automatically predicated competition for resources in a British economy which had been geared for total war to a greater degree than either the United States or Germany. However valid might be the case for giving increasing and more effective support to the Navy and the Army in the crucial years of 1942 and, regarding the U-boat campaign especially, 1943, it went by default if one accepted the necessity for some kind of bombing offensive directed at the heart of Germany. The issues therefore remained fundamental: who should control and decide strategy, and how should scarce resources be distributed? Harris fought for all he could get—and in 1943 was to get much of what he sought—because not to fight would be to surrender the strategic palm to others and see the bombing of Germany grind to a halt.

Harris could also see well enough what would happen when the mighty, if still only partly mobilised, American economy and society began to churn out bombers and crews in a seemingly endless flood. The result would be a renewal of the whole argument and a more subtle demand from the Admiralty and War Office. If the 8th and 15th Air Forces could attack Germany from North and South with armadas greater than Bomber Command could muster, what need for the latter to claim a preponderant share of resources or devote so much of its attention to duplicating the American effort?

But Harris saw still further ahead. Before becoming Commander-in-Chief he had spent nearly a year in Washington as head of the RAF Delegation; it had been absolutely apparent to him that if America joined Britain in fighting Germany its President and advisers would want to be the senior partner in the resulting alliance.[23] The bombing of Germany would become an American-controlled offensive, even if command ostensibly was shared. As it turned out, by one of those ironies which seem an especial feature of allied operations of war, Bomber Command was able to remain an independent air force with a distinctly different strategy from its American compatriots because the 8th Air Force in 1943 comprehensively failed to achieve what was expected of it. The short-range 1942 operations against targets in France and the Low Countries gave no warning of what was to happen over Germany the following year, culminating in a dreadful week in October, when virtually one third of the 8th Air Force's Liberator and Fortress strength was destroyed or disabled by the German Air Force and ground defences.

In such a situation, with the American theory of unescorted daylight bombing shot to pieces by the Luftwaffe's Focke-Wulf and Messerschmitt fighters, Bomber Command remained in the fight—for a major role in the bombing of Germany—by its capacity to survive a further four months' war of attrition more expensive even than the precision bombing attempted by its American counterparts. The so-called Battle of Berlin, which Bomber Command fought through the longest nights of late 1943 and early 1944, was a respite for Harris in terms of authority, delaying by some months the moment when the effective direction of the strategic air offensive passed to American hands. But by 'March 1944, Bomber Command was no longer in a position to sustain a major night offensive against German cities'[24] and by February the 8th Air Force had already demonstrated that escorted daylight bombing was a feasible operation of war.

This seesaw between the fortunes of the two air forces is a factor in the whole story which is usually obscured by accounts of what after the 1943 Casablanca Conference was called the Combined Bomber Offensive, an operation which was intended to achieve Anglo-American 'command of the air' through the destruction of the German Air Force in its defence of the Reich. Except however for the three-month pre-invasion phase, and other than in terms of round-the-clock attacks, there was really no combined offensive. There were two separate offensives, based on initially different ideas about the nature of air power and the function of air forces. Despite the losses of 1943, American airmen overtly kept faith with the principles of concentrated attacks on industrial targets. Moreover, the success achieved early in 1944 and before the Overlord period began strengthened their belief in the use of air forces for a wide variety of missions, and essentially as a complement to ground forces engaged in destroying an enemy's military capability.

Indeed, it may be fairly said that the 8th Air Force became an effective instrument of allied strategy once it achieved balanced offensive and defensive strength. Only then, but then very powerfully and with immediate effect on the enemy war machine, did General Doolittle's bombers, operating in conjunction with the 15th Air Force in Northern Italy and the Britain-based medium bombers of the 9th Air Force, mount an offensive which ranged from deep penetration raids on German cities, through attacks on oil and communications, to close support of General Eisenhower's armies as they sought to extend their bridgehead in Normandy and the Pas de Calais. And we may note as an example of the basic difference between British and American resources that four years were to elapse before daylight bombing was regularly resumed by Bomber Command, whereas the 8th Air Force was back in the act within months. Nor did this expression of air power lead to a demand from Spaatz for strategic independence[25]; in 1942 however Harris could repeat such a claim simply because he insisted that Bomber Command was the one thing really hurting the Germans.

It is an academic question now to ask what might have happened to Bomber Command if by early 1943 the 8th Air Force had already succeeded as an unescorted force or if the Mustang had been sent along to escort the bombers from the first. It is, however, highly relevant to any consideration of the validity of a strategic air offensive *per se* to examine what lay behind American theories—and whether they continue to affect current strategic thought and practice. Here we are in the realms of national attitudes as much as state policy. Writing in 1968 it still is just possible to say that America, as a nation and a society, does not believe in 'the military'—whatever the colour of their uniforms—taking control of national policy, particularly if this leads to permanent involvement in international commitments. Despite, or perhaps because of Viet Nam—America's first major war fought virtually alone—the national ethos is isolationist and the people's predisposition is towards a more strict subjection of strategy to political imperatives than is the case in Britain.

This tradition was a powerful, if often negative, influence on American policy in the twenties and thirties, when air power was the wave of the strategic future in so many other countries. The tradition survived the short-lived period of American nuclear supremacy in the fifties, and it did so because the years between 1918 and 1945 contain no instance of the military establishment as such stepping out of line; with a bow towards President Truman and his dismissal of General MacArthur for threatening to misuse air power across the Yalu in the Korean war we may extend the period when the tradition was not seriously impaired up to 1952. The fact that the Air Force was an integral—and subordinate—part of the Army until the late forties is explicable not only in strategic but in political terms; two military pressures could be more easily resisted than three, a fact against which General Arnold, wartime Chief of Staff of the USAAF and nominally ranking with the Chiefs of Staff (as well as being an occasional member of the Combined Chiefs of Staff Committee), protested repeatedly and with entire lack of success.

Some readers would doubtless contest this account simply by murmuring 'Hiroshima and Nagasaki', but if the record is examined it will be seen that the USAAF was to a surprising extent simply the instrument which was utilised by the proponents of the 'Manhattan Project' in the hopes of saving Americans in uniform from what, with some reason, was thought would be a bloody assault on the shores of Japan.[26] Further, this political policy, this Thunderclap strategy, was framed without the Air Force knowing much about it. Arnold was in no sense responsible for it or privy to its proponents' deliberations. Such subordination may well explain how, after the reign of General Curtis LeMay, a powerful administration was able to pull the US Air Force right back into line.

That American air forces were thus only for a short period able to dominate decision-making may account for the fact that more time and energy has been spent in 50 years on evolving strategies for the flexible use of air power rather than the dogged application of a rigid theory which could be sold to economy-minded administrations. In the years during which Trenchard was equating independence for the RAF with the doctrine of the war-winning strategic air offensive, the Air Corps Tactical School was teaching that 'the immediate mission of the armed forces may be defeat of the enemy's army, navy or air force . . ., these missions are best carried through by the co-operation of the three arms . . . each has its particular functions and limitations . . . .'[27]

This doctrine of a trinity of functions was not, it may be observed, one that evolved automatically, but by a process whereby the sometimes exaggerated arguments of General Billy Mitchell, America's leading military airman, were tempered by the realisation that Navy and Army requirements remained the main determinant of national strategy. Nevertheless, the comparative subordination of the Air Force had its surprising aspects. Mitchell's habit of stumping the country to urge more freedom for the Air Force and a bigger one than Congress thought necessary reflected not only personal aspirations and his plain man's version of Douhet, but was also in line with the growing national belief in the application of technology to the solution of diverse problems. 'We have seen the future and it works', said the American labour leader Eugene Debs in the early years of the twentieth century. General Mitchell hadn't seen the strategic future 20 years later, but he claimed nonetheless to be its prophet, and he declared that it lay with air power, something specifically available to a modern state like the USA.

But even in his most fervent periods Mitchell never claimed a wholly independent role for air forces, nor asserted that they 'won' wars. And perhaps, from the USAAF's point of view, most important of all, he never overlooked the fact that offensive forces, above all 'bombardment forces' as he called them, required to be protected in the execution of their missions. Mitchell wrote that, 'whatever the future might hold, war is still a matter of defeating the enemy's armed forces'.[28] To achieve that objective, bombardment aircraft must be able to survive, not merely destroy. Thus, without accepting the Army Department's view that 'the chief mission of aviation is the close support of ground forces',[29] Mitchell nevertheless laid down the basis for the kind of air force which would certainly be able to give the required support whenever need arose. Not more than 20 per cent of resources provided for the Air Force should be devoted to the bombardment element; the remaining 80 per cent should be spent on fighters—'pursuit aircraft'—of various types, in order to ensure that, whatever their mission, the bombardment aircraft could execute it without crippling loss.[30]

It is of course true to say that America's strategic problems were very different from Britain's, most notably in that no aerial attack on Americans was likely or, in the thirties, possible. The battle for resources therefore assumed a different form, it being feasible to build prototypes of two heavy bombers, a variety of medium and light bombers, and several versatile pursuit and ground support aircraft at a time when the British Air Staff was being forced to choose between producing heavy bombers to support Trenchard's theory or fighters to contest it. It is also certainly the case that the apparent combat quality of the 'Fortress' blinded the Air Corps between 1939 and 1942 to the possibility that practice might be very different from theory; they forgot that Mitchell's warning on the need to escort a bombardment force was based on his own experience and success in 1917 in welding these and other elements of air power into a coherent whole.

One can also say that the effectively subordinate role of the Air Corps did nothing to prevent some lively in-fighting over command and status when war broke out, particularly over that vexed issue of anti-U-boat operations. A command structure of inordinate complexity was devised to cover America's eastern seaboard and its approaches, together with the Caribbean, in the fond hope that inter-Service jealousies would be assuaged. No satisfactory compromise was reached. General Arnold led an Alice in Wonderland or snakes-and-ladders life, at one moment the confidant of President and Prime Minister, at another subordinate to commanders junior to him in rank and service. And even accepting that the decision to drop the atom bomb was not Arnold's responsibility, it is still true that the destruction of Japan's cities by fire raids as terrible as any inflicted on Germany had much to do with encouraging the belief that a difference of strategic degree rather than kind was going to be expressed on 6 August 1945.

Nevertheless the American air forces in World War Two attempted to express a more flexible and more limited notion of air power than their British counterparts, and this view prevailed strongly in the bombing of Germany. Above all, the subordination of strategic formulation, advice and decision-making to political authority was never in doubt, nor until Hiroshima was the air force expected to provide an alternative to military or, in the Pacific Ocean context, amphibious strength. It is for these reasons one can say that historically American strategic theories of air, or air-space power, still remain comprehensible and rational. As against the misuse of air power today in Viet Nam, we may set the post-war record as a whole.

Perhaps no better example of this record can be found than that set by General Lauris Norstad, for five years the Supreme Allied Commander in the North Atlantic Treaty Organisation. In retirement he has insisted on the subordination of military commanders to governmental authority; he has expressed not only a genuinely 'alliance' outlook but a conviction that the needs of armed forces are greater than the requirements of any one national service. This attitude, and the tradition which it reflects, had surely much to do with the great degree of success in achieving a strategic balance with Russia which the Kennedy administration achieved; in turn we may note the remarkable degree to which Kennedy's Secretary of Defense was able to interest the US Air Force once again in tasks that were precise and limited and formed part of a strategy in which no one idea and no service was dominant.

It now remains to be seen whether this new-found versatility will survive the demands of the Viet Nam war and the advent of another nuclear power. With the basic strategic function of deterrence based on relatively invulnerable nuclear missiles, and with a readiness to preserve this power by developing an anti-missile missile system if necessary, it might be thought that the functions of conventionally armed air forces could be determined with relative ease as part of a limited war strategy embracing all arms. But doubt must creep in when reading of the almost blind belief that air power 'will bring Hanoi to the negotiating table'. Can it be that American Air Force commanders, facing the new and exceedingly difficult problems of limited war fought with weapons much more powerful and numerous than in the days of Korea, are beginning to follow where Trenchard led? It must, after all, be said that the RAF today remains as firmly convinced as ever that air power is the key to defence policy, in terms of deterring war or fighting it more 'cheaply' than by committing troops on the ground.

Perhaps mindful of the losses endured over Germany between 1939 and 1945, RAF thinking about its European role today is relatively flexible; the commitment of its effective heavy and medium bomber forces to an interdiction role in NATO in recent years, after a decade in which Russia itself was supposedly within their effective range, may partly explain this co-operative and restrained outlook. But Trenchard's basic premise remains to fortify the Air Staff in its demand for a major part of the defence budget. The premise has survived the realisation that Britain cannot afford a missile force; the refusal of the United States to prolong the life of the V-bombers by providing the Skybolt missile for them in order to decrease their vulnerability to Warsaw Pact defences; and the decision to cancel the TSR-2 aircraft, intended to be versatile nuclear weapons carriers of considerable range.

The V-bomber force has been reprieved by providing it with some capacity to operate at low level and thus be less vulnerable to detection by radar, and by the development of a successor to Skybolt. The American aircraft known as the Phantom is being provided for the RAF as a partial replacement for the TSR-2, and to fulfil substantially the same

function. Above all, in the retention of a global deterrent role despite the
progressive relinquishment of Britain's Asian commitments, the RAF is
intended progressively to replace those surplus fleets and garrisons
which have hitherto, and particularly since 1945, expressed Britain's
contribution to international security and the preservation of national
interests.[31]

The most significant feature of this new role in the context of what this
this book attempts to analyse and narrate is that it represents that culmination of Trenchard's ambitions for the RAF which habit and the need
to provide a fighter force for the defence of the United Kingdom denied
it before 1939. Today Fighter Command, in the old 'Air Defence of Great
Britain' sense, is a skeleton force of four squadrons. Thus resources, fiscal
if no longer industrial or technological, can be devoted to the acquisition
of aircraft whose deployment outside the North Atlantic Treaty area
is intended to deter aggression against those states which Britain is still
committed to defend. Although fixed-wing and helicopter aircraft for
close support are either obsolete or in short supply, the deterrent capacity
of the RAF has been preserved, and in a geographical context which
ensures a closer identity of interest between political authority and the
Air Staff than Trenchard, Harris or any of their colleagues and successors
could have hoped for.

Whether one is comforted by this situation or not, it cannot be denied
that a service which has always rested a large part of its case on 'cost
effectiveness' has succeeded at the last in fulfilling its founder's hopes.
What is equally worthy of remark, however, is that this success has been
achieved by advocacy in the corridors of power, not by unequivocal
success between 1939 and 1945 or an active combat role since then. After
the defeat of the German Air Force over Britain in 1940, some dispassionate
analysis of the Baldwin-Trenchard premise was made by a few serving
officers and independent critics; but their probing had no effect on the
conduct of operations. Since 1945 unofficial strategic analysis has been
persistently critical of the RAF claim to provide a deterrent force in a
strategic context which demands constant development of material in
order to maintain the 'delicate balance of terror'.

But the RAF as such has eschewed any such criticism; it could hardly
be expected to write its own obituary as a major element in strategy, but
a society where strategic beliefs and assumptions were subject to rather
more stringent analysis than in Britain might have questioned whether
manned aircraft could for the indefinite future be thought of as a
major element in deterring nuclear war. Yet in the pre-nuclear era the

same belief held good, and when war came at last the concomitant belief in the effectiveness of a strategic air offensive survived loss and disappointment, the growing disillusionment of the Churchill Government and the advent of American air forces whose commanders were willing to accept a subordinate role in the execution of Allied strategy.

We come finally to what for some should be the central issue of the Battle of Germany and certainly of a book which attempts to relate it to contemporary issues. The morality of the battle, specifically the deliberate decision, at the late Lord Cherwell's instigation, to measure success by numbers of Germans 'de-housed', aroused protest then and has been the subject of debate and controversy since. The Official History of the offensive says oddly and inaccurately that debate about the moral issues enjoyed a 'vogue' for some years after the war. Dr Frankland has compounded the obtuseness of this remark by choosing to deal with moral issues in his Lees Knowles lectures and then dismissing them with two arguments which other partisans have adopted: the moralists didn't know what they were talking about; killing civilians in fire raids is no worse than killing any 'combatant'—assumed to be us all in total war—or subjecting them to other forms of suffering like blockade.

About the second of these two arguments little will be said in the pages which follow; the nuclear age has to all except the purblind rendered the argument at least suspect. But the first argument does merit mention here and will receive attention later. For the burden of this argument is that, if the moralists had known what was happening, they would have realised that the strategic air offensive could only have been conducted by means which to many seemed abhorrent and pointless. As already indicated, a strategic air offensive conducted by the Bomber Command of 1939 to 1945 had to be one based on the Trenchard premise, fashioned by a commander like Harris and executed by crews who accepted their death-dealing role with equanimity if rarely with much enthusiasm. But to say this is really to pose the moral issue in its most elemental form. If it was wrong to put Germans to the sword by the methods employed over Hamburg, the Ruhr, Berlin, Dresden and many other cities, it was a wrong which stemmed from the refusal of British governments in the thirties to provide Bomber Command with the weapons and devices to fight a less inhuman campaign. It must be stressed that less reliance on assumption and more belief in analysis by Trenchard and the Air Staff might have remedied this situation. It certainly can be said that there were few in Bomber Command who did not come to feel, if not to say, by 1945 that victory could be bought at too high a price.

But the ultimate responsibility was political—as it is today. In strategy the moral element is that which chooses right before war reduces choice to acts which may produce untoward or untold reactions. If there is a lesson in the strategic air offensive, that surely is the one.

PART ONE

Air Power Comes of Age
1918–1939

The Trenchard Legacy

Birth of a Theory

Hunting for significant dates in order to mark the birth of an idea or the origin of an historical change is a dangerous process, leading to false trails and over-simplification. This should be borne in mind when seeking the moment when aerial strategic bombardment originated, designed to play a part in or have an effect on more than purely local operations. Arguably it was when the Royal Naval Air Service bombed Cuxhaven on Christmas Eve 1914; to many, air war began not on the day following the Cuxhaven raid, when sporadic German attacks were made on two British naval establishments, nor was its inception indicated by the relatively heavy *Zeppelin* raids of the summer of 1915, but in May 1917, when heavy casualties were suffered in London and south-east coast towns from the bombing of high-flying Gotha aircraft of the German Air Service, operating from bases in Belgium.

On the other hand, one could plausibly trace the record of the Royal Flying Corps from its establishment in 1912 to the culmination of its efforts in support of Sir Douglas Haig's armies during the last German offensive of March 1918. To students of air power who hold that strategic bombardment remains essentially an adjunct of ground operations (and in an age of limited war such a view has revived), the RFC's developing role as a 'strafing' weapon reveals air power in its most useful, albeit in its most embryonic form. No subordinate commander was more loyal to the requests and needs of his chief than was Major-General Trenchard to Field-Marshal Haig in those anxious weeks of 1918. Yet it was within days of the German offensive being halted in front of Arras and Amiens that the RFC joined with the RNAS to become the Royal Air Force; two months and four days later, on 5 June, a separate element of the RAF in France, known indeed as the Independent Force, was established, with the express objective of conducting bomber operations on targets in Germany, targets broadly related to the ebb and flow of battle on the Western Front (airfields were objects of primary importance), but targets reflecting the concept of long-range penetration by aircraft selected to form the spearhead of a new branch of the armed forces.[1]

If peace had not come with some abruptness in November 1918, Berlin would have been attacked by the new, four-engined Handley-Page bombers of the Independent Air Force, flying not from French airfields within the territorial jurisdiction of the Army Commander, but from fields in the United Kingdom. In 1939, 21 years later, Berlin was so attacked, and by 1943 the German capital was to be subjected to aerial devastation by aircraft of a Bomber Command whose chief had been given a degree of freedom in the planning and conduct of operations far greater than that enjoyed by any of his contemporaries in the RAF or in the other British Services. Thus, if there is a date on which strategic air bombardment, as the Royal Air Force has construed it, truly began, it is 5 June 1918.

But to the German Air Service and the almost unscathed Air Service of the American Expeditionary Force, this date could have had no great significance. Despite the former's shock—and temporary success in making a uniformed member of the Royal Flying Corps as unpopular a sight to the British public as shot-down members of Bomber Command were to German civilians in World War Two—those in the German High Command who planned the 1917 Gotha raids had no intention of adding to the U-boat and Big Bertha a new and aerial form of 'frightfulness'. It is in fact hard to discover the strategic reasoning which governed the decision to bomb United Kingdom targets, nominally military in the broad sense, but well populated by civilians nonetheless. A reasonable speculation, if no more, is that the decision was based on the necessity to relieve pressure on the German squadrons fighting over the Western Front. By all accounts, these squadrons were far more on the defensive than their enemy; operational superiority obtaining in the first two years of the war with Fokker aircraft had been lost to the German Air Service by 1917.[2]

Whatever the reason, it is important to our whole understanding of the strategic air offensive against Germany in World War Two to realise that the origins of air bombardment saw no German strategic commitment to the idea of an independently planned and exercised offensive against the enemy and, in effect if not by design, against his civilian population. The cohesion of doctrine and the obedience to the ideas and orders of a supreme authority, which had characterised the German armed forces for generations, effectively prevented, even if they did not specifically deny, the emergence of an independent Service to prosecute an independent strategy. Equally, it should be understood that America, a democracy with a rooted distaste for the military establishment, was unlikely to provide an environment in which the theory of total war could be argued and simulated. And so it proved. Although Brigadier-General Billy Mitchell had achieved much in the short space of seven months when his squadrons were supporting General Pershing's armies, and became for a while to the American public of the 1920s something of a popular hero, his advocacy of autonomy for the air arm and a role for it characterised by bombing the enemy heartland, was sufficient heresy to ensure that the US Army Air Force remained in a subordinate position and with an infinitely more modest strategic function than was vouchsafed to the bomber squadrons of the RAF.[3]

For a consideration of the first decade of what Churchill, referring specifically to air power, called 'the locust years',[4] and which Trenchard, more bitterly, described as those in which Jonah's gourd was broken, attention must unavoidably be concentrated on the RAF, and the birth and establishment of the idea that air power was unique and should be exercised without fetters. An Italian airman, General Guilio Douhet, it is true, published in 1921 his now classic *The Command of the Air*, in which arguments were advanced for the singularity of the third dimension of war, and for 'a distinction between an Independent Air force and auxiliary aviation'. The book, moreover, bore the imprimatur of the Italian Ministry of War. But although the Italian Air Force was to behave in bombing Haile Selassie's tribesmen like the Japanese Air Force over Nanking and the Condor Legion at Guernica, there is no evidence to suggest that air forces other than the British owed their very existence to being executants of operations wholly distinct and different from those to be conducted at sea or on land.

All other air forces, while recognising the singularity of their weapons and intermittently trumpeting the uniqueness of their effects, gave attention first to support for co-operation with fleets and armies. The US Services were undoubtedly hindered in the attainment of this objective by internal jealousies; on the other hand, American industry provided aircraft to test theory against utility (if not as honestly as should have been done). The French Air Force was effete, even in the 1920s when, for a ludicrous year—1923—it was posed as a threat to the British Isles, leading, in a still more absurd reflex action, to a political demand for a '52-squadron Royal Air Force'.[5] The German Air Force was, *de facto*, an affair of flying clubs and forgotten 'aces' or men biding their time—Goering a virtual exile in Sweden, Udet a test and aerobatic pilot, Sperrle, Kammhuber and Von Richthofen in the Reichswehr, Koller in the Bavarian State Police.[6] Fronting these men and providing an incentive for continued patience was the Lufthansa, established in 1926 under the brilliant Milch and shortly to become 'the best equipped and operated airline in Europe'.[7] The Russian air arm, like its sister Services, remained an unknown quantity to intelligence staffs in Paris, London and Washington.

It appears to be one of the ironies of the history of strategy that the adaptation of a theory is geographically far removed from whoever formulated it. We see Prussian theories of the nation in arms adapted to Chinese communism; the French post-Sedan belief in '*l'audace, toujours l'audace*' adapted to American convictions about the primacy of the offensive arm or the necessity to retain offensive superiority in weapons. Little theory has flowed from British sources, other than via the genius of Liddell Hart; what is interesting and relevant to our story is the reception by the Royal Navy and the Royal Air Force respectively of Mahan's and Douhet's theories of the primacy of forces that could move at will, thus exercising a political, a strategic, a moral influence out of all proportion to their ranking in the international arms league. Thus Mahan held that the Royal Navy exercised a unique influence, wider and more pervasive than might be supposed from the number of ships in commission and their strength when measured against single enemies or those in combination. The Royal Navy, however, although it may have been collectively flattered by this foreign accolade, fortunately possessed Lord Fisher and several gifted subordinates to ensure that practice bore some relation to theory. The Royal Air Force was less fortunate in its leader during the 1920s. Lord Trenchard, remarkable as any man must be who strives to do a new thing, was no Fisher. The history of what happened to the RAF in the 1920s—and hence, bearing in mind the intellectual and physical gap in strategy between conception and realisation, what Bomber Command was like in 1939—must be sought largely in the fact that Trenchard was very nearly a great man, but lacked just that touch of greatness that might have made the infant service not only independent but strong.

This is no place to pass judgment of Trenchard; it is, however, necessary to stress that he spent five years—from 1918 to 1923—fighting to establish the RAF as a truly independent Service, with its own slice of the defence budget, its own hierarchy and methods of organisation and training, and, almost as an afterthought and lacking anything remotely resembling formulation or articulation, a strategy comprising uneven lumps of deterrence and pre-emption interlarded with woolly, incoherent and unconvincing assertions about 'moral' and 'morale' factors. Trenchard, as Sir John Slessor, a great admirer, has said, 'was very inarticulate—his mind always worked quicker than his tongue; he was almost physically incapable of expressing his thoughts on paper . . . his instructions were often a cause of puzzlement (and sometimes amusement) to his staff officers. His closest friends (or worst enemies), could hardly accuse him of being an intellectual type of officer. But he had a flair, an instinct for getting at the really essential core of a problem.'[8]

We will examine shortly where that instinct led Trenchard and landed the bomber component of the RAF (there was no Bomber Command as such until 1936). What must be stressed here is that by 1923, when the permanent establishment of the RAF was symbolised by Trenchard's *inter pares* membership of the newly established Chiefs of Staff Committee, the credibility of the force had already begun to decline. Churchill (a champion of the service in its embryo days and later to be so intimately associated with its failures and triumphs) was about to begin four years as Chancellor of the Exchequer marked by net cuts in Service expenditure, and British foreign and strategic policy was turning away from European problems to those of the Empire and the preservation of its newly acquired Middle Eastern part by what was coming to be known as 'Imperial Policing'. Retrenchment denied research; policing in lieu of administration led to the device of 'air control', a technique which could be quite satisfactorily executed by bombers of essentially World War One design and performance; since European security could not be wholly neglected by the British Government, despite the Service's profound distaste for war on the European scale, it was necessary to engage in 'Locarno' diplomacy and to fabricate a strategy. Locarno indeed symbolised diplomacy; bombing, or threatening to bomb the very heart and sinews of an enemy nation, represented the flower of British strategic thought and appeared to be a perfectly adequate substitute for occupation forces in peace and mud, machine guns and mutilated men in war. As Slessor subsequently wrote of the late 1930s, 'our belief in the bomber, in fact, was intuitive, a matter of faith'.[9]

The Trenchard Years

The singular degree to which the RAF was thus involved in both main aspects of British foreign policy and strategy may reflect Slessor's view that Trenchard's instinct and his belief in independence were 'absolutely right . . . *at that time and in those circumstances*'. This is a view which one must respect; arguably a war-weary Britain, still heavily committed on a global scale, found in Trenchard's simple beliefs about the efficacy of deterrence and the effectiveness of 'air control' an important, a necessary relief from reflecting that the war to end wars had left behind a vengeful Germany, a prostrate France, an isolationist America, and had produced a fascist Italy and a revolutionary Russia, whose disturbing convictions and acts were threatening, or seemingly threatening, the fabric of government and order, not least in that greatly enlarged Empire of suzerain states that was held to protect India and Britain's routes thereto. Maybe all these notions were valid at the time. This history is not concerned with the effect of Imperial commitments on national security. But it is necessary to point out that the locust years were really those of the 1920s rather than the 1930s; the early period, when Lawrence could write of the joys of flying over the Lincolnshire countryside and compare the enthusiasm of airmen with the dullards of the Tank Corps, were nevertheless years when the Royal Air Force ceased to be 'the most powerful air force in the world',[10] when it not only became the victim of the Lloyd George Government's Aircraft Disposal Company, but failed, through insufficient internal understanding of the scientific and technological age (of which indeed it was the child), to design or produce a single aircraft remotely similar to the stressed-skin, enclosed cabin monoplanes beginning to appear in foreign civil airlines—the aerodynamic forerunners of the bombers and fighters of World War Two.

Simply in terms of comparative numbers the record is gloomy and relevant, because offensive and defensive armament had not kept pace with aerodynamic advance. In 1930, the French, Italian, United States and British air forces possessed respectively 1,300, 1,100, 900 and 700 aircraft. Germany it may be noted, 'was already the most air-minded nation in Europe',[11] with over 50,000 members in the *Deutscher Luftsportverband*; there was a secret training centre for future air force personnel at Lipetz in the Soviet Union—and the firms of Junkers, Heinkel, Dornier and Focke-Wulf were building and exporting hard throughout Europe. By 1930 Goering had been in Germany for three years and, with some remnants of the glamour of the last commander of part of the Manfred Von

Richthofen 'circus' still clinging to him, was already an intimate of Hitler; he was shortly to be a Reichstag deputy and a strong if unwelcome influence on Erhard Milch. In Berlin, Heinz Guderian was developing theories of mobile war, derived in good measure from Liddell Hart, and requiring full and sympathetic co-operation between armour, artillery—and aircraft. In Britain Liddell Hart was still, as he was to remain, a thorn in the flesh of the Service Establishment. His 'expanding torrent' of an accelerating offensive, in which bombers in the interdiction and ground-support role played such a central part, was derided by higher authority. Instead of considering the real problem of European security—namely the survival of a vengeful state with an exceptionally strong industrial and technological base—governments and their Service advisers continued to prefer the aerial torrent on civilian populations postulated by the Balfour Committee as far back as 1922—'75 tons a day for an indefinite period'.[12] The Committee had supposed that such an onslaught on Britain would 'render London uninhabitable'. Per contra, the torrent would have the same effect on any state whose government welshed on Locarno.

These comfortable theories had nine more years to run in 1930, but before turning to the Goering era and what, belatedly, the British National governments of the 1930s did to contemplate an air force which might turn the tables and unleash a torrent of its own, it is necessary to indicate some of the particular assumptions and arguments which governed Trenchard and his fellow Chiefs of Staff. The Imperial priority has been emphasised, and it is only necessary to add that, despite the unfortunate affair at Nuseriyah on the Indian North-West Frontier—where 'the tribesmen and their families were put to confusion, many of them ran into the lake, making good targets for the machine guns'[13]—and the repeated criticisms of subordinate political officers in Iraq that bombing tribesmen did not pay, air policing remained a feature of British Imperial strategy, giving the crews of the many Royal Air Force bomber squadrons which served overseas in those years an operational experience whose irrelevance to the task of destroying major cities and industrial complexes must be unique.

It would be too much to say that the view of the Deputy Chief of the Air Staff in 1932 'that no bomb heavier than 500 lb. would be needed'[14] in major war derives from a consideration of the maximum effort needed in Iraq or India, Somaliland or the Aden Protectorate, but there is undoubtedly an element of cause and effect; the element becomes rather more pronounced when we look at illustrations of British bomber aircraft of the 1930s, virtually indistinguishable from those of 20 years earlier. The same point applies more forcefully to lack of defensive armament and most importantly to a positive indifference about the problems of following a route and finding a target by night. Although some RAF officers practised and trained their squadrons in night flying whenever posssible (Harris, when a squadron commander, was known for his belief in the importance of this technique), an atmosphere in which even the new four-engined bombers being contemplated in the 1930s were planned to operate from grass runways[15] was hardly conducive to experimenting with radio equipments of the kind commonly used by crews of the most modern civil airlines. By the middle of the 1930s the North and South Atlantic had been conquered by air, but the RAF was still navigating by methods only suitable for cross-country hops in daylight.[16]

Backing the Imperial priority was a sanguine British belief in the commitment of the United States to supporting Britain if ever involved again in a European war. Although several analysts of American strategic policy between the wars have shown that the boot was on the other foot, and that the shadow of Mahan still lay over the White House, Professor Beloff has lately revealed not only how confident were British governments that hands from across the Atlantic would be stretched out to help in time of need, but what a conveniently diverse form such assistance was supposed to take.[17] But Professor Beloff would have done well to add one American to his list of those who even in those days believed in this strategic 'special relationship', and that none other than Mitchell himself, who argued that, should America again be at war with a European power, bases in the United Kingdom would be necessary if a strategic air offensive was to be mounted in strength.[18] Whether Mitchell's views about a British alliance, plus the impressive demonstrations he had given in the 1920s of the vulnerability of warships to bombing, produced a political-cum-naval consensus of opinion which decided that the state was better off without his services must remain a matter of speculation. There is little doubt however that, although British Chiefs of Staff assumed American help, there was not the slightest intention by American administrations or their Service advisers to be so committed. The British Official History states that the Chief of the Air Staff had 'especially the task of formulating with the other Chiefs of Staff and their opposite numbers in the United States the global strategy of the war'.[19] It is important to make it clear that not even the most informal talks, let alone any formulation of objectives and methods took place between the Chief of the Air Staff and the Chief of Staff of the US Army Air Force before 1941; such contact as existed was confined to sailors on both sides of the Atlantic, and that began only in December 1937.[20]

Standing alone, therefore, with only an assumption of American eleventh-hour support, the British Chiefs of Staff in general and the Chief of the Air Staff in particular had little to comfort them when Hitler's murder of Dollfuss in 1934 forced even the most reluctant British politician's attention to the realities of the European situation. In the five years remaining before World War Two broke out, Air Staff thinking was to oscillate between simple deterrence and what in modern strategic terminology would be known as a pre-emptive counter-city first-strike strategy, followed by a brief interlude of cool reflection about operational realities when Sir Edgar Ludlow-Hewitt became C-in-C of Bomber Command in 1937; this moment of sobriety was followed in turn by a reversion to deterrent and pre-emptive notions on the eve of war which only served to complicate the already involved relations the Royal Air Force establishment enjoyed with governments and politicians. This toying with extreme methods of deterring and waging war was to have unfortunate consequences when war came, especially in 1941 and 1942, when Bomber Command was regarded by more than one Government Department as a dumping ground for discredited strategies or a test tube for experimenting with new ones.

The inconsistency of Air Staff thinking naturally had some considerable effect on rearmament, which, so far as the RAF was concerned, began in 1934, and on the various 'Western Air Plans' (as they came to be called), which were written in 1937. But what did the bomber element of the RAF actually consist of in 1934, when the Government made public a programme to increase the Royal Air Force by 41 squadrons within five years? What was it supposed to do, and what, in turn, was the strength and strategy of the enemy it was supposed to deter or fight? Finally, was there anything in the matériel and long-range plans of the US Army Air Force which might strengthen a supposition that Hitler should fear an American deterrent even if he ignored a British one?

As a matter of record, 488 nominally first-line aircraft in 42 squadrons comprised the 'Air Defence of Great Britain' Command in 1934; some of these squadrons formed part of the three designated 'bomber area commands' of which two, Western and Central, were operational, based in a ring behind the fighter squadrons. The bomber squadrons flew from stations in Wiltshire, Hampshire, Berkshire and Oxfordshire; the fighter squadrons were based on airfields in Essex, Kent, Surrey, Sussex and Middlesex.[21] 'It was a disposition based on the assumption that any attack on us in a European war could only be made by France—an hypothesis which had little reality after the Ruhr crisis of 1923, which had continued to exist for want of a better. . . .'[22] One may also add that although the period of subsequent rearmament saw more effort expended on building new airfields in Yorkshire and East Anglia than in producing a credible bomber force to operate from them, the 'disposition' obtaining in 1934 did not materially alter for several years. Not only did it reflect the ambiguity of British policy towards France, but the double ring of fighter and bomber airfields revealed rather plainly the inadequacy of an air defence for Great Britain at that time. The idea of a radar chain to give early warning of enemy aircraft had not yet been developed even to the planning stage, although the success of the raiding force in the 1934 RAF summer air exercises had shown how urgently necessary such warning could be. No anti-aircraft defences worth the name existed at all, since those established in World War One had collapsed; none were to be rebuilt until the expanded Territorial Army was given this role between 1937 and 1939.[23]

The distinction between fighters and bombers was almost academic— the last generation of biplanes for pure 'pursuit' roles, the Hawker Fury and the Gloucester Gladiator, were hardly yet operational in 1934. The Harts, Hinds, Heyfords, Wapitis and other miscellaneous types with a designated bomber role could as effectively—or with as little effect—have been used as 'air defence' fighters, as their lineal successors, the Blenheim and the Defiant, were to be used *faute de mieux* in the Battle of Britain. The loss of aerodynamic lead time in the 1920s meant that when these vintage biplane types were replaced in the late 1930s it was, for Bomber Command, by the immediately obsolescent Harrows and Wellesleys, and not by genuine twin-engined fast light bombers for an interdiction role or by four-engined heavy bombers which could execute the Trenchard strategy. In a situation where London was widely regarded as defenceless— a point Churchill emphasised in the House of Commons debate on the Royal Air Force on 23 July, when he referred to the German threat and to Britain's capital as 'the greatest target in the world, a kind of tremendous fat cow, a valuable fat cow tied up to attract the beasts of prey'—every one of those 488 aircraft might be needed.

In so far as the bomber aircraft were worthy of the name at all, not only their pitiful range but their inadequate numbers must be stressed. Twenty-four squadrons were serving overseas, in a deployment which sufficiently indicates governmental and Air Staff preoccupation with Imperial requirements. Six squadrons were in Egypt, the Sudan and Palestine; eight were in India; five in Iraq; three in the Far East; one at Aden; one at Malta.[24] In none of these areas was there an enemy, or a potential enemy other than Japan with forces requiring the presence of RAF fighter squadrons to deter or combat. And the fact of the matter is that although, as in the United Kingdom, some squadrons had a nominally defensive role and others an offensive, all were committed to a greater or less degree to Trenchard's strategy of air control. If an explanation is sought for the paradox that an independent bomber force as an expression of the strategy of deterrence or, failing that, the destruction of enemy morale, did not exist, or existed only in obsolescent form within the confines of a defensive command, the answer is to be found by studying the deployment and role of those 24 squadrons operating between Malta and Malaya. Not for the first time in the history of strategy, the sledgehammer and the nut were in absurd proximity.

The paradox is nevertheless so pronounced that, as a background to the late arrival of rearmament and of realistic appreciations by some in high places, we must emphasise the difficulties under which Trenchard's successors laboured in trying to build a bomber force (and a fighter defence) which reflected the threat facing Britain and the part in collective security which the country was supposed to play. The Imperial priority and the Anglo-American illusion have been mentioned, but there were at least four other factors quite apart from Trenchard's maverick personality which militated against the design, organisation and establishment of even a modest bomber force stationed in the United Kingdom, one capable of an interdiction or ground-support role if not one committed to long-range attacks on enemy cities or industry. These four factors were: the ten-year rule; the concept of 'parity'; the nature of the official organisation for strategic and defence policy planning; and the attitude of the Royal Navy and the Army to the RAF.

The ten-year rule was introduced in 1919 by the Lloyd George Government, and it laid down that: 'It should be assumed, for framing revised estimates, that the British Empire will not be engaged in any great war during the next ten years and that no Expeditionary Force is required for this purpose.'[25] The rule, if it can be so dignified, has been quoted in full to indicate the Imperial order of priorities, one spelled out of course by the disavowal of that European expeditionary force which Lord Haldane had striven to create, and which arguably had saved Britain in 1914. (The persistent refusal until 1939 of any British government to pledge ground forces in support of a European ally was materially to affect Air Staff planning when attention was at last directed to the practical problems of building a bomber force and giving it a role to perform.[26]) But although the rule was bad in concept, it was worse in practice, leaving a legacy of procrastination and illusion which dogs British policy-makers to this day. It gave Trenchard a golden opportunity to assert the value of the RAF as a substitute not only for expeditionary forces in Europe but for garrisons elsewhere. But the rule also prevented the establishment of a bomber force which might—it is an interesting thought—have been the policeman that Europe required.

Added to this wretched 'rule'—which was regularly revived throughout the 1920s and only formally abandoned in 1933[27]—was the notion of parity, based on simple quantitative estimates of what a given enemy might be presumed to possess in various branches of its armed forces. For no reason that has been satisfactorily explained, France—and the French Air Force in particular—was presumed for a short time in 1923 to threaten Britain. It was this threat which gave birth to the 'Air Defence of Great Britain' command, led to one of the most incoherent meetings of senior officers which even Whitehall can have seen, and which resulted in a demand for a 'parity' RAF in the United Kingdom of 52 squadrons, which, in Trenchard's view, should be composed mainly of bombers, with a minority of interceptor squadrons and *no* long-range fighters, capable either of independent action or of serving as escorts to a day bomber force. Trenchard's object was 'to obtain as many bombing squadrons as possible and thus increase the offensive power of the Air Force. This decision, of fundamental importance to the whole development of the Air Force, could not therefore be challenged, though some of those present insisted that unescorted day bombers would be likely to suffer heavy casualties.' The Official History, from which these words are taken, errs on the side of meiosis when it adds: 'From these discussions came decisions which determined not only the composition of the future Bomber Command, but also to a considerable extent its strategy and tactics. . . .'[28]

One may wonder why Trenchard's objective could not be challenged, because sitting round the table with him on that curious occasion on 19 July 1923 were, among others, the Deputy Chief of the Air Staff and the Air Officer Commanding in India. There was also a Squadron Leader Portal, of the Directorate of Operations and Intelligence, who did in fact occasionally put his oar in. But although he made some shrewd observations on the importance of a well-integrated fighter defence, able to conduct operations both by day and night, and despite the fact that a lot of time was taken up with defence generally, it is clear from the run of talk that all present shared their Chief's convictions, expressed most forcibly in his 1928 Memorandum, which has been quoted in the Introduction[29].

But although the Royal Air Force was behind Trenchard in his notion of bombers being preferable to fighters or escorts, the ten-year rule and the economic difficulties of practising the parity principle, allied to the broad strategic beliefs and assumptions already described, effectively prevented anything being done. The inadequate system of defence organisation and hostility from the Navy and Army thus only served to make a strong, independent bomber force an aspiration rather than an objective: as is the way with extreme views—and, in the light of aircraft performance in the 1920s, Trenchard's were certainly that—lack of realisation of them most often leads to a hardening of attitude, rather than the growth of moderation and compromise. As time passed this is what happened to Trenchard, and when, in 1928 he wrote his apologia for strategic bombing, the Chief of Naval Staff and the Chief of the Imperial General Staff were moved to deny their colleague's arrogation of a dominant strategic role in words not much different from those in which their successors replied to another piece of special pleading from the same unwearied source 13 years later.[30]

It is unnecessary here to more than summarise the arguments. The Sailor, Madden, and the Soldier, Milne (the latter reckoned to be something of a thinker as the Service society of those days defined the word), simply refused to approve the principle of attacking the enemy heartland or accept that his will to resist would thereby be destroyed. The rebuttal was restrained; nevertheless, although the fear that the Senior Service might be downgraded and that soldiers might find their occupation gone is not apparent, it can scarcely be denied that the Navy and Army establishment found in the Trenchard memorandum fresh evidence of the upstart Service's determination to sabotage them. Between 1928 and 1939 inter-Service disputes ran their usual acrid course, only to be exceeded by the habitual quarrels within the Services themselves. But in a decade notable for bickering, the Navy's attempt to gain and retain control of what later became known as Coastal Command and the Army's steadfast refusal to practise mobile operations with airmen—in other than an Imperial setting—stand out as sad examples of the dissipation of time and the waste of scarce resources. The 1928 Memorandum was certainly not the cause of these quarrels, but it did much to make them so wasteful and pointless.

Before considering how they ordered these things in Germany and the United States, it must be emphasised that, although the old Committee of Imperial Defence had much to recommend it in the relative ease with which ministers and their departments could consult with the Services, there was, as today in the elephantine Ministry of Defence, a basic lack of communication with Parliament or the public, and a quite inadequate machinery for the actual formulation of policy. Outside the RAF there were few in Whitehall and virtually none beyond who knew how the new Service actually worked. Trenchard's utterances boomeranged; they clouded rather than clarified problems, because, like most senior officers giving tongue, he spoke in generalities based on assumptions rather than took actual events and analysed them. Writers on strategy were few; Liddell Hart and Fuller had their work cut out trying to explain what the internal combustion engine could do on the ground, let alone in the air. An earlier decade of writers on matters aerial, F. W. Lanchester in particular, had confined themselves to principles rather than cases or to argument based on scientific and technical knowledge. The Official History was little help either; in the hands of that distinguished literary figure, Sir Walter Raleigh, *The War in the Air* followed the methods of Macaulay rather than the principles of Lord Acton or Van Ranke.

The Goering Years

What that great German historian would have made of the corruption of his country in the 1920s and 1930s by the forces of hate and disorder is hard to say; but he could hardly have been other than amazed at the profound secrecy in which Hitler, Goering and their confederates managed to shroud their preparations for war, and the comparably profound ignorance displayed by those charged with the security of a state for which indeed the Fuehrer professed admiration but which was nonetheless threatened by his ambitions to a degree never experienced before. The CID, the Joint Planning Staff (established in its original form only in 1927), the Air Staff, the Foreign Office, all seemed equally ignorant of the revival of the German armed forces, and over no aspect of the threat to British responsibilities was this ignorance and, in the literal as well as the technical sense, lack of intelligence, displayed more glaringly than over the secret air force. The apothesis of the ostrich was reached in 1937, by which time plenty of official appreciations about Germany were available. In October of that year, one of Vickers Armstrong's senior test pilots visited Germany; the time for secrecy was past; he was shown new aircraft by Udet, was even permitted to fly some. On returning home, Mr Summers, the pilot in question, assessed the implication of these new aircraft for his chairman, Sir Archibald Jamieson, who found them sufficiently disturbing to pass them on to the Secretary of State for Air, Lord Swinton. The latter promptly wrote: 'My Dear Archie, kindly tell your pilots to mind their own bloody business . . . .'[31]

Secret therefore, but apart from collaboration with the Soviet Union, not so utterly clandestine as to fail to arouse suspicion about what was afoot, or so veiled in ambiguity that no appreciation could have been made before 1936 of the threat to Britain should latent power become apparent, let alone utilised diplomatically or in war. The origins of the new Air Force have been indicated; the reluctance of the British Service establishment to take Germany seriously—or to support France in doing so, it may be added—has already been shown. But what, in 1934, was the danger in reality? In the Commons debate of July 1934, Churchill asserted that:

> Germany, in violation of the Treaty of Versailles, already possessed a military air force nearly two-thirds as strong as our existing home defence force; secondly, that at the present rate of expansion, even if the proposals for increasing the Royal Air Force were approved, the German Air Force would nearly equal our home defence force in numbers and efficiency by the end of 1935, and would be substantially stronger in 1936 . . . once Germany had established a lead, we might never overtake them. . . . In civil aircraft readily convertible to military uses, in trained pilots and in glider pilots, Germany already far surpassed us.

How true were these charges? The first point to grasp in considering them is that by the terms of the Treaty of Versailles Germany was prohibited from having an air force at all, but that by 1934 aircraft not only capable of a military role but demonstrably unsuitable for any other were being built. Churchill's figures exaggerate in suggesting a combat force equal to anything Britain could put against it, but he nevertheless starkly and accurately indicated the German potential for war. Although his assertions went by default in the 1934 debate, a central weakness in the British plans to rearm was that Government and public opinion continued to declare and believe that the German threat was not on the scale which Churchill alleged. Churchill's innate prescience about war and his rooted suspicion of Germany, plus a degree of privately supplied information which was of little value because it lacked authenticity, determined his line of argument. It was, however, still just possible to say and believe in 1934 that the Heinkel fighter was an export model or that the rapid turnover of Lufthansa aircrew was a device to give a technological training to young Germans who might otherwise find themselves on the labour market.[32]

Most of what we now know about the build-up of the German Air Force was not only unknown to the British authorities at the time, but, unless agents had been employed who could have seen Milch's and Goering's files, could not have been known—in detail. But it is no exercise in hindsight to say that the outline was unmistakable, provided one added all the other bits of evidence together—an intelligence discipline which the British authorities seemed conspicuously unwilling to practise. Shirer, for example, gives two pieces of circumstantial evidence in consecutive passages of his *Rise and Fall of the Third Reich*, which would not be especially significant if considered separately, but which, if assimilated in London at the period in question (between 1934 and 1937), would surely have led to certain inferences being drawn by minds less imaginative and prejudiced than the infinitely unpopular Churchill. Shirer writes—and it should be remembered that he is summarising what he reported at the time: 'Goering too was busy those first two years [after 1934] establishing the Air Force. As Minister of Aviation—supposedly *civil* aviation—he put the manufacturers to work designing warplanes. Training of military pilots began immediately under the convenient camouflage of the League for Air Sports.'33

Deceit, and deceit in parts admittedly hard to discover. Young Galland, and hundreds like him were leading a double life. But the following passage from Shirer indicates the difficulty of absolute camouflage for a nation bent on conquest, bloodless or sanguinary:

A visitor to the Ruhr and Rhineland industrial areas in those days might have been struck by the intense activity of the armament works. . . . Although Krupp had been forbidden by the Allies to continue in the armament business after 1919, the company had really not been idle. . . . Of the guns being used in 1939–41, the most important ones were already fully complete in 1933. Farben scientists had saved Germany from early disaster in the First World War by the invention of a process to make synthetic nitrates from air after the country's normal supply of nitrates from Chile was cut off by the British blockade. Now under Hitler the trust set out to make Germany self-sufficient in two materials without which modern war could not be fought; gasoline and rubber, both of which had to be imported. The problems of making synthetic gasoline from coal had actually been solved by the company's scientists in the mid-twenties. After 1933, the Nazi government gave Farben the go-ahead with orders to raise its synthetic oil production to 300,000 tons a year by 1937. By that time the company had also discovered how to make synthetic rubber from coal and other products of which Germany had a sufficiency, and the first of four plants was set up at Schkopau for large scale production of *Buna*, as the artificial rubber became known. By the beginning of 1934, plans were approved by the working committee of the Reich Defence Council for the mobilisation of some 240,000 plants for war orders. By the end of that year rearmament, in all its phases, had become so massive it was obvious it could no longer be concealed from the suspicious and uneasy powers of Versailles.[34]

We now know that these powers weren't suspicious or uneasy enough, partly through divisive suspicions of their own, exacerbated by different strategic priorities, but also because the fact of German rearmament as such led until 1938 to various schemes of appeasement, a factor in considering the situation confronting Ludlow-Hewitt and his like which is painfully clear from British political memoirs of the time. What concerns us here, however, is the equally disturbing fact that intelligence staffs underestimated the strength of the German industrial revival, the opportunities thus provided to accelerate the production of war material when the go-ahead was given—this was the pith of Churchill's warning, unfortunately lost in his tocsin sounding—and the difficulties of destroying centres of armaments activity by a strategic air offensive. This last point was to occur to the Air Staff only in 1938, and reality breaking in was mainly due to Ludlow-Hewitt's urgent and caustic promptings.[35] As in later days, those in command grasped the nettle of operational limitations more bravely than did members of the Air Staff. The targets which Bomber Command was asked to attack at the behest of a variety of committees between 1939 and 1941, and even those other targets which Harris chose to attack between 1942 and 1945 were securely embedded in the German industrial landscape by the time disguises were discarded and the German Air Force was openly proclaimed in 1935. Thus, setting Bomber Command's early inadequacies aside, the question of whether certain industrial complexes were important to the German war effort or not—and synthetics certainly were—was academic when so much effort had been expended to ensure that the destruction of several would hardly affect the output of the whole.

The German aircraft industry in particular was to pose singular problems of target selection, from the time that the Western Air Plans were written until virtually the end of the war. Although much German industry was dispersed to the south and east in 1942 and 1943, neither before nor during the war was there the degree of dispersal for aircraft production which would have seemed feasible in view of its importance and the relative ease with which parts could be locally manufactured and then transported to assembly centres. The explanation for the paradox that, with some notable exceptions, dispersal was not great but targets were nevertheless hard to find and harder to destroy, is that much aircraft manufacture, although sub-contracted, took place in or near main industrial centres rather than in the south and east, where communications were poor, but heavy industry could nonetheless partly recover through the assets of certain raw or synthesised materials—the Silesian coal basin and the Rumanian refineries for example. But apropos of aircraft production, as Harris several times pointed out, it was not possible to destroy every German industrial town.

It is not so surprising, therefore, that the destruction of German air-fields figured in the Western Air Plans.[36] Although confusion and dis-agreement over which airfields should be selected for attack were to arise with the French authorities when, at the eleventh hour, staff talks were held, one can understand the thinking behind the selection of such targets, even though others apart from Ludlow-Hewitt were eventually to agree that an attempt to destroy airfields in Germany itself would be pretty futile. For the fact of the matter was that, although the Air Staff came by 1939 to have a good idea of the German Air Force order of battle, it knew little about the German aircraft industry. Indeed, this very point is made by Sir John Slessor, who was in overall charge of the writing of the Western Air Plans, and the significance of his observation is emphasised if we realise that in 1938, when he made it, he was given to believe that in most respects the German industrial revival was nothing like as powerful and dangerous as some had proclaimed.[37]

Thus although we may say that the Air Staff should have known the size of the double problem it faced—an aerial offensive threat to Britain, however low this ranked not only on Hitler's list but on that of the nascent Oberkommando der Luftwaffe,[38] and an industrial strength which Bomber Command would find hard to destroy, let alone *threaten* to destroy, either pre-emptively or after a formal declaration of war—it must also be con-ceded that fully to have measured the German threat and taken comparable remedial action would have required powers of divination, assessment and persuasion which the airmen of the late 1930s simply did not possess. There was no lack of expert warning voices, from Churchill to Liddell Hart; the lack was in hard facts as to exactly with what and precisely where the German Air Force was preparing for its roles. A post-war official and classified account of the German Air Force quotes the records of the Technical Department of the German Air Ministry between 1934 and 1935 in support of the statement that:

> With the aircraft industry now tooled for producing military types in larger quantities, Milch put in hand a new production programme to commence on 1st January, 1934. In view of the needs of training, this programme contained

a very large proportion of trainers, but it provided for the production of 4,021 aircraft up to 30th September, 1935. This programme was in fact superseded in January, 1935, but by the end of that month 2,105 aircraft— 216 short of the planned programme to that date—had been produced, showing an average rate of production over the thirteen-month period of 160 per month.[39]

These figures, as given here, are impressive and disturbing. If Baldwin or Chamberlain—or Flandin or Blum—had known them, it is hard to believe that the Royal Air Force would have been strengthened largely on paper or the French Air Force permitted to moulder.

But what of the United States? American reporters have the rare experience of being read and their despatches digested by their fellow-countrymen in government and administration. Shirer and his colleagues may not have known that 'at the inception of the Luftwaffe its strength stood at 1,888 aircraft of all types, and during 1935 the new arm could muster some 20,000 officers and men'[40]; they would not have had the expertise to appreciate that 'great stress was laid on the rapid mobility of the flying units and their supporting ground staffs, and their operation at short notice from temporary landing grounds . . .',[41] but the kind of information about German industrial strength already quoted could hardly have failed to have an effect on even the most isolationist United States.

Or so one would have thought, but the record shows that until the late 1930s the political presumptions of American administrations, which have already been indicated, prevailed over warning voices. There was also the dangerous if natural tendency to believe that Trenchard was an aerial Mahan, and that his theories represented British strength and strategy, all the more attractive to an administration busy giving its people a New Deal—although the cause of some envy and occasional verbal emulation from airmen controlled by a senior Service and still wincing in some quarters from the furore of Mitchell's resignation. This American tendency to believe Bomber Command an effective instrument of war took some time to disappear, even in World War Two; pre-war there was no hard evidence to blow the mists of assumption away. All the more credit, therefore, should be accorded to the US Army Air Corps and to officers who were to achieve senior command appointments in war for striving to build an air force capable of combating a major state, even though there was no political co-operation or diplomatic initiative to warn a European aggressor that American Air power could be a force to reckon with.

By 1937 the B.17 was flying, four years after manufacturers had been

invited by the War Department General Staff to submit designs for a
bomber capable of a range of 5,000 miles, with a mean speed of 200
miles per hour, carrying a 2,000-lb. bomb load.[42] The bomber was
designed primarily for the Pacific Theatre (to which the earliest operational
aircraft were indeed despatched, although the B.17 first saw combat with
the RAF), but what is more pertinent to later events is that the 'Fort'
was intended to express a tactical principle enunciated most positively in
1933 by Brigadier-General Oscar Westover, then Assistant Chief of the
Air Corps.

> Bombardment aviation has such defensive fire power of such quantity and
> effectiveness as to warrant the belief that with its modern speeds it may be
> capable of effectively accomplishing its assigned mission without support.
> ... The ability of bombardment aviation to fly in close formation and thus
> to insure greater defense against air attack, together with improved efficiency
> of silencers and camouflage argues that no known agency can frustrate the
> accomplishment of a bombardment mission.[43]

The language of air strategy lends itself to hyperbole, especially when
expressed by serving senior officers; the beliefs they express are often
adhered to even when events have discredited them. This quoted belief
in the self-defending daylight bomber formation survived not only the
losses which Bomber Command's Wellingtons and Blenheims endured
on operations in the early months and years of the war (these unsuccessful
raids aroused rather less interest in the USAAF than Fighter Command's
achievement in winning the Battle of Britain), but also the 8th Air Force's
disillusioning middle months of 1943. Thus it is fair comment that the
thinking of General Westover and his colleagues was as much bedevilled
by unproven assumptions as was that of the British Air Staff. Certainly at
the tactical and operational level USAAF notions about strategic air bombardment were unsound; in the broad strategic field however and over
matters of research, design and procurement, the air force which from
September 1938 General Arnold was to lead through uneasy peace and
in war already had a sound and solid base.

Whatever faith was mistakenly placed in the Trenchard doctrine so
far as it was held to protect Britain and, *inter alia*, the United States, the
beliefs that governed American Air Staff thinking were built around the
role of long-range bombers to conduct operations in combination with
naval and ground forces, and strengthened by a reasonable conviction that
American designers and industry could produce the right aircraft for that
task. On the other hand, too much emphasis was possibly laid on the
heavy bombers' range and not enough on their bomb load. What,

however, is relevant to our consideration of the situation in the 1930s is that the fact of range enabled a European as well as a Pacific strategy to be formulated. And this formulation was a considerable achievement in the face of an isolationist Congress and a Naval lobby emphatically selling the Pacific requirement to such members of that body as studied national defence and international strategic responsibilities.

The formulation does much to explain how 'Germany First'[44] emerged from the early months of World War Two as the main premise of American strategy and the basis of planning with Britain, how such an aspiration became an objective—and how it survived the shock of Pearl Harbor, the renewed assaults of Admiral King and the proponents of a strategy which aimed solely at the defeat of Japan, leaving to an isolated Britain the task of fighting Hitler as best it could. The map cited in footnote 18 is an eloquent expression of American belief in the role of strategic bombardment in a European environment, rather than of air power operating in the Pacific and in isolation; the map reflects the determination of General Arnold and his colleagues to regard a threat to European peace as a danger to American security, which neither the Mahan nor Trenchard doctrines could entirely remove. It was fortunate for Britain and the United States that Hitler and his entourage appear to have been unaware of the implications of that very first B.17 flight in spring 1936 and the strategy that was thereafter built round it. The target analysis printed on the map in question is not all that it might be, but its implications are unmistakable.

Of course, there were other plans than AWPD/1; the tortuous history of the earlier 'colour' plans which the Joint Planning Committee Staffs advising the 'Joint Board' of the US Services devised in the twenties and thirties is ample evidence of the tactic of preparing on paper for every possible contingency, of the natural—and national—preoccupation with seeing the continental United States as the 'Americas', and of the fact that 'with the exception of Plan Orange, signifying Japan, these plans bore little relation to contemporary political and military alignments'.[45] Indeed, until the 'Rainbow' series in 1937 superseded those of the overtly isolationist years, ' ... no ... plan was developed against Germany, the foe in the First World War'.[46] Nor should this omission be regarded as surprising; it was not until the Munich period that either the Roosevelt Administration or the Joint Board were virtually forced by the run of global events to revise their series of plans, replacing the colour range with the Rainbow collection, where, for the first time the Axis threat to American security was considered in detail. Hitler's seizure of Czechoslovakia was significant to the United States because, although the act did not pose an obvious threat, taken in conjunction with the development of the Anti-Comintern Pact and the steady Japanese subjugation of China, it emphasised the irrelevance of an 'America first' strategy in a world of aggressive powers.

By the time of Munich the strategic thinking of the Joint Board, the plans of their Staffs and the matériel of the Services were reaching a useful degree of realism and credibility. Although General Arnold has often been quoted as saying 'we had the plans but not the planes', his own testimony qualifies that apothegm. Effective procurement was not so impressive: the Army Staff, arbitrating the Air Corps' affairs, rarely understood what Arnold and his colleagues were trying to do; the B.17 and B.24—the latter flying for the first time in 1939—were produced only in derisory numbers for some years, and 'as late as May 13, 1938, the Adjutant-General sent to the Assistant Secretary of War the following note:

> No military requirement exists for the procurement of experimental pressure cabin bombers in the fiscal year 1939 or the fiscal year 1940, of the size and type described. The Chief of the Air Corps has been informed that the experimentation and development for the fiscal years 1939–40 will be restricted to that class of aviation designed for the *close-in support of ground and light aircraft, pursuit and other light aircraft.*'[47]

But although this passage is comparable in outlook and wording to minutes circulating in the Air Ministry in the late 1930s, the fact remains that by 1939 the USAAF had a true heavy bomber flying, and another at the prototype stage; there was not only America's industrial strength but the fact that imagination and time had been expended on research into aircraft and their equipments, into what we would now call weapons systems. Despite Arnold's 'plans and planes' remark, he nevertheless has pointed out that by 1935 much of the know-how required to make the United States an air power existed and had been tested. An all-metal pursuit plane was flying by 1931; by 1934 the Martin bomber was in service—'a low-wing monoplane, it was the first all-metal bomber, the first of the 200-mile-an-hour bombers. It had a range of approximately 900 miles, and was very clean in design.'[48]

As far back as 1929 blind landing techniques were being practised; in 1930 and 1931 air exercises involving up to 700 aircraft had been held; by 1933 the far west was being used for advanced flying training, bombing and air to air firing.[49] The USAAF was not operationally committed— apart from the occasional but hazardous job of carrying US Mails in weather too rough for the ordinary service—but it was beginning to acquire skills, aircraft and equipments relevant to operations against a major power. More important than all these advances, although many airmen still resented their subordinate status, the wiser heads apparently agreed with the line that 'we didn't want an independent Air Force until we could sustain it properly'.[50] The General Headquarters Air Force had been established in 1935, designed to provide an 'attack' element of strategic bombardment and tactical support aircraft. To a country not itself threatened with an aerial onslaught (an important factor to be considered in giving the pre-1939 plans their true weight), such a force was not only the 'nearest thing to an independent Air Force yet realised',[51] but a useful expression of intent should the international skies darken still more.

We thus find that in the late 1930s USAAF concentration on matériel formed a sensible accompaniment to the plans which were evolving at the Chiefs of Staff level for the kind of war the country might have to fight; the practical and the theoretical therefore did much to offset political indifference to the international scene; within the USAAF itself, concentration on the tools for the job may also have alleviated some of the more unfortunate effects of dogmatic assertions about self-defending formations and the like. We are, however, left with an interesting mystery, as relevant to any consideration of the relationship between government and the Services per se—and to the latter's fraternal relations—as to the development of the USAAF in the years before World War Two. There appears to be no explanation of why, on the one hand, the B.17 and B.24 curtailed rather than inflated USAAF enthusiasm for a pure doctrine of strategic air bombardment—or deterrence—or why, on the other, an aircraft designed primarily for the Pacific theatre should have enabled thinking to develop on how America could exercise a strategic role over Europe's skies; nevertheless, it seems that the smooth transition of American strategy between 1937 and 1939 from a Pacific to a European order of priorities was due in large if undisclosed measure to the advent of the long range bomber. Lack of evidence on this point indicates how wayward a thing is the emergence of a feasible strategy, which harnesses resources to objectives.

Emphasis on the great strategic importance of the B.17 and B.24 does not imply that the Joint Board and its staffs supposed that a strategic air offensive against Germany could be mounted and conducted in default of ground operations; not only in respect of targets but over this equally crucial issue of whether strategic air forces were a substitute for or a complement to ground forces USAAF doctrine differed basically from Trenchard and his followers. In any case, the US Army Staff accepted rather earlier than the British Army Council the necessity to fight on Europe's soil if a European aggressor was to be defeated. It may be, indeed, the very fact that no doctrinal row affected relations between the Army and the Air Corps that enabled the new bombers to be given a role which in no sense elevated them or the Service which operated them to the dangerous level where Trenchard had placed Bomber Command— at once the darling and the butt of political fears and hopes. Although General Westover undoubtedly claimed that the American bomber would get through, there was no forum in the United States where he could have claimed that it would get through without American soldiers beneath it. Mitchell occasionally claimed the paramountcy of air power; as already indicated, the USAAF in general, and the Air Corps Tactical School in particular, did not.

Although, as we have seen, evidence is lacking as to the value of these essentially moderate views in assisting the Joint Board to frame a European strategy, it cannot be doubted that a causal rather than casual relationship obtained between those urging the merits of the B.17 and B.24 and higher Service authority, charged with advising the President. To some the point may seem obvious, but it should be remembered that in 1938 the aircraft's potential was still a gleam in the Air Staff's eye; it could not possibly mean the same to the staff triumvirate who wrote the appreciations on which the 'Rainbow' Plans were based. It was, after all, 'Rainbow 5' which got to the top of the file and stayed there, through Pearl Harbor and beyond, arguing in this wise:

> ... early projection of US forces to the eastern Atlantic, and to either or both the African and European Continents; offensive operations were to be conducted, in concert with British and allied forces, to effect the defeat of Germany and Italy. A strategic defensive was to be maintained in the Pacific until success against the European Axis Powers permitted transfer of major forces to the Pacific for an offensive against Japan.[52]

If the Air Staff had not seen a European role for the B.17 and B.24 or if it had asserted the paramountcy of a strategic air offensive in executing a European strategy, the eminently balanced evaluation just quoted might well have remained just a point of view. The Joint Board's commitment to Europe needed careful nursing; a USAAF denial of responsibility or arrogation of role might have been disastrous for healthy planning.

In short, the lack of inflated notions about what air power could do, plus a USAAF willingness to consider what its strategic bombardment element might be able to do over Europe, probably helped the Joint Board to plan for a long haul against Hitler, and may well have provided Spaatz and other commanders at his level with a useful sense of perspective, both when things were going badly and when the tide had turned. The RAF, as World War Two approached, had no such ballast. Few things are more significant for this period than the determination of the Air Staff to maintain the principle of deterrence and its inevitable coefficient of pre-emption in the face of six factors which should have indicated at the very least caution in expressing extreme views if not the total abandonment of a strategy suitable only for aggressive powers or those who had made their air force the major weapon in their strategic armoury.

The Nature of Power

Rearmament

The six factors which so plainly condemned the Trenchard strategy as merely an exercise in senior officer's rhetoric were: the wayward course of rearmament; the lack of co-operation with France, whose airfields were a necessary element in executing a deep penetration air offensive against Germany; the prudent options given in the Western Air Plans, reflecting, if unconsciously, the operational inadequacies of Bomber Command as much as they drew attention to its duty to provide some kind of support for a British Expeditionary Force; the admonitions of Ludlow-Hewitt, already referred to, based on knowledge of inadequacies in personnel and matériel, not merely in aircraft as such; the impossibility of harnessing science and technology to both offensive and defensive requirements; the German Air Force, and the variety of problems its numbers and calibre posed, particularly in the tactical arena, where the German squadrons which had lately fought in Spain were experienced and versatile. In concluding this study of the locust years, let us consider each of these six factors in turn before ringing up the curtain on a conflict in which air power was to be a major strategic factor.

First, however, the 'Appreciation by the Joint Planning Sub-Committee', dated 26 October 1936, must be given an honourable mention, because it was a brave attempt by officers of all three Services (of whom the then Group Captain A. T. Harris was one) to discuss certain problems 'in the event of war against Germany in 1939'. Despite an inherited alarmist warning note about the loss that could be inflicted on a Britain unprovided with defences against aerial assault—'. . . 150,000 casualties, it was estimated, might occur in the first week of the war', rather more in fact than were suffered by the British people from all forms of German attack in five and a half years of war—the Appreciation did attempt to get away from the strategic simplicities and naive belief in deterrence of earlier years, and grapple with some real issues. Those passages dealing with the role of Bomber Command were an exercise in counter-force strategy, not counter-city bluff, 'force' moreover being used in a narrow and classic sense of armies and their support, rather than industrial locations of obvious strategic value or in the modern sense of strategic weapons systems. Realism was also manifest in those passages dealing with the necessity to co-operate closely with the French and Belgian armies and air forces, and in the absence of any references to the United States.

The Appreciation had been two years gestating, and its circulation around Whitehall in the aftermath of Hitler's entry into the Rhineland in March can be regarded as an official, an inter-departmental recognition of the situation confronting Britain. A Committee which could, *inter alia*, argue that 'the bombing force must . . be used to attack the communications of the German Army and thus assist the land forces to repel their attack', had clearly dismissed the entire presumptions—and dangers— of deterrence and pre-emption in favour of defence and combined operations; in the process, and despite imprecise language over what attacking the German Army and supporting the British and French really involved, the Committee had given political authority and the Air Staff a guide to action which could have been translated into strategy and weapons at a time when the rearmament programme was still fairly simple.

But although the arguments of the Committee respecting the most effective employment for a re-armed Royal Air Force were to find expression in the Western Air Plans of 1937, to be cited by a Chamberlain Government fearful of German reprisals, and to reappear as protests and philippics from various quarters during the war, the implied challenge in the Appreciation for all in authority to think afresh about how Britain could fight defensively and offensively against Germany was too unpalatable to be swallowed. Defence of the United Kingdom was an imperative, an undeniable necessity; that first meeting of the Committee for the Scientific Survey of Air Defence, on a bleak January day of 1935,[1] a day conjuring up a certain quintessential Whitehall atmosphere, most fitting for the employment of greatly gifted, patriotic and strong-minded men in the resolution of an urgent problem, had already begun to show results in the visits by Tizard and his colleagues not only to Watson-Watt and other scientists but to RAF stations and research establishments in comparably bleak East Anglian locations. Defence of the heartland was clearly, demonstrably in good hands.

But if defence in this sense was imperative, was going to absorb much of the RAF budget in ways opposed by Trenchard, and was in effect going to force the new Fighter Command organisation into some kind of relationship with the proposed Anti-Aircraft Command, then a major deterrent cum pre-emptive Bomber Command must be created in addition.

Yet although one part of the Committee's recommendations were in the course of 18 months translated into plans which called for the employment of Bomber Command mainly in an interdiction and close support role, allowing for strategic bombardment only against a limited type of well defined industrial target, implied recommendations, calling either for a bomber force which could wreak casualties on a scale of 150,000 weekly or thereabouts *or* co-operate with the other two Services, were left to wither on the vine. Nothing is odder than the paucity of references to a true heavy bomber force in material relating to the *thirteen* schemes for aircraft procurement which ran their course between 1934 and 1939— indeed, only in 1936 was serious consideration given in the Air Ministry, that citadel of the Trenchard philosophy, to the characteristics of a bomber which could operate all over Germany from bases in the United Kingdom; this degree of contradiction between what Harris and his colleagues recommended, what the Trenchard-imbued Air Staff clung to and what actually found its way into Bomber Command is only matched by the Navy's determination to control Coastal Command, the Army's resentment at Anti-Aircraft Command being put under the operational control of the marginally senior Fighter Command, and the Air Force's comparable insistence that any striking force sent to France would remain an element of Bomber Command and would not be put under the operational control of the Army Commander.[2]

It may, of course, be argued that if the British Government had pledged an Army Expeditionary Force at the same time as it embarked on rearmament, and had urged its French ally to provide proper facilities for supporting an interdiction campaign along the lines spelled out in the 1936 Joint Planners Appreciation and partly formulated in the Western Air Plans, the Air Staff would have got the message, adapted their lion's share of the rearmament budget accordingly, and ordered aircraft related to a true support and limited offensive role. Such a cool look at the strategic requirement might even have seen an order for, not a rejection of, the Mosquito.[3] Alternatively if belief in deterrence and pre-emption had prevailed over political fears of reprisals, the Lancaster might have been a significant weapon by 1939 or 1940. As it was, the notion continued to hold sway until events disproved it that unescorted daylight bombing with twin-engined aircraft was a feasible operation of war. Moreover, because the paper advent of four-engined aircraft for offensive operations actually preceeded the Rearmament Programme, and because obeisance continued to be offered at the shrine of parity, aerodynamic and techno-logical developments and operational requirements became inextricably confused with a political demand for numbers. As a result, aircraft were built which conformed neither to a strategic bombardment nor to an interdiction and close support role; as Mr Divine points out in *The Broken Wing*,

> The story of the Fairey Battle bomber will serve as a type example. The Battle was, by and large, an unwanted aircraft. As early as 1933, the Deputy Chief of the Air Staff declared that it would not make a high performance bomber. Fairey's, however, were tooled up and an order for 655 (approxi-mately equal to the total of the whole air force at Trenchard's retirement) was placed. A further 500 were ordered from Austin's shadow factory which had little to do. When eventually Scheme L arrived and the Ministry still had not a suitable aircraft to put into production, 363 more were ordered from Austin's and a few months later 200 more from Fairey's. Thereafter the Battle was declared 'redundant for operational use'. But the orders continued. In 1939 it was 'definitely obsolete' but in 1940 they were still pouring out. By the end of the year over 3,100 had been produced, two and a half times the number first intended by Scheme F . . . . The Battle was one of many. Five thousand, four hundred and twenty-one Blenheims were built, a vast number of them after they were operationally useless. Long after the heavy bombers were in production the Whitleys went on pouring out— 1,812 altogether where 300 had been originally planned.[4]

It is important to understand that the real cause of this 'stop-gap orders' situation was a combination of strategic and political fallacies; it was not that the Battle, Blenheim and Whitley had no role in war; even if they were obsolete, as fighting stop-gaps they were better than nothing. The fault lay in the lack of anybody knowing or deciding what they were supposed to do. This lack of intellectual vision and practical sense to decide what to do with Bomber Command is what most distinguishes the immediate pre-war period; it was the mixture of dogma and doubt which rendered the Western Air Plans so academic. The lacuna in thought and planning was bound eventually to find some expression in operations, and, during part of 1941, to keep Bomber Command on the ground. For example, and to take our story forward for a moment to May 1940, the gallantry shown by five Battle crews of No. 12 Squadron in attacking the Maastricht bridges is well known, but less well known is the fact that they, and their fellow-crews on many other occasions in those desperate days, received no fighter cover, or did so quite ineffectively.

So strong are the feelings aroused among retired and serving members of the Royal Air Force whenever operations of this kind are described or analysed, that it is necessary to stress the fighter numbers which actually were available to support Air Marshal Barratt's Advanced Air Striking Force of ten Battle squadrons (some 160 aircraft). It was no less than 261; moreover these fighters were Hurricanes, the equal of virtually anything which the German Air Force could put into the sky in those days. But it is a fact that 66 Hurricanes flew back to England; only 74 were shot down, a rather curious statistic in view of the fact that the German Air Force committed well over 3,000 aircraft for the invasion of the Low Countries and France. No less than 121 Hurricanes were abandoned.[5] The inference is unavoidable that this fighter force was underemployed during the Battle for France, and that this was done not in order to preserve it for future use but because no concept of fighter escort had been accepted or practised before the war, whether for penetration or for interdiction raids of the Maastricht type. Fighter cover was in fact ordered for that operation; it failed to arrive over the right place at the right time, which may fairly be considered one reason why four of the Battles were shot down.[6] It is, however, worth noting that even this obsolete aircraft, carrying but four 250-lb. bombs and armed with two single Vickers machine guns, was able in broad daylight to partly damage two very heavily defended bridges. If the Royal Air Force a few years earlier had acquired by practice even a fraction of the tactical flexibility which the Condor Legion had learned the hard way in Spain, the Maastricht raid and others like it might not be recorded as just another gallant sacrifice.

The fate of 16 main and eight subsidiary Western Air Plans shows clearly however, that although the Government shuddered at the thought of a pre-emptive or a reprisal strategic air offensive—Sir Thomas Inskip, holding that curiously unreal office of Minister for Co-ordination of Defence cut Scheme E in 1937 by a 'drastic reduction in the proposed strength of Bomber Command',[7] and urged that production should concentrate on the light and medium types—the Air Staff was not prepared in 1939 to write Operations Orders to implement the arguments advanced in 1936 or related to the objectives—presumably considered attainable in certain conditions—a year later. Taking the main plans alone, the 12 for which Operations Orders were *not* written covered objectives ranging from the German Air Force and its airfields, through reconnaissance and 'counter-offensive action in defence of sea-borne trade in co-operation with the Navy', to German communications and those crucial in the defence of France and the Channel Ports. The four plans for which Operations Orders *were* written covered 'German War industry', Wilhelmshaven, 'the German fleet or a section thereof at sea', and propaganda leaflets. When war came, it was those four plans, translated into operations orders, which sent Bomber Command into action.[8] Certainly the operations were ineffectual and expensive, and the Government's order that Hitler should be allowed to bomb cities first reluctantly obeyed. But, in this context, and for a reminder of what was to happen from 1943 onwards, we should note that:

> The considered view of the Air Staff. . . was summed up in a memorandum issued early in 1938. . . . They divided the targets into two types, (1) the 'precise target', e.g. a power station. . . . (2) the 'target group', of considerable area in which are concentrated many targets of equal or nearly equal importance *on which accurate bombing is not necessary to achieve valuable hits*, e.g. parts of cities, industrial towns, distribution centres or storage areas.[9]

These observations and the Operations Orders summarised on this page should be taken together; they emphasise Sir Charles Webster's comment on the 1938 memorandum that this strategy 'was later to be called "area bombing"'.[10] It was indeed.

Thus neither lack of a consistent Rearmament Programme nor of heavy bombers nor the existence of a considered case for supporting naval and ground forces deflected the Air Staff from its steadfast belief that an independent Air Force should be employed in independent strategic bombardment. This is not an expression of opinion; the statements and the strategy are on the record. Arguably belief in the strategy nurtured hopes and convictions which were to be justified in the fire-storm raids of 1943; it is fair to say that a personality as strong as Trenchard's, but thinking along different lines, would have been necessary to make a reality of the arguments so clearly if so belatedly expressed in the 1936 Appreciation. Undeniably the Air Staffs of the 1930s got no help from Government— 'ready to wound but yet afraid to strike' would aptly characterise it in the Munich days.

Reality Breaks In

But despite this compound of dogma and appeasement, the weakness of Bomber Command and the strength—or, at all events, the size—of the German Air Force were facts which Ludlow-Hewitt, of all airmen, was least likely to ignore and most capable of pointing out to his superiors. For an airman with so much Imperial experience, he showed a salutary grasp of the realities of war among Continental powers. Slessor, recording those days, pays tribute to his 'old Indian ACC', and declares that 'his sense of reality and unsurpassed experience as a practical airman led him to express himself in no uncertain terms on these matters, particularly in relation to the training of his crews'.[11] Harris, no dispenser of bouquets, asserts that Ludlow-Hewitt 'was a man with a minute and detailed knowledge of every aspect of his job. He was far and away the most brilliant officer I have ever met in any of the three services.'[12]

The Official History is sparing of praise, but cannot forebear to devote considerable space to the analyses and criticisms which Bomber Command's immediate pre-war Commander made of the tasks confronting him, equipped in 1937 with a force of '96 . . ."long-range" bombers—36 each of Blenheims and Wellesleys and 12 each of Blenheims and Harrows . . .' to match an estimated '800 bombers technically capable of attacking objectives in this country from bases on German soil'.[13] Although by the outbreak of war Bomber Command, less Air Marshal Barratt's Force, consisted of 43 squadrons, of which 33 were operational, only 17 squadrons—of Wellingtons, Whitleys and Hampdens—could be considered as the elements of a strategic bombardment force; the remaining operational squadrons were equipped with Blenheims and Battles.[14] The German Air Force bomber strength at that time was some 1,180 aircraft.[15] Ludlow-Hewitt did not necessarily quarrel with the beliefs animating the Air Staff; he took issue not with so much their inability or unwillingness to do strategic sums but with an apparent blindness to purely operational factors. A glance at the entry 'Ludlow-Hewitt, Air Chief Marshal Sir Edgar' in the index to Volume One of the Official History reveals clearly enough the nature and degree of his anxieties: 'State of Bomber Command; on protection for Bombers; on state of navigation; on state of armament training; on bomb aiming; presses for Bombing Development Unit; on need for photographic reconnaissance; on realistic exercises . . . .'

Looking back across nearly 30 years it can be said without any exaggeration that, except in morale and maintenance standards, Bomber Command was totally unprepared for war against Germany. The unpreparedness was not confined merely to the lack of aircraft suitable for executing the kind of strategy which, as we have seen, the Air Staff inherited from Trenchard, clung to throughout the 1930s and was determined to test somehow in the crucible of war, despite political inhibitions and a large ignorance about the nature and location of German industry. This ignorance was compounded by unsupported assertions about the rotten state of the German economy and the low morale of the German people. Even the level-headed Slessor, holding in 1939 the appointment of Director of Plans, indulged in this wishful thinking about the enemy as, with a modesty most rare in senior officers, he has later admitted. The root weakness lay in the fact that, on the eve of war, the Air Staff had spent some years mulling over the concept of a bomber which could fly unescorted by day to Berlin and back from bases in the United Kingdom, carrying—in its 1938 paper incarnation—a bomb load of 12,000 lb.[16] The indecision over design and performance, compounded again by the three specifications issued in 1938, was at the root of Bomber Command being a force totally unsuitable for strategic bombardment, actually possessed of aircraft only suitable for an interdiction role, and that only when escorted. The problems to which Ludlow-Hewitt drew repeated attention followed inevitably from this separation of theory and practice. Lack of the right aircraft, lack of the right arms, armament and equipment, and sheer lack of training above the most elementary level explain why it was not until March 1943 that the Commander-in-Chief Bomber Command could say, 'At last we are ready'.[17]

It may fairly be asked by any who think a harsh assessment has been made, 'What *is* right?' There is no such thing as an ideal weapons system; those like the Mosquito, which operate in action almost ideally, seem a fortuitous bonus as much as the result of long-maturing plans; this is a view which even many scientists hold, a body supposedly critical of allowing the element of chance or luck to creep into calculations and judgements. But having said that, an objective look at the state of Bomber Command on the eve of World War Two reinforces the assessment that no serious attempt was made by the Air Staff to prepare it even for the most limited type of operations, let alone for forcing Hitler to cry quits. Public opinion was certainly no help; to prepare a striking force for war in an overcrowded island—and one moreover, not invaded for nearly nine hundred years—could never have been easy. Harris and Slessor relate with reasonable anger how attempts to find new bombing ranges were stymied by public outcry—the swans at Abbotsbury would be disturbed, said one pressure group, it was a sacrilege to disturb the ghosts of Holy Island, said another.

But aside from these symptoms of the Alice-in-Wonderland mood which afflicts the British on occasions, the evidence is clear that when keen squadron commanders, let alone an anxious Commander-in-Chief, asked for training in their trade, higher authority discouraged or refused them.[18] Ludlow-Hewitt's determination not to send his groups and squadrons into battle untrained, even though this meant rolling-up some front-line units in order to provide experienced airmen for the remainder, was echoed by many of his subordinates, who knew that their crews were unable to navigate at all by night, could do so by dead reckoning only during daylight, dropped practice bombs in ideal conditions of visibility, and were rarely exercised against Fighter Command. Perhaps, with the advent of the eight-gun fighter this was just as well. Although by 1939 power-operated turrets were scheduled for installation throughout Bomber Command in all but the Battle and Hampden—the equipment being a notable advance on that provided for the B.17 and B.24 let alone for German aircraft—fixed, free and hand-held Lewis and Vickers guns of World War One vintage were still commonly found in the squadrons designated as operational. One of my informants who served in those days, who had been a sergeant pilot since the early 1930s, and was by 1939 an experienced Whitley captain, has said that, in lieu of the promised turrets, his crew 'designed', manufactured and installed a *wooden* gun mounting to support the single gun available to the rear gunner.

This is perhaps an extreme example, although even Sir Charles Webster's studied prose occasionally reflects the fear that lay beneath the traditional British 'all right on the night' demeanour of Bomber Command. 'The training of crews in night flying, was, indeed, obviously a difficult problem and it was never really faced in the pre-war period',[19] writes Sir Charles evenly. Referring to the problems of those untrained crews, whose lives were his responsibility, Ludlow-Hewitt more tersely stated that 'he was not prepared to embark immediately on operations that went a large distance into Germany. Such a course . . . might end in a major disaster.'[20] Such a disaster, be it noted, could have resulted from faults in Bomber Command itself; it would not have required the intervention of the German Air Force or ground defences.

But the irony, or the tragedy, of this situation was that, with the exception of the Whitley, aircraft of Bomber Command were not intended primarily for night operations; on the other hand, not only Ludlow-Hewitt but other senior officers had expressed doubts about its credibility in unescorted daylight operations. Navigation in general, therefore, and navigating by night, was, or should have been, of quite unique importance.

Yet it was left to the enthusiasm of individual squadron commanders and their crews to practise as best they could the techniques of radio- and astro-navigation. The Commanding Officer of 51 Squadron enrolled some of his crews on a navigation course at Southampton University; other pilots—there were no navigators as a trade until 1941—manufactured their own sextants; those instruments that were officially provided were, it seems, either in short supply or unreliable or both. Radio direction finding by 1939 was a normal navigation technique in civil aviation; the Air Ministry made no efforts to learn from men like Bennett, whose employment with Imperial Airways added undoubted if belated British lustre to the business of long-distance flying. In Bomber Command, however, those crews led by professionals were still experimenting with primitive apparatus, whereby cross-bearings based on the strength of radio transmissions enabled a position to be approximated—in favourable conditions. But flying over the Irish Sea in good weather was to compare very favourably with seeking Hamm or Hamburg in industrial haze.[21] Even so, peace-time crashes and forced landings were frequent. During 1937–8, 'Bomber Command had 478 landings due to pilots losing their way . . . '.[22]

A catalogue of errors becomes tedious. A more fundamental point, and one especially relevant to navigation, was that the scientific and technological effort being devoted to the defence of the United Kingdom could not have been diluted in order to aid Bomber Command without the safety of the country being put at impossible risk. The consensus of scientific opinion is virtually unanimous on the necessity which obtained to concentrate on defence between 1935 and 1939. Tizard and Lindemann came to disagree about practically everything before war broke out, but although the latter's participation in the former's committee for the Scientific Survey of Air Defence was valuable or deplorable according to one's point of view, there is no evidence of disagreement on the overriding importance which should be given to the defensive requirement; inevitably the parallel Committee of the Scientific Survey of Air Offence—a body which emerged after informal talks in the Autumn of 1936—had little to do. 'We first met nearly a year ago in November last', wrote Tizard on 7 October 1937 to the then Air Vice-Marshal Freeman, the Air Member for Research and Development.

Since then we have had six other meetings and some interesting discussion covering a wide range of subjects, but time goes on, and it seems extremely difficult to get some experimental work carried out . . . . I know of course about all the difficulties of providing for everybody's urgent needs . . . . All I want is to make quite clear that the scientific people cannot really discharge

the responsibility put upon them unless the Experimental Departments get
the equipment they need.[23]

The rub was in the last observation: the 'Experimental Departments'
were pushed for time to test material that could result in prototype defensive equipment for manufacturers to produce and install in the 'Chain
Home' early warning system. As Tizard's biographer says, in a happy
phrase, ' . . . the battle of "the Few" was won with the weapon of radar,
handed to that bright company almost as the chocks were pulled away.'[24]
With such a race to provide early warning for Fighter Command against
attacks on its airfields and, should Hitler and Goering attempt that 'knock-
out-blow' so frequently prophesied, against Britain's great cities, not
much more than thought could be spared for aids to the offensive arm.
The Air Offence Committee continued in being until December 1938, and
its members enjoyed one advantage over the desperately active Air
Defence Committee, in that they reported direct to the Air Ministry—
and in practice to the understanding Chief of the Air Staff, Newall, and
to the energetic Freeman—and were spared the irritation of knowing that
another body, a sub-committee of the Committee of Imperial Defence,
was not only pursuing parallel defensive investigations but enjoyed
Professor Lindemann's presence on it as well.

On the Brink

But this relief was little help in a situation where not only were resources
lacking but where the 'instinctive faith' in the Trenchard theory of
strategic bombardment, of which Slessor has written, virtually precluded
a dispassionate, scientific examination of how it was to be executed. The
Air Staff could call, if it wished, on the Royal Aeronautical Establishment,
the Department of Scientific and Industrial Research, the Director of
Scientific Research, the Secretary of State's Aeronautical Research Committee, and for that matter, no less than ten universities or colleges where
aeronautical research was undertaken. The Aeroplane Experimental
Station at Martlesham Heath in Suffolk also conducted research—tests
would perhaps be a more accurate word—in various problems of bombing
and gunnery. Although most of the work carried out by these bodies and
in these places was concerned with aircraft or equipment, and practically
none with weapons systems, it can hardly be denied that techniques
existed for discovering whether certain things worked or did not, or could

be made to work better. But at the Air Staff level there was, collectively, a refusal to think about the need for improving existing arms and equipments, or devising new ones; this refusal reflected, however, a deeper malaise, a refusal to think dispassionately about the responsibility of chucking a lot of green young men in badly armed aircraft against a country which had for years been preparing to fight if bluffs were called. Although the probable behaviour of aircraft in war had been mathematically calculated by F. W. Lanchester as far back as 1916—leading to the unoriginal but highly pertinent conclusion that many well-armed aircraft were likely to have the advantage over fewer ill-armed ones[25]—operational research teams formed no part of Service Commands or Establishments before 1939. Bomber Command, indeed, resisted them until 1941.[26]

In this atmosphere it is not surprising that Tizard and his colleagues concentrated utterly on the defensive imperative and, having been rebuffed by the Air Staff, particularly over Bomber Command's navigation and gunnery problems, let ill alone until the Chain Home stations were well on the way to completion. It was not until 4 July 1939 that Tizard actually met Ludlow-Hewitt[27]; despite the lateness of the hour, these two dedicated men at once set about doing what they could to help the air crews who would have to pay the bill for those locust years. There was precious little that could be done, two months before war broke out. Tizard, characteristically, did not insult the courage or intelligence of his youthful audiences on his visits to bomber stations at Great Driffield, Waddington, Mildenhall and Wattisham; he was no academic, but conformed rather closely to that kind of seeker after truth in a setting described by Sir Isaac Newton, who once wrote: 'If, instead of sending the observations of able seamen to able mathematicians on land, the land would send able mathematicians to sea, it would signify much more to the improvement of navigation and the safety of men's lives and estates on that element.'[28]

The safety of men's lives in the air interested Tizard very deeply. He had many times in World War One risked his own to reduce unnecessary hazards in operational flying. Yet although in the aftermath of his visits to these Bomber Command stations he made recommendations for 'further aids to navigation, improvement of gunnery, and further research on a gyroscopically controlled automatic sight for high-altitude bombing',[29] he pulled no punches about the problem which stared Ludlow-Hewitt and his crews in the face. Tizard wrote: 'Generally considered, with proper training, it would be possible to be pretty certain of being within one's objective by a distance of *ten to fifteen miles**, even if one could

* Author's italics.

not see the ground . . . .'[30] As Clark points out, 'This was but six weeks
before the outbreak of war; the Germans were already making preparations to "bomb on the beam", a method which could, until countered,
provide them with an accuracy of a few hundred yards . . .'[31]

The crews of Bomber Command faced in fact such absurd odds that,
with the exception of the early daylight raids, the Battle of France and
isolated operations by 2 Group's Blenheims in 1941, operations were
limited and losses did not occur on the scale which Ludlow-Hewitt and
others had prophesied. But, of course, there was no strategic air offensive
worth the name in those years; it did not require the Chamberlain Government to inhibit such an operation of war. Extreme vulnerability being a
kind of insurance was, however, a notion too subtle for the crews of the
17 Wellington, Whitley and Hampden Squadrons, of Nos 3, 4 and 5
Groups respectively, on whom lay the burden of bombing Germany,
if only with leaflets. The collective personality of these crews is hard to
describe, since the characteristics with which Bomber Command later
became identified did not develop until 1941 and 1942. By then the wartime aircrew member predominated, and the new and purely aircrew
trades had become established. The regular, peace-time Bomber Command
was not only very small, but 'aircrew' really only comprised first and
second pilots. Observers were mustered as a trade, but they had ground
duties to perform as well, while gunners were junior non-commissioned
officers in ground trades, who volunteered for flying duties and flew
when not otherwise employed. A fair proportion of pilots were sergeants,
and a small number captained aircraft. But flying personnel in Bomber
Command was essentially some 600-odd officers; those who survived one
tour of operations in war could reasonably expect rapid promotion. In
fact, very few of that small band lived to get it.

Their instruction in pure airmanship was thorough enough, but, apart
from the material and advanced training deficiencies already described,
the professional outlook of Bomber Command's junior officers was
governed by the fact that since 1934 the Short Service Commission Scheme
of four years on the active list and eight years on the reserve had taken
precedence over the regular entry through the Cadet College at Cranwell.
The Short Service programme reflected the paper expansion of the Royal
Air Force between 1934 and 1939; if, eventually, Bomber Command
was to number not less than 1,631 aircraft—this was the Scheme H figure,
introduced in January 1937, and the highest of the pre-war totals—then it
was clearly necessary to train many more pilots than Cranwell could
produce. The Short Service Commission Scheme was in many ways

admirable; it utilised civil flying training capacity, helped to make young men 'air-minded', brought many fine pilots from the Commonwealth, and could indeed be considered as a curtain-raiser to that great wartime scheme for training pilots, navigators and others in Canada, South Africa and Rhodesia. But, in the nature of things, four years' regular service was unlikely to implant professional zeal in Bomber Command's pilots. Skill yes; courage of every kind, most abundantly; the incentive to get to the top and help improve the overall calibre of Bomber Command, no.[32]

The Scheme did, however, provide a link with the three popular reserve forces, on which all branches of the Royal Air Force relied so heavily in the early years of the war, namely the Royal Auxiliary Air Force, the Royal Air Force Volunteer Reserve and the University Air Squadrons. The establishment of a Reserve Command and a Training Command in the 1930s and the imaginative utilisation of civilian flying schools then did a great deal to combat material deficiencies; without exaggeration, it may be said that lacking the foundations laid by these schemes for tapping manpower and attracting it into the Royal Air Force, a true heavy bomber force would not have been created and certainly would not have endured through bitter loss and nearly six years of combat. It is perhaps equally appropriate here to mention the Air Training Corps, in which schoolboys enrolled for evening training and summer camps; this most enthusiastic of volunteer corps not only encouraged thousands of school-leavers to volunteer for flying training, but kept interest in the Royal Air Force at such a pitch that the ground trades were constantly replenished throughout the war by youngsters who, if flying was out for them, were determined to do their best in the essential maintenance and administrative tasks.[33]

But none of these native schemes would by themselves have provided the flying and initial crew training that was essential if Bomber Command was to expand. Wide open spaces and clear skies were needed if major aircrew expansion was ever to take place. The Empire Air Training Scheme, first broached by the Air Ministry to the Canadian Government in 1936, became by 1942 an 'organisation . . . capable of producing no less than 11,000 pilots and 17,000 other aircrew each year'[34] from the Dominions as a whole. Bearing in mind that the initial reaction of the Canadian Government was hostile, then, through Lord Tweedsmuir's efforts, cool, and only by 1939, co-operative, and that until war broke out the Australasian attitude to Britain was rather different to what it had been in 1914, these figures are interesting commentary on how, in World War Two, the white dominions rallied for the last time to the support of the 'mother country'.[35] Canada trained not only its own young airmen, but thousands from Britain, Australia and New Zealand in the intermediate techniques of operating twin and four-engined aircraft. By the terms of the Ottawa Agreement of 17 December 1939,

> the United Kingdom was to supply nearly all the aircraft and a nucleus of skilled men, the Dominions all other requirements. Canada, training Canadians, Australians, New Zealanders and a small number of pupils from Britain and Newfoundland, would build up thirteen Elementary Flying Training Schools, sixteen Service Flying Training Schools, ten Air Observer Schools, ten Bombing and Gunnery Schools and two Air Navigation Schools. Australia, training her own citizens, would create nine Elementary Flying Training Schools, seven Service Flying Training Schools, four Air Observer Schools and four Bombing and Gunnery Schools. New Zealand, also training her own citizens, would form three Elementary Flying Training Schools and two Service Flying Training Schools.[36]

But even the Canadian scheme as ratified in the Ottawa Agreement, expressive and effective though it was, required support elsewhere. The Governments of South Africa and Southern Rhodesia (as it then was) rallied round. 'Southern Rhodesia led the way by agreeing to accommo-date, administer and partly pay for three Service Flying Training Schools, all of which were to be, in the main, staffed by and run for the Royal Air Force.... South Africa offered a share of her expanding training organisation to Royal Air Force pupils.'[37] Thus, in terms of potential, the aircrew position was satisfactory. If these well-trained British and Dominion crews could be provided with the right aircraft, armament and equipment, the Trenchard idea of absolute air power might yet become a strategic reality. If the generally expected onslaught of the German Air Force on Britain when war broke out could be discovered by radar and broken up by Fighter and Anti-Aircraft Command, sustaining an Air Raid Precautions Scheme which, by 1939, had caused a fair number of young Londoners to be evacuated while their parents contemplated a troglodyte existence under fire, time might be bought for East Anglia to become a complex of airfields from which the return match could be played.

After 3 September 1939 this balance of possibilities, this policy of the long haul, rapidly acquired a kind of reality which peace in the locust years of extreme strategic views and fabric-covered biplanes had wholly denied it. Despite the air-raid sirens wailing over London on that first Sunday of the war—in false alarm as it turned out—one discerns in the private records of that time a feeling of release; either our defences would stand up or the dyke would be breached.[38] But buttressing this further stage in simplifying the issues to a degree where the Royal Air Force was bound to achieve great significance in both its defensive and offensive roles, was an inherited conviction that once the balloon went up British tenacity would overcome German aggression. Little thought was spared for the French, just as little time had been spent on the Czechs or the Poles or much intelligent consideration given to a strategic relationship with the Soviet Union. There was an inchoate feeling that Britain was alone, but that America would 'come in' at some unspecified time. As Col. Fleming has pointed out in *Operation Sea Lion*, these were attitudes which the island race preferred to entangling alliance, and which were to reach their fullest expression during the Battle of Britain and the Blitz.

But the attitudes are mentioned here because, in their embryonic form on the eve of war, they reflected among the Government and its advisers, and not only with the man in the street, a preference for assumptions about the course of events, however sombre these might become, rather than a willingness to analyse their probable development. To this obfuscatory process, the idea of absolute air power had also made a notably unfortunate contribution. Although by 1939 the German Air Force was in terms of all-round capability easily the largest and most formidable in the world, and had demonstrated some part of it in Spain, there was no evidence that Hitler and Goering intended an aerial Blitzkreig on Britain once war with Germany had been declared. The year 1943, when in Hitler's view Germany would be 'fully rearmed', was tentatively set as a date when all strategic options in Europe were open, and from this date such an offensive might have been contemplated. But the air offensives actually waged in Poland, the Low Countries and over Britain in 1939 and 1940 were strictly counter-force; the Polish and Dutch Air Forces were knocked out in a few days, Fighter Command's airfields were the primary objects of attention in the opening rounds of the Battle of Britain, when they were badly mauled. Even Warsaw and Rotterdam were the objects of limited attack, not elements in a sustained offensive.[39]

At the level where weapons of war are considered as instruments of state policy and not merely as expressions of national aspirations or resources, the evidence up to 1939 would, if analysed, have shown that Hitler was determined to acquire territory, to do so without fighting if possible, to invade on the ground if 'opposed'. *Lebensraum* was Hitler's obsession, next to personal fulfilment and pathological racialism, and it was an obsession he had demonstrated long before the German Air Force became an instrument of policy or a weapon of war. Bluff, which played so large a part in Hitler's approach to international affairs, is, of all things, the easiest of techniques to expose by hindsight. Nevertheless, as Mr A. J. P. Taylor says of Hitler, in one of the few studies of those days to have been published: 'In 1939 he was still master of the art of waiting . . . . The war of nerves was his speciality.' Never once before war broke out—was 'forced on him', as he, like Kaiser Wilhelm in 1914, declared—was the threat of aerial blitz in the form of 'terror bombing' invoked against Britain, or, for that matter, against any other of the Third Reich's intended victims.[40]

The reason for this policy was not fear of reprisal, but cunning plus a tincture of realism. Such a threat would have had to be swallowed or met; but the essence of Hitler's technique was to present a threat which appeared to offer room for compromise or negotiation, in situations coloured by ambiguous factors like demilitarised zones, and 'corridors', 'free' cities, the Sudetan Germans and the 'common language and inheritance' link with Austria. Air power aimed at civilians and their industrial wealth would have rubbed out these convenient ambiguities. On the eve of war, Hitler laid it down that

> . . . the Air Force is, in the first place, to prevent the French and British Air Forces from attacking the German Army and the German *Lebensraum*. In conducting the war against England, preparations are to be made for the use of the Luftwaffe in disrupting British supplies by sea, the armaments industry, and the transport of troops to France. A favourable opportunity is to be taken for an effective attack on massed British naval units, especially against battleships and aircraft carriers. Attacks against London are reserved for my decision.[41]

The sting, certainly, is in the tail, but it should be emphasised again that until he attacked Poland Hitler did not overreach himself; attacks on London *followed* the bombing of Berlin; the '800 estimated bombers, technically capable of attacking objectives in this country from bases on German soil' as early as 1937, had risen by 1939 to nearly 1,200, but it will be seen that their designated role was counter-force not counter-city; the passages quoted above *followed* the signing of the Nazi–Soviet Pact on 21 August 1939. Thus although Hitler had secured his rear and avoided, at least temporarily, the German fear of 'encirclement', great caution was still the keynote over plans for dealing with Britain, should 'a peaceful settlement' prove impossible.

It may be thought ironic that the absolute weapon, lord of the third dimension, should be considered so inappropriate, so inflexible by one who corrupted Germany and savaged Europe over 12 long years. Ironic or not, not only does this control of air power by Hitler tell us much about his pre-1939 technique, but it gave Goering and the Luftwaffe Air Staff a brief on which to establish an air arm which could best serve the many different strategies open to a ruler who retains the initiative. That brief may be summarised thus:

> The German Air Force . . . although constitutionally an independent arm of the armed forces, was . . . not expected to conduct an independent war. It was intended to operate tactically in support of both the Army and the Navy, as well as conducting, at certain stages, strategic warfare of its own in defence of German cities and industries or in the attack on enemy shipping, industry and communications.[42]

A long-range bombing force was certainly developed—but so was a troops-carrying element, both physically derived from civil transport types; the latter, however, was conceived as an element in political warfare and not merely as an aid to mobile armies. From the same fertile source came also a powerful force of long-range reconnaissance and maritime aircraft, weapons systems unmatched, indeed scarcely found, in the British armoury. In still narrower strategic and tactical terms, the disparity between the British and German capacities to utilise air power in support of ground operations is clearly illustrated by the latter's sole possession of over 400 dive bombers and ground attack fighters. Moreover, not only had the German Air Force some 1,200 fighters of the pursuit type on the outbreak of war, compared to Fighter Command's 600-odd, but the former could be considered available for employment on several fronts, while still retaining a comfortable numerical margin.

Nevertheless, despite this clear, if unexpressed concept of air power's strategic limitations, coupled with a well-articulated doctrine for the German Air Force's role in war, weaknesses existed, and they revealed that, from Hitler downwards, the concept of the long haul was, as ever in German strategy, anathema. Although Milch had delivered the goods demanded by Goering (aided by the acquisition of Austrian factories in 1938),[43] neither production rates nor aircraft design when war broke out was in a state which allowed for significant improvements in quantity and quality. The notion that Germany had fully mobilised its industry for war by September 1939 was propagated by Hitler; but it is not borne out by the facts. ' . . . Aircraft production, in spite of all contrary foreign views, did not exceed a few hundred aircraft a month. At the same time the usual errors of modern armament—multiplicity of types, equipment complicated to produce and service—were by no means avoided.'[44] Above all, and the most significant indication of the 'short and easy war' outlook shared by Hitler and his generals alike, no integrated radar, fighter and ground defence system had been developed, even although elements of all three existed. Only in undeveloped industrial resources combined with technical skill, plus a mounting enthusiasm for Hitler (a bonding process, as it were, to the extraordinary toughness and hardness of the German city-dweller) could the Third Reich be considered as prepared for defence. Despite the number of fighters available to Generaloberst Jeschonnek, Chief of the General Staff of the Air Force in 1939, they were none too many should Britain, at last galvanised into action, decide in desperation to execute a Trenchard offensive while German armies and their Luftwaffe supporting elements were rolling east and west.

Once the point is grasped that the striking power of the Luftwaffe was intended essentially for interdiction, tactical bombing and ground support operations, and that, moreover, escorted bombing had been the rule even in Spain, it can be seen that a fighter arm comprising only 25–30 per cent of the whole did not allow for all of Germany to be defended. The British Government, in expectation of terror bombing on London, had ordered Fighter Command to be concentrated in the south of England; the radar stations gave early warning only to the south, east and north-east. These dispositions revealed several interesting emotions affecting the British Government's sense of priorities and its appreciations of Hitler's intentions, resources and method; by the varying fortunes of war, his unexpected success in forcing France's surrender after a matter of months, led him, if most nervously, to consider invading England, a strategy which required the destruction of Fighter Command and its bases before all else. In the event, therefore, the radar and fighter shield for London proved, with the great success of Bomber Command in sinking the barge concentrations, an effective defence against invasion.

Hitler, however, had no problems on this scale. In 1939 Germany was virtually immune to all but an aerial Balaclava; Berlin was a distant and difficult target; other major cities were not apparently considered as vulnerable; aided, therefore, by an impressive network of airfields and by a command and administrative structure which reflected the concept of swift movement and adaptability to changing circumstances, fighter forces could be rapidly despatched to defend the one industrial area, namely the Ruhr, which was relatively close to East Anglian airfields—and very close to those in France—and contained such concentrations of 'workers' that even the severest critic of the Trenchard strategy could scarcely afford to ignore them. As we have seen, the Air Staff, selecting four of the Western Air Plans for translation into operations orders, was not inhibited by any such critical attitude, and earmarked the Ruhr for attack when opportunity afforded. It is an interesting speculation whether the theory of air power as the dominant weapon of modern war would have been so strongly held to in Britain if the Ruhr industrial complex had been located in Silesia.

The defensive screen for the Ruhr was a very straightforward affair. 'The defence of Germany by fighter aircraft was a secondary consideration and no night fighter units had been formed; the major burden of the permanent home defences was in the hands of the anti-aircraft units.'[45] But it should be borne in mind that, out of the one and half million men in the Luftwaffe on the outbreak of war, nearly *two-thirds* were anti-air-craft personnel—' . . . an elite body of men . . probably more effective in hindering enemy air operations and shooting down or damaging enemy bombers, fighters and reconnaissance aircraft than any other anti-aircraft organisation in Europe.'[46] A force of nearly one million well-trained and armed flak gunners and searchlight operators enabled a powerful static defence to be provided for the Ruhr, which could be reinforced as need arose or if other areas or the German Fleet in harbour required heavier fixed defences by fighters from home based air fleets, groups and squadrons. The heavy emphasis on flak defences does much to explain the frequency with which they figure in Bomber Command accounts of the early stages of the strategic air offensive.

So confident was the German High Command in 1939 of the effective-ness of such a defence in a context where Bomber Command was every-where at a disadvantage, that only some 25 squadrons (about 250 aircraft, less reserves) were allocated for the defence of the Ruhr and western Germany. These squadrons consisted principally of the Me. 109 single-engined fighter, armed with a zoom Oerlikon cannon, with an all round performance not inferior to the Spitfire. Like its twin-engined partner the Me. 110 (intended as much for offensive as defensive operations), the 109 represented an interesting stage in German aircraft design and pro-duction. Unlike the other basic operational aircraft manufactured by Junkers, Heinkel and Dornier, the Messerschmitt had come late to pro-duction for military purposes. It had not been tested by service in the Condor Legion, but neither had it been saddled with performance char-acteristics which became obsolescent by 1942–43. The Messerschmitt types were to prove more than adequate in 1939; they were still going strong as late as 1944.

A combination of scepticism about Bomber Command's capacities, and the establishment of very strong ground defences plus mobile fighter support, does much to explain why the third element in the defensive chain—early warning—was not linked with the other two. It should also be appreciated that the comparably efficient and flexibly organised signals organisation in the Luftwaffe was intended primarily to support offensive air and ground operations. Thus the day of close co-operation between aircraft, guns, searchlights, early warning and communications was not yet. The apparatus for early warning, the *Freya* and *Wuerzburg* systems, covered the North-Western approaches to Germany, and were technically and in terms of range the equal of the British Chain Home system. But the radar and fighter control systems remained quite separate, indeed fighters, intended to fly in a support role *and by day only*, were not organised for sector or 'box' operations at all. Squadron commanders trained their pilots hard in various tactics, particularly variations on the 'arrow head' formation, as Galland describes in his memoirs, but nothing approaching the Fighter Command defensive system was considered necessary by Jeschonnek and his colleagues.

Fundamentally this attitude was based on confidence. Although not every German senior officer, in the Luftwaffe or anywhere else, thought that Britain would be easily defeated, the prevailing belief was that the Third Reich was unstoppable. This conviction was especially strong in the Luftwaffe, which had given thousands of young men a first-class technical education, and whose Condor Legion had been imaginatively and intelligently led in Spain, where young commanders had been given plenty of chance to show initiative. Now the confidence was about to be tried; the seconds were out of the ring; two fundamentally different concepts of air war were about to be tested; in the last analysis, however, the young men on both sides would decide the issue; in one corner, Galland and his like, at concert pitch, strung up by success, arrogant with certainty of victory; in the other, young men, epitomised by Guy Gibson, who went to battle in a manner that now seems as dated as a faded snapshot:

> In the Officers' Mess there was a dim sinister bluelight. You couldn't possibly see to read, but then there were not enough black-out curtains for every building. As I was having my breakfast and about to go to bed, all the boys came in. Normally there is no one about in an RAF Officers' Mess at 6 o'clock in the morning, but this was different. They had been standing by since dawn. They had not changed; they were cheerful in their greetings.
> 'Good leave, old boy?'
> 'Hullo you old so-and-so, so you've come back for the war, have you?'[47]

PART TWO

The Years of Aspiration
1939–1942

The Issues
1939–42

Bomber Command as an Instrument of Politics

The war which Guy Gibson had 'come back to' was for over three years one fought largely in Whitehall and in semi-secret scientific establishments scattered about the remoter parts of southern England. The first three years also witnessed occasional British successes in the offensive as well as the defensive aspects of this type of war; the gloomy operational picture is belatedly relieved not by technological advance but by tactical innovation; gallantry in the face of ludicrous odds never failed. But the main interest of the period from the outbreak of war until 'the end of the beginning' must centre on the Whitehall battle for control of Bomber Command and for a valid role for it to perform.

The United States Army Air Force was uncommitted in Europe for all but the last few months of the period, and then only notionally; the Luftwaffe's task in defending Germany was light and, excepting the Kammhuber Line, required, or at all events, produced little worthy of record, especially as the aircraft-locating and gun-ranging radar systems of *Freya* and *Wuerzburg* were installed well before war broke out, and proved perfectly adequate for their purpose until well into the summer of 1943. This chapter, concerned with issues, will not be concerned, except incidentally, with either the American contribution to or the German reaction to Bomber Command's efforts to maintain itself in the political and strategic line of battle between 1939 and 1942. The concepts of air power held in both countries bore little relation to Bomber Command's particular Whitehall battles. These concepts have been described in the chapters covering the inter-war years, and will be dealt with fully in the chapters concerning the last three years of the Second World War.

In terms of operations, the picture is slightly different. Confidence was the characteristic both of the American bomber squadrons arriving in England during 1942 and the Luftwaffe fighter squadrons defending the Reich during Bomber Command's dark days. The reasons for that confidence lay on the one hand in the belief and on the other in the knowledge that equipment superior to that possessed by the enemy would make a decisive impact on the strategic air offensive. We shall see in Chapter 4 how, as 1942 drew to a close, both attitudes remained quite unimpaired by events. The United States 8th Air Force commanders were indeed all the more confident that the accurate daylight bombing of selected industrial targets by unescorted squadrons of Fortresses and Liberators would be a feasible operation of war in 1943, and that German targets could and would be struck with as trifling a loss as had been sustained over France in four months of operations.[1] The commanders of the Luftwaffe's fighter groups were equally sure a major Bomber Command offensive would be defeated; as to the threat from America, they recalled the fate of Bomber Command's squadrons whenever unescorted daylight raids had been attempted, and saw no reason to doubt that the 8th Air Force would learn its lesson also.[2]

It is first of all necessary to grasp the fact that the overwhelming requirement for Bomber Command in these three years was to display its suitability as an instrument of political and psychological warfare. Few aspects of this phase of the strategic air offensive are more striking in retrospect or revealing to the student of the history of war as an instrument of policy than the disparity between the claims made for and the hopes entertained about mass bombing before 1939 and the virtual absence of all reference to it at the highest policy-making levels for many months thereafter. The memoirs of Britain's leaders in World War Two are remarkable for neither reticence nor charity; candour about Bomber Command's operational failures and criticism about its strategic premises and those who formulated them would, one thinks, have been right up Churchill's or Alanbrooke's street—as, equally, would have praise for a sound plan and its successful execution. Failures at sea and on land have been treated harshly enough by these and other chroniclers, and it may also be remarked here that there was between 1939 and 1942 no lack of controversy on bombing policy within the Air Ministry itself should critics in more elevated positions have felt the need for corroborative evidence.

Instead, we have, except in 1942, virtual silence about the strategic air offensive, against which the propaganda claims of Air Ministry spokesmen, the Ministry of Information and the British Broadcasting Corporation now strike many a discordant note.[3] It is of course true that countries fighting defensive wars do frequently misread the evidence—the figures for German aircraft destroyed in the Battle of Britain and of U-boats sunk in the early stages of the Battle of the Atlantic are cases in point. But the first battle was an unequivocal victory for the defending forces, while the latter was, paradoxically, fought at no crippling disadvantage to Britain's overall prosecution of the war because of the expedient of mulcting Bomber Command of aircraft so that U-boats might be attacked at the beginning or end of their patrols. If spokesmen from the Air Ministry between 1939 and 1942—and specifically in 1941 and 1942—had emphasised the great contribution which bomber aircraft were making to the elemental defensive war of national survival at sea, historical truth would have been well served. It is a matter of the record, however, that Bomber Command in these lean years was not only virtually ignored in terms of grand strategy; it suffered at the hands of its partisans also, these being too much imbued with Service convictions to spend time describing the Royal Air Force in a role complementary to that of the Royal Navy.[4]

Bomber Command was, of course, not alone in being a branch of the armed forces for whom a feasible *offensive* role could only with difficulty be found once the collapse of France was followed by a version of American neutrality which ensured that Britain and the Commonwealth would stand indefinitely alone against a Reich whose potential power was at last being dimly apprehended. The Royal Navy clearly had to fight a defensive battle; the Army would be in no position to mount an offensive on the Continent for many years—a truth not made more palatable by the widely held belief that a British Expeditionary Force should not have been committed to the support of France in 1939 and should never be deployed on the Continent of Europe again.[5] This belief was strongly expressed up to the levels of the Chiefs of Staff Committee and the War Cabinet; it frequently provided the champions of a strategic air offensive with the argument that Germany should—and could—be defeated by area bombing alone. The argument was found to be particularly useful in 1942 and 1943, the years in which Roosevelt and Stalin pressed the case for a 'second front' on an obdurate Churchill.[6]

Bomber Command, of its nature, was an offensive weapon, whose unsuitability for a variety of strategic and tactical defensive tasks or those to be undertaken in co-operation with the other Services had become an

GROUP
HEADQUARTERS   AIRFIEL

2 GROUP   ○   ○

3   "   ●   •

4   "   □   □

5   "   ■   ■

6   "   △   △

□ Dishforth

□ Linton-on-Ouse

□ YORK   □ Driffield

■ Doncaster

Finningley ■

■ Hemswell

■ Scampton

■ Waddington

△ Hucknall

■ GRANTHAM

○ West Raynham

△ Cottesmore

• Marham

○ Watton

• Feltwell

△ Upwood   • Mildenhall

Alconbury ○   • Honington

○ Wyton   ● EXNING

○
HUNTINGTON   • Newmarket

○ Wattisham

Stradishall
△ Bassingbourn

Upper Heyford △

△ Bicester

ABINGDON △

⚑ HIGH
WYCOMBE
△   H.Q. Bomber
Benson   Command   LONDON
△
Harwell

0   10   20   30   40   50   Miles

Bomber Command, 15 May 1940

article of faith with the Air Staff and virtually a fact of policy because of the neglect of basic operational requirements in the inter-war years. Once France had fallen, some offensive role, however nominal, had to be found for Bomber Command, and while it might lie more in the realm of gesture than objective, clearly had to be rather more militant than the curious policy which governed its night operations before May 1940. One basic problem facing the War Cabinet in the autumn of 1940 was quite simply to find a role for Bomber Command: the preceding year had witnessed one clear operational failure—unescorted daylight bombing—and a protracted experiment in the use of Bomber Command as an instrument of psychological warfare—leaflet raids by night over German cities. Whatever misgivings perusal of such leaflets may have aroused in the German breast, propaganda from the skies had clearly failed to impose any checks on Hitler; once the Battle of France had been joined, it was unlikely that the proponents of leaflet raids would get much of a hearing in Whitehall.

Indeed, once Mr Churchill had become Prime Minister, such timid pokes at the coiled spring of the Reich were soon replaced by the development of Bomber Command in a role by night which marked the end of the Chamberlain era and the notion that Hitler might just go away if he was not provoked. On 15 May, five days after Churchill had succeeded Chamberlain, 'the War Cabinet authorised Bomber Command to attack East of the Rhine, and that night 99 bombers were despatched to attack oil and railway targets in the Ruhr'.[7] The Official History continues in a strain where the dreadful note of preparation is muted in tacit recognition that area bombing offered no quick road to victory:

> Thus began the Bomber Command strategic air offensive against Germany. For many years it was the sole means at Britain's disposal for attacking the heart of the enemy, it never ceased until almost exactly five years later when Germany, with many of her cities in ruins, her communications cut, her oil supplies drained dry and her industry reduced to chaos, capitulated to the invading armies of the Grand Alliance. It was probably the most continuous and gruelling operation of war ever carried out.[8]

Before turning, however, to a detailed account of how the strategic air offensive gathered momentum, it is necessary to consider some aspects of the aptly named 'phoney war' so far as it affected Bomber Command. In the essentially political considerations which governed its tasks in that period are to be found the seeds of several issues and disputes which were to germinate in later years, to check or choke, according to one's view, a total reliance on area bombing, and to produce at least as much verbal recrimination between those in high places on both sides of the Atlantic as was to be found over the conduct of maritime or land operations.[9] Two issues in particular germinated in that first year: was Bomber Command an instrument at the disposal of a Grand Alliance or one in the gift of a British Prime Minister, to be employed in ways designed to show Britain's allies that it still possessed singular strategic power and intended to wage independent strategic offensives? Was area bombing effective in operational terms and as an element in the overall conduct of the war, or was it an uncertain, frequently an ineffectual and arguably an immoral way of trying to frighten and pulverise the Germans into surrender? To these issues that of whether Bomber Command should devote most of its resources to supporting the Royal Navy and the Army was essentially subordinate.

The first issue is infinitely the more important for our understanding of some of the considerations which at the Prime Minister's level governed the use of Bomber Command throughout the five years of its offensive. In historical terms the second issue is very probably of greater importance, but between 1939 and 1945 those who wished to employ Bomber Command 'selectively'[10] were constantly overborne by two factors: bomber aircraft, their crews and their equipment formed a weapons system only exceptionally capable of hitting selected targets accurately; Mr Churchill advised by his scientific grey eminence, Lord Cherwell, decided very early in his premiership that 'dehousing' and killing Germans of whatever degree was an effective and indeed essential use of Bomber Command. Churchill discounted exaggerated claims for area bombing; he gave it *carte blanche* nonetheless.[11]

When war broke out no clear understanding had been reached with the French Government and General Staff on how Bomber Command was to be employed. The establishment by January 1940 of Air Vice-Marshal Barratt's 'British Air Forces in France' as an element in General Lord Gort's British Expeditionary Force did nothing to clarify either the command structure under which aircraft detached from Bomber Command to France would operate, or to suggest what role they could usefully perform. Not only Air Marshal Barratt, but Air Vice-Marshal Playfair, commanding the 'Advanced Air Striking Force', were subject to directives and commands from Lord Gort on the one hand and Sir Edgar Ludlow-Hewitt on the other. Air Marshal Playfair's squadrons were linked both by systems of communications and by warning voices to High Wycombe; similarly, it may be noted, the 'Air Component' of fighter aircraft under Air Vice-Marshal Blount's command, remained a detached but integral element of Fighter Command, could therefore be

1   Bombing practice, Royal Air Force

THE INTER-WAR YEARS

2   Pilot training, German Air Force

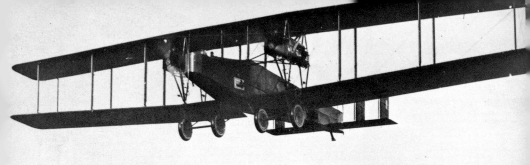

3 (*top*) Handley Page bomber, 1918   4 (*above*) Hawker Hart, 1936

AERODYNAMIC DEVELOPMENT—A TWENTY-YEAR SPAN

5 (*below*) De Havilland Mosquito, 1939

6 (*right*) Lord Trenchard

THE CHAMPIONS OF AIR POWER

7 (*below*) Air Chief Marshal
Sir Charles Portal, Chief of the
Air Staff

8 (*bottom right*) Air Chief Marshal
Sir Arthur Harris, Commander-
in-Chief Bomber Command

9 (*top*) Bristol Blenheim   10 (*above*) Vickers Wellesley

LIGHT BOMBERS—VICTIMS OF CIRCUMSTANCE

11 (*below*) Fairey Battle

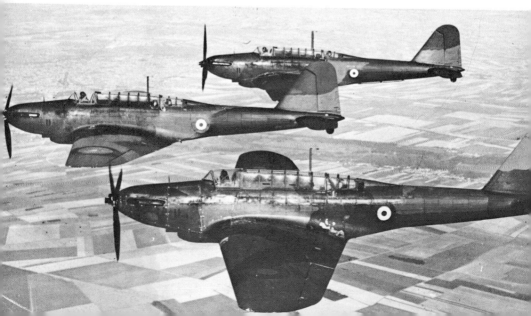

12 (*above*)
Vickers Wellington

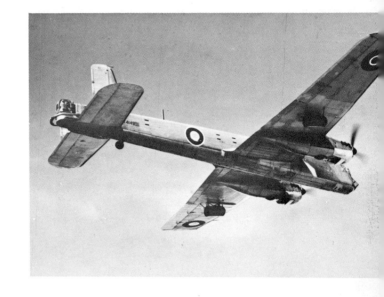

13 (*right*)
Avro Whitley

MEDIUM BOMBERS—
THE STOP GAP

14 (*below*)
Avro Manchester

15 Air Chief Marshal Sir Richard Peirse

16 Air Chief Marshal Sir Edgar
Ludlow-Hewitt

BRITISH COMMANDERS, BOMBER COMMAND AND 5 and 8 GROUPS

17 Air Vice-Marshal the Hon. R. A. Cochrane

18 Air Vice-Marshal D. C. T. Bennet

19 Briefing 1940—youthful enthusiasm

BOMBER COMMAND

20 Debriefing, Bomber Command crew 1943

21   (*above*) Short Stirling

HEAVY BOMBERS—INCREASING SUCCESS

22   (*below*) Handley Page Halifax   23   (*bottom*) Avro Lancaster

withdrawn at any time, and was so withdrawn by Churchill's order on the eve of France's defeat, to expressions of French—and not only French—disgust, but in order to provide Britain with further defensive strength for meeting the expected German onslaught from the skies.[12]

Air Marshal Playfair's squadrons were, however, withdrawn only as a shattered remnant; his force had consisted of ten squadrons of Battles, organised in five wings. In considering the nature of such a force may be found at least one of the clues to Anglo-French misunderstandings; these ten squadrons, a numerically substantial but operationally obsolescent force, were quite unsuitable for conducting even a limited bombing offensive from French soil. Escorted, the Battles might have been temporarily effective in an interdiction role; it was in such a role that the French General Staff wished them to be used.[13] It must, however, be admitted that the reasons for this request had their roots in a hope comparable to Chamberlain's—that the commitment of bomber aircraft in war would not provoke the Germans to retaliate or to initiate mass bombing provided Allied air operations were conducted on a modest scale and well away from German cities.

The more central point, however, is that Bomber Command siphoned off her squadrons of second-rate aircraft and sent them to be destroyed in France, leaving in the United Kingdom 17 operational squadrons of Wellingtons, Whitleys and Hampdens. These aircraft were by no means all that was required, and the test of battle was soon to show that the Wellington could not operate by day without escorts. But compared with the Battles, these aircraft represented some British capacity to strike at Germany should the chance arise or the necessity be unavoidable. But the capacity was to be exercised from East Anglia, not from Flanders or Picardy. The strategy of 1918, when the Independent Air Force bombed German targets from French airfields, was not to be repeated in 1939 and 1940. The British Government under Chamberlain had two neuroses which destroyed any consideration of such a strategy, and rendered the Trenchard philosophy null and void: it was frightened of its enemy and mistrustful of its ally. The Churchill Government was to suffer from only the second of these neuroses, and then in terms of who should be the senior partner in the Grand Alliance; there were no fears about America's will or capacity to fight once Pearl Harbor set its people on the road to war.

Certainly we can now say that Chamberlain's neuroses were quite understandable, perhaps inevitable. But although Churchill's leadership and the pace of events from May 1940 produced a more robust British attitude, it led to a notion of reserving Bomber Command as an instrument of peculiarly national strategy. Later, the need, real or not, to comfort blitzed British families with the thought that the Germans were suffering also, coupled with the necessity of convincing a neutral America and an invaded Russia that Britain could attack as well as defend, strengthened the Churchillian conviction that Bomber Command was too valuable a national weapon to be adapted for merely Allied purposes.[14] The Prime Minister's short-lived but considerable intimacy with Air Marshal Harris— who possessed to a rare degree not only bellicose attitudes but a capacity for explaining what his aircraft and crews could and could not do, rather than what they should and should not do—gave Bomber Command a special place in the former's preoccupations during 1942 and 1943, when the strain of prosecuting the war and the glory of standing alone had been complicated and changed by the advent of two immensely powerful partners.

One of those partners, and that Britain's supposedly 'natural' ally, had developed among its higher military command concepts of a strategic air offensive and the control thereof markedly different from those fervently held at High Wycombe and, with ineffectual reservations and qualifications, endorsed by the Chief of the Air Staff. The Casablanca Conference of February 1943 was to herald the planning and execution of a Combined Bomber Offensive, in which, theoretically, American notions of unified command and the bombing of selected industrial targets, preparatory to a grand interdiction campaign in support of invading Allied forces, were given a new authority. As we shall see, the Combined Bomber Offensive became in practice two national campaigns, reflecting different national strategic beliefs and, on the British side, a determination to go on fighting Germany in an independent way by incinerating its cities at night.[15]

Bomber Command as an Instrument of Policy

The independent strategy just summarised had its seeds in an older soil than British mistrust of the French capacity to wage war, but the events of 1940 saw the conviction flower that the virtues of national strategic independence were immeasurable. It is not surprising therefore that the case for a particular expression of that independent strategy, namely area bombing, should be developed from that time onwards, although, setting the merits and demerits of the case aside for the moment, it was more than unfortunate, it was desperately wrong, that its advocates should have become so partisan while its analysts became officially discredited. The controversy between Sir Charles Tizard and Cherwell will be examined shortly—it was not to reach its bitter depths until April 1942, when the whole future of Bomber Command had temporarily set Whitehall by the ears[16]—but it is essential to note here that what Lord Snow has curiously described as the clash between 'normal' and 'abnormal' personalities had its origins in Cherwell's effective replacement of Tizard as the principal scientific adviser on war in the air in June 1940.[17]

It is also necessary for a true understanding of how, between 1940 and 1942, the Whitehall arguments about Bomber Command were lost and won, to stress that at the level of scientific advice the case for area bombing was analysed by Tizard and his associates on matters of detail; although in these years some scientists were revolted or distressed by the moral implications of area bombing—as obviously were many reflective men and women privy to the issues—Tizard and company were not. As Mr Clark and others have shown, Tizard was not that kind of man. More to the point, Tizard had spent enough time before 1939 discovering in Ludlow-Hewitt's company Bomber Command's collective inability to find and bomb targets accurately to prevent delusions about the amount of damage that could be done to the German war effort by picking selected vital industries from a list (always assuming the list to have been based on reliable and recent intelligence sources and to have been compiled by officials with some knowledge and appreciation of the operational problems inherent in a strategic air offensive) and then attacking them methodically until the cost of their repair was greater than dispersal—or surrender.

Tizard in these two years of declining personal influence criticised the Cherwell case for 'dehousing' the German population with the arguments that it was wildly overstated, that Cherwell's arithmetic was wrong, and that there were conceivably better ways of using Bomber Command elsewhere; Tizard did not say that it was morally reprehensible to put the enemy's women and children to the sword. But there were many who wished bombing policy to be adapted to their views and who prosecuted these views without much regard for facts and analytical processes. Between the late summer of 1940 and December 1942 the Cherwell case for area bombing was opposed in Whitehall's proliferating wartime committees by four main groups advocating other roles: the oil group; the transportation group; the anti-submarine—and anti-'sea raider'—group; advocates of the selective bombing of German targets chosen by a variety of strategic or war-industrial criteria—rubber, synthetics of all kinds, even agriculture. There were also two sub-groups, although these appear to have made little impression anywhere: that which advocated more bomber aircraft being sent to support the British and Commonwealth campaigns in the Mediterranean and North Africa; and that which urged greater support to the resistance movement in occupied Europe and the ostensibly secret forces which were being sent from Britain to stiffen it.[18]

With the exception of the oil group, none of these assorted bodies and spokesmen got much of a hearing at the level where, until Air Marshal Harris' arrival at Bomber Command in February 1942, bombing policy was decided—by the Prime Minister himself. It is of course the case that Bomber Command 'lost' many squadrons to Coastal Command in 1941 and 1942, and that much effort was devoted to bombing targets of special concern to the Admiralty—in April 1941 Air Marshal Peirse complained to Portal that one-third of his squadrons' attacks were being made on *Scharnhorst* and *Gneisenau* at Brest[19]; Peirse thought these attacks a waste of time, much as Harris was to regard the bombing of U-boat pens two years later as a stupid distraction from his appointed task.[20] It is also true that Bomber Command sent six entire squadrons to the Middle East in 1941 and 1943 to support the Wellington and light bomber squadrons attempting to interdict the enemy's movements at sea and on land.[21] But the point to remember in considering these 'losses' is that, compared with the fact that the Royal Navy and the Army were always being redeployed to other theatres, Bomber Command kept the large majority of its squadrons in the United Kingdom, and operated them as its commanders thought fit.

Oil was in a special case, and on paper remained so, although it was not until 1944 that anything effective could be done—or, at all events, was done—to give oil targets real priority. The notion that Germany's oil stocks were low and could not be made good persisted throughout much of the war[22]; the oil committees under Lord Hankey and Mr Geoffrey Lloyd persisted in their belief that this commodity should be the priority for attack; oil targets had a fascination for those who saw strategy in terms of severing jugular veins, a view opposed to those who saw it in terms of the bludgeon and the battering ram. Well before the opening of the night offensive in May 1940 and its resumption in September, oil had been placed high on the list of industrial targets enumerated in the Western Air Plans.

Thus the oil committee definitely had the edge over its rivals so far as the approval of the ruling few was concerned. But it made no odds in the end. Cherwell's views were Churchill's views, and for long remained so;

they were also the Air Staff's view, although decreasingly that of the Directorate of Bomber Operations.[23] The techniques of propaganda were employed to tell the world it was German industry, not the German people, which received Bomber Command's attentions.[24]

Although, as we shall see, various ideas were offered an operational run on occasion ('precision' attacks by day were also made in 1941 and 1942, without proving or disproving anything significant), none superseded for more than a few weeks the regular process whereby the crews of Bomber Command were given German industrial towns as a target, told to attack given industries in and around those towns, sought to find them, sometimes found the towns—or *some* town—and, according to whim, practice or view, either unloaded their bombs in the general target area— or what they supposed that to be—or, if uncertain of their whereabouts, struggled back to base with a full bomb load.[25] When Harris became Commander-in-Chief, he rejected targets put up to him by the Air Staff (acting as unconvinced agent for minority groups) if he thought them impossible to reach or pointless to attack—'requests' to bomb Ploesti and Schweinfurt, representing oil and ballbearings, were simply brushed aside.[26]

Two points should be noted in this connection: the Ruhr, as a 'battle area', and as aircrews in 1943 and 1944 came to see it, was given a wide berth; hence, in part, the industrial targets listed for attack during the period in question covered a pretty wide range of manufacturing processes; it is doubtful whether these scattered raids much affected German war production, as did the heavy and sustained area raids of 1943. What is certain is that the Ruhr's virtual immunity to attack until the spring of 1943 rendered the bombing effort of the preceding two years null and void. The Ruhr contained more people as well as more industry than any other part of Germany. We must also note that the Ruhr's immunity was provided by an operational factor which reflects discredit on British governments and Air Staffs before 1939 rather than credit on those responsible for Germany's defences. As the Dickens Report on German night defences reveals,[27] it was not only the effectiveness of fighters and flak which troubled bomber crews over the Ruhr; it was the sheer size of the area, a livid lake of searchlights, which, in those pre-radar days of visual identification, prevented the establishment of one's whereabouts or the location of even the most broadly defined target area. Yet the bomber element of the Luftwaffe was equipped with target-finding radar by 1938.

Few of these operational problems were known to or appreciated by the Whitehall committees which urged that Bomber Command should cease bombing Germany much as one might cease to throw stones at a haystack in the dark.[28] However, the atmosphere in which lengthy discussions of amended or alternative strategies took place must be appreciated before too definite an assessment is made of the wide gap which existed between what might be theoretically feasible or strategically desirable and what was operationally possible. A number of those concerned between 1940 and 1942 with advising or assisting the deliberations of the various bodies involved with the strategic air offensive have confirmed what the Official History quietly implies—that critics of Bomber Command's methods of waging war were ill provided with evidence which could suggest a valid alternative. This was a characteristic of such pressure groups which was to excite Harris greatly in later years, and a weakness in them which he turned to good account.[29] The Admiralty was better provided with statistics—but that was hardly surprising, since U-boat sinkings were stark evidence of a desperately hard and unrelenting battle for Britain's survival. Further, when critics, not necessarily opponents of bombing policy, tried to find out what was happening at High Wycombe or in the air, they were rebuffed. Tizard was in the know, because he was Tizard, and had developed over many years the practice of tapping the far from reticent Service mind. His long-standing entrée into the higher levels of the Service world was possibly one of the reasons why he was ousted by Cherwell.

But the newcomers to Whitehall were inhibited and checked in their enquiries by two further factors, over and above their ignorance of the labyrinth and the passwords. These wartime ministers and civil servants made their début on a stage firmly occupied by Churchill and the Service Chiefs, a group which bickered among itself but which resented keenly any outside interference. Not only was this a formidable, frequently an implacable foe to any who questioned the efficacy of a given policy. A war-time convention of unnaturally but presumably inevitably rapid growth equated dissent with disloyalty. Most critics eventually shut up, or were shut up. A few lonely spirits refused to be silenced—that oddly assorted trio of Parliamentarians, Mr Bevan, Mr Shinwell and Lord Winterton come to mind—but they were sustained by a dislike of secrecy and by Churchill's assumption of strategic omnipotence rather than fortified with telling facts or damning evidence. Least of all did anybody outside the War Cabinet and the Air Staff know what was happening over Germany night after frozen, fruitless night.[30]

Nevertheless, the oil and other committees ploughed on and certainly kept a strategic dialogue going in these lean years. The dialogue was in any case given some sort of an impetus by the hesitations of openly accepting the fact that Bomber Command was a bludgeon—and one moreover wielded in the dark against an almost invisible foe—rather than a rapier. Such hesitations characterised the Government and the Air Staff in the early months of the war. Following the Government's apprehension about the counter-effects of unrestricted air warfare, the Director of Plans wrote on 7 September 1939: 'Indiscriminate attacks on civilian population will never form part of our policy.'[31] But on 21 October he also wrote: 'One must think very hard before beginning the air war against industry.'[32] The indecision and uncertainty about objectives revealed by these two statements was for nearly a year thereafter to be lessened in their effects by the fact that Bomber Command had first to abandon daylight raids as the preferred strategy, then turn to assist in checking the German flood-tide before it hit Britain's shores. But throughout this period of the reluctant—and indeed very partial—commitment of Bomber Command's Main Force to attacks on airfields, invasion barge concentrations and ports, the proponents of 'economic warfare' were preparing their case for selective industrial attack.

It appears that they did not argue in committee as to the success which Bomber Command had made of its essentially defensive raids on invasion targets, despite the fact that the latter comprised in the tactical and logistic sense just those elements of vital matériel and the means to transport it which some urged could be bombed at the higher, the strategic level. Bombing invasion barges and troop concentrations was costly, but effective, partly because Air Marshal Portal (who succeeded Ludlow-Hewitt in April, only to be made CAS in the following October) was prepared to use up the half-dozen or so effectively operational Blenheim squadrons in this manner—as indeed his successor, Air Marshal Peirse was to do with the remnant, until mid-1941, in strikes against shipping and coastal targets.[33] Industrial targets in Germany were, however, a different proposition, lying within or behind the glacis of the Ruhr.

Further, Bomber Command's Hampden, Wellington and Whitley squadrons could not be allowed wholesale destruction, as had been possible with the obsolescent Battle and Blenheim squadrons. Whatever the indecision of the Air Staff as to particular objectives, the conversation of Bomber Command's long-range force until the four-engined types came into service was a principle allowing of no contradiction or dispute. It should be remembered that, although by November 1941 the effective front-line strength of Bomber Command—excluding Battles and Blenheims—had increased from the September 1939 figure of just over 200 to something over 500, the numbers of four-engined aircraft was still minimal: only 18 Stirlings and 17 Halifaxes were in front-line service.[34] With so slow a change from aircraft of the 1930s to those built to deliver really heavy attacks on German targets, it is understandable that the average monthly night sortie rate in the 29 months from September 1939 to January 1942 should be but 1,625,[35] a figure which by no means rose steadily throughout this time of preparation, but which fluctuated considerably as Bomber Command strove to adapt itself to major war.

Although for the period in question the Command suffered an average of just under three per cent losses until December 1940 and just over three per cent thereafter—percentages which compare very favourably with those encountered when the bombing of Germany started in earnest—it must be pointed out that this was due at least in part to the commitment of the front-line force on an average of only three nights in each month.[36] To be sure, the incidence of day raids against all targets remained high throughout this period (although the Wellingtons, Whitleys and Hampdens were never regularly engaged on them after December 1939), and to have committed Bomber Command 'nightly', as Harris declared that he committed it,[37] would have been virtually impossible. But the facts show that for over two years the bombing of Germany was a sustained operation of war only in a rather generous interpretation of that phrase.

The committees which urged the merits of various industrial targets were ill provided with information on operational factors. Whether the Air Staff chose to reveal to them that Bomber Command could not, or at any rate did not, mount a sustained offensive must remain a matter of speculation. It is not however in dispute that those who urged the destruction of oil refineries, marshalling yards or U-boat pens were in like case, in that their appreciations lacked the kind of hard fact which might have forced the Air Staff to take them seriously. In such circumstances the dialogue referred to on page 92 was useful principally in reminding airmen that strategic air power was the proper concern of all with responsibilities for advising on the most effective conduct of operations and assessing the weakest joints in the enemy's armour. Although the Air Staff in general succeeded in convincing higher authority that area bombing was inevitable, the weary wrangles in the dark days of the war about alternatives to it did bear some fruit when the tide had turned. By that time the planning of Overlord was well begun, and airmen who had succeeded in refuting the case for selective attack were compelled by the advent of a powerful ally whose air force had a different concept of air power to study the kind of targets which they had formerly ignored.

Bomber Command as an Instrument of Strategy

In chronological terms the first three years of the strategic air offensive fall into three distinct phases: September 1939 to May 1940; May to September 1940; October 1940 to December 1942. There are those who may consider the last phase too lengthy to be considered as one and that some distinction must be drawn between the events of 1941 and those of 1942. But it must be stressed that, once area bombing had become tacitly acknowledged as Bomber Command's sole technique and the various precision targets enumerated by the Air Staff and urged by interested parties had been pigeonholed, events in this last phase are to be found and recorded at the operational level, not at that where, ostensibly, bombing policy was made. The major difference in real events between 1941 and 1942 is in the rising sortie rate for the summer months and in the fact that in the third year of the war four-engined aircraft, new navigational aids and new tactics enabled Bomber Command for the first time to drop enough bombs on any one night to cause sufficient destruction over a 'target area' for subsequent photographic reconnaissance to suggest a mounting and increasingly effective campaign.

It is equally important to stress again, however, that these aids to Bomber Command's operational credibility did not in the Air Staff's and Air Marshal Harris' view do more than enable the area campaign to be prosecuted at all. So far as Portal and Bomber Command were concerned, 1941 had been notable principally for a series of critical comments and reports by outsiders[38]; there was little disposition in 1942 to seek further criticism by attempting to utilise the new techniques in support of precision bombing. In any event, with the exception of a few lone and distant voices, most of the argument about alternative targets had died away by the time Bomber Command set out on its first raid openly designed to demonstrate what area bombing could achieve—the attack on Lübeck on 28 March 1942.

There was one notable voice which was certainly neither lone nor distant, namely Sir Henry Tizard's: just one month after the Lübeck raid he was to comment sharply and statistically on the assumptions about the rate at which and the force with which Germans of the industrial working class could be killed and rendered homeless.[39] His comments led to what is still known in some quarters as the Tizard–Cherwell controversy; a phrase suggesting a major clash of personalities and principles. In fact, however, Tizard, although he detested much in Cherwell's character and behaviour, and had allowed his detestation to affect his judgement on at least one major issue,[40] was concerned in this instance mainly with his opponent's arithmetic, and not with his strategic insight or his moral standards. But Tizard failed even to upset Cherwell's arithmetic, although this was demonstrably faulty. Tizard failed not only because he was fallen from grace, but because the mood of 1942 was not conducive to appreciating his approach to war. Much more than in 1940, the mood was to give Bomber Command its head and to ignore awkward questions about what, precisely, it was trying to achieve.

We have seen how the use of Bomber Command as an instrument of politics was inseparable from the first phase; the second phase covers the Battles of France and Britain; the third must now engage our attention, particularly since the Official History devotes many pages to analysing a 'crisis' in the strategic air offensive. Sir Charles Webster suggests that 1941 and 1942 were crisis years for Bomber Command because of its repeated failure to deliver the strategic goods and the rising clamour from the Admiralty and the War Office for its squadrons to be put to better use. In fact there was no crisis for Bomber Command in this sense; it continued to deliver the political and psychological goods, particularly in the darkest days of the war and those most humiliating to British naval and military prowess—the first ten months of 1942.[41] Although Bomber Command's strategic successes were as negligible in 1942 as in 1941, the latter year ended with an unequivocal endorsement by the Chiefs of Staff of the objective and methods conceived by Trenchard and pursued by Harris.

The Chiefs of Staff said on 31 December 1942 that the aim of the bombing offensive was 'the progressive destruction and dislocation of the enemy's war industrial and economic system, and the undermining of his morale to a point where his capacity for armed resistance is fatally weakened'.[42] This endorsement of area bombing as Bomber Command's prime function in war—taking Germany apart was not something which could be done by a constantly depleted force—was particularly satisfying to Portal and Harris for three reasons. The First Sea Lord, Sir Dudley Pound, and the Chief of the Imperial General Staff, Sir Alan Brooke, had made between 15 November and 26 December several last-ditch attempts to upset the idea of an independently executed strategic air offensive, and one which absorbed most of Bomber Command's resources. They had not only failed, but Portal defeated them without recourse to argument. He successfully opposed the idea of an 'objective scientific analysis', intimating that a committee established for this purpose 'would probably roam about over a very wide field', and that 'their deliberations would certainly cause much further delay'.[43]

'Delay' is the important word in this context, and it brings us to the other two reasons why the last day of 1942 saw Bomber Command's British critics finally off the course. The Casablanca Conference was scheduled for January 1943; that conference was to decide Anglo-American strategy for the defeat of Germany; much time, it was thought, would be devoted to a combined aerial offensive; it was essential for the Air Staff to get its case for Bomber Command's role accepted by the British Chiefs of Staff before a conference at which American ideas would freely circulate and might indeed lead to the Prime Minister acquiescing in objectives set by the American President and put in the hands of American commanders to attain.[44] Secondly, Bomber Command was, at long last, and as the 'beginning of the end' was heard on men's lips, ready to strike hard. The number of aircraft available for operations at the end of 1942 was approximately the same as 12 months before, namely about 500 of all types.[45] But the aircraft destined to strike in 1943 were predominately four-engined; of infinitely greater significance were the facts that a special force had been established to guide squadrons to their targets, and to do so with equipment enabling the night, the dark and the cold to be defeated at last. Of 5-6 March 1943 when *Oboe*-equipped aircraft of Bomber Command struck hated Essen with deadly effect, Harris was to say, 'At long last we were ready'. It had been a very long wait.

The many reasons why Bomber Command had survived not only campaigning loss but the greater threat from its critics in Whitehall have been discussed. There were, however, four additional reasons which should be described for a full understanding of how the Command was preserved for the time when it could operate without let or hindrance. These four reasons were: the quadrilateral of Churchill, Cherwell, Portal and Harris; the rejection of critical evidence; the disasters of 1942; Bomber Command's slow increase in size. Let us take these facts together.

'Quadrilateral' may seem an odd phrase to apply to four men who had such different responsibilities and characters. But they shared a conviction that bombing the German people was the most effective way of pro-secuting a British strategy; this conviction they shared to a degree found nowhere else, and, although Churchill expressed reservations and had publicly to support the American belief in fighting Germany in France and the Low Countries, he consistently backed Portal and Harris; he listened to Cherwell and believed—or, at all events accepted—what he was told. Churchill in September 1940 believed that 'only the Air Force ... could win the war'.[46] Part of that belief reflected his tribute to Fighter Command; much of the surviving conviction was eroded by American

pressure; the destruction of Dresden in February 1945 led him to wonder
where it would all end.[47] But in June 1941 Churchill deplored 'a policy
expressed in terms of principle'[48], that of selective bombing; he equivo-
cated the following September when Portal, most uncharacteristically,
overplayed his hand by suggesting that a 4,000-bomber force could break
Germany in six months,[49] but in July 1942, when the Admiralty and War
Office were trying to succeed where the Ministry of Economic Warfare
and its committees had failed, the Prime Minister wrote:

> We must observe with sorrow and alarm the woeful shrinkage of our plans
> for Bomber expansion ... we must regard the Bomber offensive against
> Germany at least as a feature in breaking her war-will second only to the
> largest military operations which can be conducted on the Continent until
> that war-will is broken. Renewed, intense efforts should be made by the
> Allies to develop during the winter and onwards ever-growing, ever more
> accurate and ever more far-ranging bomber attacks on Germany. In this
> way alone can we prepare the conditions which will be favourable to the
> major military operations on which we are resolved.[50]

Sir Charles Webster interprets this sonorous declaration of intent as a
rejection of 'Sir Arthur Harris' advice as to the major strategy of the war'.[51]
It is difficult to accept that interpretation, unless one gives undue weight to
the qualifying phrase, 'at least as a feature'. But such a qualification is
surely more than outweighed by the Prime Minister's ruling that the
strategic air offensive was to be regarded as 'second only to the largest
military operations', and one which 'alone (could) prepare the conditions'
for their victorious conclusion. Churchill did not publicly agree with
Harris that a second front was unnecessary, but he agreed with him on the
far more substantial point, the very one which the Admiralty and War
Office disputed, that Bomber Command's resources were not to be constantly diluted by the demands of other Services and theatres. This support
by the Prime Minister is all the more significant if we recall that he remained adamant about Britain's Imperial role and saw in the North
African and Mediterranean campaigns a means of retaining one in the
Middle East which had been secured in a scrambling and ineffectual manner
in 1918. Yet Churchill remained deaf to Wavell's pleas for the despatch
of heavy bombers and ignored the latter's fairly bitter comment after the
first '1,000' raid in May 1942 that 'when, after trying with less than
20 light bombers to meet an attack which has cost us three important warships and several others and nearly 100,000 tons of mer-
chant shipping, we see that over 200 heavy bombers attacked one town in
Germany'.[52]

Confident of Churchill's support over priorities, Harris had been able in the earlier months of 1942 to conduct an offensive framed largely in terms of effect. His year of scarce challenged command was 1943, but in 1942 he not only nursed his groups and squadrons through long months of negative bombing but, at isolated moments, well calculated to achieve the maximum propaganda effect, 'laid on', as he would phrase it, operations designed to remind the world that the lion had claws as well as wings. Thus Lübeck and Rostock, ports surrounded by wooden houses, were destroyed in March and April.[53] The targets were relatively easy to find and once found could scarcely avoid destruction from incendiaries. Thus much of Cologne's residential areas was destroyed in the first '1,000' raid of 30 May. The two subsequent '1,000' raids of 1 June on Essen and 25 June on Bremen were failures, except in respect of the acclaim which greeted them.[54] Ironically but most suitably, from Harris' point of view, that acclaim was loudly voiced by sailors and soldiers seeking to divert Bomber Command to other tasks, but forced to laud its achievements to their American opposite numbers during months of otherwise unalleviated defeat.[55]

Portal and Cherwell went about their task of promoting the role of Bomber Command in a more sophisticated way. Churchill and Cherwell, Portal and Harris are often bracketed together. Temperamentally, however, Portal and Cherwell had more in common and achieved their results by similar means, most notably by an acute understanding of the techniques of manipulating men and a pretty resolute indifference to the laws of probability. Both men were aloof, strengthened by convictions which were never made apparent to their Whitehall colleagues. Of the two Portal is by far the more interesting character, the more enigmatic, the less consistent over strategic or tactical principles, the more skilful in arguing the case for area bombing while appearing to be impartial about its merits and sympathetic to the case for alternative. It would be interesting to know what Churchill and his peers really thought about him.

However that may be, the record shows that for five years Portal moved carefully from one position to another without ever leaving a flank which could be turned by Pound, Cunningham or Brooke. In July 1940, while C-in-C Bomber Command, he made a case for not seeking to attack aircraft assembly plants, but did so in language so deferential that the issue was allowed to lapse.[56] By September, he was the author of a letter to the Air Staff which supported the Prime Minister's suggestion that selected German towns should be devastated. Portal provided a list of such towns together with recommendations for their destruction.[57]

By December 1940, Portal was Chief of the Air Staff, and had become an enthusiastic supporter of the Lloyd Committee's case for concentrating on oil targets, and the 'quick death clinch'[58] which would supposedly result. Indulging in a habit which today is still more strong among the proponents of a strategic air offensive than other practitioners of the art of war, Portal began his memorandum to the Chiefs of Staff Committee recommending adoption of the Lloyd Committee's proposals by '*Assuming* that we can hope for an average of nine clear nights a month . . .'.[59] This assumption was followed by a set of figures which quite failed, whether deliberately or by an oversight, to take account of the fact that Bomber Command's crews found it hard enough to find a town, let alone a particular industrial target.

Criticism of Portal's techniques of persuasion would be less in these pages if the above set of figures was an isolated example of confusing what might be achieved with what probably could be achieved. But Portal indulged in this practice during a phase of the war when Britain's survival was still an entirely open question, and this point must be appreciated in relation to the intervention which Cherwell was to make in March 1942. The issue is not whether Portal was right to bat for his side—he would have been unique among senior officers if he had not. The issue is not even whether Portal was right to resist so far as lay in his power the diversion in March 1941 of part of Bomber Command in support of maritime operations or to comment on the Prime Minister's directive in language which reveals the degree of antipathy to others' problems which lay behind his outward manner. Nor finally is the issue one of consistency—by February 1941 Portal was lukewarm about oil and had reverted to the case for 'mass attacks on industrial areas'.[60] Consistency in war is pretty hard to achieve when there is no basis of information about an enemy's strengths and weaknesses which can serve as a guide to policy and action.

The issue is one of moderate or exaggerated claims about what a given force can achieve. Portal not only advanced figures in 1942 which bore no relation to the operational feasibility by which, on his own account, he set such store, but he supported Cherwell's figures also. Anybody who could do that was clearly determined to see an independent strategic air offensive waged at all costs. Portal (and Sinclair) found Cherwell's figures 'simple, clear and convincing'.[61] These were certainly simple, hence clarity was not difficult to achieve. Conviction was a matter of *a priori* rather than *a posteriori*; all that the figures lacked was, as with Portal's earlier set, any relation to what Bomber Command possessed in the way of aircraft, knowledge or skill in 1942, or what it was likely to possess

thereafter. By 'saving the Prime Minister the trouble of making arith-
metical calculations',[62] Cherwell saved Portal the trouble of warning the
Chiefs of Staff Committee that Bomber Command would remain a
propaganda force for months to come.

What matters in the light of strategic history is not that Cherwell
indulged in absurdities about numbers or ignored on the one hand the
very heavy dilution of Bomber Command which was currently taking
place (510 aircraft were transferred between January and September),[63]
or on the other that US officials were making it clear even as he did his
sums that American aircraft would not be available to the Royal Air Force
in the numbers earlier given.[64] The importance of Cherwell's intervention
is that when Tizard pointed out their fallacies nobody in power took the
slightest notice. Tizard and Cherwell argued, their supporters took sides,
every aspect of the issue was discussed by those engaged in trying to
advise the services at the scientific level—but it was virtually ignored by
senior officers themselves.[65] Cherwell's figures were proved utterly
wrong by the events of the following three years, but the bases for them
were completely false at the time—certainly as seen by most of the defence
scientific community. The figure of 10,000 was indeed one designed to
save the Prime Minister trouble. 'Target E' called for Bomber Command
to maintain a force of 4,000 aircraft by spring 1943. In spring 1942 that
target had been put back by a year[66]; more to the point, even a large American bomber force, supposing production and distribution problems to be
soluble, did not provide for 6,000 aircraft at the disposal of Bomber Command and the enthusiasts of area bombing. The Joint Chiefs of Staff had
very different ideas about the role of air power in war.

Tizard's destruction of Cherwell's case therefore involved nothing
arduous in the realms of higher mathematics or strategic appreciation. He
was ignored nonetheless, as many of his fellow scientists were ignored
or rebuffed if they presumed to argue that the conduct of war was directly,
not marginally, influenced by scientific or technological factors. There is
little doubt however that, in Tizard's case, his final defeat was not only
due to the fact that Cherwell was 'in' and he was 'out', but to the latter
being dead right about German target finding radar in 1940 and Tizard
being dead wrong. These things happen. Tizard, whom his champions
tend to see as the good man attacked by a bad one, could make major
mistakes in scientific interpretation. He made one when his stock was
declining, Cherwell's rising. Fair-minded men of power, deciding issues
calmly, would have continued to use Tizard's services in other than trivial
and occasional ways; men of independent judgement might well have

decided that a strategy which required to be supported by such wild exaggerations and such phoney statistics as Cherwell's deserved to be replaced by one which enabled a defensive war at sea to be won and an offensive war on land to be planned. In 1942, much more than in 1940, men in power were neither calm, objective nor possessed of independent judgement. They were anxious, above all, about Britain's place in the new alliance; they wanted *their* Service to be given the lion's share. Portal appears to have judged the temper of those times very well. It is not surprising that Harris could afford to plan and wait, confident that Bomber Command's day would come.

4

Daylight Operations
1939–1942

The Background

The most important point to grasp about the operations of Bomber Command between the outbreak of war and the end of 1942 is that they were sporadic and varied. Night bombing became the established pattern by autumn 1940, but daylight raids against land targets continued to be mounted, while mining, anti-submarine patrols and anti-shipping strikes contributed rather more to the fortunes of war at sea than most historians of maritime operations seem prepared to allow. The 8th Air Force's early operations were sporadic too, but there was little variety among the sorties; they merely picked up the option of daylight raids at the point where nearly the last of the major Bomber Command operations of this type left off. General Eaker's squadrons bombed from high level and suffered a missing rate of no more than two-and-a-half per cent between 17 August and 31 December 1942;[1] Air Marshal Stevenson's 2 Group and the squadrons of other groups intermittently engaged on daylight operations throughout 1941 and 1942 bombed from low level and endured an overall missing rate of five per cent.[2] With the exception of two imaginatively planned and gallantly executed operations—Augsburg on 17 April and Eindhoven on 6 December—the attempt to bomb vital targets accurately by day in 1942 was as insignificant as the search for town targets by night. The early American raids were virtually ignored by the German defences[3]; having devoted scant attention to defence against Bomber Command the Luftwaffe saw little need to exert itself over the newcomers.

The main reason for German complacency—in which the 1942 Lübeck,

Rostock and Cologne raids by Bomber Command made but a slight and temporary dent[4]—was due not only to the early discovery that Bomber Command was vulnerable by day and frequently lost at night, but to the possession of a large and modern day and night fighter force, guided to its victims by a simple but efficient early warning and control system. The German flak defences were also well organised and effective; German gunlaying, although initially lacking radar-controlled height/range finders and predictors, was of its usual high quality; searchlights were used from the outbreak of war with tactical ingenuity, not only to drench areas with light and to cone aircraft but as horizontal beacons in different colours, signalling to more distant targets course and height of the attacking force.[5] By July 1940 searchlights and fighters were combined in order that the latter could be given an approximate indication of the bombers' position, and then close with them visually. By such somewhat rudimentary means did Germany defend itself. Yet although after three years these defences remained sufficient against bombers whose crews were still groping in the dark, the balance did slowly shift in that time away from the position of virtual invulnerability which the Reich enjoyed until the spring of 1942. After the establishment of the Kammhuber Line German tactics underwent no fundamental change; too little thought was given at the most senior levels to applying technical improvements in radar to the growing requirement for the defeat, not merely the discouragement, of Bomber Command.

By contrast, arduous efforts were made by British scientists and technologists throughout the period to provide Bomber Command with the means to be guided to targets, if still rarely to see them on radar screens when they did arrive. *Gee*, *H₂S* and *Oboe* were developments which, although belated, the enemy did not match; it was not until late 1943 that the riposte came, when German commanders fundamentally changed their tactics and drew on some powerful new equipment in the process.[6] If 1942 was the year when Bomber Command slipped through the net spread by Whitehall critics of a strategic air offensive, it was also the year when those responsible for defending Germany figuratively slept at their posts. It was these two factors in combination which made 1943 the first year of strategically significant operations for Bomber Command. It must again be said, however, that the nature of the war of scientific wits was as little appreciated by Sinclair and Portal as it was by Goering and Jeschonnek. It was accepted that radar enabled an area campaign to be waged; it was not understood by the Air Staff that the tactical corollary to reliance on radar by Main Force crews was the establishment of a force which could operate over Germany directly in support of them, jamming and confusing the German control system. Not until November 1943 was such a force established.

For the 8th Air Force 1943 was to be a year of mounting loss and growing frustration, as we shall later describe. The reason for this unhappy year lay not only in a dogmatic adherence to the doctrine of unescorted daylight bombing, but in a comparable belief that the Norden bomb sight put bombs on target with infallible results.[7] These *simpliste* beliefs were in no way tested by the events of 1942. Nor did those 27 operations over lightly defended France and the Low Countries suggest any need for tactical innovation. The self-defending formation was enough; it was useful to have short-range fighter escort from the Royal Air Force; it was not essential, nor would it be required when Germany came fully to feel American power. Portal's warnings about unescorted daylight operations (one of the very few matters on which the Chief of the Air Staff was both consistent and right) were ignored.[8]

Intelligent thought about defensive tactics was, however, infrequently found either in Bomber Command or the Luftwaffe. The latter had so clear a margin of superiority that little energy was devoted to concentrating a fighter force in a given area in order to deal the bombers such a blow that an unescorted *night* offensive might also be abandoned. There is no evidence that the 15 per cent missing rate which Bomber Command suffered on 7 November 1941—its heaviest loss in night operations since the outbreak of war and one not to be matched until late 1943—was due to co-ordinated fighter attacks. Indeed, since on the night in question Peirse ordered 'attacks on Berlin, Mannheim, the Ruhr, Cologne, Boulogne' and was also ordered 'to carry out mining and intruder operations',[9] and lost aircraft over most of these widely scattered targets, little in the way of co-ordinated fighter attacks can have been planned. They were not needed. The result of 7 November 1941 was a demand, originating from Churchill, that Bomber Command be conserved until more opportune days had come.[10] For three months thereafter area bombing of this type virtually stopped, although the night sortie rate only slightly declined.

The necessity for tactical flexibility in Bomber Command as the operational problems became apparent hardly admitted of argument. Yet there were two inhibiting factors, apart from the fact that 1941 and 1942 were years of dribbling losses, not outright defeat. Fighter Command could not provide even short-range escort by night, since its night fighters were required, or thought to be required, at home.[11] The best that could be offered was 'intruder', plus 'Circus' diversionary operations by day. The former was designed to damage German fighters on the ground, and to damage too the airfields covering the approaches to Germany from which some defensive sorties were undoubtedly flown; the latter was designed to engage German fighters in the hopes that Bomber Command's squadrons setting out on daylight raids or at dusk would fly over the approaches to Germany comparatively unscathed.[12]

Both tactics failed, because neither had much relevance to the fact that most of Peirse's aircraft were lost on the run in to the target, over it, or as they left it. The only hope for crews in these critical areas was to adopt the tactics of the hare when closely pursued by the hound, or by the wing-threequarter with the enemy to his front and on his flank. Yet twisting and turning destroyed any chance of a 'straight and level' approach to the target; if the third dimension was called on, accurate bombing ceased even to be an aspiration. Peirse's squadrons were not sent over Germany to emulate the Stuka technique.[13] It might be thought that, since bomber crews frequently despaired of finding their targets, they would scarcely bother to fly straight towards an approximation of, or an alternative to, it in order to drop their bombs in some kind of pattern. The evidence of squadron operational record books is that they resolutely sought a target[14]; the evidence of mounting loss is that they sought to fly straight and level towards it. It was believed in some quarters that, by the time Bomber Command four-engined aircraft would be guided to their target by radio emissions and when crews could see it on a radar screen, bombing would not only change from 'area' to 'precision' but that losses would decrease[15]; airborne radar to warn of approaching enemy fighters was as feasible an equipment as that to identify the target. This was to be the case technically; it was not to be so tactically, since a bomber equipped with two radar sets turned out to be a gift to the German defences.[16]

The second inhibition on new tactics being developed arose from the situation just described. Once a fighter had a bomber in its sights the issue was rarely in doubt.[17] This was so throughout the entire course of the war, and it will be necessary to describe later in this book how Bomber Command's destructive triumphs of mid-1943 cost so much to repeat in the following winter and spring. The reason lay mostly in the fundamental disadvantage which the crew of a large, slow, noisy aircraft flying straight and level faces when attacked by a small, fast aircraft, which darts about the sky and, even when twin-engined, is as hard to detect by sound as by sight. But the aircraft of Bomber Command were also badly armed. Machine guns were outranged by cannon; an increasing number of gun turrets did not increase the defensive power of a bomber flying alone, particularly if more than one fighter attacked it.

There were four principal measures which could theoretically have been taken to alleviate a situation where all crews were at maximum danger over the target area and many (the inexperienced, the incompetent, the stale, the tired and the wounded), when plodding towards or struggling back from it: better armament; shorter time over target; improved standards of navigation and gunnery: jamming and spoofing. The last measure has a particular relevance to what Harris would describe as the 'real' opening of the offensive in March 1943, or rather to the scientists' battle which followed it. The other three measures are particularly relevant to the first three years of the war, the years covered by the Dickens Report on German night defences. This report which was a series of comments on Bomber Commands fortunes at the hands of the German defences between December 1940 and December 1942, presents, if unwittingly, a battle scenario where defensive tactics of evasion were sufficient to keep the missing rate within acceptable limits. No attempt is made in the report to analyse or evaluate the odds against the bomber or to describe the German methods of control. No attempt is made to suggest alternatives to the practice of allowing each crew to make their own way to the target in their own time, a practice which gave maximum opportunity to the German fighter and searchlight defences on the coast, maximum opportunity to fighters looking for stragglers and meant maximum time over target—another gift to the enemy. Instead of analysis, one is offered in the Dickens Report a running commentary based on individual accounts of combat and the average of a given number of actual or probable types of encounter—attacks made singly or in pairs; attacks from various positions; attacks by single- and/or twin-engined fighters; attacks on nights of different degrees of visibility; the defensive advantages of different heights; of particular evasive manoeuvres.

The basic weaknesses of the Dickens Report are thus threefold: it eschews analysis; it concerns itself solely with tactical factors which might almost be described as of World War One vintage; and such assessments as it does make are based on reports of sightings and attacks. At all times during the period in question this was an insignificant percentage of the total number of sorties flown on any one night—never more than five and usually under two. Obviously this percentage could not give an accurate picture of what was really happening, because it excluded aircraft attacked and destroyed. The 'Dickens' percentage and the missing rate taken together gave a reasonably accurate figure for the total number of aircraft attacked on any night, but there was nothing particularly useful to be gleaned from that. The significance of the missing rate was almost always in its cumulative effect, or how long it would take, as the jargon had it, before a given force was 'turned over' or a given squadron suffered such losses that its operational credibility was destroyed and its morale damaged. The significance, such as it was, of the Dickens figures, lay in their indication of the reasons why a fighter broke off an attack.

What does emerge is a picture in which evasive action was preferred to a gun battle. Bomber Command's crews knew they were outgunned, and although many a brave fight did take place, none showed how the inequalities described on page 106 could be remedied. If the United States had not entered the war in 1941 ·5 armament would have been available to Bomber Command by early 1942, since four factories had been built there to manufacture such weapons for the Ministry of Supply. When the United States entered the war, the factories were commandeered.[18] Hence it was necessary to protect Bomber Command's crews in other ways. The argument then developed, most empirically, that what might reduce losses, particularly in the target area, would be to shorten the period of maximum exposure and minimum manoeuvrability. If bombers could be flown in a stream, so as to reduce the overall time over the target area, losses might be reduced. But concentration of this kind in place of the 'make your own way' tactic required higher standards of airmanship or a system whereby the majority of crews would be guided to the target by a specially selected minority. The cumulative effect of the missing rate had virtually destroyed the pre-war Bomber Command by early 1942, when these operational problems became controversial issues; the rapidly expanding wartime Command hardly allowed a training time scale which would enable new standards to be reached, whether for pilots or navigators.[19] The establishment of the Pathfinder Force in August 1942 at the urgent prompting of the Directorate of Bomber Operations, coupled with the introduction of improved navigation and target-finding aids earlier in that year appeared to produce solutions to the problems of loss and innaccuracy. As we shall see the solutions were never to be more than partial.

The Early Daylight Raids

If the chapters on the inter-war years and the background to this chapter are read together it can be seen that an economic offensive in terms of crews and aircraft demanded an understanding of enemy capacity and intentions somewhat greater than the Air Staff and Bomber Command did in fact possess. Bearing that fact in mind, one must view in retrospect the daylight operations of Bomber Command in the first three years of the war as exercises in self-confidence and esprit rather than as a serious attempt to initiate and execute a strategic air offensive on the one hand or to fly in an interdiction role on the other. (The missing rate in the major raids which took place between April and August 1940 was all but six per cent. Nevertheless major daylight raids continued to be mounted on occasion until December 1942; throughout the period as a whole 9,223 sorties were flown as against 77,501 by night. The missing rate throughout averaged six per cent.[20] Although a high proportion of these daylight sorties is accounted for by the operations of 2 Group, whose light bombers performed mainly against short-range targets, the figures show that successive Commanders-in-Chief of Bomber Command did not entirely abandon the conviction that results could be achieved by day which could never be achieved at night. But Harris was always more sceptical than his predecessors, and was not displeased when, in May 1943, 2 Group was detached from his command to form the nucleus of what was to become the 2nd Tactical Air Force. Bomber Command as such carried out no more daylight raids until February 1944.

Daylight bombing operations appear to have a precision and clarity about them which is lacking at night. This characteristic was true certainly of World War Two accounts. The actual confusion and uncertainty inseparable from any operation of war, and the strain and monotony peculiar to night bombing are replaced in the mind's eye by a series of definite images; by day one could at least *see*, whether it was your comrades, the target or the enemy. In reality many daylight operations were flown in poor visibility; the necessarily repetitive pages of squadron operational record books are a litany of cloud, mist, rain, that combination which produces the sudden and dangerous lack or loss of visibility so frequently found in the North Sea and the English Channel. All too often a fine start ended in fading light or lowering cloud—and heavy loss. The four main daylight operations of 1939, flown on 4 September and on 3, 14 and 18 December, possess all these characteristics abundantly.

It will be recalled that the opening months of the war limited Bomber Command's operations in political as well as strategic terms. The four daylight raids in question were therefore an attempt to circumvent both inhibitions: specific targets in or near ports would be attacked, while the feasibility of flying in formation without escort would be demonstrated.[21]

On 4 September, therefore, Bomber Command went to war. Fifteen Blenheims and 14 Wellingtons took off to attack the German fleet, reported to be lying off Brunsbüttel and Wilhelmshaven. This somewhat comprehensive target was attacked through rain and cloud, the Blenheims diving low and losing formation as their crews sought individual ships. From 19 aircraft attacking, seven were lost. No firm conclusions were drawn from this scrambling encounter, flown largely at the behest of the First Lord of the Admiralty to demonstrate that the lion had wings.[22] Fighter opposition had been negligible, and the vulnerability of the Blenheim to flak was disregarded. Nevertheless the three December raids were confined to the Wellingtons of 3 Group. The targets remained German North Sea naval bases and the fleet. The difficulty of searching for the latter—a precise yet elusive target—only accentuated an unequal struggle. The German early warning system, though not linked to fighter control or pilots as was the case with Fighter Command, was adequate enough to despatch strong forces—the actual numbers were not given by crews experiencing war in reality, but they were clearly too many for even the most disciplined formation.

Formation flying, if it is to be tactically effective in defensive terms, cannot be a low-level affair. Only very exceptionally can even brave, disciplined and experienced crews stay together when streaking along at wave or roof top height. This factor was not revealed by the 3 December raid, since fighters made no determined effort to attack; no bombers were lost; nor, for that matter, was any specific damage done to the German fleet. On the 14th, however, 12 Wellingtons, whose crews had been briefed to 'carry out an armed patrol of the Schillig Roads', were attacked off Heligoland when flying at 600 feet in atrocious visibility. A hitherto unappreciated feature of the German defences, effective even in bad weather, was soon revealed. Flak and fighters fired alternately at a formation losing height and cohesion. Five Wellingtons were shot down and another crashed on landing.

Because these three raids had been flown in bad weather, making it difficult for crews to report accurately, the staff at Bomber Command was reluctant to decide that fighters had the edge over a bomber formation. Air Commodore Bottomley, the Senior Air Staff Officer at 3 Group, and later in the war the member of the Air Staff most cautious in drawing firm conclusions from any event, went so far as to assert that formation flying was 'the equivalent of the old "thin red line" or the "shoulder to shoulder" of Cromwell's Ironsides'. Be that analogy as it may (and the 14 December battle led the 3 Group Commander, Air Vice-Marshal Baldwin to compare it with the charge of the Light Brigade), the events of the 18th settled the matter until the invasion of France six months later. Again, Wellingtons, 24 this time, were sent on a search for the German fleet. Crews were, however, ordered to fly at a minimum level of 10,000 feet as well as to stick together.

Survivors' accounts suggest that formation was maintained for as long as possible, although its nature and the rapid and heavy losses suffered [precluded] any equivalent of covering fire being provided. After 'a desperate battle' at in fact 15,000 feet, the Wellingtons returned to base. But of the 22 Wellingtons which had actually engaged, only ten returned. Although crew reports suggested that up to 24 German fighters had been destroyed, bomber losses on this scale at any period of the war would have brought a temporary halt in operations. In 1939 they stopped them dead. Unfortunately, however, the estimate of German fighters destroyed was accepted without demur, thus enabling the proponents of unescorted daylight bombing to have, for the time being, the last word. A similar optimism was to prevail among the Commander and Staff of the 8th Air Force in 1942, and was later seen to be based on comparably inaccurate figures of fighter loss. But the reluctance in 1939 to accept that unescorted daylight bombing was not feasible by any criteria of war, was, in a sense, more dangerous than the optimism of the unblooded or unscathed Americans, rich in resources and armoured in confidence.

Although the events of September and December forced the Air Staff to contemplate a night offensive if and when Germany itself was to be attacked, they did not sufficiently convince it of the fact that, night or day, the bomber was at a disadvantage. The failure of the German bomber force to achieve strategic success over Britain in the summer of 1940 later tended to convince the Air Staff that night operations were both inevitable and feasible. Too much attention was paid by Bomber Command to the Battle of Britain; too little to the blitz which followed it, and the failure of the Luftwaffe night bomber squadrons to achieve by killing civilians what the day bomber squadrons had failed to achieve by attacking Fighter Command Stations. The 'acceptable' missing rates suffered by Bomber Command throught most of 1941 and 1942 did little to shake convictions. Indeed, despite the scientific effort by then being devoted to assisting Bomber Command, it would be now true to say that the inherent menace of the German fighter, at night as well as by day, was overlooked. For long it was believed that flak destroyed more bombers than did fighters; the partial evidence and tentative conclusions of the Dickens Report did nothing to weaken that belief.[23]

The more immediate danger of failing to consider bombers and fighters objectively in 1939 was that the daylight operations of 1940 were flown unescorted on most occasions; such shattering losses were suffered that faith in daylight bombing operations *for whatever purpose* began to wane. The further losses suffered by Blenheim squadrons in 1941 had the effect, arbitrarily and for the duration of the war, of finally dividing the proponents of 'strategic' and 'tactical' bombing into two verbally hostile camps. This did not happen to the Americans, because faith in the principles of interdiction and close support of ground forces was never for a moment destroyed by the 8th Air Force's losses in 1943. But when Bomber Command once again resumed daylight operations in 1944, Harris made it clear that not only would they be escorted but that they would, where possible, be flown against 'strategic' targets which he had selected. A new technique of daylight *area* bombing through cloud was indeed introduced by 3 Group, leaving 1 and 4 to fight their night battles in the old ways.[24]

In 1940 these complexities were absent. Once France and the Low Countries had been invaded, Bomber Command had to be involved, at least in part. The brunt fell on the Battle and Blenheim squadrons; no better indication can be given of the fact that even in those desperate days dogma prevailed over necessity than recording that the Hampden, Whitley and Wellington squadrons continued to concentrate on targets in Germany as the first two had done from the outbreak of war and the latter since January 1940.[25] What is more surprising is to find that, when these aircraft were committed to the battle for France and the salvation of the British Army, their operations took place at night, although directed at targets as 'precise' as cross-roads or forward airfields.[26] To compound this odd role, 2 Group squadrons in the United Kingdom were overworked during June and July, bombing targets in Germany as well as supporting their hard-pressed comrades in France.[27] It is an academic question now whether escorted daylight attacks by these aircraft on interdiction targets would have prevented defeat on the ground. At all events, the Battles and Blenheims were left to themselves. Not only were they unescorted or inadequately escorted by British or French fighters on virtually all their operations, but their low-level attacks precluded more than a semblance of formation flying. The attack on the Maastricht bridges is famous; less frequently recalled is the fate of the Blenheims of 82 Squadron over the Gembloux airfield on 17 May. Flying at 8,000 feet, they were attacked by fighters and flak; the formation dispersed seeking cloud; only one Blenheim, heavily damaged, returned to base.[28]

By the end of 1940 daylight operations were, of necessity, scattered and infrequent. Anti-invasion sorties had been flown mainly at night since August. Anti-shipping strikes and 'sweeps' indeed continued through a 2 Group version of what later became known as 'tip and run' tactics, and a useful tonnage of vessels destined for or leaving German ports was sunk before Coastal Command became responsible for all these offensive maritime operations in May 1941.[29] But a specific role, daylight role, for Bomber Command in general and 2 Group in particular was becoming increasingly difficult to define or play. The Blenheim was especially vulnerable, as a compromise aircraft attempting especially difficult tasks is likely to be, but all Bomber Command's aircraft were the products in one way or another of pre-war neglect of operational realities. The Wellington was at least capable of taking much punishment due, it was thought, to its 'geodetic' frame,[30] but that advantage was more than outweighed by the fact that the petrol tanks were unprotected.

Despite all these problems day operations could not be abandoned entirely. Although by 1941 those who believed in daylight precision bombing had become as rare as those airmen who believed in providing support for the Royal Navy and the Army, an increasing number began to argue in late 1940 and early 1941 that escorted daylight operations could engage the enemy and, as it was later argued, support operations at night. At this time, it must be remembered, the Luftwaffe day and night fighter squadrons in France and the Low Countries were at their maximum establishment. 'Sea Lion', although postponed and, in the eyes of the OKW and OKH, a non-starter, had not yet been officially abandoned; headquarters and units had not yet moved east and south in preparation for 'Barbarossa' and lesser campaigns in the Balkans, the Mediterranean and the North African desert.[31] Hence the Luftwaffe in the west remained a formidable strike, support and defensive force. It was understandable, therefore, that Bomber Command appreciations in 1941 for what was hoped would be an expanding campaign of area bombing should take account of the large number of German fighter squadrons lying athwart the routes which the Wellingtons, Whitleys, Hampdens, Manchesters, Halifaxes and Stirlings would have to fly. Initially the idea was to engage the German fighter *tout court*, although for what purpose it is hard to say. But by mid-1941 hopes were being entertained that, if these German fighter squadrons could be diverted to other tasks while Bomber Command's Main Force was crossing the North Sea and the Dutch coast, the latter's losses might well be reduced.[32]

This was a faulty appreciation on two counts. 'Circus' operations—as the original attempt to draw the German day fighter squadrons was called —had no clear objective and no appreciable result. The subsequent notion, strongly urged by Churchill on the rather pliable Peirse, that Circus operations would give cover to Bomber Command's Main Force, was misconceived in that it assumed most bombers were lost in the coastal area. The number of German fighter squadrons stationed in them lent weight to the notion. In fact, however, as the Scientific Intelligence branch of the Air Staff—or intelligent scientists—discovered in 1942, attacks on bombers crossing the coast were made by a comparatively small number of aircraft. In 1941 General Kammhuber's fighter strength totalled some 200. Of these approximately 50 were committed to operations over the coast.

It must be said at this point that the account of 1941 notions just given was not that openly proclaimed at the time. Overtly the developing role of Circus operations, involving 2 Group of Bomber Command and 11 Group of Fighter Command, was to support Peirse's Main Force in daylight operations against major German targets or those of particular importance in the Battle of the Atlantic. And indeed, one major operation of this type was flown on 24 July, when 99 aircraft attacked Brest in daylight. This raid, which probably played its part in immobilising *Gneisenau* and can thus be considered a necessary operation of war, achieved a missing rate of 14 per cent.[33] This figure rubbed in what the pessimists had said. It was nothing to the argument that the new Halifaxes and Stirlings were occasionally bombing by daylight without serious loss. Their luck had held prior to the Brest raid, but on 24 July, while the Main Force was attacking Brest, 15 Halifaxes sought out *Scharnhorst* at La Pallice.

> Fourteen of them reached the target and were met by what appeared to be between 12 and 18 Messerschmitt 109s. Every one of these 14 Halifaxes was hit by fire from the fighters or by flak. Five failed to return, five more were damaged to an extent which required about three weeks to repair. Two were damaged to a lesser extent and the remaining two were superficially damaged.[34]

This quotation from the Official History has been given at length because it starkly illustrates what an 'unacceptable' missing rate can mean. It is not surprising therefore that when the day and night sortie figures for July and August 1941 are checked we find they come to 6,587 and 1,050 respectively.[35] The respective missing rates, exclusive of aircraft which crashed on returning to or attempting to land at base, is just under three and ten per cent. In short, for much of the summer and indeed the autumn of 1941, 2 Group continued to fly operations with crews whose expectation of life was around two months.[36] This figure is hardly surprising when one considers that, by regarding 2 Group as expendable, its squadrons could be sent to attack targets totally outside their capabilities, and only worth attacking for propaganda purposes. The attack on Bremen on 30 June, following a Main Force raid the preceding night, enabled Air Ministry spokesmen to speak of the beginning of round-the-clock bombing of German cities; but the wish was father to the thought. More to the point, of 12 aircraft attacking four were shot down and 'many of the aircraft were written off after landing'.[37] That attacks continued to be pressed home in such circumstances reflects the fact that those bombing by night in dark and cold had no monopoly of courage. The raids in themselves achieved little but the spirit with which they were executed was all part of a process whereby the truth was hammered home that bombing was a very costly business.

The expense was such that 1942 is at least partly notable for the fact that daylight operations continued at all. The reason for this continuance is twofold: 2 Group was beginning to get aircraft faster and better armed than the Blenheim[38]; occasional attacks by Main Force squadrons were designed to answer charges that Bomber Command played no part in the U-boat war. Although the Official History argues that daylight bombing in 1942 tied down considerable fighter forces and led to 'Royal Air Force superiority over the nearer parts of France',[39] the truth surely is that it lingered on largely because nobody had decided whether it was feasible strategically or tactically. Tying down day fighters was no help to those bombing by night; the phrase just quoted has little meaning, since Fighter Command intruder operations actually preceded the Circus plan.[40] More to the point is the fact that 1942 saw the end of daylight operations by Bomber Command until its unavoidable if partial resumption in 1944. The explanation, dogma apart, may be found in the fact that the cost, even with greatly improved aircraft, continued to be high. Indeed this factor only made things worse: the two-man crew Blenheim was expendable; the seven-man crew Lancaster was not, or rather not so on the scale of the Augsburg raid.

We shall return to this raid later, but here it should be considered in conjunction with the daylight operations of 11 July, 17 October and 6 December 1942, in which Danzig, Le Creusot and Eindhoven respectively were attacked.[41] It is important to get one thing clear at once about these raids. Like Augsburg, all were directed at precise targets, and in discussing the operations one can use that word in its proper context. For Augsburg read the MAN diesel works; for Danzig, read submarine yards; for Le Creusot and Eindhoven read electrical components. For them all, in fact read Harris' own highly individual, cynical and, in the context of personal choice, short-lived contribution to the Battle of the Atlantic. But the raids should not be regarded as a chapter in the history of the strategy of bombing. They proved nothing except the cost of such operations and the difficulty of destroying targets when travelling at high speed and at low level. The last point is of particular importance in considering operational feasibilities; although 617 Squadron and Mosquito squadrons occasionally achieved dramatic success with low level raids later in the war, they by no means did so invariably.

None of the daylight raids laid on by Harris achieved much in the way of accuracy or destruction, with the partial exception of that against the Philips works at Eindhoven. The Danzig raid, by 44 Lancasters from 5 Group, was an impressive demonstration of long-range flying and target finding—a round flight of 1,500 miles, and Bomber Command's most ambitious undertaking of that sort to date. But although only two aircraft were lost, the distance flown made the raid virtually one by night, and attacks were scattered over a wide area and in no sense were 'precise'. The Le Creusot raid, again a 5 Group affair of 44 Lancasters, was flown on a 'dog leg' course well out to sea, and thus involved a round flight of 1,700 miles. Only one Lancaster failed to return. Flak and fighter defence was, however, weak. Subsequent reconnaissance photographs showed, moreover, that the Schneider works had hardly been damaged. The Eindhoven raid, by contrast, was more positive in all its results. The attack was made by 93 aircraft, all from 2 Group, consisting of Bostons, Mosquitoes and Venturas, harbingers of better things to come, albeit in a different operational context. The crews of these fast and manoeuvrable aircraft were able to pick their target, make repeated runs and inflict severe damage. But the net missing rate was over 13 per cent. Whatever the importance of the target—and the Philips factories were reckoned then to be making one-third of the really crucial electrical components for Germany's advanced weapons systems and equipments[42]—the cost of attacking it could be too high. Were there alternative targets? It is necessary now briefly to examine the nature of maritime operations to answer that question in part.

Bomber Command and the War at Sea

Sir Arthur Harris once complained to the Prime Minister that it took an average 7,000 hours for an aircraft to find and sink a U-boat. In that time, he said, his Main Force could destroy one third of Cologne.[43]

It is comparisons of this kind, to which senior officers are always much given, which makes any discussion of Bomber Command's contribution to the Battle of the Atlantic so extremely difficult to assess. It might be thought in any case that the subject was better suited to 'issues' rather than 'operations'. But in 1941 and 1942 the short point was not whether the Royal Air Force in general and Bomber Command in particular should help fight the U-boat—Churchill settled that by placing Coastal Command virtually under Admiralty control and diverting obsolescent British Wellingtons and the new American Liberators from Peirse and Harris[44]— or whether the strategic air offensive should have been postponed until the U-boat had been defeated. Such a decision was theoretically feasible, but, as the Introduction and preceding chapter have endeavoured to show, the situation in terms of aircraft, equipment and training obtaining in Bomber Command before 1939 and the necessities of political and psychological warfare which developed after that date effectively precluded such a fundamental strategic change.

All therefore that one can usefully do in a work of this compass is to describe some of the operational factors involved in the Battle of the Atlantic and see whether Bomber Command's contribution might have been more effective with the resources which were actually made available for operations against land targets and patrols over the Bay of Biscay by squadrons *transferred* from Bomber to Coastal Command. The question of allocation of resources was essentially a decision which only Churchill could take, since the relentless pursuit by the Services themselves of vested interests made them quite unfitted for the task, even at the Chiefs of Staff level. The tart, not infrequently acrid, exchanges in the Chiefs of Staff committee on this and related matters in 1941 and 1942 are instructive only in so far as they remind us that the Services perform their most useful functions when they are executing strategy, not when they are devising or attempting to allocate the resources for it.[45]

The operational factors are surely these: targets, aircraft, equipment, crews. The operations in themselves merit no especial scrutiny: whether by sea or land they shared the critical factor that targets were hard to find and dangerous to attack. Attacking a U-boat usually anxious to submerge was, by the law of averages, less dangerous than attacking Augsburg or, in the wider context of maritime operations, bombing major units of the German fleet (whether at sea or in harbour), or factories making the long-range aircraft which co-operated with U-boats at sea. The Augsburg raid, indeed, in which no less than seven of the 12 aircraft attacking were shot down, ranks singularly high for courage even in the records of Bomber

Command. But finding a U-boat was obviously harder than locating a ground target, and, given the psychological truth that bomber crews needed to attack *something* to keep going, it was small comfort for those transferred to Coastal Command to be told by sailors that their infinitely wearisome patrols over blank waters were probably keeping submarines submerged on their way to the 'wolf pack' concentration area, thus forcing them to run down their batteries and fuel supplies. Bomber crews were motivated and trained to drop bombs, not act as beaters for warships; for this task they lacked the aircraft and the temperament.

Bearing these points in mind Harris had a case which is not without force when he argued that for Bomber Command to fight as Coastal Command fought was a waste of resources and time.[46] By reluctantly bombing warships, occasionally attacking factories making vital components or even the submarine shipyards themselves, Harris could instead claim that he was making a major contribution to the Battle of the Atlantic. Further, he records with particular pride the effectiveness of Bomber Command's mining operations in virtually destroying Germany's coastal and short sea trade, and in accounting too both for a useful number of submarines and for a progressive restriction of safe areas for their crew's training and working up.[47] On the other hand, the author of *The War at Sea* and many senior naval officers who fought in the Battle of the Atlantic argue that the addition of even a relatively small number of aircraft made a crucial contribution to the tactic of forcing the U-boat to dive when its crew wanted to stay on the surface.[48]

There are several factors here which must be carefully distinguished. More U-boats were sunk by the Royal Air Force than the Royal Navy.[49] Bearing in mind that aircraft in those days had no 'dipping sonar'[50] and could only detect a U-boat on the surface (for which the ASV radar was provided by 1940[51] and an extra powerful searchlight, known as a 'Leigh Light', by summer 1942), this is a remarkable achievement. It is an achievement, moreover, which emphasises what a key factor the submarine's need to conserve energy and recharge batteries was; by travelling on the surface whenever possible even the smaller, 700-ton U-boats could operate off the New England coasts for a fortnight to three weeks.[52] Effective hunting of U-boats from the air, however, required long-range or very long-range aircraft, and this was especially so if convoy escorts or warships in the search area were to co-operate in what was by definition an operation requiring patience and persistence. Moreover, once German scientists had assessed the importance of ASV radar, they produced a search receiver which detected the former in ample time for the submarine to dive[53]; there were, of course, purely visual sightings, but inevitably they were few, given the conditions frequently prevailing, summer and winter, in the Bay of Biscay, and the fleeting spectacle a well-handled U-boat presented as it surfaced, at night if possible, at dawn or dusk if only then did weather allow.

Hunting for submarines therefore required particular aircraft with special equipment, specifically the very long range Liberator and the ten-centimetre ASV. These aircraft and equipments did not become available until 1943,[54] and when the Battle of the Atlantic reached its climax in the summer of that year the outcome was a major and virtually final defeat of the U-boat. If Churchill had decided to produce a Coastal Command version of the Lancaster and equip it with progressively more sensitive ASV additional submarines would probably have been sunk in 1942, but such success in those truly grim summer months would have required this weapons system to have been conceived and prototyped before war broke out. There is some circumstantial evidence that Avros were dissuaded from producing a 'maritime' Lancaster in 1942,[55] and if this was so, the point about the intensity of inter-Service rivalry acquires, alas, an extra validity. But Churchill was essentially the arbiter of these matters. Strongly as he felt about the Battle of the Atlantic, he was not prepared to slow the increasing momentum of the strategic air offensive to see the former fought more vigorously.[56]

Bomber Command was the sole recipient of the Lancaster, certainly the most successful four-engined aircraft built during World War Two, in terms of payload to range and, no less important, capacity to take and survive punishment. Of equal significance, the Lancaster formed part of a triangular operational plot: aircraft; war-time crews of very average quality in terms of navigational skill and overall airmanship; *aids* to help them. And H_2S, enabling crews to see, was, in Harris' thinking, the base of that triangle.[57] That the development of H_2S and its use on operations enabled the enemy to nullify for a time the effectiveness of ASV worried Harris not at all. He was the more concerned to point out that the enemy knew about ASV by the time H_2S came into service, consequently re-ducing the latter's value, indeed making it a double-edged weapon. Bereft of H_2S and thus forced to endure loss in darkness the morale of Bomber Command might well have declined to a point where its ability to mount a sustained offensive was rigorously curtailed if not absolutely destroyed.

It can be seen from the above, therefore, that there is little point in asking *here* whether Bomber Command might have made a bigger contribution to the Battle of the Atlantic as fought at sea. A different Command, differently equipped would almost certainly have done so. Bomber Command as led, with Churchill's support, by Harris could not have done so. To see whether the Command might have struck harder at the U-boat by attacking its production vitals, we must shortly turn to a narrative of how it operated at night during the first three years of the war. The daylight attacks described on pages 114-15 may have done some significant damage, although nothing comparable to the raid on Friedrichshafen on 20 June 1943.[58] But daylight attacks rapidly became counter-productive, above all in the loss of the most expert crews. Only by night could Bomber Command strike again and again, whatever the target.

The American Entry on to the Stage

It is not proposed in this final section of the chapter dealing with the operations of Bomber Command and with the US 8th Air Force between 1939 and 1942 to delve too deeply into how the latter made its entry on to the stage. As will be apparent from any study of the ebb and flow of the war in 1942, many strategic premises which governed American thinking before 1939 were sharply effected by what happened at Pearl Harbor and the course of events thereafter. Among the enforced changes in thinking caused by the surprise Japanese attack was a revision in the time scale for any assault by Anglo-American forces on a defended European shore in order to effect the defeat of Germany. Thus, although that defeat remained on paper an American strategic priority, and had as one of its principal elements a bomber offensive directed at Germany's industrial heartland, sheer necessity and the demands of other theatres meant that in practice nothing very dramatic was achieved by the US Air Force over European skies in the late summer and autumn of 1942.

Considerable space has been devoted to a narrative and an analysis of American strategic thinking in respect of British air power in the chapters devoted to the inter-war years; far greater space is given to describing American air power in battle in the chapters for 1943; when we come to 1944 and 1945 it will be seen that not only the concepts and practice of American air power had come to dominate what was formally known as the Combined Bomber Offensive, but that General Arnold's determination to place his commanders in positions of unchallenged authority led to a direct clash with their British opposite numbers and certain notions of how air power should be formulated and expressed. Thus, 1943 was a year of battle in the skies; 1944 and 1945 saw battle too, but it was at its most intense at the higher echelons of command in the Anglo-American strategic community. For the US Air Force operating over Europe, 1942 was a half year of preparation, inconclusive combat and somewhat misleading optimism as to what the future might hold. Moreover, it should be noted that although the two main strategic premises in the American air power canon remained—that accurate bombing of industrial targets was a necessary prelude to major ground operations and that this could be carried out by the 'self-defending formation'— little occurred in these five months to cause much debate as to their validity; the interest of the period, such as it is, resides principally in watching the fledgling air force attempt to address itself to war in practice rather than at the training camp.

We therefore have seven aspects of this introductory phase to consider: the strategic premises (in so far as they obtained at all); the operational objectives; the operational tactics; the command structure; the material factors; the logistic factors; the operations themselves. Before, however, embarking on a narrative of how these seven factors were assessed by Generals Spaatz and Eaker, respectively commanding the 8th Air Force and the 8th Bomber Command, the following figures should be noted, because without in any way derogating from the promising debut which the latter commander's crews made from the time of their first raid, they do form a clear contrast with the growing momentum of Bomber Command raids, sorties, tonnages—and losses in men and aircraft. Between 17 August, when 12 B.17s first attacked the marshalling yards at Rouen and Sotteville, and 30 December, when 77 aircraft attacked the U-boat pens at Lorient, 27 operations were mounted; 1,547 sorties were flown; 32 aircraft were lost—a missing rate of under two per cent. Marshalling yards were attacked on four occasions; airfields on 15; shipyards on four; 'industrial, aviation' targets on three; 'targets of opportunity' on three, 'industrial, transportation' targets on three; U-boat pens and bases on 11. Diversionary attacks were made on 11 occasions.[59] These figures, the targets attacked and the proportions in which they were attacked, should be compared with the objectives set out in the directives summarised on pages 326–38.

The foregoing summary should not be taken as a criticism of the American approach to the staggering problems of striking a decisive blow at Germany's industrial strength, or doing so without loss which would fairly rapidly prove unacceptable. It is true that great confidence reigned among those who were responsible for expanding the US Army Air Force once war was declared, and their confidence extended to the belief that the B.17 and B.24 were weapons of war which the German Air Force would find rather more formidable than the medium and heavy bombers of the RAF Bomber Command, operating at the mercy of the enemy in all its strength, the weather and their crews' fatigue. But this natural confidence apart, the US Air Force did accept, if more by implication than expressly, that no sudden or massive assault on Germany's industry could be launched. It has been well said: 'AAF leaders most intimately concerned, made soberly aware of the difficulty and the significance of their task by intensive study of British and German experience, were prepared to devote their earliest combat missions to testing American techniques and equipment in the war's toughest air theatre.'[60] Thus, although strategic premises of industrial destruction remained and although Germany's main targets in this category were listed and analysed, the first operational plans made by General Eaker's staff were confined to targets in France and the Low Countries. It is possibly the warnings that 'Torch' had effectively superseded 'Bolero' and 'Roundup' that accounted for this readiness to test the German defences in a sector where they were unlikely to be particularly strong. But however that may be, and while the 8th Air Force remained theoretically committed to Bolero, deployment of General Eaker's groups went ahead rapidly on the understanding that minor targets would be their first concern. This appreciation was welcome in a number of ways to the British Air Staff, who were 'politely sceptical'[61] of the ability of the Bomber to survive aerial combat by day, and had no wish to see Air Marshal Harris' offensive altered in any direction by the advent of a bomber force developed round fundamentally different concepts.

It is true that as late as 21 July 1942 General Eisenhower, who by then had been appointed to the somewhat unreal post of European Theatre Commander, had ruled that the objective of the 8th Air Force was the destruction of 'carefully chosen strategic targets'[62]; by no stretch of the imagination could many of the targets in France and the Low Countries come into this category; the U-boat bases and pens possibly did, but already senior officers on General Spaatz's staff had been made aware, by comments from their RAF colleagues that attacking these targets was prohibitively expensive in terms of time, cost and results achieved. It is interesting to note that from the first a certain doubt reigned at General Spaatz's Headquarters as to the likelihood of achieving anything of significance against such virtually impregnable targets.[63]

Before the 8th Air Force could embark on operations one purely operational issue had to be resolved, and in theory it was so resolved by the 'joint American-British directive on day bomber operations involving fighter co-operation',[64] dated 8 September 1942. The purpose of this directive was clear enough; it was to ensure that the early and shallow penetration raids carried out by Eaker's crews would be escorted by aircraft from Fighter Command; after the initial period of familiarisation, the 8th Fighter Command would replace the British fighter squadrons. It is at this point that a great lack of clarity appears in the appreciations which were written and the detailed plans which were worked out for the employment of these joint forces. In the first place, Craven and Cate are surely at fault in suggesting that the directive implied anything in the way of Anglo-American approach to this minor aspect of the strategic air offensive. The authors of the formidable history of *The Army Air Forces in World War Two* are rarely at fault and their treatment of the complex relationships which existed in the Grand Alliance is sympathetic if astringent. But it is not true as is stated in the History, that the RAF in any of its manifestations provided the 8th Air Force with information about targets in France, although some information may well have been provided about those in the Low Countries. The targets in question had, with very few exceptions, never been attacked by Bomber Command, and even less was known about them than those in Germany. The truth is that the criterion of target selection was much simpler. It was governed by the effective operational range of Fighter Command's Spitfires. This meant that if these aircraft were to escort the bombers throughout the length of their mission, no target further south than Paris or further east than Rotterdam was at all feasible.

But here another issue must be settled: Craven and Cate state, they do not merely imply, that the commander and senior officers of the 8th Air Force accepted that the bomber groups must be escorted. The experience of the Pacific Theatre in which the unescorted bomber had suffered heavily may indeed have led to this fundamental review of what I have called a canon of American theories of air power; but if this were so, it is odd that no provision was being made at the time when the 8th Air Force was about to go into action for the design and production of an escorting fighter which could carry out its assigned mission however deeply into Germany the bombardment groups and wings were ordered to penetrate.

The truth seems to be, however, that no revision of strategic thought or dogma took place, either at General Arnold's level or among his subordinates; the destruction of Germany's industrial potential and the execution of that task by the unescorted 'self-defending' formation remained as clear and unequivocal expressions of military competence and airmanship.[65] The belief was put to the test in 1943 and was utterly shattered. It was not put to the test in 1942, although sights were lowered in that French, Dutch and Belgian targets were attacked by heavily escorted fighter formations. A far more probable explanation of the decision to co-operate with Fighter Command is that many of the latter's squadrons were virtually unemployed by the late summer of 1942, and an opportunity presented itself for their earlier 'Circus' operations to be resumed, albeit in a different form.[66]

The early missions flown by 97 Group were thus heavily protected, both from the enemy and from any objective analyses.[67] This is not to say that they had no value, indeed it seems probable that the second mission, on 19 August, and planned as part of the air operations undertaken in connection with the Dieppe raid, did have a useful diversionary effect. The missions themselves, however, attracted little attention from the German Air Force. The first occasion on which combat ensued was on 21 August; there was a muddle over rendezvous times with the RAF fighter escort and hence the bombers flew on unescorted to attack shipyards at Rotterdam. On the way to the target the formation was attacked by a fighter force estimated between 20 and 25 Me. 109s and Fw. 190s. An inconclusive combat took place, resulting in the death of one American pilot and the first of what were to become persistently exaggerated claims by the American air gunners that enemy fighters had been destroyed or damaged.

The fighter reaction, however, continued to be limited, and until the mission on 9 October no German communiqué was issued about the new arrivals on the bomber offensive scene. A more serious reaction came from the civilian population of France and the Low Countries, which began to endure casualties as American bombs rained down with rather less accuracy than predicted when the Norden bomb site came into service. It had been appreciated from the first that chosen targets in enemy occupied territory meant risking losing the goodwill of those who silently supported the Allied cause, and who were prepared to risk torture and prison in order to provide information. The risk may be called a considered one, and it was taken, not only because no viable alternative presented itself, but because of a real if unsupported belief that precision bombing was more than a figure of speech. The very earliest results appeared to corroborate this belief, although it must be pointed out that evidence of accuracy was provided by crews rather than the camera. General Eaker had predicted that 40 per cent of all bombs might be expected to fall within a radius of 500 yards from the aiming point. This was demanding a really fantastic degree of accuracy, from aircraft bombing at 12,000 feet or above, however clear the weather, however weak the opposition, and however skilful and resolute the bomber crews; and it must be said that although some interesting results were achieved in the early missions, nothing corresponding to Eaker's prediction ever came to pass.

Even when bombing by any standards was of commendable accuracy the fact that no bomb heavier than 500 lb. was dropped virtually precluded more than incidental damage being caused. When photographic reconnaissance began at the beginning of October it was quickly realised that damage with bombs of this weight could only be superficial, and was quickly repairable. In the first two months of the 8th's missions, the weather remained clear and fine; and remained so for long enough for these unpalatable facts to be recorded on the camera. Information of a more worrying kind came from intelligence sources, posing the question of whether a raid should be judged successful if it killed civilians at the same time as it wrecked locomotives and marshalling yards.[68] On 5 September for example, when the target was again Rouen and Sotteville, 37 bombers did do appreciable damage to the yards and the locomotives; but later reports from inside France stated that approximately 140 civilians, most of them French, had been killed, while some 200 had been wounded. In war's hideous scale of values these casualties were, however, of decreasing account as the 8th Air Force began to learn the business of flying by day over enemy territory.

The mission following that in which Frenchmen died for the Allied cause saw Eaker's crews meeting real fighter opposition for the first time, and losing their first aircraft in consequence. On this occasion 41 bombers were despatched to attack the Avions Potez aircraft factory at Meaulte and airfields at St Omer. Despite this early tactic of flying a diversionary raid, crews reported encounters with Fw. 190s. On 7 September what is somewhat prematurely described as 'a bitter aerial battle' took place, but in fact no aircraft were lost from 29 despatched; high claims were, however, made for the number of enemy aircraft destroyed. So it continued through September and early October, with intelligence staff at General Spaatz's Headquarters beginning to believe that his crews had already taken the measure of German fighter opposition, and the initially sceptical RAF began to wonder too whether there might not be something in the American approach, provided the day bomber force transported itself into one supporting Air Marshal Harris' groups.

We need not trouble ourselves with suggestions put out by Churchill and the Air Staff that this transformation should take place[69]; there was never the slightest chance of it happening, and if it did it is inconceivable that the Joint Chiefs of Staff would have been prepared to have the show run by British airmen. Moreover, although confidence and admiration were beginning to surround the missions flown by the B.17 and B.24 crews, there was as yet nothing conclusive which could lead to any fundamental strategic reappraisal. Although German fighters had yet to make their presence seriously felt, bombing accuracy was certainly not on the increase, while the more objective among Eaker's staff were becoming aware that claims of enemy aircraft destroyed were not only very far from the truth, but, if accepted and fed into higher level appreciations, might lead to a totally unwarranted optimism about the scale of effort required to meet the objective of so weakening Germany industrially in 1943 that an assault on Europe could be mounted with relative ease thereafter.

Thus by late November the staff of the 8th Air Force was in something of a quandary; and the attempt which was made to analyse the results of the first 23 missions shows this very clearly. On the one hand escorted daylight attacks had been mounted and executed with only trifling loss; even when bomber formations had found themselves temporarily unescorted, German fighters had either hesitated to close for the kill or had been driven off with, apparently, heavy loss. On the other hand even a moderate fighter attack at once affected bombing accuracy. Combat reports of General Eaker's crews are inconclusive on this point, but it seems probable that, although formation flying in a tight pattern was laid down as a standard procedure, the early missions saw much individual combat between bomber and fighter crews. The courageous tactics of 1943, when crews carried on unflinchingly in tight echelon in order to put the bombs precisely on target was the result of dissatisfaction with bombing accuracy, not the reflection of the effectiveness of German fighter attacks in 1942. In the event, however, neither optimism nor reservations about how a daylight offensive could develop was to be tested until a serious check to experiment had been overcome.

By the beginning of November the 8th Air Force in both its bomber and fighter elements was being drawn on heavily in support of the operations mounted by the 12th Air Force in North Africa.

In addition to four fighter and two heavy bomber groups, the 8th Air Force [by this time] had turned over trained personnel to the extent of 3,198 officers, 24,124 enlisted men and 34 warrant officers, of whom 1,098 officers,

7,101 enlisted men and 14 warrant officers came from the 8th Bomber Command alone. The remaining heavy bombardment groups (the 44th, 91st, 92nd, 93rd, 303rd, 305th and 306th) suffered considerably from loss of such essential equipment as bomb-loading appliances and transport vehicles. They suffered even more from complete lack of replacement of both crews and aircraft, a fact which made it impossible to keep a large force in the air even when weather conditions permitted.

This passage has been quoted at such length because it reveals that the 8th Air Force was virtually grounded until spring of 1943, first by demands of the North African campaign and secondly, as we shall see, by a winter of the utmost severity. Although in fact the size of missions between early November and the end of year had been materially increased, the crews which had begun to learn their way about in war were replaced by those with no operational experience. That the loss continued to be derisory is simply a reflection of the fact that the operations flown by the 8th Air Force in these four months were interesting as tactical exercises, and gave abundant proof of the American airman's determination to stick to his job. But they gave no proof at all of what might happen when the German Air Force rose to the challenge of American air power.

5

Night Operations
1939–1942

Shots in the Dark

Between the outbreak of war and the end of 1942, Bomber Command flew 77,501 night sorties for the loss of 2,859 aircraft; some 80,000 tons of bombs were dropped[1]; two towns were devastated—Lübeck and Rostock; others were damaged in those working-class areas of closely packed homes, by whose destruction Lord Cherwell set such store as a method of simultaneously sapping morale and reducing industrial output. The '1,000' raid on Cologne on 30 May was reckoned to have laid 600 acres of the city flat,[2] but half of this was its centre; it was not until mid-1943 that crews began methodically to bomb German city suburbs reducing them to rubble, and treating city centres as aiming points. 'Area bombing' in fact gradually acquired a particular, if never precise, meaning: although any urban destruction had its value, some accuracy was required to destroy the areas of greatest human density; it was the task of the Pathfinder squadrons of 8 Group to find and mark those areas in order that the Main Force should not waste its bombs on the city as a whole.

In the first three years many German cities were attacked or, at least visited by Bomber Command; but many escaped even a 'dusting' or a 'browning' until 1942 and its twin developments of *Gee* and the Pathfinders; some damage was done to the German war economy, but in a way exactly and paradoxically the opposite of that intended. The sporadic nature of the night offensive not only produced complacency and overconfidence in the Luftwaffe and its associated defensive services, but allowed the economy as a whole to operate at a pitch which compared oddly with the objectives and methods of total war. Both the German defences and the Germany economy ignored the air offensive in those first three years as a strategic factor in the war. When the hammer blows began to fall in 1943, an enormous amount of untapped resources was available to enable production to be maintained and, as by Hitler's folly the German armed forces became hopelessly over-extended on all fronts, to increase.[3]

These first three years of the offensive must be seen therefore in this somewhat paradoxical light in assessing its effect on the enemy; it was an ostensibly negative effect, which nevertheless, and in ways certainly not intended, had its value. For Bomber Command as a whole, however, it was three years of frustration, and it is interesting in this connection to note that Group commanders and their subordinates seemed to be more concerned with morale when crews were failing to find even what was euphemistically called a 'target area' than when, in 1943 and 1944, they were enduring heavy loss because they had found it all too well.[4] Air Commodore Coningham (as he then was) expressed the problem of frustration very well when he said in December 1939, 'I foresee a never-ending struggle to circumvent the law that one cannot see in the dark'.[5] Yet night operations began immediately war broke out with leaflet and reconnaissance flights to 'Hamburg, the Ruhr, Münster, Osnabrück, Stuttgart, Mannheim, Nuremburg, Berlin and many other parts of Germany'.[6] Crews reported that they identified targets and that opposition was light—indeed between 10 November and 16 March it was so light that 4 Group lost no aircraft from enemy action at all. Several aircraft were lost due to icing, and many crews endured greater hazards and indeed suffering on what were aptly named 'ice flights' than they did from the German defences. It is certainly the case that at this period these were unco-ordinated; it is also the case that the professional Germans have rarely wasted powder and shot on trivial or elusive targets; 20–30 aircraft flying all over Germany scattering leaflets neither demanded a reaction—nor easily allowed of one —although it it interesting to speculate what might have happened to the concept of a strategic air offensive if the Whitleys had been shot out of the sky in those early months.

This did not happen, however, and it is thus understandable that hopes should be entertained at Bomber Command, even by the cautious Ludlow-Hewitt, that a night offensive was feasible, provided crews could find 'the general area in which the objective lay'.[7] Some of 4 Group's Whitley crews were undoubtedly capable of doing this; their unfortunate experience in seeking French bases was due to the inefficiency or the bloody-mindedness of their Allies on the ground, not to navigational weaknesses aloft.[8] But it should be borne in mind that their reconnaissance flights, in which quite detailed information was given (although not by camera) of German towns, were made without opposition; moreover to be sure of identifying their so called targets, crews on reconnaissance flights dropped down to as low as 1,000 feet.[9] But night bombing from 1,000 feet would invite a strong defensive reaction; more to the point, and setting the effects of enemy opposition aside, navigational standards as a whole in Bomber Command were not only low and known to be low, but few senior officers seemed to care about improving them. The Official History records without comment that at a Group Navigation Officers' conference held on 12 November 1939, the Chairman remarked on 'the fact that "less than half of the Groups had replied to notification of the Conference" '.[10] Conferences being what they are, this might not have mattered so much, although the symptoms of indifference to technical problems and the means of overcoming them should have disturbed higher authority. In the case of this particular conference, however, the Chairman also reported that, in his estimation, 'only 35 per cent of the bombers despatched were reaching their primary targets',[11] so it was unfortunate that this figure, surprisingly accurate in the event, should not have been pondered.

'Primary target' is another euphemism, meaning in fact an urban concentration sufficiently large to suggest that, by dead reckoning and visual observation, one had reached what should have been a given area within which lay the target announced in that night's operation orders. If 65 per cent of crews were not even going to find that, it might seem desirable to improve navigation before committing other groups to night operations. Yet on 6 March the Wellingtons of 3 Group and the Hampdens of 5 Group were ordered to carry out operations similar to those already being performed by 4 Group.[12] The preparations were being laid by Bomber Command if not by the Chamberlain Government for the night bombing of Germany. Since in 1940, as opposed to 1941 and 1942, the Staff of Bomber Command laboured under illusions about the navigational and target-finding problems involved in a night offensive, we may say that area bombing of the crudest kind was being contemplated if not openly announced. The small size of the force which could be committed—rarely more than 100 aircraft were over Germany in any one night in 1940 and 1941, due in part to Ludlow-Hewitt's decision to 'roll up' 14 operational squadrons to form the basis of an expanding training organisation[13]—and bombs which were both puny and defective,[14] ensured that virtually no notice would be taken of these raids; in these years Goering's boast was not called to account.[15]

That *area* bombing would be made probable rather than possible when the first of the new navigational aids were introduced is illustrated by some notes made at a Bomber Command conference on 6 November 1939. After discussion, it was agreed that crews should reach an area of ten square miles around a designated target, and with flares succeed in recognising some landmark, provided they relied on astro-navigation.[16] Now, in fact, the opportunity to navigate by the stars in weather which crews mostly experienced was extremely limited, and the number of navigators who could use a sextant accurately more limited still. The conference referred to 'precision bombing' but did so in a sentence which said in full: 'It was not considered unreasonable to assume that this size target area [that is, ten square miles] could be reached because it was felt that by the time the necessary illumination aids to precision bombing had been developed, improvements in navigation would enable a target area of the size indicated to be made good.'

This is certainly a muddled sentence but the inference is clear: if crews could identify a target area of ten square miles it was hoped that some method of illumination would further identify the designated target within it. A timed course would then be flown in the hopes of bombing more 'precisely' within the area. This, of course, is not 'precision bombing', although it is the nearest to it that most Main Force crews ever got. The sentence quoted is a clumsy description in effect, although not intentional, of the technique initiated in 1942 and developed in 1943 of marking the target area and particular points on the way to and inside it by differently coloured flares or, as they came to be called (when, very belatedly, production got under way), marker bombs. The technique was initiated in March 1942, when *Gee* was introduced, but only became a central *tactical* feature of the night offensive when Group Captain Bennett (as he then was), an Australian pilot of unusual navigational skill and experience—and pronounced views on the inability of the average Bomber Command navigator to get from A to B without getting comprehensively lost—was ordered by Harris to form a special force for the purpose. Pathfinders, as the marking force became known as from the date of official establishment in August, got hopelessly lost too on occasions,[17] but Bennett's crews did become skilful at marking the target *area*; within that area Main Force crews bombed, having found it or its approaches, not by 'astro-navigation', but by the radio and radar aids of *Gee* and, from December 1942, *Oboe*.

Thus as early as November 1939 and long before Whitehall arguments about the purpose and technique of the strategic air offensive, the Staff of

Bomber Command had outlined just how 'precise' the actual bombing was going to be—and that after certain 'improvements' had been effected. The first open admission of an area offensive did not, however, occur until 16 December 1940, when Mannheim was bombed by 134 aircraft, and crews were told at the built-up areas.[18] Indeed, the object of the raid was 'to concentrate the maximum amount of damage in the centre of the town',[19] and this was to be done by sending on 'a fire-raising force of Wellingtons flown by the "most experienced crews available" and armed with incendiary bombs'.[20] The preceding months had seen a gradual yet steady rise in the number of night operations and sorties, reflecting Bomber Command's great part in deterring an invasion of Britain and its growing commitment to a long-range offensive. Sir Arthur Harris, writing of the period when he commanded 5 Group, has said that crews became so familiar with anti-invasion targets they felt almost personally concerned to destroy particular concentrations of barges.[21] Wing Commander Gibson, Bomber Command's most famous pilot, *chevalier sans peur et sans reproche* of the strategic air offensive, has written in similar terms.[22]

Bomber Command's contribution to the postponement of Sea Lion lay however in demonstrating the perils of an opposed Channel crossing rather than in the destruction Peirse's crews wrought. Unlike Napoleon, Hitler had not got to the stage of large barge concentrations before he turned his attention elsewhere.[23] Bomber Command's contribution to deterring him was valuable, but its commander's main intention remained what it had been once daylight bombing of Germany was seen to be hopeless. As 1940 drew to a close and the winter nights lengthened, Bomber Command began to exchange leaflets for bombs on targets as distant as Berlin,[24] and those to become as familiar in communiqués and casualty lists as Hamm and Essen, Düsseldorf, Hanover, Bremen, Cologne and Hamburg.

These raids afforded no chance to Dr Goebbels to speak of 'terror bombing' and made no effect on German war production. They did however initiate among various interested parties in the United Kingdom a pointless, sterile and frequently hypocritical debate about the accuracy or otherwise of the offensive. Ostensibly the debate was concerned with demonstrating that crews had bombed specific targets—this was an exercise in propaganda, in which some thumping lies were told, despite the fact that the crews themselves reported with admirable candour their repeated inability to find the target area, let alone hit the designated target[25]; specifying a town centre in the case of Mannheim was an exercise in realism which was not to be repeated until, later in 1941, German towns were listed for attack as a retaliation for the blitz on Britain. In early 1941 the furthest which Bomber Command would go in this direction was to specify 'town centre'.[26]

The debate in actuality went on and on for two years—with occasional interventions by a surprised and worried Churchill and odd investigations by people totally ignorant of operational factors[27]—because few in Bomber Command would openly admit, least of all to higher authority, that finding, let alone hitting, a target remained the great headache. Some extraordinary reports were submitted by Bomber Command Headquarters about the raids on Berlin on 7 October 1940 and on Essen on 7 November, which created a totally false impression to an Air Staff and a Ministry of Economic Warfare beginning to pick over the issue of how Germany's war potential could best be damaged—by attacks on oil targets or transport targets.[28] There is no direct evidence that Bomber Command's unfortunate propaganda exercises led to the War Cabinet urging that either type of target be bombed; the propaganda details did not reach that far, nor did that elevated authority much concern itself with specific targets, or indeed with the offensive at all. It is not unreasonable to suppose, however, that claims of 'considerable damage'[29] and the like had some influence on an Air Staff which asked Peirse to list oil targets and thus satisfy Portal's belief in this new method of shortening the war. Peirse and his Group commanders managed to come up with Gelsenkirchen, Leuna, Pölitz, Magdeburg and Homberg.[30]

Looking back over nearly three decades in which air power has become permanently associated with the largest possible scale of destruction and loss of life and not with the elimination of a key element in strategy or war, one can see the dilemma confronting those connected with the bombing of Germany. To their credit, nearly all wanted to tell the truth—that, as the Butt Report[30] said,[31] most crews were lucky if they bombed within five miles of their target; practically nobody felt that the truth could be told; nobody was consistent in what he said. Portal, fighting in Whitehall, had to do, or at any rate chose to do, what men in his position usually do—to say different things at different times, all designed to keep the offensive arm of the Royal Air Force in being. Peirse's Group commanders stilled or stifled some of their earlier warnings about the limitations to and the cost of night bombing. Coningham, for example, replied in January 1941 to Peirse's questions about the feasibility of bombing oil targets, by saying that his pilots could 'operate' even on moonless nights,[32] that is they could 'find, not just a town target, but a specific oil installation'. Air Vice-Marshal Baldwin thought that some of his crews could 'take on' oil targets.[33] Air Vice-Marshal Bottomley was more sanguine; he was prepared to send all his crews to bomb certain oil targets in the dark.[34]

What the crews of 1, 3, 4 and 5 Groups thought about oil targets has not been recorded; their recollections today as middle-aged men of those distant events is inevitably coloured by particular experiences or dulled by lapses of memory in which only the cold, the dark and the relentless searchlights remain. The record shows however that oil targets as such received little attention from Bomber Command in this time of dogged endeavour. Transport targets were attacked far more frequently, Hamm being bombed no less than 80 times between June 1940 and 1941[35]; *Scharnhorst* and *Gneisenau* were attacked by night as well as day[36]; Kiel, Hamburg, Wilhelmshaven, Emden and Bremen were bombed too in an effort not only to curtail U-boat production but that of the long-range aircraft which were also being committed to the Battle of the Atlantic.[37] With the effective front-line strength of Bomber Command rarely more than 100 aircraft, much latitude was allowed to the Groups to find what can be best be described as targets of opportunity; 5 Group, for example, whose operations have been recorded with more fidelity than the other Groups, had aircraft flying all over Germany in the summer of 1941 and the winter of 1941–42, a period of exceptionally bad weather, which doubtless accounts partly for the fact that some gross errors in navigation were made.[38]

It has been argued that these scattered and sporadic attacks did much to create 'alarm and despondency' in Germany, and were, if, unintentionally, more of a challenge to Goering's boast of invulnerability than a concentrated raid on a particular town. There is no evidence to substantiate this assertion[39]; it was Harris in 1942 who demonstrated that a town must be heavily damaged and known to be so damaged for 'alarm and despondency' to occur. Even then this emotion was short-lived. Nor did scattered bombing of towns present problems to the defence. The Kammhuber Line, of which more shortly, remained in 1941 and 1942 essentially as a defensive screeen on the coast; not until July 1943 was the line extended to protect the Ruhr on all sides.

Yet while Bomber Command endured this period of trial and error, losing all the while some of its more skilled and persistent crews, changes were occurring which were bound to increase the effectiveness of the front-line force eventually, even though many failed to appreciate at the time that this would be measured mainly in the numbers of Germans killed, rendered homeless and put out of work. The Butt Report, which showed, by a rather narrow sample, that most of Bomber Command's crews never got within five miles of the target, was sent to Bomber Command Headquarters in August 1941. It was at once criticised there[40]; Churchill, on the other hand, found it depressing and disquieting.[41] But the effective answer to the Report was made in two ways; by default, as on a larger scale and in a more acrid Whitehall atmosphere happened in 1942; secondly, the answer was made by the fact that new aircraft, high-capacity bombs and radar aids to navigation and target finding were, at last, strengthening Bomber Command, and by growing evidence that some Germans were beginning to take the night offensive as an operation of strategic significance.[42]

Thus, by the end of 1941 Bomber Command was in an interesting position. Cherwell and Portal skilfully assuaged Churchill's doubts and suspicions about the purpose and effect of the offensive during an autumn and early winter marked by bad weather and mounting loss; in retrospect it may be said that Churchill's reaction to the losses suffered on 7 November gave a necessary breathing space at the operational level. When the offensive was resumed in 1942, Bomber Command was on the threshold of advances which were to make the achievements of 1943 possible. When Harris became Commander-in-Chief on 23 February 1942, 69 heavy bombers were available in the front line out of a total of 378 aircraft serviceable with crews.[43] This was not much, but it was a sign of the times, and of the opening of a year which was to see the Lancaster added to the order of battle to the tune of no less than 178 aircraft.[44] However, 1942 was also to be a year in which the contestants first began to exchange blows in earnest, to prepare, albeit with no settled or precise objective, for deadlier combat, and above all to turn the scientist from someone with a walk-on part to a star performer. To that transformation and to its effect on the strategic air offensive at the operational level we must now turn.

The Scientists' War

No simple comparison can ever be made of the merits of an offensive system in relation to the defence against it, or vice versa. Throughout the strategic air offensive the balance tilted in favour of one or the other, although remaining for most of the time in a position where the offensive forces struggled courageously, uphill, achieved a temporary balance and then found the seesaw of contending factors inexorably pushing them downhill again. For the first three years it was all uphill for Bomber Command; but in 1942 the possibility of a balance being struck began to be felt, even while Whitehall was bowing its head to further global blows or preparing for new arguments at the grand strategic level. Much of this passed over Bomber Command's head; what mattered at High Wycombe and on the mist-cloaked airfields of eastern England was the advent of new material with which to pierce the blanket of the dark and set Germany alight, to make, not merely find, targets which would be a beacon and a guide rather than a coldly military objective.

If, however, we are to appreciate how weight of numbers, size of bombs and use of radar were to set Bomber Command on the path of fire raising and area bombing, it is first necessary to appreciate the defensive system which had to be challenged. Typically, and indeed inevitably, Bomber Command discovered by trial and error how formidable those defences could be when put to the test. But the discovery was not made in 1942, because the German response to the challenge of a force developing an undeniable destructive power was uncharacteristically slow and tentative. Why was this so? Bomber Command's losses certainly rose in 1942, although it must be remembered that its overall losses throughout the war contained a very high proportion not directly attributable to enemy action.[45] Of greater significance is the fact that nothing which the defence achieved in 1942 deterred the Command from increasing the number of raids or the tonnage of bombs. If Bomber Command remained insignificant in the strategic terms set by its most committed proponents, this was due to its strategic inadequacies, not to the quality of the defence or doubts about the need for the offensive as such.

The answer to the questions just posed must be found in the fact that the German forces committed to the defence of the Reich possessed, by 1942, a combination of aircraft, early warning, flak plus searchlights and ground control of all four which appeared to be sufficient when, in fact, further development was needed, both individually and collectively. The feeble challenge posed by Bomber Command between 1939 and 1941 may be much of the explanation, but some of it will also be found in the fact that in Germany, as in Britain, higher authority remained fundamentally ignorant of certain factors, specifically that the Luftwaffe and the ground defences would one day face a challenge they might be unable to meet.[46] Above all, the fruits of victory in Russia and the North African desert were still sweet, and the campaigns there appeared to justify a drain on German resources which spread even to matériel which should, were prudence ruling, have been provided for the defensive arms.

It is true that in 1942 the Luftwaffe possessed types of fighter suitable for night operations much more formidable than in 1939—the Me. 109 was in quantity production, but more to the point, so was the Me. 110, while the value of the Ju. 88 as an AI-equipped interceptor was beginning to be realised. Nevertheless, only 65 of these aircraft were in front-line service by December 1942; of greater significance is the fact that, after three years of war, the German Air Force as a whole was little larger than at its outbreak—3,960 aircraft, as against 3,750. Although the number of aircraft committed to the defence of Germany by night rose from 180 to 350 aircraft in 1942, this 95 per cent increase would have been significant only if other fronts had ceased to claim the lion's share. But on the Russian front alone, 2,000 aircraft, including a large fighter element, were committed to an offensive which Russian toughness and courage had only temporarily halted.[47]

So much, at this point, for the night fighter. Guns and searchlights would have become an increasing menace to the bomber in 1942 had not many of the latter, on Hitler's personal order, been transferred from the Kammhuber Line in May 1942 on the grounds that early warning and other radar-controlled defences there were so developed that one element could be removed for operations elsewhere.[48] The removal of a crucial link in the defensive chain (and one moreover, of considerable psychological as well as tactical importance) inevitably weakened the whole. Hitler paid an unconscious tribute to the Commander of the night fighter force and the Luftwaffe's Director-General of Signals, Generals Kammhuber and Martini, in supposing that the defensive system which they had established could survive with vital parts missing, but it was one singularly ill received by those gifted and perceptive men. For an understanding of why the defensive system was so weakened by Hitler's arbitrary act it is necessary to consider for a moment the radar position in Germany at the outbreak of war.

It was then a satisfactory position indeed.[49] The bomber force was equipped with navigational and target-finding aids which Bomber Command was not to receive for another two-and-a-half years. These aids, working on the principle of transmitted signals which either had to be synchronised for a true course to be flown or regarded as cross-bearings for it to be plotted, had been in commercial use in Germany since 1935—a sufficient indication of the industrial and technological achievements of a modern state. Further refinements with flying on the 'beam' were introduced on the outbreak of war, enabling the navigators of German bombers to listen not only for the transmissions but to know when the

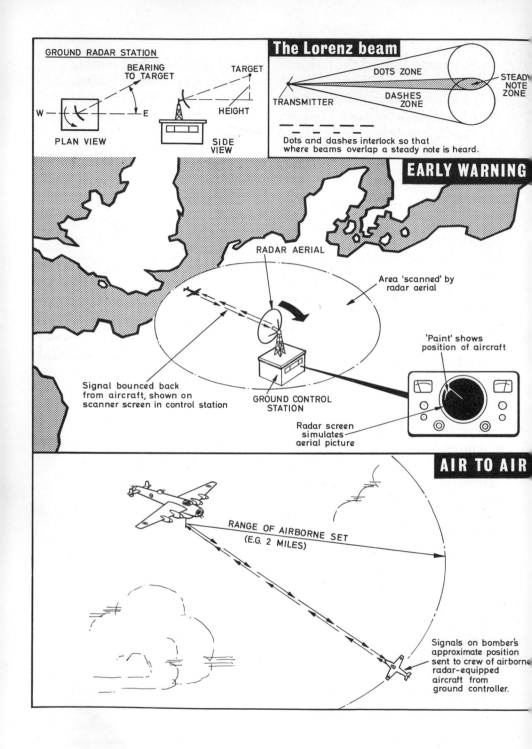

GROUND RADAR STATION

BEARING TO TARGET

TARGET

W ——— E

PLAN VIEW

TARGET

HEIGHT

SIDE VIEW

The Lorenz beam

DOTS ZONE

STEADY NOTE ZONE

TRANSMITTER

DASHES ZONE

Dots and dashes interlock so that
where beams overlap a steady note is heard.

EARLY WARNING

RADAR AERIAL

Area 'scanned' by
radar aerial

'Paint' shows
position of aircraft

Signal bounced back
from aircraft, shown on
scanner screen in control station

GROUND CONTROL
STATION

Radar screen
simulates
aerial picture

AIR TO AIR

RANGE OF AIRBORNE SET
(E.G. 2 MILES)

Signals on bomber's
approximate position
sent to crew of airborne
radar-equipped
aircraft from
ground controller.

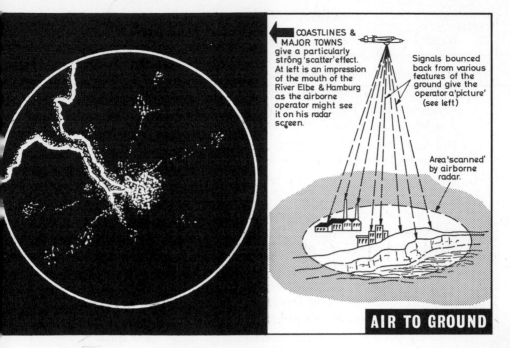

Four Main Radio Systems

The four systems shown here are presented chronologically, indicating the development of one basic technique—radio transmission and reception as a measure of distance and location—to the point where the reflection or echo of transmission from ground objects presents an outline of the latter on a screen. The main equipments embodying variations of the systems are given in Appendix 1, together with a summary of the counter measures equipments. Although opinions differ on which systems should be described as 'radio' and which as 'radar', the difference is semantic, and of degree, not kind. 'Radar' was, in any case, evolved from 'RDF'; an early example of this cover name will be found in correspondence within the Air Staff in March 1938 (*Strategic Air Offensive*, Vol. I, p. 102 fn. 1).

target had been reached; a timing device released the bombs at a given moment; if true course, height and speed had been maintained, accurate area bombing of a designated target theoretically followed. It rarely did, because blind bombing on a radio or radar frequency is only one stage removed from dead reckoning or astro-navigation. Moreover, the *Knickebein*, *X-Gerät* and *Y-Gerät* systems were pretty successfully jammed and distorted by No. 80 wing, Royal Air Force, commanded by that Group Captain Addison who, later in the war, was to show the enemy what *offensive* jamming could really mean.[50]

Nevertheless, it was clear to perceptive Royal Air Force officers and their scientific and technological colleagues in 1940 that German radio and radar as such might be as good, possibly better than anything in Britain. Indeed this was so; the fundamental difference, when comparing the relative merits of the two defensive systems was that Fighter Command utilised its radar to the point where ground control could put interceptors right on to the attacking force; the German radar chain gave excellent early warning—as we have seen—but there was no co-ordinated system enabling ground control to direct fighters on to their quarry, whether individually or by concentrated forces. It must of course be stressed that the comparisons are inexact, because Bomber Command so rapidly became a night bombing force that the defences, although not troubled *at the time*, were nevertheless forced to think again. The German system, like the British, had been designed to operate against a daylight offensive. British defences, it should also be remembered, took months to tackle the German bombing offensive in the winter of 1940–41, and really satisfactory co-ordination of all elements was never achieved. Success came largely when AI radar improved and its operators grew so skilful at identification that several night fighter crews achieved high scores, a factor which, in combination with others, had much to do with the termination of that campaign.[51]

There was as little basically wrong with German AI radar as there was with British, but research and development in this quarter had lagged; hence the defensive concept for its use was rather different and the attitude of many night fighter crews to it markedly so. Moreover, in late 1940 and 1941 Fighter Command had to win the night battle or possibly see a British defeat despite the defensive victory of the summer. In the same period the German defences could afford, or so it appeared, to rely on a simple sector system which sought to deter, dishearten and defeat Bomber Command over the coast, in order that the cities of the Reich might remain unvisited, not merely unscathed. That defensive system was known as the Kammhuber Line, to which reference has already been made, and of which a basic description is given on page 142. Something more must now be said about the genesis and development of the system, because it was effective enough for the period under discussion; its basic weakness, an extremely understandable one, is that it was not designed to deal with fighter concentrations, only with individual sorties.

Between 1939 and 1942 the German defences relied on three main types of radar: the *Freya*, the *Wuerzburg* and the *Lichtenstein*. These three types, and the several improvements and variants on them, were designed to give early warning, fighter or fire-plus-searchlight control, and sighting of one aircraft from another. In the opinion of those qualified to judge, the quality of much of this radar surpassed anything to be found in Britain, although the *Freya* system had not been developed to anything like the extent of the 'Chain Home' stations when war broke out in 1939. At that time only eight *Freya* stations had been installed. The effective range of *Freya*, 'the most important German early warning radar up to the middle of the Second World War', was however increased from 36 to 75 between 1939 and 1942. The *Wuerzburg* was not only reliable but was a small highly mobile set with the ability to plot aircraft within very fine limits at ranges up to 25 miles. The set worked on what was at that time an extremely high frequency—560 megacycles—much higher than anything under development in Britain. It was this that gave it its excellent resolving power. *Wuerzburg* was in consequence the first radar device to come anywhere near to meeting the exacting requirements of the anti-aircraft gunners, who needed to be able to engage unseen targets. It was the *Wuerzburg* which controlled the master, a blue-light searchlight in a given sector or 'box' and, in conjunction with radio-telephony links to night fighter crews, eventually provided them with the basic information on which they began their search for bombers, whether they used their (two-mile range) *Lichtenstein* AI sets or not.

The development of *Wuerzburg* allied to the notion that a co-ordinated defensive system was strategically unnecessary, plus the fact that German AI radar remained comparatively undeveloped until 1942, goes much of the way to explaining why the Kammhuber Line was established and why it functioned the way it did, passing from the first stage, when there was no machinery 'for channelling reliable and up-to-date information based on radar plots to fighter pilots by radio', to that of its apotheosis in July 1943, when its controllers still limited the deployment of the night fighter force to an area governed by the *Wuerzburg's* range. That range, at its greatest and in the Giant *Wuerzburg* mark, reached 40 miles: provided a bomber could pass through or fly round a 'box' of 40 by 40 miles with-out being attacked by a *Wuerzburg*-controlled combination of searchlights, flak and aircraft, it was comparatively safe until it reached the target area. This relative safety diminished as time went by, not because the Kammhuber concept became intrinsically more efficient but because, as the map on page 178 shows, it grew in size, and because the defences around major German cities increased and also improved in performance. The greatest danger to the bomber crew, or at least to the conscientious bomber crews, remained in the target area, when level flight was required before bombing and evasive action was virtually impossible; although a crew caught in a 'box', and especially caught by surprise was usually lost, one which had its eyes skinned had some chance of evasion and escape.

The Kammhuber Line was nevertheless a formidable barrier. When on 17 July 1940, Goering summoned the 43-year-old Colonel to establish a specialist night defensive system, nothing more than his brains and good material lay to hand. By the end of 1940, he had worked out his schemes; by the end of 1941 the Line was not only operationally formidable—given its inherent limitations—but, in the opinion of more than one Group commander in Bomber Command, was a barrier which few crews contemplated crossing or seeking to evade with feelings other than of dread. Kammhuber benefited from the existence from the first not only of the *Wuerzburg*—the key to the entire concept—but from a nucleus of experienced Me. 110 crews which, in June 1940, 'were despatched . . . to Düsseldorf airfield in the Ruhr area, for training and operational trials in night fighting. The unit, which was reinforced by newly trained aircrew, was provisionally known as the *Nach und Versuchs Staffel* (night and experimental squadron) and its commander, Major Falk, set about the task of developing night fighting tactics with all the energy of the pioneer.'[52]

Falk's unit was not to remain long in the Ruhr, or to operate 'with some success' there by simple tactics of searchlight and radio-telephony, known indeed as *Helle Nachtjagd*, or 'illuminated night fighting'. Three days after his appointment, Kammhuber formed a night fighter division of two *Gruppen*, of which Falk's was one, and established his headquarters at Zeist, near Utrecht. By October, Kammhuber and Martini were effectively in business, with *Freya* coming under command and a procedure being worked out whereby most of the new *Wuerzburg* sets would be provided for the 'box' system which was being established. The inland cities lost their searchlights and guns, which were deployed along the coast; illuminated night fighting went into cold storage for three years, while

Falk and his compatriots strove to perfect a system whereby each 'box' had its night fighter patrol, operating within the *Wuerzburg* range.

In August 1941 Kammhuber was appointed General of night fighters, and had sufficient material, including variants on *Freya*, to control a sickle-shaped line, which ran from Denmark to the Swiss Frontier and was divided into overlapping 'boxes', each some 20 miles wide. Further, by the summer of 1942, the *Lichtenstein* set's early deficiencies had been over-come, largely because technical developments had produced lighter aerials which hardly slowed the fighter's speed. Although in one sense AI radar became less important in 1942, as bomber 'streams' began to appear, and identification became either obvious or, on the screen, confusing, the improved *Lichtenstein*, plus longer-range early warning sets and in-creased expertise in all departments, gave Kammhuber justified reason to feel satisfied. By the end of 1942, the ascendancy of the night fighter had not been entirely established, and as has been said, Bomber Command was redressing some of the imbalance; but the night fighter as the prime destroyer of the bomber was a fact of operational life. In late 1943 that fact was to be demonstrated with deadly effect.

Moreover, it is doubtful if the imbalance would have been redressed even with *Gee*, H_2S and *Oboe* if Kammhuber had developed, or had been allowed to develop, his theories of controlled night fighting to the point where concentrations of fighters were able to attack the bomber stream en route to and over the target.[53] It is of course the case that the bomber's aids were by themselves no defence against the fighter, despite the fact that variants of airborne radar were progressively installed in order to give the crew an 'eye' on who might be attacking them. The point is one of psychology, or morale: *Gee* and its fellows were crucial in giving Bomber Command crews the feeling that they were getting *somewhere*; to put it bluntly, radar aids came none too soon, because a feeling of hopelessness and futility was beginning to affect the Command at the end of 1941. Losses were endurable; losses and futility might not indefinitely be so. The thought of, and the advent of, aids enabled Bomber Command to carry on through its worst period of high-level disenchantment and pointless loss, the winter of 1941–42, and then to fight through a year which ended with it poised for a real strategic role. If, in 1942, these advantages had been destroyed by Kammhuber so developing his forces that the missing rate rose to five or six per cent, the air offensive might have been stopped in its tracks before it reached the stage of strategic significance. The end of the offensive would have been brought about by the loss of bombers, not by the immunity of targets. In that sense it would have been a more decisive result than was achieved over Britain in the winter of 1940-41; in the opinion of some who lived through and bore responsibilities in those days, the bombers of the Luftwaffe were not so very far from victory at one point—the concentrated bombing of Liverpool in April 1941, and its effect not only on the citizens of that great port but on the crews of convoy-protecting warships who saw their familiar skyline wreathed in flames and smoke.[54]

Fortunately for Bomber Command, Kammhuber's plan to keep the Line but make it virtually impenetrable—through extent, depth and a greatly increased fighter force operating outside as well as inside the 'boxes'— was subordinated to Hitler's demand that German cities be protected.[55] The Line could never be extended so as to become a total protection to Germany; the cumulative effects of Lübeck, Rostock and the '1,000' raids distorted objective analysis of what was required to stop the offensive in its tracks; but concentration of resources—and the Kammhuber Line was emphatically that strategically, if not so in the precise tactical sense—would almost certainly have seen Harris go the way of Peirse. Harris did not succeed in making 1942 a watershed for Bomber Command which it safely crossed because the Lancaster came into service, because *Gee* and *H_2S* were introduced, and least of all because on 14 February the War Cabinet delivered a singular Valentine by announcing the decision to launch an 'intensive air offensive'[56] against German cities. The watershed was not crossed because of Portal's and Cherwell's bargaining power, or because much of 1942 was otherwise a bad time for Allied arms; the watershed was not even crossed because of the extraordinary courage of the men from many lands who formed the aircrews of Bomber Command by this time. All these things had a part in the offensive achieving strategic status, and in all these things the embattled Harris was fully engaged. All except one—Hitler's refusal to listen to expert advice on *defensive* measures, a sign of his growing detachment from reality.[57]

Against this background of the wider issues, the operational record of Bomber Command's night offensive in 1942 can now be described and assessed. They cannot be achievements measured by effect on the German economy or even by continuously mounting destruction, although, considered in isolation and by examining the results of individual raids, it is the case that some factories were severely damaged and some towns were partly destroyed. With very few exceptions, accuracy, by any meaning of the word, is irrelevant to this assessment. The achievement must be measured by the criterion outlined at the beginning of this chapter, namely the ability to stay in the line of battle, to reach and then to bomb without crippling loss a target *area*. The negative element has been summarised above; the positive elements, in material terms, were four—namely the Lancaster bomber, the Pathfinder Force, the radar aids and the tactics which were developed to take advantage of this growing capability. Let us see how the major raids of 1942 benefited from this quartet, first by presenting the growing operational strength of Bomber Command chronologically; then by discussing certain aspects of the positive elements.[58]

The chronology is thus:

14 February	Air Staff Directive that concentrated six months' offensive should be mounted against German cities.
21 February	Bomber Command instruction on target marking and illuminating by *Gee*-equipped Wellingtons, and the division of attacking force into marking and main.
3 March	Renault works in Paris bombed on target marking principle, but not with *Gee*-equipped aircraft. An accurate raid on an important industrial target.
8 March	Essen bombed with aid of *Gee*; first use of this equipment, initiating operational use of *Shaker* (illuminating) and *Sampson* (blind bombing) tactics.
28 March	Lübeck bombed and heavily damaged. Lancaster introduced to operational service on this raid.
23–26 April	Four consecutive attacks on Rostock, destroying much of the city and effectively damaging U-boat and aircraft plant.
30 May	Cologne bombed by 1,046 aircraft from Bomber and Flying Training Commands; overall period of raid reduced by 'streaming' from an average of approximately seven hours to two and a half. Missing rate relatively low (3.8 per cent), due to 'plate rack' height variations, but none below 8,000 feet. Very heavy damage to city centre and suburbs.
1 June	Essen bombed by 956 aircraft from Bomber and Flying Training Commands, using *Shaker* tactics; missing rate of 3.2 per cent: little damage.
25 June	Bremen bombed by 1,006 aircraft from Bomber, Coastal and Flying Training Commands; bad weather and head winds; virtually total reliance on marking and *Gee*; missing rate of nearly five per cent. No more raids of 1,000 or more aircraft until 1944.
5 July	Group Captain Bennett appointed to command special target finding, marking and illuminating force.
31 July	Düsseldorf bombed by 630 aircraft from Bomber Command; this number not exceeded until the Dortmund raid of 23 May 1944.

10 August	*Gee* jammed during raid on Osnabrück.
15 August	The Pathfinder Force officially established; no priority in aircraft but priority supply of *Oboe* and H_2S for operational testing and use.
20 December	*Oboe* first used on operations, although not yet in full operational use. The occasion was a raid on Lutterade.
31 December	Sky-marking techniques first employed—target Düsseldorf.

For a full appreciation of this record of change, of new purpose and above all, new matériel and methods, we should also note:

April	Four squadrons of Lancasters in front-line service.
May–September	Hampdens, Manchesters and Whitleys withdrawn from service.
June–July	The case for a Pathfinder Force fought and won by the Directorate of Bomber Operations, against Harris' initial beliefs and against his Group Commander's absolute dislike of the entire concept.
15 June	Churchill insists that Coastal Command 'plays its part' in Bremen raid.
17 June	Harris minutes Churchill that 'victory, speedy and complete awaits the side which employs air power as it should be employed'.
28 June	Appreciation by Harris for the War Cabinet and at Churchill's request on Bomber Command's strategic role, the resources it employs and the contribution it makes on various fronts.
17 August	The 8th Air Force mounts its first operation from the United Kingdom; target: Rouen/Sotteville marshalling yards plus diversions: 18 aircraft despatched; 12 aircraft attacked; no aircraft lost.
September–November	Approximately 80 Lancasters available for front-line service, 'teething troubles' overcome.

and in early 1943:

16 January	Target-indicator ground-markers first used—target Berlin.
30 January	H_2S first used operationally—target Hamburg.

From this deliberately tabulated and compressed account it will, I hope, be apparent to the reader that momentum had come at last to the bombing of Germany, and that the offensive was on the way to finding its place in the strategy of world war largely because it could no longer be overlooked or regarded as a thing of fits and starts. The record just summarised compares rather oddly with the fortunes of Bomber Command as analysed and narrated at the Whitehall level; we can see something of what Harris saw and why he could write to Churchill in words which would be bombast if they did not spring from conviction.

From this summary five specific elements in the nature and execution of the offensive also emerge, and it is with them, rather than with the raids themselves, that the final assessment of Bomber Command's night operations in 1942 must be concerned.

First: it will be seen that the February directive's objective of a 'six months' offensive was met by Bomber Command, if not quite in the same terms or for exactly the same reasons as were seen by the Air Staff. Because Bomber Command waged a continual struggle for so long there is a tendency at times to assume that operations continued at the same pitch of intensity for months on end; at no time in the war was this so, even in its last stages there were periods when weather grounded aircraft, or did so at all events in respect of the targets which Harris thought worthy of attack. In 1942, weather was perhaps the least of the operational problems, but this was more than matched by increasing loss and by all the problems inherent in expansion and the introduction of new material. There were also the demands of other theatres and Services which Harris, for all that he was so rapidly becoming a powerful and assertive commander, could not absolutely ignore.

Indeed, the apparent gap in the chronological account between August and December is misleading; the offensive as conceived in the February directive was halted, but Bomber Command remained committed to waging war against German industrial towns. The demands of the Admiralty did not cease; to support the landings in North Africa, targets in Italy were attacked in a minor interdiction campaign which appears to have been conceived at the political rather than the strategic level. In September Bomber Command despatched 3,489 aircraft on operations, compared with 2,621 in the same month in 1941. But figures by themselves indicate little. In October 1941 Bomber Command actually despatched more aircraft than in October 1942. But we should note that the respective tonnage figures for these months are 2,984 and 3,809.

Second: the ascendancy of Harris as Commander-in-Chief must be appreciated as a factor of direct and immediate relevance to the actual conduct of the offensive. The fight Harris waged was not to keep the offensive as such in being or to ensure that it was regarded as of strategic value. Harris had patience, a virtue which is not only rare but of little use unless it is bred out of confidence that all things come in due season. What concerned Harris in 1942 was to revive Churchill's waning belief in the offensive as a feasible objective in itself; to win Churchill's confidence

Bomber Command had to demonstrate destructive potential. The '1,000 plan' was seen, as Harris admits, not only as a means of heavily damaging urban centres and of testing new material and tactics, but as a propaganda exercise. This last objective was met in the Cologne and succeeding raids.

Harris' influence with Churchill has been exaggerated in some quarters, and it is necessary therefore to stress that, temperamental factors apart, it lay in the airman's ability to deliver some useful political goods to the statesman and to behave pragmatically over urgent, operational issues. The Prime Minister's famous injunction to his subordinates—that they should express objectives and requirements on a single sheet of paper —was as little met by Harris as by any other senior officer living, at least in part, the life of the bureaucratic apologist. Harris overplayed his hand in his minutes and appreciations, leaving a record of seeming conceit and verbosity which was to be used against him at the end. But among his great virtues as a commander was a lack of dogma about practical issues, and therein is the explanation for much of his power over subordinates and superiors and of his influence with the Prime Minister.

The issue of the Pathfinders is a case in point. Harris agreed that targets must be marked; so did everybody concerned in the operational side of the offensive. Harris did not believe that target marking required a special force, least of all one drawn from Main Force squadrons and made into what he sourly referred to as a *corps d'élite*. Harris suspected that the Director of Bomber Operations, Group Captain Bufton, wanted to form such a force and, moreover, wanted to do so not merely, as he said, because he was concerned at the continued inability of Main Force crews to find their designated targets, but because he believed that a marking force could pave the way for accurate bombing of selected targets of specific value to the German war effort. Harris was right both about the supposition and the suspicion. He could therefore have used the vehement dislike of his Group commanders to the establishment of a separate marking force (a dislike, it must here be said, residing in prejudice and the prevalence of dog-in-the-manger attitudes in the higher reaches of the Services rather than due to one founded on analysis of requirements and resources) to delay if not utterly to thwart Bufton and his colleagues.

But on 5 July, after four months of bad-tempered debate, Harris nominated Bennett to command the Pathfinder Force. The important thing to note, however, is that Bennett's squadrons began to train as the spearhead of an area bombing Main Force, not as one committed to the destruction of targets which Bufton (and many others in Whitehall) had in mind. Harris had seen the practical value of a special marking force to assist in the attainment of *his* objective; his prejudice against a *corps d'élite* quickly disappeared. His power was such that it became a settled matter by the time Bomber Command was 'ready' that the Pathfinder Force and all its new material should be directed towards causing fire and death at the heart or at the extremities of German cities. One of the most successful demonstrations of marking on *Oboe* occurred on the night of 24–25 June 1943, when the Coventry-sized town of Wuppertal-Elberfeld, an extremely difficult target to find and destroy, was utterly devastated—870 acres out of 929. In 20 minutes Bomber Command's Main Force of 517 had bombed on markers laid by *Oboe*-equipped Mosquitoes. After the raid 'the town was no more than a memory of the day before'.[59]

Third: tactics depended on material, and above all on the fact that an increase in marking shortened time over target. This was so by virtue of the simple truth that Main Force crews increasingly came to rely on their radar to get and stay on the right course and on the Pathfinders to light their way to, as well as over, the target. The chapter devoted to operations in 1943 will bear this truth out very plainly; by then navigation standards had declined to the level that even Pathfinder crews went astray. The principal tactical requirement was to tax the defence over the target, where it enjoyed the advantage that bombers were flying straight and level. But there was a second factor and it was the two taken together which led to the tactics adopted and, in all essentials, practised by the Main Force until the end of the war.

The second factor lay in the nature of the Kammhuber Line itself. As the map on p. 178 shows, the Main Force could be routed to fly round the Line to attack all but the most important target of all—the Ruhr. However, as more became known about the Line, its central weakness became apparent. From an appreciation of that weakness came the tactics which are so well described in the following passage:

> During the first two years of the RAF Bomber Command's night offensive, the bombers had invariably to make their own way to their targets. There was no attempt to keep the force together—indeed many crews attributed their survival to the fact that they did something different from everybody else. A large number of bombers crossing the 'Line' at widely separated points over a period of several hours—this was the grist for which Kammhuber had designed his mill. But the standard unit of the 'Line' was the 'box', patrolled by one radar-guided fighter aircraft; so the one great weakness which was realised in England the moment that the Line's workings became clear was that it could be easily overwhelmed at say one point.

Each defensive box could only engage one bomber at a time, and during each engagement—an average of ten minutes—there was an unguarded gap in the Line. If the raiders were to fly in a tight mass all would pass through the Line unscathed bar the one or two unfortunates upon whom the German fighter controllers focused their attention.

Hitherto the bombers' navigation had not been precise enough to enable the bombers to be 'streamed'; the advent of *Gee* had changed all that. The concentration-in-time of bombing attacks promised a further advantage, for it would reduce the effectiveness of the German anti-aircraft guns: the *target's* defences would be saturated. . . . The new tactics were first tried on the night of 30 May 1942, during the famous Thousand Bomber Raid on Cologne. The attacking aircraft all took the same route, and the period of attack was cut from about seven hours to two and a half—an average of seven aircraft bombing each minute . . . The 'bomber stream' had been born.[60]

Unlike *H₂S* and *Oboe* and some jamming devices, it was always the Air Staff's intention to introduce *Gee* into operational service for Main Force crews as soon as it was in quantity production. Although the marking and 'illuminating' Wellingtons which preceded the Pathfinders were the first to get *Gee*, it was decided as early as August 1941 that it would be a standard equipment, not one confined to specialist crews. By January 1943, despite the jamming which began five months earlier, the Main Force was 'extensively equipped' with *Gee*. Hence, as *Gee* came into quantity production and became a standard equipment, Main Force crews learned to 'stream' through the Kammhuber 'boxes'. By the time the target areas was reached little cohesion remained, but the increasing effectiveness of the Pathfinder technique drew the scattered band together. In 1942 the refinements of master bombers and the complexities of 'back up' marking were unknown; the aim was confined to passing as many aircraft as possible as quickly as possible through a given area; the one element of complexity in 1942, but one which called for nerves and skill by pilots, was to fly bombers at different heights, in order to confuse the flak and searchlight operators.

Mention of this last factor does, however, lead to the crucial point, and one which has tended to be overlooked in some analyses of this phase of the offensive—that the German night fighters were not yet in 1942 concentrated around major German cities. They were between seasons, so to speak; the Kammhuber Line was still claiming its victims, and, not yet being susceptible to jamming, could relay information to fighter controllers further east. But those controllers had neither the number of aircraft nor the technique to concentrate an interception force. Hitherto fighters in the target area had enjoyed one thing in common with those patrolling the Kammhuber Line—what might be called the leisurely or piecemeal destruction of elements of the Main Force as it struggled along. The bombers' concentration ended that phase; in 1942 the lack of a technique to replace 'illuminated night flying' over the target extended the life of the new phase until, in late 1943, with the Kammhuber Line also reduced to ironmongery, a tremendous effort was made to introduce new aircraft, equipment and tactics into the defending forces.

Fourth: although the actual jamming of German defensive radar did not begin effectively until mid-1943 and the use of *Window* did not become a major factor in the offensive until the establishment of 100 Group in November of that year, cracking of the Kammhuber Line in April 1942 (largely due to the efforts of Dr. R. V. Jones, the Deputy Director of Scientific Intelligence) was a necessary stage in enabling Bomber Command to fight on temporarily level terms. The more that was known about the Kammhuber Line, the more it followed in reason that German radar was formidably good. This meant two things: *prima facie*, good radar either indicated or could lead to good fighter control; if Bomber Command came increasingly to rely on radar, then increasingly would it be probable, although not inevitable, that this would be jammed or distorted or that enemy fighters would home on it. It must be said that this appreciation is one based on hindsight; the scientific community involved in the strategic air offensive may have grasped all these implications; it is more realistic to suggest that some members of it did so at various points in time. That airmen of varying degree did not in 1942 realise the relationship of radar to the next phase in weapons and tactics may be inferred from Harris' lack of a reaction when Jones told him that the secrets and much of the details of the Kammhuber Line were known at last. The short point is this: when the Bomber Command missing rate started getting into double figures, *then* its chiefs got interested in the scientific war of wits; but not before.[62]

Fifth: the Mosquito, whether used for reconnaissance, target marking or as a bomber. Introduced into Bomber Command in 1942 as a 'light bomber' and as a reconnaissance aircraft in support of the Main Force, it was seen by some of the more discerning airmen by the end of the year as a natural, one of those happy chances which occasionally occur in aerodynamics as in more mundane fields. Excluding 2 Group, only 17 were available for front-line service in the Command at the beginning of 1943; nearly 300 were on 'unit charge' by the end of the war. Thus although the Mosquito was flying as a service aircraft in 1940, having been developed from one designed five years earlier, indecision about its function—or rather insufficient awareness of the operational value of its versatility delayed introduction of it in quantity to Bomber Command, and particularly to squadrons charged with target finding, for over three years. For long, nobody seemed to know what to do with the Mosquito; the concept of the 'light bomber' still obtained in 1940 and 1941, as the rather unhappy history of 2 Group bears witness. Unfortunately there was little for such a bomber to do when there were no ground operations to support. The notion of the Mosquito as exactly the kind of aircraft for the Pathfinder Force was not immediately acceptable either; in December 1943, only four squadrons were in service in 8 Group, although by December 1944, ten were committed to many different tasks. Like everything else about the strategic air offensive, the positive elements were very slow to emerge.

PART THREE

The Year of Struggle
1943

The Combined Bomber Offensive

The year 1943 opened with a widely held belief among the Allies that it would be the one in which, at last, the strategic balance would tilt decisively in their favour, leading possibly to that collapse of the Axis which would enable the appropriate spoils to be picked up without further damage to the national interests of the victors.

These hopes were to be confounded. 1943 was indeed a year of achievement, but in terms of attrition, most notably with the strategic air offensive. The hopes, we can now see, were founded on the reaction to striking victories—Midway and El Alamein, to be joined shortly by Stalingrad. But these battles halted the enemies at the gates; they gave no indication of what would happen when Germany and Japan were forced on to the defensive, or how long it would take to liberate their captives. Moreover, the alternative to such a campaign of liberation—whose length and cost might prove too much for an alliance forged only by direst necessity— was the reduction of German and Japanese cities to rubble and ash. Yet there was little in the record of events for 1942 to suggest that the Axis would be defeated by bombing alone. Only one man among the Allies' commanders continued to proclaim aggressively and repeatedly that the war could thus be won. Yet again, as the months of 1943 passed and the first flush of enthusiasm for a *combined* bomber offensive faded in the face of painful, operational reality and the obduracy of national attitudes, Sir Arthur Harris became once more a lonely figure, and it may fairly be said that as the year ended he, and Bomber Command, continued to fight their war alone, and in their own particular way.

But what of the enemy whose walls were as yet hardly battered? As little was known in London or Washington about the German capacity for continued struggle in 1943 as had been known or learned at any other stage of the war. Much was known about 'occupied Europe'; little about Germany, the morale of the German people, the capacity of this wealthiest and largest of Europe's states to shorten its front, draw on its untapped or little-utilised manpower reserves and industrial resources, to fight on the defensive until such time as the Allies should sue for a negotiated peace. Indeed, despite well-founded optimism in certain Allied quarters, there was no absolute certainty that Russia would finally defeat Germany on the ground. And until such a defeat was plain to all, the great Anglo-American contribution of a return to Europe across the English Channel would not take place. Such at least was Churchill's resolve,[1] and he forti-fied it by the most determined advocacy of a Mediterranean strategy—and an aerial offensive against Germany which would serve the double objective of assuaging Russian demands for a second front, while pre-paring the way for its opening at a time most suited to British strategies and resources. If, in the process, such an extension of the strategic air offensive brought a bonus in the shape of a crumbling German industry or an impotent German Air Force, so much the better. But, in Churchill's mind, what Portal and the Air Staff subscribed to without much doubt and Harris believed in against all evidence to date, was essentially a political weapon.

The Casablanca Conference

It is in this context that we must view the Allied war leaders, their com-manders and staffs as they assembled at Casablanca in the second week of January for a conference which was eventually to be distinguished by the considerable amount of time which was devoted to the strategic air offen-sive—although for reasons as much connected with its control as its nature. But before Casablanca and its aftermath are discussed, and the American insistence on a combined air offensive for purely strategic reasons is given its place in the history of the campaign, it is necessary to glance at what took place at a meeting in Berlin at the end of January. Although this meeting was held while Casablanca's deliberations were being processed as draft directives, its genesis was the growing awareness in 1942 among the Luftwaffe's abler and more resourceful senior officers that the main task of their service would soon be to defend the Reich from aerial attack of the kind which not even Hitler could ignore.[2]

The January meeting in Berlin was based on fear of such an aerial offensive rather than its wider strategic implications in terms of the Allies' return to Europe and their occupation of Germany. The Casablanca demand for unconditional surrender probably did little to affect the views of airmen like Galland and Milch; they were used to rhetoric from another source, and had trained their minds to ignore it while concentrating on their professional tasks. But US heavy bombers attacked a German target —Wilhelmshaven—for the first time on 27 January; it was neither a well-executed nor an expensive operation. No definite conclusions could be drawn from it—except that, if Bomber Command was to be joined over Germany by aircraft poured from the vast American industrial cornucopia, then something equally in earnest had better be done to defeat this combined offensive. The January conference, although it based some of its deliberations on a vastly exaggerated estimate of what Britain and America would put into the German skies, was essentially concerned with finding out the best way of defeating this threat in its own terms, not as the precursor of worse to come.

It is true that by January 1943 most of the members of the German High Command and their immediate subordinates had reached the stage of covertly worded scepticism as to the possibility of victory, an attitude which some were to express in an attempt on Hitler's life 17 months later. But there remained a well-founded belief, grounded in the precedent of 1918 and strengthened by careful study of rifts within the Allies' lute, that a resolutely conducted defensive strategy could result in a negotiated peace and preserve a good chunk of Germany's conquests physically or economically intact. The key to such a defence was not to be found exclusively in resurrecting the Luftwaffe after the losses it had suffered in 1942 and in turning it into a force for protecting the Fatherland. Nevertheless, unless such a change was urged, and made despite Hitler's plans for an aerial 'counter-offensive', largely directed at Britain and employing both bombers and missiles, it was likely that no co-ordinated strategic defence would be established.

In the event, a variety of factors prevented Milch and his associates in 1943 from switching the Luftwaffe over to a predominately day and night fighter force deployed around the Reich and its western frontiers. The change was made on this scale in 1944, too late to prevent the march of Eisenhower's armies or the destruction of Germany's defences and the communications and resources on which they depended. But if the change had been fully made in 1943—and it would have been physically possible to do so—it must remain an extremely nice question what the outcome would have been for the Anglo-American Combined Bomber Offensive. German armies on the Eastern fronts, bereft temporarily of their air cover until intensified fighter production got under way, might have suffered the defeats that were to be reserved for them late in the year and throughout 1944; on the other hand, all types of Luftwaffe aircraft on those fronts did decrease throughout 1943, both by losses and redeployment, yet German armies mounted new offensives during the summer.[3] All that can be said with certainty therefore is that the Allies must be considered fortunate that Bomber Command and the 8th Air Force were defeated tactically, not totally, and not at the same time. If the German Air Staff and their masters had grasped the full meaning of the air strategy which emerged from the Casablanca Conference—that the destruction of German industry and the 'German will to resist' were the essential prior conditions for Overlord—the complete switch from offence to defence might well have been made, with incalculable consequences for the eventual outcome of the war.

As it was, and if we extend the period under review to March 1944, Bomber Command and the 8th were to suffer and endure a great deal. The early months of 1943 saw the Luftwaffe prepare itself for a new role, witnessed a programme of increased production which went ahead despite the fact that its location rendered it 'peculiarly vulnerable to air attack'.[4] While Harris and Eaker, in the first half of the year, were sending their bombers to U-boat pens, the cities of the Ruhr or a variety of insignificant targets in France and the Low Countries, fighter production in Germany was accelerating to the point where, by June, output reached 1,000 monthly, compared with a mere 300 at the end of 1941 and for much of 1942. In short: 'Hence, allowing for all exceptions, it is fair to say that the Luftwaffe which, until the end of 1942 had been essentially an offensive striking force, became, beginning in 1943, a defensive force with limited striking power.'[5]

It must be a considered criticism of the discussions on the Combined Bomber Offensive at Casablanca that so little attention was given to what the enemy might do to prevent its execution. For this paucity of analysis there are six main explanations: a mood of optimism which, among other things, appears to have inhibited Portal from reiterating his views on the prospects of fatally weakening Germany by a full-blown strategic air offensive, always provided the problem of unescorted daylight bombing by the USAAF was overcome; the absence of evidence to project Portal's fears into deliberations between Churchill and Roosevelt; the political factors—already referred to—governing the Prime Minister's (and the

Chiefs' of Staff) outlook; and the treble determination of Americans at Casablanca to push for Overlord, to push therefore for a Combined Bomber Offensive directed at Germany's capacity to wage war, and to push, if discreetly, for a command and control structure which would ensure that, when Overlord arrived the conduct of such an offensive would either be in American hands or in hands belonging to someone in full agreement with American theories of air power and quite willing to accept that its final execution must be at the behest of an American Supreme Commander. Tedder, Eisenhower's loyal colleague in the North African campaign, and an experienced and articulate exponent of the complementary roles of armies and air forces, was present at Casablanca, waiting in the wings for an Overlord appointment in the American gift.[6]

In such circumstances it is not surprising that Harris, the apostle and architect (although *not* the progenitor) of city bombing at night, should not be present at Casablanca, but that Generals Spaatz and Eaker were, and that they were allowed to indulge in some highly optimistic forecasts about what their bombers would do to German industry once deep-penetration raids were mounted in strength from Britain and the Mediterranean theatre. The directive of 21 January, known as the Casablanca Directive, summarised in one version in Appendix 2, bears all the outward marks of a 'consensus', but it was essentially a reflection of the following conviction:

> Given a force of 300 heavy bombers flown by trained crews, General Eaker believed he could attack any target in Germany by day with less than four per cent loss. Smaller numbers would naturally suffer more severely. Despite all problems and currently effective limitations he stoutly maintained that 'daylight bombing of Germany with planes of the B.17 and B.24 types is feasible, practicable and economical'.[7]

The Casablanca Directive

It is not therefore surprising that the Casablanca Directive, having paid consensus lip-service in Portal-like language to the doctrines first enunciated by Smuts, Trenchard and Douhet, went briskly on to give the following order of priorities:

1. German submarine construction yards
2. The German aircraft industry
3. Transportation

4. Oil plants
5. Other targets in enemy war industry.

It is also not a matter of surprise that Harris chose to ignore this directive once he had contemptuously demonstrated the waste and the cost—including the devastation of 'two perfectly good French towns'—of bombing the U-boat pens hidden beneath many feet of concrete at St Nazaire and Lorient.[8] To all but the most fervent believers in the B.17's and the B.24's 'self-defending' capacities when flying in a tight formation of the largest possible size, it was no surprise either when belated Allied awareness of the results of that other conference in Berlin revamped the Casablanca Directive into one issued finally on 10 June and known as the 'Pointblank' Directive, in which were inserted as 'intermediate objectives' the revealing words 'Depletion of the German fighter strength must be accomplished first'.[9] Finally, it will occasion no surprise either that Harris paid as little attention to this Directive as to its predecessor, even though by this time Portal was the appointed Combined Chiefs' of Staff 'Agent' for the execution of Pointblank, or what both official histories like to call the Combined Bomber Offensive (although in fact that title was decided at Casablanca and its purpose defined in the subsequent Directive).[10]

Before we condemn Harris for a course of action which, although perhaps operationally unavoidable, was eventually to damage Bomber Command far more severely than the 8th, and to strengthen the Joint Chiefs of Staff in their resolve of welding all American 'strategic' air forces based in Europe into one organisation subordinate only to their direction,[11] we must consider just why the bombing of Germany in 1943 proceeded along separate lines, achieving 'combination' only on paper. The hard lessons learned by Eaker's crews were preceded by the opening of Bomber Command's long-awaited and carefully planned 1943 offensive. Despite the degree of independence which Harris was able to achieve in mounting this offensive, it must be emphasised that he was fortified, if unconsciously, by a growing feeling among the British party at Casablanca that their American colleagues were taking altogether too much on themselves and endeavouring to push their Ally's affairs in a direction inimical to Britain's best interests.[12]

Although the Chiefs of Staff knew well enough that Overlord in 1944 was inevitable, even if 'Roundup' for 1943 could be postponed in favour of a Mediterranean strategy as successfully as 'Sledgehammer' in 1942 was forestalled by 'Torch', no British account of Casablanca shows the slightest conviction of the cross-channel operation's supreme importance and necessity if Germany was to suffer defeat at other than Russian hands. American accounts, by contrast, do little else than to criticise the Mediterranean strategy and extol that of 'Germany first'. Hence, although Portal and his colleagues were also well aware that Overlord required the Combined Bomber Offensive if it was to succeed, their attitude was ambivalent, on the strategic objectives, their attainment and the ally with which the whole affair was to be conducted. Portal indicated this ambivalence in uncharacteristically pithy language when he said: 'We are in the position of a testator who wishes to leave the bulk of his fortune to his mistress. He must, however, leave something to his wife, and his problem is to decide how little he can in decency set apart for her.'[13]

With this distinction between the attractions of a Mediterranean strategy and the necessities of a European one, Portal's colleagues were in virtually unhesitating agreement. Harris should, therefore, be regarded as the executant of a strategy which his chiefs were loath to analyse. They might, paradoxically, be the more aware of the need for Overlord to be launched only after Germany was already dazed and reeling from aerial attack than their American colleagues because, as Lord Ismay has revealed, all on the British side were haunted by memories of the Somme and similar occasions when British armies had been bled white.[14] The 1940 débâcle was also fresh in their minds, and even Montgomery's desert victories, to which the Royal Air Force had made so direct a contribution, had not allayed fears of a disaster among the defences of the Atlantic Wall.

Given these attitudes—so lengthily documented in many an unofficial account of the Alliance—it is indeed odd that neither the central pre-Overlord issue of 'command of the air', nor, in short, the defeat of the Luftwaffe in battle to complement its castration on the factory floor, nor Harris' belief that an armada of 4,000 heavy bombers would win the war, received discussion, let alone merited analysis at Casablanca. It could be said that, in respect of the latter, the Chiefs of Staff regarded Harris as a crank and a bore, essentially most useful to keep the Russians quiet. Only in the Official Histories will be found detailed discussion of the strategic air offensive, and there, as is natural, 1943 is seen as a year of the battle's ebb and flow rather than one in which the Chiefs of Staff failed to devote the attention which they should have done to the increasing burdens which Bomber Command assumed.

Nevertheless, although the Command's front-line numerical strength as 1943 opened was effectively no greater than when Harris took command, the omens for a mounting offensive, even without benefit of night-fighter escort, were at last propitious to airmen who had acquired patience in a hard school. Although the year was to close with Bomber Command a significant strategic factor because of a battle being fought temporarily alone than because of a battle won, it was reasonable to believe, as the first H_2S-equipped Stirlings and Halifaxes of 7 and 35 (PFF) Squadrons marked Hamburg for the Main Force on the night of 30 January, that a new era was beginning; an era when four-engined bombers with increasing bomb loads, flying in a protective stream to concentrate for a brief, catastrophic spell in the city target area, would be crewed by a largely Commonwealth force, supported by all that tactical and technological ingenuity could devise.

The Pathfinder Force had been expanded as No. 8 Group, after four months of preliminary operations, on 13 January; target indicators, bearing little resemblance to the old, inept flares, had been used first in an operation against Berlin on the 16th; *Oboe*-equipped Mosquitoes had first flown operationally only a month before: the 4-lb incendiary bomb was achieving recognition as a destroyer of cities more terrible than any high-explosive weapon, and a sure guide to crews despondent at losing their way or doubtful about their purpose in war; above all, although the mean missing rate of four per cent in 1942 was not something to brush aside, the Luftwaffe had as yet shown neither the disposition nor the capacity to replace it by one 'unacceptable' at Bomber Command Headquarters or among the sceptics of the Directorate of Bomber Operations. And if the German defences did attempt to shoot Bomber Command out of the sky, it would be found that the Lancaster and Halifax were a different proposition for the night fighter than the Wellington and other bombers of comparable obsolescence. Finally, there was *Window*, still supposedly a secret device.[15]

Fortified by all these additions to his Command, Harris planned 1943 as knockout year, the vindication of the long days and nights of 1942, when his search for solutions to the problem of finding, let alone destroying targets, seemed constantly to be thwarted or doubted by inadequate resources or unsympathetic superiors. Although on 1 January 'aircraft available for operations' were only 839, compared with 802 twelve months earlier (of which only around 500 at one time were fully crewed up), the proportion of four-engined bombers had risen to well over half, compared with a mere eight on the earlier date. More to the point, no less than 274 of the 'heavies' were Lancasters; there had been none a year earlier.[16] The Stirling was already as much a disappointment as the Manchester had been, and the Halifax was to be withdrawn twice from operations before it was found fit to fly in the line of battle. But to Harris, as to others, the Lancaster was the bomber which mattered, the aircraft with the significant bomb load and the toughness to survive in battle, and the doubling of Bomber Command's numbers in the course of the year was seen less as evidence that, at long last, *something* approaching his original demands was being met, than as a net increase in the tonnage which the Command could disgorge, predominantly over Germany itself, and within Germany, mostly on the cities of the Ruhr. Only as the year ended did Berlin begin to rival the Ruhr as the target on which Harris set an unblinking, if arguably a blinkered, gaze. In December, 11,802 tons were dropped by Bomber Command, compared with 4,345 in January, and a total of 45,661 tons for *all* of 1942. These, to Harris, were significant statistics.[17]

Development of Area Bombing

The loss of 2 Group in May 1943 was certainly not regarded by Harris as any weakening of his Command; if anything, he saw it as a sign that the Main Force and No. 8 Group were girding their loins for the battle, and that short-range operations and the like could pass to commanders committed to the use of bombers for anti-shipping strikes, anti-submarine operations or tactical support for the Army. If ever Harris was going to be criticised for neglecting his Command's duty to participate throughout at least the first six months of 1943 in maritime operations, he could point to the impressive number of mines his Main Force groups had laid, and to the useful amount of shipping destroyed, bottled up in harbour, or otherwise checked in running cargoes from ports in neutral Spain and Sweden, let alone up and down the Atlantic seaboard of Hitler's empire.

Yet although mining sorties might be cited whenever Bomber Command was thought by higher authority—British or American—to be 'an independent air force', the development of area bombing in 1943 is only worth consideration in this history if its exclusion by Harris from anything approaching a combined offensive is fully understood. Harris' crews neither bombed 'submarine construction yards', nor 'the German aircraft industry', with the steady repetition which such difficult targets demanded. It is true that the Casablanca and Pointblank Directives contained escape clauses to the effect that night raids should be against cities 'associated' with these sinews of war; nevertheless, whether or not one regards the priorities as sensible and the targets as feasible, the fact of the matter, as the *Bomber Command Quarterly Reviews* and the *Bomber's Baedeker* of targets make all too clear, is that Harris chose different targets to bomb. He did so in the spring, in the summer, in the autumn and in the approaching winter. In the last quarter of the year his bombing reached for 'distant targets', but the phrase will be found as descriptive most often, most *repeatedly*, of Berlin, not of those areas to which the German aircraft industry was at last dispersing—in order to meet new demands, rather than under the threat of sustained attack by day or night, from either Britain or beyond the Alps. It was to be the 8th and 15th Air Forces in 1944 which would destroy the Luftwaffe day fighter in battle and, by attacking such targets in Austria and Czechoslovakia as well as in Germany, repay Bomber Command for its solitary fight in the longest nights of the preceding winter.

It could also be said in Harris' defence that he had dutifully bombed Lorient and St Nazaire, yet another diversion from what, until Casablanca, and despite occasional interventions from the Ministry of Economic Warfare and that nagging oil committee, had been tacitly or openly agreed to be his main role—'dehousing' the German worker. In 1942 bombers had been 'lost' to Coastal Command and the Middle East, even although Harris was convinced that, in the latter case at least, crews had not been used as economically and intensively as the scale of operations and the Army's pressing need for support warranted—a conviction, or rather, a suspicion which Lord Tedder has now shown to be not as baseless as Harris' critics thought at the time.[18]

Surely, therefore, ran the train of Harris' thoughts, 1943 must be Bomber Command's year. Much as he might dislike the prospect, he knew that the Command was always likely to be diverted to other tasks, and if Overlord was launched would inevitably be concentrated for a time on interdiction targets. Harris could also judge, however much he might have been excluded from Casablanca's deliberations, that American power meant an eventual American say-so; he had not spent 1941 in Washington without learning that fact.[19] But Casablanca Directives not withstanding, it would be months before the 8th Air Force was a significant operational force; it was small, inexperienced, depleted in respect of escorts as well as bombers by the demands of the North African campaign; nobody *knew* what it could do over Germany; above all, although given top priority among all the combat formations of the USAAF, it was in competition with the claims of the Pacific theatre. General Eaker had spoken confidently of what a fleet of 300 B.17s and B.24s could do. But at the beginning of 1943, the 8th numbered barely 100 operational bombers[20]; it was not only a daylight force, it was a fine weather one too, because no radar aids for bombing through overcast were yet ready. And the weather in the English winter, as the Americans were gloomily discovering, was a different proposition from that in their training areas in the far and sunny west. The skies over occupied Europe remained cloudy too. Eaker and his fellow commanders had to sit and sweat it out, make what they could of inconclusive raids, with insignificant losses (mostly, but occasionally with disturbing hints of a different tale later), against targets either trivial or impervious to destruction.

But in Bomber Command the mood and the objectives were very different.

At long last we were ready and equipped. Bomber Command's main offensive began at a precise moment, the moment of the first major attack on an objective in Germany by means of *Oboe*. This was on the night of 5–6 March 1943, when I was at last able to undertake with real hope of success the task which had been given to me when I first took over the Command a little more than a year before, the task of destroying the main cities of the Ruhr. In the interval, however, the scope of my instructions had been enlarged, as a result of the Casablanca Conference, when it was decided to proceed with a joint Anglo-American bomber offensive against German war industry. The subject of morale had been dropped, and I was now required to proceed with the general 'disorganisation' of German industry, giving priority to certain aspects of it such as U-boat building, aircraft production, oil production, transportation and so forth, *which gave one a very wide range of choice and allowed me to attack pretty well any German industrial city of* 100,000 *inhabitants and above*.* But the Ruhr remained a principal objective, because it was the most important industrial area in the whole of Germany, which was why it had been originally chosen for morale-breaking attacks: *the new instructions therefore made no difference*.* Essen had been named as the first town for destruction a year before, as it was the largest and most important manufacturing centre in the Ruhr, and Essen was the target on the night of 5–6 March.

A force of 442 aircraft was despatched. In the Main Force there were 140 Lancasters, 69 Halifaxes, 52 Stirlings and 131 Wellingtons, while the Pathfinder marking force consisted of 22 heavy bombers and 8 *Oboe*-Mosquitoes, on which and on the equipment they carried everything in the last resort depended. They flew to Egmong on the Dutch coast, and thence directly to a point 15 miles north of Essen, which point Pathfinder heavies had marked with yellow markers on the ground as a guide to the Main Force. From there the bombers began the run-up to the target, which they were to reach at the rate of 11 a minute, the whole attack lasting 38 minutes. The Mosquitoes dropped red target indicators, not visually but by means of *Oboe* on the aiming point before the bombing began, and thereafter at intervals alternately of three and seven minutes.[21]

* Author's italics.

I have quoted extensively from Harris' own account of the opening of his long-awaited offensive, because, aside from its revealing summary of strategic independence, it describes so clearly what was in Bomber Command's capacity to achieve, a factor on which at all times, and not merely in the last resort, all other considerations and plans depended. With variations of no great significance, the raid pattern which Harris describes, following the strategic and operational justification for it which he had laid down, was repeated until the closing weeks of the war against Germany. The Main Force was to become dominated by Lancasters; the Mosquito, not only in Bennett's Group but in 5 Group, commanded by Air Vice-Marshal Cochrane, an airman much given to tactical innovation, was to become a marvellously flexible instrument of air power; marking was to assume complexities and permutations, in order to guide the Main Force and confuse an always vigilant and expert defence, which at times led to confusion among the less expert and careful of Bomber Command crews. And the losses exacted by the Luftwaffe in the early months of 1944 did lead to a rather overdue change in the concept of the bomber stream and the requirements of electronic counter-measures; by mid-1944, many new varieties of diversionary raid and mock attack had given an extra edge to a force whose tonnages dropped on German city centres were to make even the 1943 figures seem derisory. But in all essentials, just as 5 March 1943 rather than May 1940 or May 1942 marked the true beginning of the strategic air offensive (as February 1944 and not August 1942 or January 1943 did for the 8th Air Force), so we may say that on this night was set a pattern for targets and their destruction from which Harris deviated only as a gesture or by express—and repeated—order.

The purely operational aspects of the Essen and subsequent raids must be considered in more detail in Chapter 8, where it will be seen that the improving quality and increasing quantity of Bomber Command's equipment and weapons could only disguise or temporarily diminish the challenge of the German defences. In one respect at least, but that the most important of all, the Essen raid was untypical; the missing rate was just over three per cent, whereas for 1943 as a whole it was to be more than four, over two per cent below the Directorate of Bomber Operations figure of what would be 'unacceptable' if suffered over a three months' period, but a warning for 1944 nonetheless.[22]

In the other major respect—damage inflicted on Germany, by whatever criterion one selects—the Essen raid and those which followed were typical of the strategic air offensive as a whole, not only for the incidental industrial destruction which Bomber Command wrought, but for its failure to seriously disrupt the belated effort to put Germany on a full war economy. Speer's testimony is eloquent enough in this respect—not least his central point, made not only during his 1945 interrogations but after his release in 1966, that *repeated* attacks were necessary on selected targets or selected city areas if significant loss of or damage to production and resources was to ensue[23]; but perhaps as revealing is the fact that even in a city as heavily bombed as Essen, it was virtually impossible to knock out the basic industrial process, even if factory roofs and walls went up in flames and thousands of Krupp's workers were driven to exist in conditions little better than the helots of the Todt Organisation. Moreover, not only Hitler had an Empire; Krupp's was the biggest, not the only industrial looter from Germany when 'in 1943 the Russian's modern electro-steel mill at Mariup was broken down to be re-erected as part of their new Berthawerke near Breslau in Eastern Germany. Towards the end of the war Krupp's despoliation of the occupied countries became quite wilful. In France for instance most of the Austin factory at Liancourt, the Almag plant at Mulhouse, and the Alsthow works at Belfort, were manhandled bodily back to Essen.'[24]

Despite claims in the (restrospectively written) Bomber Command Quarterly Review for January to March, that in the March and April attacks on Essen 10 and 27 per cent respectively of Krupp's was destroyed, resulting in losses of output measured by time of two weeks and two months, the record shows that throughout the war this unique heavy engineering complex only received 30 per cent damage as far as the capacity to produce went.[25] The last major attack of the war—on 11 March 1945—left but half the complex standing, but although it did not seem apparent at the time to either photographic interpretation experts or those from Whitehall or High Wycombe, destruction of buildings did not automatically produce a cut-back, still less a halt, in production. What brought Krupp's to a standstill in 1945 was destruction of roads, railways and canals: '... it was no good producing the stuff if you could not ship it.'[26]

These factors should no doubt have been more objectively assessed than they were by those responsible for planning and measuring the progress of the strategic air offensive. They must certainly be remembered when the roll is called of the mounting attacks on the Ruhr and adjoining cities which lit the German skies in the shortest nights of 1943 with the lurid glow of the fire-storm; so fierce and prolonged were these fires that to one pilot at least looking down from the cockpit of his Halifax, 'the clouds were like cottonwool soaked in blood'.[27] From March to July and beyond Bomber Command endeavoured to make 'happy valley' a hell for those below. In what the Official History calls '43 major actions', Harris' crews bombed Aachen, Krefeld, Duisburg, Oberhausen, Bochum, Dortmund, Gelsenkirchen, Essen, Mülheim, Wuppertal, Düsseldorf, Cologne and Münster, with attacks on Kiel, Rostock, Stettin, Berlin, Mannheim, Nuremberg, Frankfurt, Stuttgart, Munich and even Pilsen in far Czecho-slovakia as reminders to German and sceptic alike that this new and terrifying fire-bird could destroy wherever it chose to fly.

Most raids in this new kind of air offensive were mounted by between 300 and 700 aircraft.[28] The largest force, 826 aircraft, bombed Dortmund on 23 May—clear indication that Bomber Command was reaching towards that number by which, in default of his impossible demand for 4,000 heavies, Harris set such store. In this Ruhr offensive, 18,406 sorties were flown; 872 aircraft failed to return; a further 2,136 were damaged. There was no set pattern in the losses on which to base firm conclusions as to how and when the German defences would exact co-ordinated punish-ment for this offensive of attrition. The highest missing rate was from the Pilsen raid of 16–17 April, one of two attacks (the other was in May) undertaken to test accuracy at very long range. Unfortunately the marking accuracy was poor—and, from the first raid by 327 aircraft, 36 failed to return. On the other hand Nuremberg, certainly another distant target, was bombed on 8–9 March by the usual 90 per cent of 335 aircraft despatched; only seven aircraft failed to return. The bombing was in-accurate—H_2S, being required at this range, showed itself a vague guide for blind bomb aiming although invaluable for navigation—but it was still a startling improvement from anything obtaining in 1942.

Although the crucial factor of the missing rate seemed elusive and arbitrary so far as forecasts went, there was no escaping the mean figure after the last raid of the battle proper (against Aachen on 13 July): ' . . . slightly over 16 per cent of the bombers ordered into these actions became casualties of one sort or another and 4.7 per cent of them were lost over Germany.' For aircraft missing read 6,000-odd men killed, or wounded or prisoner; for those aircraft damaged but brought home by discipline and courage, read a like toll, not least in crews broken up and dispersed. As the Official History remarks: 'These were grave losses and the margin left to Bomber Command with which to preserve the future fighting efficiency of the force was narrow indeed.'

Yet all that had been proved by the battle was the increasing relevance of *Oboe* and marking to the conduct of an offensive dictated by targets comprising cities 'of 100,000 inhabitants and above', endowed with prominent aiming points—like Cologne Cathedral. However much

Germany had or had not suffered between March and July, nothing catastrophic had yet occurred, nothing to make the Germans cry halt or to force Hitler's advisers to rub his nose in the evidence of the destruction of the Third Reich. Not enough Germans had been killed, no city had been so shattered as to be erased from the target list. But after the attacks on Essen, a city always marked by Harris for the severest treatment, 'the number of people rendered homeless was estimated at 50,000, of whom 40,000 belonged to the working class . . .'.[29] Before we turn to what higher authority was making of this battle of the Ruhr and wondering where, if at all, it could be said to form part of the Combined Bomber Offensive, we must describe what happened to Hamburg between 24 July and 2 August. Not only was it Harris' attempt to make Essen seem paltry, to make Germans cry enough, but at long last *Window* was used to render the night fighter impotent and to suggest that other cities could be burned alive with impunity. It was also the first (as it was for long the only) occasion where the 8th Air Force joined in at the point where Bomber Command left off, endeavouring to stick to its brief by bombing U-boat yards, but adding to the general holocaust nonetheless.

A holocaust it was.

> The rapidity with which the fires and firebombs developed, made every plan and every prospect of defence by the inhabitants purposeless. Houses, which in previous raids might have been preserved by the courageous efforts of self-protection and other personnel, now fell victims to the flames. Before the necessity of flight could be realised, often every path to safety was cut off. . . . People who now attempted to leave their shelters to see what the situation was or to fight the fires were met by a sea of flame. . . . There was no water. . . . None knew where to begin firefighting. . . . The heat, which was becoming unbearable, showed plainly that there was no longer any question of putting out fires but only of saving their lives. Escape from the sea of flame seemed already impossible. . . . The fire had become a hurricane which made it impossible in most cases to reach the open . . . to cover long distances in the redhot streets of leaping flames was impossible. . . . The destruction was so immense that of many people literally nothing remains. . . . The enemy attacked with ceaseless raids until the work of destruction was complete. His hate had its triumph in the firestorms which destroyed mercilessly men and material alike.

Thus one of the more restrained accounts, by the Hamburg Police President the following December, of an operation given by Harris the code-name 'Gomorrah', where the fire-storm, or furnace-like air from fires turned to a hurricane, killed a conservatively estimated 30,000 people, destroyed 70 per cent of the city, and rendered homeless nearly a million survivors. And the cost to Bomber Command? Fifty-nine aircraft failed to return from the four major raids of 24, 27, 29 July and 2 August, from 2,318 despatched—a missing rate of under three per cent. Here, despite the rapidity with which the German defences recovered from the effects of *Window*—the heaviest loss, 30 aircraft missing, occurred on the third raid—seemed to be the way to end the war, here surely was the chance of continuing the slaughter, the devastation, the industrial damage, right through the autumn until the longer nights set in and the Command, backed by further improvements in equipment, could defy the weather and reach out to Berlin with like repetition. And, indeed, despite the accumulated losses of Bomber Command in men and material through-out 1943, despite the shortcomings of H_2S and the vigour of the Luftwaffe's ripostes, nothing is more impressive than the way in which this momentum was sustained.

Pointblank Directive and the Overlord Objective

Attacks of comparative intensity to those of the March to July period were made in September and October, further stages along the road to Berlin, a battle royal, which began in November. Moreover, despite a seemingly unrelieved programme of city destruction, there were occasional operations which showed tactical experiment and still evolving equipments directed on to targets which had a particular strategic importance and required to be destroyed at a particular moment in time, in conformity with the requirements of Pointblank, and hence, indirectly, of Overlord. On 17 August 597 heavies attacked Peenemunde, on the Baltic coast, where the flying-bomb research and experimental station was located.[30] That 'severe damage' was achieved may be attributed in part to the first operational use of a 250-lb. marker bomb. Given that 'it burst and ignited at 3,000 feet and burnt on the ground as a vivid crimson fire for about ten minutes', it is not surprising that 'its appearance was easy to recognise and difficult to simulate'.[31] But Peenemunde is surely more significant for the introduction of the master bomber technique, first employed by the specially trained and equipped 617 Squadron in its operation against the Mohne and Eder dams on 16 May; after 17 August there was growing need to direct the Main Force on to targets over which increasingly inexperienced crews so frequently became confused, uncertain and innaccurate.

Peenemunde, however, cost 40 aircraft missing and 32 damaged. Although an exact correlation was never established at any stage of the war between a target's inherent difficulties and dangers and losses sustained, Harris was never short of evidence to demonstrate that it was not operationally feasible to mount a sustained offensive against the kind of targets which could be drawn up on the basis of mere directives. As if to rub that truth home for the daylight bomber also, the 8th, only a few hours before Peenemunde raid, and on the anniversary of its first operation, had lost 60 aircraft out of 376 despatched in a double attack on the most carefully selected targets of all—the ball-bearing plants at Schweinfurt and the aircraft factories at Regensburg.[32] The Pointblank Directive had been the Combined Bomber Offensive's text for just over two months; already for its most committed supporters it had become a test to which dutiful adherence meant disastrous loss in combat.

Nevertheless, Eaker was to persist in the attempt to adhere to a directive which expressed so clearly the American notion of air power. He did so until that terrible week between 8 and 14 October when, in combat alone, 148 of his bombers were destroyed attacking targets as far afield as Gdynia and, again, Schweinfurt, variously denominated as 'industrial areas, U-boat yards, industrial-aviation, port areas, railroads, waterways, industrial transportation'.[33] In the nine months of the 8th's first efforts to establish itself over Germany, the results were most impressive, if least important, at Hamburg, where the port area was comprehensively wrecked. But all too often the early loss of the lead plane in a formation not only gave the fighter swarms their chance to rip it apart but destroyed the bombardier on whose bombing his comrades bombed as well.

Yet the 8th struggled on. Whereas a few occasions in 1939 had sufficed to convince the British Air Staff that unescorted daylight raids over Germany were not a feasible operation of war, weeks were to pass before that painful truth was driven home to Arnold and his subordinates. While Bomber Command was setting the major cities of western Germany alight, the 8th was stabbing at targets in France or venturing into Germany.[34] In the first case, losses were light, but results hard to determine; occasional examples of 'pickle-barrel' bombing showed up in the next day's photographic plot (Marienburg on 9 October, for example), but although targets in France could be squeezed in the Pointblank list (which in most respects was the same as that in the Casablanca Directive), the real enemy and the big prizes lay deep in Germany itself. And when the 8th went over Germany they got a pasting. Not always—the losses from the attacks on Kiel on 14 May and 'industrial targets in NW Germany' on 17 July were light and accuracy was fair—but more often than not.

The attacks were not so frequent—between that on Wilhelmshaven on 27 January and Schweinfurt on 14 October, approximately 65 targets were attacked on 33 days—and they lacked momentum and consistency. Ports, which were relatively easy to find, obviously contained something on the Pointblank list and offered approach and departure routes not unduly menaced by fighters or flak, figured on no less than 26 occasions; 'targets of opportunity' appear frequently on the list of those attacked; inland German targets appear only 30 times, compared with 102 for France and the Low Countries. Of really significant targets within the Pointblank list, and if we exclude those abortive—and detested—attacks on the submarine pens, only those on ports known or likely to contain U-boats in various stages of *fitting-out*, plus the 22 June attacks on Hüls and those on Regensburg and Schweinfurt, merit much attention.

Targets outside Germany can be considered as largely a waste of time, indeed, as warnings to green crews of what happened over Germany, they were positively misleading. Yet even if all operations between the two dates are taken together, we get these sobering figures: 16,210 sorties were flown, with an average of a fraction under 112 sorties per raid; 10,740 aircraft succeeded in attacking their targets, a figure which allows for a number of completely abortive missions, but which still leaves us with only 60–70 per cent successful missions in terms of this rather rudimentary criterion; the missing rate from all sorties was just under five per cent, and from aircraft attacking, just over seven per cent. Figures for damaged bombers vary and are not always consistent (a factor, it must be emphasised which applies to all calculations of this type). But the 8th in this respect not surprisingly suffered more heavily than Bomber Command. 'It is normal', wrote Eaker at the end of 1943, 'for from 25 to 50 per cent of aircraft on a deep-penetration mission into Germany to suffer some form of battle damage.'

These are daunting statistics, and across two decades and more of post-war history and from a strategic environment which bears only an incidental resemblance to that of 1943, we must salute the courage and resolution of the commanders and crews of the 8th Air Force as they sent their groups out and brought the battered remnants home. But although the armed forces of a young nation can endure losses which their older allies shun, and although the 8th's crews fortified themselves with (wildly inaccurate) figures of enemy fighters destroyed, there was a limit to what even American optimism could accept. Men might be prepared to fight on—there was no evidence that they were not or could not—but aircraft replacements were not keeping pace with losses. With his groups reduced to not more than 200 aircraft fit to fly by the end of 'black week', Eaker reluctantly called off the deep penetration raids on Germany, and sent the 8th back to its original targets; attacks on those in Germany continued, but they were heavily escorted and hence of limited range duration—and value.

With Harris by November beginning his assault on Berlin, and with the 8th reduced to a holding operation, the Combined Bomber Offensive was, through the unwillingness of the Commander of one element to participate and the inability of the other element to do so, reduced temporarily to a dead letter. Most disturbing of all, the acknowledged primary strategic objective of the offensive by late 1943—or acknowledged at the level which finally arbitrated the air forces' fortunes—which was the destruction of the combat and productive capacity of German air power, was further than ever from achievement. Indeed, the breathing space afforded by the failure of the Combined Bomber Offensive, and the rapidity with which the German defences came to terms with *Window* and its like, meant that the whole balance was by November tilting against Bomber Command and the 8th. The effect of concentrating German fighters in the Ruhr carried comparably grave implications for the German High Command, but this was little consolation to the Combined Chiefs of Staff or to Lieutenant-General F. E. Morgan and his 'Cossac' staff who, since April, had been planning the operational strategy of the return to France. Without command of the air there could be no Overlord; to set Berlin ablaze as the Ruhr had been fired was not the way to achieve this command, and daylight raids on targets within the range of fighter escorts was not going to achieve it either, unless of course the fighter's range could be increased to that of the B.17 and B.24, operating moreover from Italy as well as East Anglia.

Just as it must surprise us that the Casablanca Conference spent so little time in reasoned discussion of the problems involved in meeting the real requirements of Overlord, so the remainder of 'Conference Year', as Lord Ismay aptly calls it, must occasion a like dismay that the relatively straightforward but crucial issue of the long-range fighter escort was not tackled urgently and at the highest level. Although 'the fighter support slowly became an acknowledged necessity of a day bomber offensive',[35] it was not until February 1944 that this *belated* realism was fully translated into practice, which sufficiently indicates that pre-war dogma about the 'self-defending formation' held sway for longer than was healthy. Many factors contributed to this delay—Torch; the unsuitability of the P.38 (Lightning) as an escort; the failure of bombers up-gunned to act as escorts;

the delay in building up American fighter squadrons as replacements for those in the RAF Fighter Command which, through much of 1943, continued to provide most of the cover for the 8th's short- and middle-range raids[36]; not least, one suspects, a total lack of conviction that fighter escorts for daylight raids were really essential. The B.17 and B.24, bristling with .5 cannon and machine guns, tended to convince the impressionable, dogmatic or inexperienced that the self-defending formation still made operational sense. There was a persistent tendency in the 8th to underrate the enemy; the intermittent habit of British senior officers, from Portal downwards, of commenting pessimistically on the 8th's chances on deep-penetration raids against determined opposition, doubtless stiffened the natural American desire to prove such sceptics wrong.

Thus the long-range escort failed to appear in 1943, and even its experimental or prototype version—existing models equipped with drop tanks—evolved by fits and starts. The P.47 (Thunderbolt) arrived in Britain in January, but did not become fully operational until April; not until May was an escort range of 175 miles achieved—enough for France and the Low Countries only.[37] Meantime the design and supply of fuel tanks became stuck in the logistic pipelines, and it is instructive to survey, however briefly, a factor whose details may appear boring, but which relate directly to the whole concept of air power as it was disputed over Germany in those days.[38] In January, the 8th, which in the preceding October had already asked about drop tanks, queried whether tanks could be manufactured in Britain for the P.47. But in February, 60,000 tanks of 200-gallon capacity were ordered from the United States. In March a 125-gallon tank was suggested as better suited to operational conditions, essentially manoeuvrability in combat if this occurred before jettisoning. Subsequently a steel 125-gallon tank was designed, and it was decided that 43,200 of them would be manufactured in Britain.

The Ministry of Aircraft Production then proposed instead a 106-gallon paper tank; anxious to acquire this tank, the 8th tested it in June and asked for a production run. American production was therefore cancelled. By July some of the original 205-gallon tanks were in operation—but neither paper tanks nor an additional supply of steel 100- and 250-gallon tanks had yet arrived from British sources. By August the 8th over Germany was suffering serious loss; in response to urgent pleas, by October about 10,000 75-gallon tanks had reached the 8th from the United States; by the 12th of that month—two days before the great and costly second raid on Schweinfurt 450 paper tanks had been supplied. 'But not until the middle of December did the supply begin to approach requirements. Thereafter supplies grew rapidly, and in March 1944 the American fighters flew over Berlin for the first time—thanks to the jettisonable tank'.

It would push the argument too far to say that Overlord succeeded because of the drop tank, even though it is undeniable that this humble appendage of war has hitherto not received the recognition it deserves. Nevertheless, we can unhesitatingly say that the lack of fighter cover, and the limitations of those aircraft which were available, reduced the Combined Bomber Offensive from an objective to an aspiration throughout most of 1943. German aircraft production was unimpaired; indeed such raids as did take place were but a stimulus to expansion. German fighters in combat *tactically* defeated the 8th. The combined effect of this double failure was to increase the tactical burden as well as the strategic load on Bomber Command, which not all the counter-measures devised and operated were able to alleviate. The weight of this burden gave the German defences a chance they were not slow to seize. Before we close this chapter with an account of how the progress of the Combined Bomber Offensive was viewed towards the end of 1943 by the Allied High Command, and how Harris set about his assault on Berlin, it is necessary to consider how the German defences responded to the double challenge of the night and the daylight raids. In the former case, these defences passed through and surmounted a crisis which at one time threatened to overwhelm them; in the other, victory was enjoyed—before early 1944 saw a total reversal of fortune.

Crisis for the German Night Fighter

The decisions taken by the Luftwaffe at the beginning of 1943 have already been discussed, as have their efforts in terms of production and redeployment. Impressive as was the former and flexible, by virtue of internal lines of communication, though the latter became, the combined effect of *Window* in the July Hamburg raids and the drain on fighter strength caused by the Sicily landings of the same month, was a definite double crisis for the Luftwaffe.[39] Resourcefulness met and largely overcame the first crisis; but it is arguable that the loss of 'not less than 850 German operational aircraft . . . in the central Mediterranean area during July, 1943, of which approximately 600 were single-engined fighter types' was a blow to the new defensive strategy, which allowed Bomber Command and the 8th Air Force to survive as instruments of war between October and the following March, albeit very badly damaged in the process. By 1 January 1944, the Luftwaffe had approximately 1,650 fighters of all types distributed around Germany (including Austria) and the Western Front (including Denmark and South Norway), compared with 1,045 for a year earlier—and 790 as 1944 opened for the Russian, Mediterranean and Balkan fronts together.[40] Another 600 fighters added to the first figure would possibly have defeated even the long-range Mustang escort or at least still further delayed that moment when Spaatz and Portal could tell the Cossac staffs that command of the air had been won and that Allied invasion forces could land and fight under the umbrella of total air supremacy.

But whether or not the initial Luftwaffe losses which were suffered when the 'soft under-belly' was pierced reprieved the 8th, the essential dilemma of Bomber Command was certainly not solved. Well before the German day fighter was defeated by the Mustang, Bomber Command was fighting its way to its winter distant targets through defences which had made a remarkable recovery from the effects of *Window*. The Command's 100 Group was in operation by November 1943 with the express objective of introducing further refinements of jamming; but between the Hamburg raids and that month the German defences revived in a manner comparable to the earlier transition from an offensive to a defensive strategy. As we shall see, although the Berlin loss rate between 18 November and 30 December averaged under four per cent, those between 1 January and 25 March the following year averaged 6.5 per cent.[41] The foundation for that latter figure was the decision by Schmid and others to combine a variety of defensive techniques with an intensive programme of scientific and technical innovation, welded together for operational purposes by master controllers, who nightly conducted the whole.

To refer to this recovery is not to minimise the British scientific skill which, however belatedly utilised, led to the emasculation of the original German night fighter defences, or the courage and skill with which Bomber Command's crews tackled the increasingly complex tactics of late 1943. The point to grasp is simply that in this period a perfectly classic battle between the offence and the defence was being waged, with the balance constantly tilting. That to conduct such a battle had hitherto been beyond Bomber Command's capabilities merely illustrates the truth that in the 1940s war in the air was still in the phase of requiring such a battle at some point in time to be joined and waged. It is only in this sense that the technical ingenuity which both sides displayed is relevant to the history of the strategic air offensive.

Although *Window* was an immensely satisfactory achievement, the *Rise and Fall of the German Air Force* does remind us that 'it is not true to say that the German signals organisation was taken by surprise when the British first employed it'. The idea of metal strips to simulate the wavelength emissions of bombers picked up on the *Wuerzburg* (short-range for ground control interception) radar had occurred to the Technical Office of the Luftwaffe in 1942.[42] But, just as *Window* was only belatedly introduced for fear of premature disclosure to the enemy of a device which derived from an invention of great significance and potential, so too was Goering, on hearing of the Technical Office's researches, loath to take remedial action. His notion that to do nothing would somehow preserve the conspiracy of silence about *Window*, of it remaining an experiment rather than an operational tool, may have delayed the moment when the latter role became inescapably necessary, but it certainly made a counter measure pretty difficult for the Luftwaffe Signals Staff to devise.[43]

Nevertheless, General Martini, the Director-General of Air Force Signals, appears throughout 1942 to have been as anxious to plan for the day when the war of wits and the battle for command of the air would be joined as were his comparably far-sighted superiors.[44] The essence of the pre-*Window* German defences against night operations has already been described: given that the German High Command only began to take Bomber Command seriously in 1943, it is to Kammhuber's credit that his 'boxes' were increased as the years went by, until, by July 1943, they extended from southern Norway to south of Paris and, in depth, well to the east of the Ruhr. Most distant targets were outside the Kammhuber Line (but Frankfurt, Mannheim and Stuttgart were not). Berlin may thus appear to have been unprotected, but the routes which Bomber Command took when attacking it provided the opposition with a reasonable notion of the intended target and how it would be reached.

The fact that Bomber Command Headquarters and Groups routed raids where possible round, rather than through, the Kammhuber Line not only in its heyday but after July 1943, is not only evidence that the bomber stream was not an absolute answer to German fighters being guided on to the attacking forces; it reveals also that *Window* tactics failed to dispose of this defensive scheme in its entirety. After the Hamburg raid (of 27 July), there were a few days of confusion, and doubtless, of recrimination among the German Air Staff. But almost immediately the strongest endeavours were made to combine the substance of the Kammhuber plan with three other measures.[45] Aircraft would be flown off when bombers were picked up by the long-range (*Freya*) early-warning system—which was not jammed

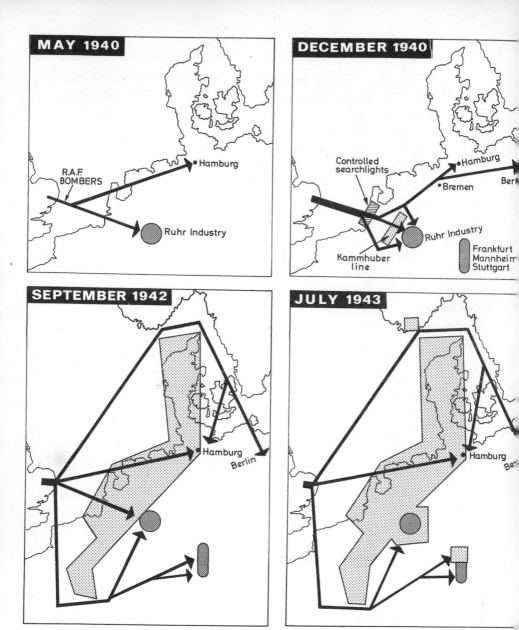

The Kammhuber Line

These four maps show the development of the Kammhuber Line before it was rendered useless by *Window*. The depth and extent of what was a system of linked sectors rather than a linear defence indicates the size of the task confronting those responsible for the German defences once *Window* had been used. The maps also indicate that the Kammhuber Line was comparable in scale to the early warning system established around the south and east coasts of the United Kingdom before 1939.

effectively until the *Mandrel* equipment was used operationally by 100 Group in 1944; these fighters would search independently for the bomber stream, and for this tactic the Germans coined the phrase 'wild sow'. Fighters equipped with airborne radar (*Lichtenstein*) would search in a comparably independent fashion; the hope, which was realised at the turn of the year, was that new wave-lengths outside the *Window* band would enable GCI to be revived.

Over and above these 'wild sow' tactics developed the concept of the Master Controller, whose powers eventually reached the stage where 'cases occurred in which a unit based in northern Denmark intercepted Allied raiders over Stuttgart'.[46] These controllers led a life of fantastic strain and responsibility (one of the most skilled, Major Ruppel, claimed the destruction of no less than 782 bombers between 1941 and 1944)[47]; on occasions, and from a variety of fortuitous or consciously planned reasons, they scored great successes. On others, and increasingly throughout 1944, Bomber Command's capacity to mount a Main Force operation on any given night, *plus* diversions and spoofs, told against them in a situation where sending fighters to the wrong place meant a total waste of precious fuel. Increasingly too, internal divisions, especially over signals, intelligence and flak co-ordination, made the controller's tasks too taxing for continued success within the terms necessary for an effective defence— that if the destruction of German cities could not be prevented, then the cost to Bomber Command must be such as to call a halt to the offensive before command of the air had been achieved. For by the end of 1943 it was clear to the High Command on *both* sides that in that battle lay the key to Overlord.

Controlled fighters were part of the 'tame sow' tactics, whose full development depended on a fully integrated ground control system, whose objective was to destroy all elements of a raid which were flying outside the main stream—the Pathfinders, which in early 1944, were suffering heavily after months of slight loss[48]; the diversion elements, including 100 Group—which in fact rarely suffered loss, so scattered were its aircraft employed on the manifold subterfuges of electronic warfare[49]; and above all, aircraft which flew slap through the Line on their way home, with crews, as often as not, failing to keep the right kind of watch or adopt the most sensible evasive tactics. But controlled tactics and all their variants (like 'squadron attacks' led by one airborne radar equipped aircraft, interception of the bomber stream over the North Sea, and shadowing of the stream by reconnaissance aircraft),[50] depended for success on freedom from jamming, not only for all varieties of radar but for contact between controller and the hundreds of fighters he directed. German technologists succeeded by the beginning of 1944 in producing airborne radar *SN2*, operating on frequencies not easily susceptible to jamming[57] (*Window*, although used for the rest of war, became less of a problem to the defence as other tactics and techniques improved and evolved), leading to 100 Group's ascending importance, not least to Saundby, Harris' deputy, who guided its operations with a mind unclouded by any belief in the inevitability of the strategic air offensive's success. By early 1944 so many wavelengths were in use and had been jammed or were likely to be, that controllers were sending messages via German civil radio stations, using regional songs and the like to indicate a probable area of attack.[52]

Victory for the German Day Fighter

From all the above it is clear that the battle between Bomber Command and the German defences was bound to approach a mutual crisis point sometime in 1944. No comparable situation in 1943 existed or appeared to be developing between the 8th Air Force and the enemy, because the struggle had not reached so intense a stage, nor was it then on the German side seen so directly to menace the Reich itself. Although Speer and others have testified that it was the USAAF daylight bombing in 1944 which struck most deeply at Germany's industrial vitals, the picture in 1943 was very different, and the 8th then was regarded pretty much as Bomber Command had been before the week of Hamburg. Moreover, although it is doubtful whether Hitler, the OKW or the German Air Staff realised the full implications of the Casablanca and Pointblank Directives until late in 1943, the purpose and nature and target pattern of daylight bombing was hardly a mystery which required much study by anybody who had pondered the tactics of American bomber operations in the European theatre before the combined offensive (on paper) got under way.

The first raid undertaken in that theatre as such had in fact not only preceded the 8th's on 17 August 1942, but spelled out in advance what such operations were intended to achieve. On 11 June 1942, 13 B.24s of the so-called Halverson detachment, flying from RAF Fayid in the Canal Zone, bombed oil refineries at Ploesti in Rumania.[53] The operation was neither successful nor expensive; it was nevertheless a portent of American strategic beliefs and operational intentions, different in kind and not merely degree from the 1939 daylight raids of Bomber Command on the German fleet and its bases. Over a year later the Ploesti operation was repeated, with somewhat different results. Out of 177 B.24s sent to bomb the refineries from North African bases on 1 August 1943—well before 'first' Schweinfurt—54 were lost and many seriously damaged.[54]

Thus, however much Arnold and Spaatz might plan for the day of an American strategic air offensive, combining operations by the 8th in East Anglia and the embryonic 15th in the Mediterranean,[55] to the German Air Staff it seemed plain as a pikestaff that deep-penetration raids were simply a chance for their forces to wreak havoc on a weak enemy which virtually announced its intentions in advance, especially as 'favourable weather was an absolute prerequisite to successful day bombing at least until more efficient methods of blind bombing had been discovered'.[56] Bomber Command's daylight raids, in no sense being 'precise', had *required* cloud in order to give crews a fighting chance of evasion and survival. It is true that many aircraft in the 1943 Ploesti raid were lost through poor navigation and airmanship, and that the low-level tactics adopted proved disastrous in view of the extra-heavy flak concentration of many calibres around the refinery. There is also some evidence to suggest that those responsible for defending so important a target were told when the raid was to take place.[57]

No such comments apply to either of the Schweinfurt raids, or others by the 8th where many aircraft were lost. On such occasions bombers kept above 12,000 feet, stuck together and achieved as much accuracy on target as could be expected in circumstances well described by the reminder that, 'Except for the few seconds of the bombing run, when the purpose of the heavy bomber is realised, all phases of a bombing mission are dominated by considerations of defence'.[56] But it was just before the bombing run that the German fighters struck. Later in 1943, their tactics suggested that Luftwaffe commanders had cottoned on to the USAAF practice of a formation bombing on the signal of the bombardier in the lead plane. This plane, and indeed the lead group in large formations, were singled out for particularly ferocious attack by fighters, so much so indeed that on at least one occasion ('second' Schweinfurt) the lead formation was virtually annihilated.

By September blind bombing with airborne radar had begun[58]; bombing through overcast became safer, relatively, provided the most distant targets were avoided, and the 8th ended the year bombing 'Crossbow' (flying-bomb) targets in the Pas de Calais area, an unidentified 'blockade runner', 'air depots' in various parts of France, together with what by implication was little more than a light area raid on 'Paris, Ivry and Bois de Colombes'.[60] These missions, on 24 and 31 December, saw 1,294 aircraft despatched; 1,134 attacked; 25 were lost, a missing rate of just over two per cent. But in a raid on Ludwigshafen on 30 December, 23 aircraft were lost from 698 despatched and 647 attacking, a missing rate of over three per cent. This percentage was preferable to 'black week'; it was 'acceptable'—but the difference in the figures for raids which were little more than a gesture and one which was intended to be an integral part of the Combined Bomber Offensive are nevertheless indicative of a problem which was as yet unsolved. No longer did the British Air Staff mutter about using the 8th on night operations; now it was not so much a question of an unacceptable attrition rate—although the Casablanca figure of 2,225 heavy bombers to be deployed in the European theatre by 1 January 1944 was clearly not going to be realised, the 8th as 1943 drew to a close mustered almost 1,000 aircraft available for operations, compared with under 300 in mid-year[61]; the problem was not even one of growing numbers of German fighters or of the superiority of new types—it was not until 1944 that these appeared in the Heinkel and Messerschmitt jet series and then not in significant numbers.[62] The problem was simply that fighters could shoot down unescorted bombers.

Anglo-American Relations and Pointblank

Clearly such a state of affairs had to be resolved in some way; whatever premonition Spaatz and Eaker may have had that a solution was just round the corner in the shape of the P.51b (Mustang) fitted with the Rolls Royce Packard Merlin engine in place of the original Allison, the pressure of Overlord, in which the Army and Air Force members of the Joint Chiefs of Staff took as collective a proprietary interest as Admiral King and the naval lobby took in the Pacific war, required that the daylight offensive be maintained, and that no failures to date should be allowed to lessen Arnold's determination to establish a 'European' strategic air command under American control. Although of 3,259 missions flown by the 8th in September, only 1,571 could properly be described as directed on to 'CBO' targets[63] (and September was not an especially difficult month), belief in the singular leverage which the crucial role of air power could exercise in Overlord continued to dominate USAAF thinking.

To Arnold and his like, air power was but one element in strategy; this was a reasoned and reasonable belief, but a degree of vehemence was

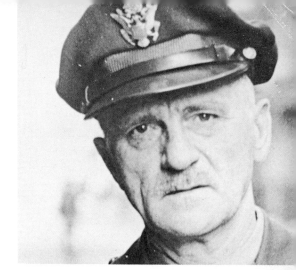

24   (*above*) General Ira C. Eaker

25   (*top right*) General Carl Spaatz

26   (*right*) General H. H. Arnold

AMERICAN COMMANDERS AND
CHIEF OF STAFF—AND ONE REBEL

27   (*below*) Major-General
James Doolittle

28   (*bottom right*) Brigadier-General
William Mitchell

29 (*right*) B.24—
the Liberator

THE AMERICAN
TEAM, 1942–45

30 (*above*) P.51—
the Mustang

31 (*right*) B.17—
the Fortress

32   Goering and Udet in 1938

GERMAN COMMANDERS, WHEN THE GOING WAS GOOD

33   Galland and Milch in 1943

34 (*above*) Junkers 88

35 (*opposite*)
Messerschmitt 109

THE GERMAN TEAM
1939–45

36 (*below*)
Messerschmitt 110

37   The Mohne Dam is breached

THE PRECISE STROKE, BRITISH

38   The Dortmund–Ems Canal is put out of action

39 (*right*) Air Marshal Sir
Robert Saundby

HARRIS' RIGHT HAND—THE
DAM BUSTER—PROPONENT OF
PRECISION BOMBING

40 (*below*) Wing Commander
Guy Gibson

41 (*bottom right*) Group Captain
Leonard Cheshire

42 Hamburg 1943: Operation Gomorrah

43 Bremen: piecemeal destruction

imparted to it by the fact that the organisation of that power was not left entirely to airmen. Arnold's memoirs display considerable restraint and tolerance about the fact that he was not among his peers in the armed forces hierarchy when he attended meetings of the Joint or Combined Chiefs, an attendance indicative of air power's significance, not of a command structure which enabled it to be wielded in freedom. Harris, by contrast, believed in city destruction for its own sake; it would win the war, and save the lives of countless Allied servicemen. He had command, as much as he wanted; he was left alone; in 1943 he still enjoyed Churchill's confidence and a degree of freedom to frame strategy, plan operations and see them executed which few other commanders have enjoyed. Provided he was left alone, Harris was as little interested in the Anglo-American struggle for command as he was in the argument that a strategic air offensive was but a preliminary, albeit an essential one, to Overlord. The memoirs of Sir Arthur Harris are somewhat intemperate, but only about issues where he found obstruction on strategic grounds; who ran the show ostensibly was of little moment since he believed that he ran a large chunk of it in reality.

The close of the year therefore saw the Combined Bomber Offensive as little an accomplished weapon of war as it had been when the Pointblank Directive appeared in June. Craven and Cate understate the case when they say mildly: 'For the integration of RAF and USAAF operations in the combined offensive the "CBO" directives made only a surprisingly informal provision.'[64] There was, in effect, no provision. Portal's position was anomalous; through his own Air Staff he could theoretically issue guide-lines for the prosecution of the offensive, but he never chose or saw any need to do so. There was no other machinery, formal or informal, for the co-ordination, let alone the planning, of operations, although there were committees of one sort and another concerned with targets and the exchange of information, and it must be said that over the latter the Ministry of Economic Warfare and its opposite number, the Committee of Operations Analysts, enjoyed a degree of unanimity not found elsewhere. Over certain technical and operational matters informal co-operation was satisfactory—the 8th was understanding about Bomber Command's fear of *Oboe* being used prematurely on daylight operations; Fighter Command provided ample cover within the limits of the Spitfire's range; the Air Ministry and the Royal Air Force in general gave much help to the 8th, ranging from major servicing facilities to the supply of protective clothing for air crews.[65]

Personal relations among senior officer appear to have been cordial, although some American surprise was evinced at the preponderance of RAF officers on the Cossac planning staffs.[66] Harris, Spaatz and Eaker were apparently fast friends. But all this had nothing to do with the two central issues: who was to run the CBO? How, with the 8th troubled by lack of escorts and Bomber Command pursuing an independent course, was it going to be run, specifically for the vital three months prior to Overlord? By this time there would be an air deputy to Eisenhower, and a commander of the Allied Air Forces as well, to control the operations of both 'strategic' and 'tactical' aircraft immediately before, and for some while after D-Day.

The last issue was to be debated energetically early in 1944, particularly in respect of a further variant of CBO, namely the attack on German communications, and for the moment we may leave it there. But the immediate CBO issues had to be settled. Ironically, or perhaps inevitably, all the paraphernalia of target priorities had by the end of 1943 boiled down to one, at least for that period preceding the Overlord three months, of support operations, about which most in authority were by now getting rather exercised. If the German Air Force in being could be neutralised, better still defeated, 'command of the air' established, and the Allied Armies subsequently put firmly ashore and thereafter provided with air cover and tactical support, air power would have been satisfactorily exercised—and vindicated—if not within the all embracing terms of the Casablanca Directive, then certainly within the classic definition in warfare of the offence asserting its superiority to the defence. The 'systematic destruction of selected vital elements of the German military and industrial machine through precision bombing in daylight' would have to wait—and it did, until well after D-Day. The case is well stated in the following terms: 'The CBO only achieved momentum late in the campaign when the weight of the American attack had made the distinction between pinpoint and area bombing a shadowy one and when the importance of enemy oil and transportation had become so apparent as to leave little doubt regarding its primary objectives.'[67]

If this assessment appears harsh, it is only necessary to turn to the pointed questions asked about the progress of the CBO by the Combined Chiefs of Staff in November. The course of the offensive, so far as it had one, had been reviewed at this level (Roosevelt and Churchill never displayed much interest in the precise application of air power) during the Washington and Quebec meetings of April and August. At the second of those meetings full support for Pointblank was evinced,[68] but as the weeks of autumn passed it became increasingly clear that it was a support governed by the

Overlord requirements already discussed; the use of air power to smash Germany, the Germans and German industry receded into the background. Despite the great destruction undeniably wrought by Bomber Command (so much so, indeed, that an uneasy feeling began to gather momentum in some parts of Whitehall that the post-war effects might be to Britain's disadvantage)[69]; despite isolated and heroic feats like the attack on the Mohne and Eder dams; despite the use of Mosquitoes for a variety of increasingly successful operations; despite, or perhaps because of, the brilliant success which detached units of the 8th had enjoyed on anti-submarine operations in the Bay of Biscay during July and August— despite all this, plus some isolated outright successes in daylight raids over Germany, such as the attack on the synthetic rubber plant at Hüls in the Ruhr on 22 June, only one issue animated the Combined Chiefs:

> The target date for Overlord had been set for 1 May 1944. Would the CBO have done its work by that time? To this question both British and American planners gave an increasingly pessimistic answer as the weeks passed. In a note to the Combined Chiefs of Staff dated 3 December 1943, Air Chief Marshal Portal stated bluntly that Pointblank was at that time a full three months behind schedule.[70]

But it was in this very month, with a major strategic objective still to be met and only simplified to the extent that it now resided in achieving command of the air, that General Arnold decided to effect a basic change in the command and organisation of American Air Forces in Europe. Formally coming into being on 1 January 1944, a new command, US Strategic Air Forces Europe, was established, thus fulfilling the strategic conviction that ' . . . the AAF was content to strike at Germany from any available bases',[71] by placing the 8th and 15th Air Forces under Spaatz's operational control. But given the immediate strategic task facing the senior and much the most committed of these two air forces, it cannot be said that this apparent rationalisation of command structures, ostensibly justified in part by the concept of shuttle bombing and even the idea of operations from Russian soil, together with the undoubted increase in Spaatz's power and authority, had much to do with real problems. But the change did have a great deal to do with a move in the disposal of senior appointments for the Overlord campaign.

The Cairo Conference in December settled most of these appointments, including that of Tedder as deputy to Eisenhower, with special responsibility for the co-ordination of ground and air forces and the arbitration in part of bombing priorities.[72] But the conference made somewhat ambiguous choices on the appointment of commanders of Allied Air Forces as such. As already mentioned, early 1944 was to produce much argument on the role of those air forces, who should be in over all charge of them, and indeed their composition for varying periods. But a careful reading of the evidence from sources on both sides of the Atlantic leaves little doubt that Arnold's move in December 1943 was designed to put Spaatz strongly in the running for the Allied Air Forces Supreme Command. His qualifications were outstanding; he had been in the closest touch with the Royal Air Force in Britain and the Middle East since America entered the war; he had commanded the 8th Air Force in its salad days; he had been regarded as a theatre commander by his superiors throughout that time; and by the Joint Chiefs of Staff he had indeed been given the title of 'Air Officer ETOUSA' from the time that operations by US forces first commenced over Europe; at the moment of Arnold's move he was deputy to Tedder in the Middle East Air Forces as well as Commander of the 8th Air Force in Italy, and it was natural for Arnold in particular and the American Service hierarchy in general to suppose that a colleague with such a record, and an active exponent of co-ordinated ground–air operations to boot, would fulfil a comparable role in Overlord. By so doing he would firmly put the seal of American air power and its associated strategic principles on a campaign American in conception, largely American in the zeal which had informed the plans for its execution from early in 1942, and demonstrably American in the person of 'Ike' to fulfil the pledge of 'Germany first'.[73]

But Spaatz didn't get the job; a British airman quite unknown to most Americans got it instead; he was Air Chief Marshal Sir Trafford Leigh-Mallory, C-in-C Fighter Command at the time of his formal appointment early in 1944. Mr John Ehrmann, in volume five of *Grand Strategy* in the British Official History of the Second World War states that Leigh-Mallory was provisionally appointed at the Cairo Conference. His revealing phrase is: 'The sea and air forces for Overlord itself had already been placed initially under British officers; the naval forces under Admiral Sir Bertram Ramsay, and the air forces under Air Chief Marshal Sir Trafford Leigh-Mallory.'[74] Hence it may be inferred that since Spaatz's new command had just been approved—it was in fact 'moved' by Eisenhower, at the Conference, although the impetus came from Arnold and the Joint Chiefs—the British airman's promotion simply fitted into the pattern of alternating American and British commanders at the most senior levels. But although it was reasonable for the British representatives at the Cairo Conference to see the matter in that light, and although it may be proper for a British historian to have done so later, the manoeuvres that characterised the control of Allied Air Forces in the spring of 1944 show that more was at stake than an alliance version of Buggin's turn.

The Cairo Conference failed to decide, or did not choose to settle, exactly what Leigh-Mallory should command, or for how long and under whose direction. If Spaatz had extended his purely American theatre appointment to this Allied command, there is little doubt that *all* available air forces, including Bomber Command, would have been placed directly, if not necessarily indefinitely, under his control. In the event, Leigh-Mallory's authority was disputed, his command came to possess but the size and composition characteristic of 'tactical' air forces, while the strategic air forces continued to pursue a much more independent line than any proponent of co-ordinated effort would have wished. Leigh-Mallory was in fact formally designated Commander in Chief of the Allied Expeditionary Force; the key word here is 'expeditionary', indicative of control for a limited period, and, by implication, with limited responsibilities. The Official History and Craven and Cate agree that, by comparison, 'General Spaatz had been placed in a position which, for an Air Commander, was unprecedented. . . . his influence . . . presently came to rival that of Sir Charles Portal himself'.

Thus Bomber Command, except for April to June of 1944, escaped the net of the combined offensive planners, yet it is no exaggeration to say that, as on previous occasions, less time spent on the juggling for position just described, and more attention given to strategic requirements might well have seen Bomber Command brought firmly within the ambit of the CBO directives. Should such a situation have arisen late in 1943, Harris would doubtless have deployed all his familiar arguments, which, from long practice, could range ingeniously from criticism of targets selected by such bodies as the Ministry of Economic Warfare, through statements about a willingness to comply with such requests when the time was ripe, to citing instances when attacks of the desired type had in fact been executed. He had also growing evidence of the skill and versatility of Bomber Command in executing that part of the Casablanca–Pointblank Directives, described with such convenient vagueness as ' . . . the undermining of the morale of the German people to a point where their armed resistance is fatally weakened'. However, unlike the argumentative days of 1942, Harris in 1943 was spared the need to sell or justify his conception of Bomber Command's role. Such proselytising as was necessary was done, indeed, by the Ministry of Home Security (by this time virtually a branch of the Air Ministry), which, on 19 October, surveyed the three months between July and September, and produced grim and presumably satisfying figures of Germans dehoused and, almost as an afterthought, the estimated 'production loss in factories', computed by a new and exceedingly vague criterion apparently based on destruction of or damage to 'worker dwellings', namely 'production loss in man months'.[75]

But aside from these useful weapons in the verbal battle that seems inseparable from war at the top, and apart from the convenient excuse for Harris provided by the American determination to get the best commands, there was the inescapable fact that daylight precision bombing had not come off—or at any rate not yet. Hence night area bombing must go on. It was all very well for the Ministry of Economic Warfare to declare after the 8th's raid on Schweinfurt–Regensburg on 17 August that these targets were 'ready for immediate re-attack'. Eaker knew that what was strategically feasible was operationally impossible. But Harris knew it better, and therefore proceeded in the last two months of 1943 to give his biggest demonstration to date that what was operationally possible was in itself the determinant of a strategic air offensive.

Due to several causes, including some trouble with labour in factories which in August affected the production of Lancasters,[76] late summer and early autumn had been a relatively quiet period for Bomber Command, although there was little change in the overall rate of city burning operations, complemented by an increasing number of Mosquito sorties and the continuous development in even heavier bombs, better marking aids to the Main Force stream and the establishment and rapid growth in responsibility of 100 Group. In the *Bomber Command Review* for the third quarter of 1943 (by which time it had patently become a vehicle for Harris' views, even utilising his curious phraseology, wherein 'the Hun' or 'the cities of the Plain' had a sort of Old Testament justice meted out to them), 17,902 sorties are recorded, as against 8,516 for the same period in 1942. Interspersed with an assertation that the Bomber Command campaign had prevented a German summer offensive in Russia, and a declaration that 'bombing, in a word, has all but won the war', were cold statements to the effect that 'many of the towns . . . such as Aachen and Remscheid . . . needed no second visit'.

Nevertheless, although Harris found no necessity at this time to defend his strategy to higher authority, the *Review* contains one of his most characteristic philippics. After quoting from (unnamed) newspaper reports in neutral countries about the 'cripples' which had once been proud German cities, those on the Allied side who dared question the efficacy of Bomber Command's achievements were denominated as 'sentimentalists, unceasing advocates of the Second Front and vendors of panacea

targets'. Perhaps an overall missing rate of over five per cent just prior to
and for the last quarter of 1943 had something to do with this point of view.
Bomber Command was not suffering the kind of losses on specific
occasions which was inhibiting the 8th's operations, but the missing rate
was creeping inexorably upwards and, for three raids on Berlin between
23 August and 4 September, it rose to seven per cent. Moreover the *Review*
made no claim that these attacks achieved any particular success. That,
however, was not the *Review's* function; as a vehicle for the Trenchard/
Harris philosophy, assertion was infinitely preferable to analysis.

The Road to Berlin

Despite the figures just recorded, it was in November that Bomber Command set out in full force on the long road to Berlin. On 3 November
Harris had said in a memorandum to Churchill: 'We can wreck Berlin
from end to end if the USAAF will come in on it. It will cost us between
400–500 aircraft. It will cost Germany the war.'[77] Although only the first
part of this prophecy proved accurate—and that possibly in a sense which
Harris would not wish to have claimed (Bomber Command alone lost
523 aircraft attacking Berlin between November 1943 and March 1944,
or most of its front-line operational strength for that period)[78]—he
could claim with some justification that the German capital was a target
which transcended nice distinctions between area and precision targets—
as the 8th Air Force in late 1944 and in 1945 was to demonstrate by inflicting casualties on the Hamburg and Dresden scale. Churchill ordered
Berlin to be bombed in 1940 as a defiant gesture; although unscathed
then and virtually immune from attack in the difficult nights of 1941 and
1942, the Casablanca Directive ensured that 'provision was also made for
bombing such essentially *political** objectives as Berlin'.
   Although this phrase was typically diffuse (Berlin and its environs
ranked with the Ruhr in industrial importance and outweighed it in the
manufacture of precision instruments, electrical components and the
like),[79] Harris had here, as on other occasions, a text which he could put
to good use. His winter campaign, the battle for Berlin as it came to be
known, may even have aroused some envy among the commander and
senior officers of the 8th Air Force. 'There were those who were so convinced of the value of blind bombing that they advocated adding to the

* Author's italics.

CBO plan a frankly stated programme of area bombardment, for the winter months at least which would be similar to and supplementary to the area bombing campaign being carried on by the RAF.'[80] By the time these sentiments were uttered, the 8th was using blind bombing radar; Berlin, although frequently obscured by overcast, would have presented a problem mainly for German fighters. Moreover, the capital was easy to find and it would have been hard to miss hitting *something* down there. From this distance of time one can see that the temptations for American commanders to subject Berlin to what we may call the Tokyo treatment were hard to resist.

They were resisted however at the time, and Bomber Command set out alone. Between 18 November and 30 December Berlin was attacked eight times; 14,074 tons of bombs, or more than one third of the total for the last quarter, were unloaded; 4,081 sorties were flown; 3,646 aircraft attacked; 183 aircraft were lost—a missing rate of less than four per cent, or not much more than half of that which was to be endured between January and March 1944. For this relatively economical loss rate, the claim was made that 40–70 per cent of the built-up area was damaged. No claims were made for industrial loss, except within the very broad definition of 'man months'.[81] Nevertheless, although use of such a term after four years of war is a revealing indication of the impossibility of accurately measuring industrial loss caused by area bombing (however vastly different this was during 1943 in material, planning and execution compared with the preceding months of trial and error), it was reasonable for Bomber Command headquarters to suppose that the urban sprawl of Berlin, comparable in its mixture of housing and industry with London or New York, was suffering in this respect as well as in all others. And post-war investigation by the British and American strategic bombing teams has proved this assumption to be right.[82] Nevertheless, it was left to Harris himself to sum up the battle when it was halted in March 1944: ' ... the strength of the German defences would in time reach a point at which night bombing attacks by existing methods and types of heavy bomber would involve percentage casualty rates which could not in the long run be sustained.'[83]

Although former members—and in some cases, serving members—of Bomber Command from Harris to senior staff officers, with whom this central issue has been discussed, have all claimed, looking back over 20 years, that they would have gone on, the C-in-C's own summing-up is on the record. What crews were prepared to endure and what Harris was forced to accept are not the same thing at all. Even though it can fairly be said that the battle's overall loss rate was increased by the defeats suffered over Leipzig and Nuremberg in February and March[84] rather than by the attrition endured over Berlin, the summing-up is still a damaging comment on an area compaign postulated in Harris' terms. A variety of partial alternatives were open, including the notion of an all-Mosquito Main Force.[85] But it is clear enough now that, although in March Bomber Command was on the verge of great success, its dilemma then was comparable to that of the 8th in the preceding October.

Thus though we have moved a little way ahead of our narrative, and to 1944 properly belongs a description of how further tactical and technical developments in Bomber Command[86] enabled all elements to switch to Overlord targets in April with more success and less heart-burning than might have been imagined earlier, it seems appropriate here to attempt an assessment of the area bombing strategy after its most sustained 12 months of operations.

It is first of all necessary to stress again how little interference Harris enjoyed in evolving a strategy whose immediate dividends even in late 1943 reflected the fact that something devastating was being inflicted on Germany rather than anything which could be precisely related to the requirements of Allied strategy—specifically the destruction of the German Air Force in production and in being. Secondly, it should be noted that, although the Ruhr, Hamburg and Berlin are the 1943 landmarks, one object of the Harris strategy was to give 'area' the widest possible geographical, not merely topographical, meaning. The last quarter witnessed an increasing number and a mounting weight of attacks on 'distant targets'. These attacks had begun substantially in the third quarter, and in citing them to higher authority—most often Churchill himself—Harris was able to argue that not only was Bomber Command spreading destruction far and wide but that more attacks were being made on cities which contained elements of the aircraft industry than were even being contemplated by the 8th.[87] Thirdly, we must engage in some simple statistical calculation in an attempt to draw up a balance sheet of profit and loss, not in terms of effort made to damage caused but in terms which we now can see are the only ones which are meaningful for the 1943 offensive and the objectives it was designed to attain.

Harris' 'freedom' has already been described in one negative sense— that the jockeying for appointments on high excluded the Commander-in-Chief Bomber Command and served but to underline the convenient (to him) isolation in which a demonstrably independent strategy could be pursued; this rare independence was further underlined by Harris' private hot line to Churchill. In 1943 that line was in full use, as Harris records with open satisfaction in his memoirs. But it should also be understood that Harris enjoyed a comparably unique degree of freedom from his Service superiors. The genesis of this relationship has already been described, but it must once again be emphasised that Portal and the Air Staff were loath to direct a commander who was performing prodigies of destruction, even though these might be rather hard to define in terms other than those of *Götterdämmerung*. 'The Air Staff directives had tended to become commentaries upon what was already being done rather than instructions about what ought to be attempted .... Any departure from this principle met with short shrift at High Wycombe.'[88] But in 1943 a more subtle element crept into this factor. Harris was by then a successful *British* commander. A suggestion by Arnold in September that Harris and his Bomber Command be placed under American control was given the curtest refusal by Portal[89]; Sinclair, when commenting on Portal's related exposition of what Bomber Command was achieving and of what, by inference, the 8th was failing to achieve, referred to the 'salutary drubbing'[90] which Arnold had received. This was not a sentiment confined to the Secretary of State for Air.

Portal, indeed, pursuing his usual wayward course where the nature and objectives of a strategic air offensive were concerned, found it convenient on occasion to utilise Harris' arguments and figures, thus further strengthening the latter's position. It was at the Cairo and Teheran Conferences of November and December that Portal drew attention to the 'tremendous importance'[91] of the Bomber Command area attacks. He pointed out that 38 German towns had been 'more or less seriously attacked'[92] and that, from their total built-up area of 133 square miles, some 32½ square miles had been devastated. Sir Charles Portal estimated that:

> perhaps 6,000,000 people or more have been made homeless and have spread alarm and despondency in the areas into which they have gone. The replacement of clothing and movable goods destroyed in these devastating attacks was, he believed, either impossible or 'can only be done at the direct expense of the war effort'. He had 'no shadow of doubt' that German morale was 'at an extremely low ebb', and he believed that Bomber Command might be 'at least half-way along the road of industrial devastation towards the point where Germany will become unable to continue the war'.[93]

This was another text good enough for Harris; with Portal's American colleagues musing over Schweinfurt and its like, with the unkind reminder too that not only were CBO targets being avoided by the 8th, but that precision bombing was sometimes more apparent than real (the city centre of Münster had been bombed from a clear sky on 10 October),[94] Harris was given a virtual mandate for a straight run to his particular targets. Portal was very shortly thereafter to qualify his praise of area bombing, and to say on 23 December ' . . . if it had been tactically possible to concentrate one quarter of our total bombs dropped on Germany upon any one of several classes of target, e.g. oil, ball-bearing, aero-engines or airframe factories, and possibly many others, the war would by now have been won'.[95] Portal was governed in this 'iffy' remark by figures of a dramatic increase in German fighter production, shown to him in November by Air Vice-Marshals Bottomley and Inglis, Deputy Chief of the Air Staff and the Assistant Chief of the Air Staff (Intelligence).[96] Although these two senior officers differed in their views about Harris' campaign, Bottomley being at best lukewarm and Inglis a convinced supporter, they were forced to join with Portal in agreeing that a situation where, 'on the eve of the planned date of Overlord, it was expected that the total front-line strength of the Luftwaffe would be 5,450 and, of the fighter force, 2,865',[97] could not be allowed to remain buried beneath verbiage about the morale of the German people being at an extremely low ebb.

But by this time Harris was in full cry once more. Moreover, not only was he bombing Berlin with, as yet, no damaging losses, but he could fairly claim that, in bombing Munich, Leipzig, Stuttgart, Hanover, Kassel and Frankfurt as well, he was the only commander making an effective assault on the cities around which a large part of the expanding German aircraft industry was believed to be concentrated. In September Bottomley had deplored the lack of Bomber Command attacks on such centres, and in a minute to Portal had listed Leipzig, Kassel, Brunswick, Gotha and Bernsburg as towns 'whose destruction . . . would be particularly valuable to the reduction of the German fighter industry'.[95] Only Kassel at that time had been attacked by the 8th Air Force (on 28 July),[99] and in fact the rest were to remain immune from daylight attack until the balance tilted sharply in January and February 1944.

But Harris had not only covered his front, he counter-attacked in a minute to Churchill of 3 November, in which he listed 20 towns as 'virtually destroyed'; 19 as 'seriously damaged'; and nine as 'damaged'. Among these 48 targets lurked four of the towns on Bottomley's list; Kassel was in the 'virtually destroyed' category, while to Brunswick, Leipzig and Augsburg was reserved further treatment implied in their being but in the 'damaged' category. Only Gotha and Bernburg remained, but if required, Harris could have pointed to comparably 'selective'—although single—attacks on Peenemunde and, earlier in the year Friedrichshafen.[100] Although one can pick holes in most of Bomber Command's claims for this, or any other period, and although significant variations in the area strategy might have been possible—specifically in the use of Mosquitoes, had they been available in greater numbers—there can be no doubt that Harris ended the year in a position of real authority and with some impressive achievements and arguments to fortify him for 1944.

But the net cost had been high, and the strategic gains hard to determine. In outline, through 1943, Bomber Command, in two main campaigns and continuous support and subsidiary raids twice lost its effective nightly front line strength of 500 heavies, or approximately half of those theoretically available for operations. Approximately 1,000 aircraft were lost outright, predominantly from enemy fighters, thus producing a mean missing rate over a period of 25 major operations of more than four per cent, exclusive of damaged aircraft which were written off.[101] The German Air Force suffered comparable losses of aircraft (and of experienced fighter pilots), although not in a straight numerical reckoning, and the German defences as a whole were forced to commit increasing resources in men (and women) and material, even although the youngest and the fittest military manpower was not affected—as has been claimed.[102] 1943 was thus a campaign of attrition so far as the strategic air offensive was concerned, whose outcome at the year's end was quite undecided. In that sense, Bomber Command, like the 8th Air Force, had not achieved the Pointblank Objective—by the end of 1943.

According to tables in the final report of the British Bombing Survey Unit, of any major force of an average 500 sorties attacking, 250 bombed inside the target area and 200 within three miles of the aiming point as marked by the Pathfinder Force with ground or sky markers released from high altitude.[103] Since the aiming point in 1943 increasingly became a prominent feature in the city centre, the criterion for target selection for a major attack, or a series of them, mostly required a city with a central built up area of at least six miles radius. Definitions of 'built-up' varied, enabling cities of 100,000 and upwards to be included. It should be noted therefore that, with notable exceptions—but invariably on single occasions —and setting aside the progressive devastation of German cities as such, the measurement of industrial damage could only reside in the crude criterion of 'man months' already referred to. We know now that area bombing in 1943 did do much damage to German industry, especially in U-boat construction and specialised equipments, like new types of airborne radar; the former were largely fabricated well inland and the latter came into the 'light industry' category which was common to any large city, most notably Berlin.[104]

Equally, we now know that German heavy industry and basic manufacturing capacity was not seriously damaged in 1943; despite the devastation of the Ruhr, foundries and the like continued to operate; there was no shortage of machine tools; there was no grave shortage of raw materials, although Speer and his associates feared the day when Allied intelligence would grasp the fact that much of German industry, like its politics, was founded on synthetics.[105] But above all, aircraft production was virtually unaffected in terms of aircraft which had to be destroyed before command of the air was secured. Hence the growing tonnage of bombs dropped by Bomber Command in 1943 is a measure of effort; it cannot be regarded as significant if it is intended as a measure of industrial damage or strategic success. But finally, although bombing accuracy in 1943 increased to the point where approximately half the crews in all aircraft despatched found and bombed the target area, only three-fifths bombed within three miles of the aiming point. And although this percentage was an improvement on 1942 (approximately two-fifths bombed within three miles then),[106] the number of dud high-explosive bombs remained at a steady 25 per cent.[107] Given the primary role of incendiaries, this percentage is perhaps not important.[108] Nevertheless, we are still left with the unavoidable fact that, on the most generous reckoning, only 300 sorties out of an average 500 on a night's operation succeeded literally or figuratively in achieving their aim. Arguably, this figure is insignificant in a history of an offensive based on strategic theories deriving from notions of 'moral' and 'morale'. But, by March 1944, such a figure was to be but another weapon in the hands of those who forced Bomber Command, at last, on to a new course.

The Price of Attrition

War in the Air—Fourth Year

As the war settled into its fourth year, the strategic air offensive against Germany began to assume some of the characteristics of any protracted and indecisive campaign, relying for its continuance on the disciplined stubborness of its human participants at the combat level rather than on strategic imperatives or striking advance in weapons and equipment. Although to Britons, Americans and Germans at the levels of decision making, the strategic imperatives did become clear as the months went by, and although weapons and equipment did acquire new dimensions of destructiveness and scope, the war in the air to the men who fought it did not change much, except to become bloodier and, to the small minority which interested itself in tactics and technology, more complex and challenging. The large majority found the going tougher, the complexities more bothersome. A briefing of night-bomber crews in the summer of 1943 was a very different affair from the brisk, inaccurate summary of route, hazards and target, which typified those of 1939 and 1940, and even the more painstaking but hardly more informative sessions of 1941 and 1942. Debriefings were comparably involved and protracted, as Bomber Command reached out at last for hitherto elusive targets and encountered in consequence a ferocity of opposition previously unknown. But the numbers of operational aircrew in any of the three air forces who simply gave up or were grounded for what the Royal Air Force understandingly if imprecisely calls 'lack of moral fibre' was small indeed.[1]

It was not, never had been and was never to be a war in which much room was available for independent action, a role traditionally welcome to the British fighting man and capable of affording relief even to services more trammelled and respectful of authority—characteristics of the US and German Air Forces. Service in the few special units in Bomber Command like 617 Squadron, the low-level marking squadrons in 5 Group, 100 Group and the Mosquito squadrons of the 'Light Night Striking Force' of 8 Group, could and did afford such relief; the 8th and later the 15th Air Forces had nothing comparable to these units, although Pathfinders were given an increasingly important role.[2] The German fighter pilots and, in the airborne radar-equipped aircraft, the fighter crews certainly sought out their enemy; even with 'tame sow' tactics, much of the fighter pilot's dash and initiative was required if success was to be gained. Indeed, when the 'wild sows' were introduced in August, they appear to have quickly, if temporarily, acquired some of the characteristics of the fighter pilots of fiction.

> These single-engined night fighter units formed a motley collection, loosely organised and rather like guerilla bands in their attitude to authority. They were composed of volunteers drawn from all sections of the GAF including highly qualified ex-bomber pilots, pilots in disgrace seeking reinstatement, social failures, etc. However, the éclat of their early success was undoubtedly achieved by Herrmann's original band of ex-bomber pilots, whose individual scores were considerable and who continued to secure victories as long as they survived.[3]

But, this British account concludes: 'The vast majority of the single-engined night fighter pilots had no such tale of success to tell, but lived on the reputation and glory of the skilful few'. Not only that, but the German fighter pilots and radar operators had no sense of eventual victory to sustain them. Men in combat are not much interested in issues outside their immediate ken, and those who fought over Germany were no exception. Nevertheless, the German Air Force had been designed and trained for offence and had operated in that role for three years. The bombing of Germany as late as 1942 had been a matter of concern to (some) senior officers, not to the average flying man. In 1943, for the first time, the latter could begin to see on his daily or nightly sorties, just what his country was up against. It must be accounted to the credit of these men that despite such a realisation, coupled with the demoralising effects of lower training standards and, eventually, crippling shortages of fuel, they stuck to their enemy and, except for the final days, could never be regarded as a spent force. The bomber crew which did so usually paid the price pretty quickly.

These factors apart, there was, of course, the one essential difference between the métier of those attacking and those defending, and it has been well expressed by Craven and Cate:

> The heavy bomber offensive was an impersonal sort of war and monotonous in its own peculiar way. Day after day, as weather and equipment permitted, B.17s and B.24s went out, dropped their deadly load and turned homeward. The immediate results of their strikes could be photographed and assessed by intelligence officers in categories reminiscent of high school 'grades'—bombing was excellent, good, fair or poor. But rarely was a mission or a series of missions decisive . . . Thus there was little visible progress, such as Allied troops could sense as they pushed Rommel's forces back from El Alamein towards Cap Bon, to encourage the 8th Air Force. . . . A few missions stood out because of the size of the force despatched (as Ludwigshafen, 30 December 1943), or because of ferocious defence (as Schweinfurt, 14 October), or because of brilliant bombing (as Marienburg, 9 October). For a mother who lost a boy in the 8th's 121st mission, that operation was uniquely and tragically important, but for a more detached reader (as for many of the participants) it was pretty much like another.[4]

Such an epitaph on collective endeavour finds no place in the British Official History; tribute there takes the form of a bare summary of casualties suffered—approximately half of all those who flew on operations.[5] But the privilege of interviewing the British and Commonwealth participants in this most impersonal of campaigns does bear out very closely the truth of the perceptive words just quoted. And just as the campaign was impersonal, so too written recollections of it seem muffled. The passage of time accounts for much of this but, as noted in the Preface, it is a curious fact that the campaign lacks a chronicle to rank with *Winged Victory*, *The Last Enemy* or *Flight to Arras*. The survivors of the strategic air offensive seem more remote from their experiences than most men who have pitted courage and skill against death or mutilation. The few personal narratives which were written have a curiously unconvincing air, even when modestly, sometimes artlessly describing operations calling for a very rare combination of qualities. *Enemy Coast Ahead* by Guy Gibson, hero of the dam raids, is a case in point, with its schoolboy jokes and suggestions that the whole thing is a kind of party. *Serenade to the Big Bird* by a B.17 co-pilot, Bert Stiles, by contrast, is written in a sub-Hemingway prose, which nevertheless effectively conveys the mingled fear, nausea, shock and relief on returning, experienced in a daylight raid over Germany. Perhaps only the bizarre *Catch-22* by Joseph Heller, woven round the experiences of a bombardier serving in a medium bombardment squadron in Italy, breaks through the impersonality barrier, and then in a peculiarly subjective way.

The clue to why, from nearly half a million men, virtually nothing of significance has been recorded lies in the fact that bombing operations were impersonal in the sense that the enemy was too big—'Germany'—and that even when it appeared in sharp focus in the form of the sudden fighter attack at night or the headlong assault by day, bomber crews could do little but fight their way through as best they might. Bomber crews, individually and collectively, were fatalists on the whole; you 'bought it' or you didn't. Although a better than average squadron or station commander would argue the dangers of this attitude and endeavour to train and lead their crews into exercising some choice—even the limited but essential one of keeping alert and ensuring that all crew members could size up and communicate to each other a combat situation, quickly and clearly—repeated operations and the physical mental and emotional toll of each made it hard to get such messages across, particularly to battle-happy crews, that subversive minority. For the daylight offensive crews the strain was maybe greatest of all; there was nothing to do at all but try to stick in formation; 'From the day you first get in a B.17 they say formation flying is the secret. They tell you over and over. Keep those planes tucked in and you'll come home.'[6] But nearly 80,000 young men did not, or did so wounded.

No such formula was applicable to night bombing; the concept of the concentrated bomber stream, first operated in 1942, was designed to pass as many aircraft as possible as quickly as possible through the boxes of the Kammhuber Line, thus presenting an embarrassment of choice to the fighter, not a chance for the bombers to defend themselves by covering fire, as with the B.17s and B.24s. The stream, however, only flowed out to the target; thereafter it was every bomber crew for itself. But in making that point—which was of far greater significance in terms of aircraft lost than the operational research section of Bomber Command ever appears to have realised—one comes close to the explanation of what kept men flying. The crew was everything; the individual as such, and in combat, was very little. The pilot in a British bomber (the first pilot in an American) was the captain, whatever his rank, but this meant far less to him and the men who flew with him than the title suggests. Unlike the captain of a gun turret, commander of a tank or of a section of riflemen, the captain of a heavy bomber in the Royal or American Air Force in World War Two was usually but *primus inter pares*, although he could certainly be the captain of the crew in fact as well as name if he wished or chose, or had the character for it.

The most effective crews would appear to have been led in this way;

from the evidence of many interviews, it also seems likely that such crews did stand a better chance of survival than their less-disciplined or more fatalistic comrades. One very experienced former Halifax pilot who served in the hard-hit 4 Group, went so far as to say that when the 'good crews', as he called them, began to be lost towards the end of 1943, morale was affected to the extent at least of the survivors becoming grimly aware of the mounting odds against them.   Halifax squadrons were suffering particularly heavily at the time compared with Lancaster squadrons, and this comment, like every scrap of evidence based on personal experience, must be evaluated accordingly. Nevertheless this pilot's notes, made at the time and supplementing the recollections, log books and letters of many others, make it clear that the crews which evoked respect and whose survival or loss was a kind of yardstick of the squadron or the station's fortunes, were those which continued to train that bit harder in non-operational periods and were determined to keep together wherever and whenever possible—but equally, were crews whose captains had no hesitation in getting rid of any member who didn't measure up to his standards.

There was no absolute measurement for a good crew member, other than basic discipline, technical competence and a conscious willingness to merge his individuality into that of the crew as a whole. There was no formula for leadership, but this truth was peculiarly relevant to relations between seven or eight men, all NCOs or above, predominantly from the same kind of social and economic background (differing, in the Royal Air Force, markedly from the Royal Navy and the Army in this respect), cooped up for hours on end, enduring monotony shot with sudden and extreme danger, performing duties which called for vigilance, common sense and, excepting the special units, a modest degree of technical flair rather than individual dash or expertise. Born navigators, air bombers (bombardiers in American parlance), wireless operators, flight engineers or gunners were as rare as born pilots, and those who tried to pretend they were so endowed not infrequently flew their aircraft into the ground, lost their way, missed the target, failed to maintain communication or watch their dials—or spot, let alone report, the fighter coming up fast from a nearly blind corner. There were naturally gifted men, just as there were a few naturally outstanding leaders at all levels. But for every Bennett, Walker, Gibson or Cheshire there were hundreds of captains whose leadership was but the highest common factor of disciplined courage in their crews. These were the captains who maintained the standards of their squadrons, who had taken the trouble before going on operations of picking and welding a crew together, who kept Bomber Command and the 8th Air Force in the front line when the going was at its roughest. And between late summer 1943 and spring 1944 the going was very rough indeed.

There were, however, some other factors peculiar to the combat side of the bombing of Germany, and to understand them we must let the mind's eye rove over the battlefield. In a sense there were two battlefields, that of England's East Anglia, stretching north to Lincolnshire and the East Riding of Yorkshire, and a rarely seen but everywhere potentially hostile Europe, of which Western Germany was the hated and dreaded major sector. The contrast between the two could hardly have been more absolute, yet in a way it was oddly similar to the rear areas and the trenches of Flanders and Picardy in an earlier war. East Anglia, the counties of Norfolk, Suffolk, Essex, Huntingdon and Cambridge was, like Lincolnshire and the East Riding, the rear area, an analogy which is the more apt if we compare the solid country houses that formed the headquarters of formations within Bomber Command and the 8th Air Force to the châteaux in which the subordinates of Haig and Pershing lived in that earlier campaign of attrition.

The rear area in the later war has always been one of special peace and individual beauty. Although in winter the wind from the North Sea blows across those flat lands, shallow valleys and unimportant hills lying under enormous skies with great and seemingly infinite severity, the prevailing impression is one of peace. 'Now we came to the most beautiful country in the world', wrote an American pilot in 1917, echoing an Englishman whose words must bring buried experiences flooding back to any who served in this campaign and who may read these pages.

> From any point of vantage, the gentle landscape of farmland and woodland rolls away, mile after mile, to the dim horizon or the sea. Slowly and subtly the colours change with the seasons and the crops; corn and roots, stubble and ploughland, olland and pasture, gorse and bracken, the beechwoods and the ash-carrs and the oaks in the hedgerows, all contribute to build up a scene which increasingly alters as the months go by. Unchanged against the ever-varying background of colour stand the grey flint towers, rising in every village above cottage roofs or from groups of ancient trees. Each tower represents many centuries of history; it stood there before the cottages and the trees, and it will outlast them, an emblem of the continuity of English life.[8]

It was from such a countryside that the crews left for their flights to the unknown, from Downham Market and Upwood, North Creake and Little Snoring, Woodhall Spa and Pocklington, Ludford Magna and

Elsham Wolds and many more; Snetterton Heath and Thorpe Abbotts, North Pickenham and Framlingham, Grafton Underwood and Alconbury, and again as many more, the stations for the night and day campaign spreading across all eastern England, until by the time of Overlord well over a hundred were operational, backed by the bases of the parent formations up to Bomber Command and the 8th Air Force headquarters at High Wycombe, joined in this location if little else, discreetly hidden in a fold of the Chilterns, yet conveniently remote from the sometimes bitter exchanges among higher authority in London, only 40 miles away.

But when crews had taken their last look at England they were on their own. Crews of the 8th could see their comrades in formation, but steel and plexiglass isolated them nonetheless. Bomber Command crews saw their compatriots at dusk, wheeling and turning, seeking their place in the stream,[9] hastening east or south, over a grey North Sea or blacked-out London, but soon night fell and the sense would strain for the first flak, along the Dutch coast maybe or from the occasional ship. In daylight raids, though Western Europe was spread beneath, there was little time to look down at the larger chequerboard of northern France or the faint details of the Westphalian Plain. At night, although, as one former air gunner said, 'you could read a book over Berlin' by the glow of spreading and ascending fires, few details of the land beneath appeared. 'We lost our way once after bombing Nuremberg', recalls one Stirling pilot. 'Came back over Germany in daylight. It was funny, seeing Germany down below.' Crews of the low-level Mosquitoes which marked 5 Group targets maybe had some sense of place, 'racing to and fro over the rooftops', in Mr Irving's exact phrase,[10] and the Lancaster crews, which flew at 20 feet to bomb Augsburg in April 1942, certainly experienced it in 'a spectacular journey across half of Europe',[11] where workers in the fields were seen clearly as spring pasture, wood and village streaked by. Squadron Leader Nettleton, leading the attack, recalled 'a fat woman wearing a blue blouse and a white skirt, and horses bolting at the roar of his engines, with the ploughs to which they were attached bumping behind them'.[12] But mostly the front line was seen dimly, through smoke and cloud or a hellish glow.

It is not surprising, therefore, that England in the dawn or as the B.17s and B.24s limped back in the darkening afternoon or sunset was a sight which acted on even the most stolid and experienced of crews. England was—or looked—beautiful, a sanctuary to men who rarely lived to complete an operational tour. In issuing that reminder, however, of the unique odds against survival entailed in the bombing of Germany, we come up against a morale factor which, allied to the youth and resilience

of the crews, explains a good deal about how they kept going. Unlike
the man in the gun turret, the tank or the slit trench, they returned to hot
food and warm beds, to quiet, or to sounds and sights that could be heard
and enjoyed before sleep came, ordinary things, reminders of normal
life, a combine harvester or bird song, a dog barking or peaceful clouds.
Around them lay villages and towns where they were especially welcomed
—and where, in the stained glass of Lincoln Cathedral and in many less
illustrious memorials, their sacrifice, their operations and their missions
are recorded. It was the wife of a Bomber Command Group Commander,
someone in an unusually good position to observe these young men,
who thought that at 20 or so shock and fear are soon erased in such sur-
roundings.

The collective outlook of Bomber Command crews reflected this curious
alternation between war and peace. So far as one can discover, only a
quite unrepresentative minority concerned itself with the issues or war and
peace. 'A good blaze' raised morale; not letting fellow crew members
down preserved it when other factors might have destroyed it; a good
night's sleep restored it. Not only were the wider issues ignored; the moral
issue of total war executed in an uniquely savage way left most minds
untroubled. Some, in retrospect, have said that the bombing of Dresden
was a 'mistake'; in one instance a former navigator, himself most perceptive and imaginative, recalled that when, after briefing for a raid on a
demonstrably non-industrial target, 'one man, at the back of the room,
called out "women and children first again", nobody took any notice.'
Obviously this incident does not tell the whole story; there were troubled
minds and uneasy consciences. But not many, and fewer as the years
went by. There was a widespread feeling, which Harris skilfully propagated to crews who believed in a commander so toughly fighting their
battles, that bombing would save Allied lives and shorten the war, even
though few seem to have believed that their efforts would win it. It is a
measure of Harris' gifts and the power of discipline and comradeship that
so many in Bomber Command died or were maimed in order to try and
prove the truth of their commander's convictions.

By 1943 the best of these young men were 'an enthusiastic body of
very ordinary people', in the words of a former Pathfinder, himself a
regular, who nevertheless recognised the overwhelming contribution of
the wartime airmen. Air Vice-Marshal Martin, one of Bomber Command's
outstanding pilots by any criterion, pointed out to me in this context
that by 1943 most of the pre-war regulars were 'dead, prisoners, or engaged
on staff duties or training'. The night battle was fought by the very young

and, moreover, by a majority from the Commonwealth, aided by the most gallant contribution from French, Polish, Czech and some other Allied air forces, whose members did not hesitate to bomb their own countrymen if the cause demanded it. So great was the Canadian contribution—and, it must be said, so keen the desire of the Canadian Government to have that contribution recognised—that on 1 January 1943 No. 6 (RCAF) Group was formed.[13] The Royal Australian and the Royal New Zealand Air Forces contributed squadrons entirely manned by their countrymen; but, like their Commonwealth and Allied compatriots, Australians and New Zealanders were found throughout Bomber Command as a whole. It is the considered verdict of the majority of former aircrew which I have interviewed, that the best crews were a small commonwealth in themselves.

By 1943 too the training of these Bomber Command crews had become an American–Commonwealth programme, which far outstripped the original Empire Air Training Scheme of 1939. Not only Canada, but the United States, South Africa and Southern Rhodesia (as it was then) received embryo pilots, navigators and air bombers. In the United States, potential Bomber Command crew members in these three categories (Royal Air Force wireless operators, flight engineers and air gunners were trained in the United Kingdom) learned their trades indeed with those earmarked for the 8th or 15th Air Forces. Although Craven and Cate, referring specifically to the inability of most of the 8th's pilots to keep their aircraft steady on course during the bombing run, comment sharply on 'the hasty training programme into which the AAF had been forced',[14] there is no evidence to suggest that operational standards differed much in the two air forces. The 8th's bombing accuracy was never all that it was cracked up to be. For that matter, navigation in Bomber Command continued to arouse criticism, particularly from a few vocal regular members, retired or still serving, of the Royal Australian Air Force, notably Air Vice-Marshal Bennett. The criticisms were harsh, but just, as the widespread desire among the crews to be issued with H_2S bears witness, despite the fact that it revealed their position to the enemy.

Gunnery by night and day was poor or fair in the vast majority of cases, although Bomber Command gunners could be excused their lack of success, bearing in mind that only in 1 Group, and there but partially and belatedly, was a .5-inch armament fitted. More surprising is that the inadequate .303-inch armament did not arouse gunners to a greater sense of vigilance. It must be emphasised again that in the vast majority of cases a successful fighter attack on the night bomber was due to intelligent stalking by the former, with the latter's crew quite unaware that its fate was about to be sealed.

Gunners in the 8th, however, despite the 'Fort' and the B.24 with their array of weapons, never scored anything like the successes claimed, even although the enemy was plain to see. But it may be mentioned here as a curious thing in the aerial battle that, although formation flying was fine in theory and lame ducks certainly were shot down very speedily, actual successes against German fighters were quite often scored by crews of isolated bombers. The point applies with greater validity to anti-submarine operations, where the heavily armed Royal Air Force Sunderland, or Liberators in either air force, frequently surprised intercepting German aircraft with their fire power and manoeuvrability. But aircraft in night and day bomber operations over Germany had their moments against the fighters too.

Yet unless the essential fact that the odds of surival were stacked against the bomber crews by night and day is firmly grasped, the nature of what was attempted and achieved cannot properly be understood. We have seen something of the strategy and something of the men who were put to its execution; the aircraft and equipment planned for or coming into service in 1942 with Bomber Command and the 8th Air Force have already been described, as have the tactics of night and day bombing which they made possible. The 8th Air Force development was simple and swifter. Although it was in 1942 and early 1943 weakened by Torch, and subsequently by heavy losses and the demands of competitors, the 8th was potentially and, by the end of 1943, actually a larger force than Bomber Command, with far greater resources to command as compensation for its more rapid wastage of crews and aircraft. Moreover, the 15th Air Force, whose operations, although not considered here in detail, were integral to the USAAF concept of the strategic air offensive, was, by the end of 1943, building up to around 24 groups, or a force not far short of Bomber Command's daily average operational strength.[15]

The Nature and Extent of Bomber Operations

With these various facts and factors in mind, let us now take some of the major night and day operations of 1943, namely:

Essen	5–6 March
The Dams Raid	16–17 May

Friedrichshafen	20–21 June
Hamburg	24 July–2–3 August
Marienburg	9 October
Schweinfurt	14 October
Wiener-Neustadt	2 November
Berlin and other distant targets	November–December
(Main Force and Mosquito attacks)	
Ludwigshafen	30 December

To some extent this selection is, and must be, arbitrary. There was no single operation and no series of them in 1943 or any other year of the offensive which conclusively proved a strategic, tactical or operational argument one way or the other, and thus introduced an entirely new dimension into aerial warfare. The selected operations merely represent phases in a campaign of attrition. Obviously, for all concerned, from the Commander-in-Chief and the Commanding General to an aircraftman second class or a private engaged in the humblest duty, each operation differed slightly, certainly demanding unvarying concentration, but inevitably producing differing psychological reactions or requiring particular application to meet a specific tactical or technical requirement—bombing on sky markers one night, or ground markers another and so on. Because night operations at this level were by 1943 much more involved and varied than daylight operations, the brief accounts of the nine selected raids is preceded by some description of how Bomber Command crews prepared for and executed their attacks during the most arduous period of the entire offensive.

The strain of participation was not confined to the eight or nine hours which a journey to Pilsen or across the Alps and back might take, or to the five hours or so of the average night's operation. The strain was always latent and, so far as individual operations were concerned, it dominated the lives of all involved, from the moment around 10 a.m. that crews knew they were 'on' for that night barring some last minute change in the weather. Unwittingly, certain books and films have given the impression that crews simply climbed into their aircraft as dusk fell, droned across Germany and back, and then landed in early dawn with the thought of bacon and eggs in the mess to sustain them. But in order to understand the strain and the complexity of heavy bomber operations it must be realised that the hours preceding take-off were in many ways far busier for aircrews than when they were airborne. Between the first crew enquiry at the flight office at 9 a.m. to that weary, thankful tumbling into bed the following morning, a whole 24 hours could pass, each minute of which made its particular demands.

From the moment that Harris 'laid on' an operation, and in the 'hole' at High Wycombe (as the underground operations room is still known) announced, that 'the target for tonight is Leipzig!'—or wherever it might be—the momentum quickened until the 4,000 or 5,000 aircrew who were to fight that particular night's battle were absorbed into a machine—Bomber Command at the peak of its operational effort. By the middle of 1943, certain routines and habits were well established, so that the flow of decisions, from Harris' final choice of main and alternative targets to Sergeant Jones in the air bomber's compartment of his Lancaster releasing 6,903 lb. of high explosive and incendiaries on target (he hoped), took on an apparent pattern of inevitability. Operations were frequently cancelled, and not infrequently at the last minute, especially as meteorological officers at all levels through Command, Group, base and station, came to exercise an influence reflecting their skill, experience and understanding of operational limitations; such cancellations obviously added to the sense of strain which affected the newest-joined member of an operational station, even if she was only a WAAF who made beds and polished buttons. But, if not this night, then the next, or another, and it was the wise member of a crew who could accept the inevitability of his lot once he had decided to be one of the 'bomber boys', and who, in consequence, set about his preparations for the battle in a calm and methodical fashion. In this he was helped not only by his individual experience or knowledge of the target selected, but by a growing corpus of information and precedents.

By the time of the Battle of the Ruhr in 1943 there were few targets of any importance in the *Bomber's Baedeker* which had not been visited by aircraft from Bomber Command. Even those seemingly fruitless and aptly named 'ice-flights' from French fields in 1939 played a modest part in yielding information about conditions, of weather, if little else, likely to be encountered in connection with a particular target at a given time of the year. The absolutely crucial information on the target's strategic significance and how it was defended obviously needed constant revision so that the intelligence officers' briefings (and subsequent debriefings) would bear some relation to the truth. But two caveats must be entered here in order that we may understand yet a little more of the operational factors governing any measurement of success or failure. 'Strategic significance' in Harris' mind first meant size of city; and whether it could be attacked with acceptable loss at a particular time of the year in the weather likely to obtain on a particular night; having decided to visit a city of (usually) 100,000 or more, its local attributes in terms of industrial importance could be described for the benefit of higher authority and the target's executioners—who were always briefed on factors of this kind, rarely that, as in the case of Dresden, it was full of refugees or was similarly suitable in terms of German lives which could be taken. But although crews were given all the information available about the target's importance, and given it in terms which organisations disenchanted with Bomber Command like the Foreign Office, the Ministry of Economic Warfare and (increasingly) the Anglican hierarchy could accept, they were rarely given much which could stand up to stringent examination on the basis of known facts.

As in 1939 (or 1945), little was *known* about German targets in 1943, other than that some were large and had clearly marked aiming points, and that others were the very devil to find and were just an urban sprawl covered with industrial haze when you got there. Photographic evidence told a great deal about dehousing but little that was conclusive about much else.[16] The evidence of Allied agents in Germany was usually fragmentary or unreliable, or out of date, or all three.[17] There was no reasonably secure means of warning them that an attack on a particular target was imminent, so that they might transmit information on its current place in the German war effort and therefore how it was defended. Obviously, it was the second point which interested crews. But information of this calibre came from signal intelligence and the deductions and inferences which the Air Ministry's Department of Scientific Intelligence drew from their interception, from captured equipment and from the reports of crews at their debriefings or at subsequent and larger-scale intelligence conferences for the more senior members of operational units and formations. Although by these methods a great deal was learned about German defences—and the Director of Scientific Intelligence and others could also forecast likely developments in this war of wits—not much was ever known about the defences of a particular target.

It is of course possible to argue that all the information in the world would not have altered the essential weakness of the bomber versus the fighter. To know that the target for tonight was defended in a certain way, that a given combination of coloured searchlight beams and flares meant a particular set of tactics by fighters or a new fire pattern by flak, was little help to a tired crew whose bomber was lumbering along at 180 m.p.h. belching flames from its exhaust and, in all probability, giving its position away by emissions from the array of devices with which it was equipped. A German fighter, one of the force directed from all over the Western Front and Germany on to the attacking stream, flying at twice to thrice the bomber's speed, had a sitting duck in its cannon sights—if eyes or radar picked it up. Fortunately, as bomber crews discovered, the sky is very large. It is not surprising that the blessed cry of 'bombs away' sent the bomber diving off into the haven of the dark, away from the flickering fingers of searchlights, the exposure of flares and the sudden thud of exploding shells. All too often, alas, it seems as though such release and relief led to a fatal relaxation of concentration. All too often then, or on the weary slog home, the fighters struck. But, that factor notwithstanding, crews wanted the best information they could get on what they might encounter on the night's operation.

Hence disciplined crews accepted the tedium of concentration on such information as was recorded in intelligence summaries and marked on target maps, and, while throughout the day the teleprinters were churning and their seniors were conferring, imprinted on their minds as much as possible about fighters, flak, flares and searchlights. There was, however, another reason why it made sense to check up on the defence as early as possible. By 1943 much of the available time before take off was absorbed by preparing a tolerably complex weapon, the four-engined bomber, for action, and on the main briefing, which was mostly concerned with the complexities of bombing on markers and all the other factors which that technique (plus the requirements of 'counter-measures') set in train. Also, and in late 1943, master bombers were introduced for the Main Force. Although none of these techniques imposed on bombing the rigid adherence of 8th Air Force crews to do what the lead plane did, they required a fair amount of hard work from all but the gunners, at the afternoon briefings, and required it with notebook, pencil and exactly synchronised watches.

There were three main aspects of the night's operation which crews were briefed on, other than the target's importance and enemy intelligence and intentions, namely, Pathfinder Force tactics (marking, and diversions by the 'Light Night Striking Force'), Main Force attacks and, after November 1943, 100 Group bluffs, feints, diversions and spoofs.[18] From June 1943 onwards, there was also occasional fighter cover, a development of the 1941 'Circus' operations, whereby Beaufighters, equipped with radar known as Serrate and designed for homing on the AI transmissions of German fighters, sortied in the assumed area of the main defensive concentration.[19] These tactics were unsuccessful, and the story of adequate fighter support to night bomber operations properly belongs to 1944. Nevertheless, the bomber crews had plenty to absorb, and had to do so on top of a day spent on their own squadron preparations (specifically the course which would be flown and the times for each check point or turn), quite apart from the matters already referred to. Before the main squadron briefing, usually at 1500 hours (there were separate briefings earlier for navigators and air bombers), each crew had checked their aircraft armament and fuel load, instruments, and above all, radar. Each aircraft had its own ground crew, under an experienced NCO. These men, unsung, unknown, unrewarded by any campaign medal (despite Harris' protestations and the merits of their case), kept the bombers flying, worked on them in the worst of winter weather and had a bond with their aircrew which was maybe some compensation for playing Martha's part. Then after aircraft checks and in the words of one who experienced this particular Chinese torture many times:

> ... at 1200 you join the others in the mess for lunch and eat what you can ... after a smoke you go to your room and try to rest for an hour. At 1430 you get up and put on flying kit ... then you go down to the briefing room and join the rest of the mob. A quick glance at the wall map and there is your target—Leipzig. Not so hot—or probably too hot!
> At 1500 in comes the Wing Co. and all is silent.
> Then on with the briefing—first the Intelligence Officer—giving targets, bomb load, routes, times, any spoof raids, supporting night fighters, method of target marking, diversion airfields on return.
> Then Met.—you hope for lots of cloud but the best you can get is 1/10 which is no use to anyone.
> Navigation goes over the route.
> Bombing leader gives you bombing gen—markers, etc.
> Signals for the w/ops.
> Engineer leader for revs, etc.
> Gunnery special gen to gunners.
> Finally the Wing Co. sums up the whole briefing and tries to give you some tactical gen but tactics are already laid down for you so you haven't much scope.
> Briefing over you troop out to flying control. ...

The key phrase in this laconic recital is, of course, 'tactics are already laid down for you so you haven't much scope'. It is the key phrase for two reasons. The marking procedures governed all that was done on the way to and over the target, and unless they were rigidly kept to you would miss the way, or miss the target, or get out of stream, or arrive early or late—any one of which could lead not merely to one careless or incompetent crew being shot down but could, and on more than one occasion did, give the route and target away prematurely to the defence, with inevitable consequences of a high missing rate and possibly lagging and a lack of concentration over target; moreover, the whole elaborate system would be called into question and the verbal battle between Bennett and the Main Force Group commanders would break out afresh. For in 1943 bombing on markers, despite the growing independence of 5 Group and the advent of master bombers, meant bombing on 8 Group marking; and there were many in Bomber Command then who resented Bennett's high-handed ways, disliked his power and criticised his squadrons' efforts. Some Main Force crews, who were convinced that the 8 Group squadrons rarely suffered serious losses, thought that Pathfinder marking was outright bad.

The second reason for the comment on tactics being so relevant to purely combat factors was that there *was* some scope for individual action once the target had been bombed. It seems likely, however, that many crews found the transition from being led to the target to pursuing evasive tactics after leaving it too great and the demands made too heavy. The pilot, gunners, navigator and wireless operator were the members most immediately affected here. It was a lot to ask of a bomber's solitary pilot (although the engineer was trained to fly the aircraft in an emergency) to weave steadily from side to side for hours on end while flying on course so that no prowling fighter pilot would have a fixed object to aim at; it was a comparable strain on gunners to keep staring into an impenetrable sky for a faint and fleeting glow from a fighter's exhaust or for a tiny and almost invisible silhouette; the captain who decided to fly a new route back to base presented a tired navigator with an unwelcome problem which, if unsolved (for radar aids might have become unservicable, have been switched off or be no guide for the route in question), would raise the option of breaking wireless silence and asking base for a 'fix'. If, in short, evasive tactics were too clever, a crew might find itself well and truly lost, with the blanket of the dark removed, the flight engineer juggling with fuel and engine revolutions, the whole thing a 'sticky do' indeed. Even so, aircraft whose crews favoured the long way round as the safest way home often made it back to base; there was always a crew or two in every squadron, usually one which had held together throughout a tour, which would be given up for lost as their surviving comrades trooped to bed or rose for breakfast, whose aircraft would be all of a sudden heard faintly over the surrounding fields and fens, louder over the perimeter, lights winking if it was still winter dark, coming back, better late than never. 'That's old F—Freddie' somebody would say as the late arrival settled down on the runway, maybe with fuel gauges that had stood at empty for an hour or more.

Thus, although the flight to the target was decided in advance and the way home offered choices which gave only marginally better chances of survival, there remained an area of controversy on tactics and techniques. Theoretically there was nothing complex about marking; the idea was straightforward, and had in fact been outlined by Air Vice-Marshal Slessor (as he then was) when commanding 5 Group in 1941. Difficulties arose because not every crew was equally competent, marking was not always accurate, and it became sufficiently complex by mid-1943 to make the target area a sea of colour (including enemy flares of every sort) among which main force crews hunted, and sometimes in vain, for the particular sky or ground primary markers which had been laid visually or by radar by the PFF squadrons (themselves, on occasion, marking on target finding flares laid by even earlier arrivals). To this was added as time went on the 'backing up' and 'centre' markers of selected Main Force aircraft. In the middle of all this, there was, one hoped, the fire from the target indicator for the aiming point—if the Germans hadn't spotted it and lit a spoof of their own. Crews hoped therefore that the master bomber had got the aiming point too—he should have, arriving ahead of the Main Force for this very purpose—and that bombs were raining down on the right part of the right target, from aircraft concentrated so closely that a few minutes more would see them all out of it.

It will be readily appreciated, therefore, that the master bombers and their deputies were not only important people—'in effect the personal representative of the Air Officer Commanding in the target area', as one of them has said—but welcome advisers to bemused crews. 'It's not always the instructions you notice so much as the relief at hearing a good English voice getting things organised ahead of you after that long slog through flak and dirty weather',[20] was one pilot's comment on the quiet and lucid instructions which brought some order into chaos. But aside from achieving that relief for Main Force crews, master bombers had to ensure precise timings for the successive waves and layers of bombers converging on the target. Different heights and speed (the Dresden raid in 1945, mounted by 722 Lancasters, had the appropriate code name of 'Plate Rack' for the Main Force) presented problems which crews of the small numbers of aircraft available before 1943 had at least been spared. Collisions over target were sadly frequent; crews of aircraft in the bottom layer had the unpleasant experience of 'friendly' bombs whistling down on them from above; left to itself in these conditions, with the always deadly flak and well-handled searchlights pumping shells and thrusting fingers of light into the sky, with 'tame' and 'wild' fighters in full cry, the Main Force would quickly have been reduced to shambles. Master bombers did not figure regularly in Main Force raids until late 1943, but they certainly made their presence felt thereafter very quickly.

So crews at briefings noted with extreme care every single detail of times, markers and target indicators; the notes were cryptic, and jotted down on the back of target maps: 'PFF Paramatta; RED TI at H-4; backed by GREEN; No skymarking; 23.15-23.18' or for a raid on Chemnitz in 1945, where, despite H_2S-based ground marking (thanks to mobile transmitters in France) it was obviously necessary to skymark as well: 'H-2100: PFF Controlled Newhaven ground marking + emergency Wanganui; Bombing order: M/Bs Instruction; centre of RED 8 GREEN T I; Centre of RED T I; Centre of GREEN T I; sky markers as GREEN/ RED stars; 15,000 ft; Hdg 055 (r).'[21]

The target maps themselves gave help only in the context of the marking plan; like their predecessors in simpler days, these maps were 1:100,000-based outlines of built-up areas, black against grey, with distances from the city centre marked in concentric circles representing one mile; railway lines likely to be visible at Main Force bombing heights of 10,000 feet and over were marked in white; occasionally, some particularly important feature, whether identifiable or not, was marked in cerise. But the general effect was little more definite than many an impression on the H_2S screen. For some major raids crews studied relief models, and photographs were available always to imprint details on the memory. But most Main Force crews went solely by the target indicators and the markers, and although the conscientious air bomber would ask for a second or even a third bombing run in order to bomb on *them*, there was a premium on delay which limited this kind of attention to detail to the most determined and resolute 'operators'.

But all crews, whether resolute or not, were subservient to the Bennett system in 1943, and it was for his squadrons' markers that their eyes strained in the long hours to the target. Each phase of the outward stage made its individual demands, especially on the navigators, who throughout the whole offensive used dead reckoning and visual checks—'that's Texel to port'—as well as wireless telegraphy, rudimentary astro-navigation and increasingly sophisticated radar. The classic, sailor's methods were needed because use of both wireless telegraphy and true radar alerted the enemy, and also because failures in the latter were frequent; moreover, until 1944 H_2S and *Oboe* sets were scarce. Indeed, it will simplify matters considerably if radar, especially *Oboe* and its later variant *G-H*, are regarded as blind bombing rather than navigational aids, which were issued to

Pathfinder squadrons, and subsequently to the more experienced Main Force crews; in a more specific sense, and in the hands of specially trained operators, H_2S was also primarily useful for target location and marking purposes.

The navigator, therefore, was hard at work in his curtained off compartment as the first flak came up and his comrades could see the searchlights springing to life, warning the fighter and gun controllers that the bomber stream was on its way. Constant time checks were being made to ensure the aircraft was keeping in stream—to bump another's slipstream and sight dark shapes about you was disconcerting and could be dangerous, but was evidence that a rough formation was being maintained. Many captains discouraged chatter, but as the heavily defended areas inexorably approached and the bomber began to shudder from the shell bursts, few gunners could resist commenting, and nobody could miss a bomber exploding or falling in flames.

Time passes; Leipzig, the target, is still far off but things begin to happen: ' . . . some clot decides to test Hanover's defences all by himself; there must be 40 searchlights, he's just like a silver moth in a candle, shells bursting all round him. He surely can't survive that hell for long, and he doesn't. A direct hit and down he goes. Not a hope.' The parachute flares begin to float down the sky, stripping night away. Parachutes from crews baling out can also be seen. The survivors press on, swinging southeast of Berlin, which is receiving the attentions of a diversion attack. Leipzig looms up—in the navigator's mind; cloud has banked up, good for cover, bad for identification; and this aircraft, as so often happens, has arrived early, ahead of the Pathfinders, with their loads of markers. Every passing minute means a greater likelihood that the German master controller will have correctly calculated that Leipzig is the primary target and that he will act accordingly.

At last down go the markers and in goes the Main Force—'like the clappers', as one survivor of Bomber Command's most costly raid on the city put it candidly. And in another's recollection:

Nose down, speed is building up. Still too damn slow. Left, left, right steady. Hold it. Come on Johnny drop those blasted bombs. OK, bombs gone. Queenie bucks like a horse. Close the bomb doors—get to hell out of here. The sky seems to be full of flying bullets and kites on fire . . . looks like cloud ahead. Must get into it. There we are. Feel a bit safer now . . . on our way home, but still a long way to go. . . . Musn't relax, still the odd fighter about.

But for crews who got this far there was inevitably a desire to relax, and intense desire to sleep after hours of preparation, the flight out, the trapped feeling over the target and the relief that at least those —— bombs had been dropped. Many a pilot has fallen asleep at the controls, only to jerk awake and find the 'kite' in a wild dive; many times chat or comments from the crew would die out as sleep became the new enemy, especially insidious for the gunners in their lonely turrets, cut off from the rest. But for the strong-willed crews, or the lucky ones, the English coast loomed up at last. Hazards were not yet over; many aircraft crashed on landing, even in 1943, when ground controlled approach was introduced, 30 being put down in one hour when first tested in July. But this final hazard of fatigue and weather overcome, relief comes at last—'... down you go ... the lights rush past and you taxi off the runway to your dispersal .... let's have a fag'.

It is not surprising that after such a challenge and in a state of fatigue and release, debriefing taxed the intelligence officer's skill and tact to elicit information which might provide evidence of success or prove useful on future occasions. There was a set debriefing procedure, which enabled a summary to be made for Night Raid Reports and intelligence files, and which could be checked against the accounts subsequently given in Squadron Operational Record Books. The cross-examination was verbal, no reliance being placed on log books, and each crew was debriefed separately, adding to the length and tedium of the whole business and, arguably, decreasing its effectiveness. By 1943 most aircraft were equipped with cameras, and there was a natural tendency for crews to suggest that the answers would be found in them, rather than in dealing with a string of questions about time over target; observation of target; state of target; quality and quantity of flak; and frequency of interceptions. Debriefing was clearly necessary, and necessary immediately crews landed, given the natural desire to forget and the infinite capacity, even in trained minds, to report details inaccurately. As usual, it was the most disciplined crews which provided the most useful information, but that, like the intelligence they had been provided with the previous afternoon, was fragmentary and of short-lived value.

The Fruits of Attrition

Nine Major Operations

Against this general background of night operations, let us see how Harris and Eaker set about mounting the nine operations listed on pages 205–6. Although Eaker enjoyed nothing like Harris' freedom of action, and was seen by Arnold and the Joint Chiefs mainly as the top American executive in the Combined Bomber Offensive, it must be remembered that both commanders enjoyed more power to decide the dates and immediate objectives of operations than their colleagues in other Services and theatres. In 1943, the Air Staff issued only seven directives to Harris, namely on: attacking U-boat bases (14 January and 6 April); the Combined Bomber Offensive (21 January); the 'desirability' of attacking Berlin (16 February); the Pointblank target list (3 and 10 June and 3 September).[1] Apart from the fact that only four basic issues were dealt with in these directives, and that none of the latter could be construed as more than broad strategic guide lines, we have already seen that if Harris disliked either the main objective or any subsidiary or detailed objectives indicated in communications from the Air Staff or the Ministry of Economic Warfare he ignored them—or gave them short shift.

Harris was even more independent in respect of his own Command. The group commander, who said 'I just put my head down in the scrum and shoved with the other chaps', certainly did not speak for Cochrane and Bennett, and there were officers at the Air Ministry—and especially in the Directorate of Bomber Operations—who disagreed with Harris and made their disagreement plain. The Air Staff was divided in their views about Harris' operational objectives; so were scientists, though by 1943 the controversies of the preceding year were smouldering, awaiting Tedder's touch to fan them alight. Saundby, in his quiet way, could add a little finesse to the C-in-C's sledgehammer approach. But when all that has been said, the fact remains that Harris chose the targets himself, on his own estimate of their importance. Of the five Bomber Command targets we now discuss only the Dams Raid and that on Friedrichshafen owed anything to outside advice or pressure—the first was primarily the test of a new bomb by low-level attack, the second, one of Harris' artfully timed concessions to the proponents of 'panacea' targets.

Eaker's situation was very different, in that until 1944 no personal antipathies or differences of strategic fundamentals affected his relations with Arnold or his Air Staff. The dogmatic tendencies of American military thought, the resources that lay to hand and the optimism that governed the overall conduct of operations were common to 8th Air Force Headquarters and Washington. Nevertheless, as 1943 took its course and the toll of the 8th's losses mounted, one senses that Eaker's letters and signals to his superiors progressively reflected an appreciation of operational factors which they did not share or could not understand. Indeed, as Craven and Cate state:

> Through the summer, as the operating force increased in strength and the pitch of the air fighting rose, General Arnold became increasingly anxious to see the 8th send out larger forces more frequently and more consistently against objectives in Germany, especially against the big aircraft factories. He was prompted in his impatience not only by his very understandable desire to see the primary task of the AAF done speedily and decisively; he was also under pressure, as he had been from the beginning of the bomber offensive against Germany, to interpret to military and civilian authorities in the United States the contribution being made by the heavy bombers. . . . As Arnold put it, he hoped to see a whole series of Regensburgs with hundreds of bombers smashing German fighter factories so decisively that the enemy would find it simpler to build new ones than to repair the old ones.[2]

No doubt, and the account continues:

> General Eaker would himself have liked nothing better than to send forces of 500 bombers repeatedly to the aircraft factories in central and south-eastern Germany. That and much more was the objective toward which he and his command were striving. But he also had to think of the future. Part of his task was to build up the bomber force to planned strength, and that objective could not always be reconciled with the policy of striking the enemy with everything he had, regardless of the cost.[3]

What all this boiled down to in practice was that Eaker, far more than Harris, wanted his campaign to chime with his superior's objectives, but, like Harris, he was not prepared to make repeated attacks on the same target, when doing so seriously, if temporarily, weakened his forces, not least in the loss of experienced crews who were daily enduring extreme danger. When Arnold wrote to Eaker in the middle of 'black week' congratulating and exhorting in the manner of Chiefs of Staff, Eaker can only have felt that the operational message was not getting across.[4] When the Committee of Operations Analysts repeatedly listed the same targets for him, Eaker was bound to feel that operational imperatives were being overlooked[5]; loyally, he attacked the type of targets listed; sensibly, as time went by, he attacked the 'safe' ones or not at all or at best, did so once—only Schweinfurt, of the priority targets, was attacked twice in 1943. Indeed, one important factor governing the rapid build-up of the 15th Air Force was that pressure would simultaneously be removed from the 8th and increased on the German Air Force in production and in being. The 15th in fact continued as it began, as a force far more capable of precisely expressing the intentions of the Pointblank Directive and its admonitory amendments by the Joint Chiefs, than was the case with the 8th. Of the four USAAF targets we discuss, it now can be seen that Wiener–Neustadt was, in the conditions prevailing in 1943, one of the most damaging, as it was one of the least costly, attacks mounted under General Spaatz's overall direction.[6]

The same point could be made in an absolutely different strategic and operational context of the Essen attack on 5–6 March.[7] The broad details and particular features of the raid have already been described in Harris' words, and it only remains to emphasise here that the importance of this 'opening' attack derived from the intensity of effort which had been devoted to the city in the past year and its success, in Harris' terms, from the careful preparations which had been made in the two months immediately preceding. Essen was bombed seven times in January, and although the numbers of bombers engaged was relatively small, they included 355 Lancasters and 25 Oboe-equipped Mosquitoes. The latter, operating at the limits of Oboe range, were an indication that Bennett's four months' probationary period was ended; although no appreciable damage to Essen was inflicted in these seven raids, the rudimentary marking techniques of 1942, mere visually sought guides to target areas, were exchanged for permutations of blind aiming-point marking for the benefit of the new Main Force crews and their big new aircraft.

Essen was throughout the offensive unavoidably a blindly sought target in any case; the January raids, in which Musical Wanganui made its full operational bow, was a crucial development in the Harris strategy and an essential factor in his plan to destroy the haze hidden Ruhr. Nevertheless a substantial campaign throughout 1943 required that Main Force crews should familiarise themselves with all the radar, visual and marking techniques open to 8 Group; on 2 February Cologne was bombed on a combination of *Newhaven* (11 Halifaxes and Stirlings) and *Wanganui* (two *Oboe*-Mosquitoes), backed up by 12 Pathfinder Lancasters dropping green target indicators. There were no concrete results, even by the easily satisfied criteria of the *Quarterly Review*, and equally indecisive effects were recorded from attacks on Hamburg and assorted Ruhr targets on the 6, 7, 9 and 11 February. On the last date, however, Wilhelmshaven was also attacked in bad weather; the target being beyond *Oboe* range, H_2S was necessary, and the weather being unco-operative, blind identification and blind sky marking were resorted to. The result was one of the most destructive raids on Wilhelmshaven to date, against all the odds and in contradiction of any theory that an ideal Pathfinder technique existed at any time of the year for any target on Harris' own list. Hamburg was attacked by the same methods on 15 and 19 February, with derisory effect, as was Berlin on 1 March.

Thus although an inconclusive raid on Essen on 5-6 March might not have diminished Harris at the political level, it was very necessary in operational terms and for the morale of his crews that the most carefully picked Pathfinder technique should do the trick. In the event, Paramatta was selected for a moonless night, with five-tenths cloud and average haze. Eight Mosquitoes, controlled over 250 miles at 30,000 feet from the east-coast ground stations of Walmer and Worth, dropped their red target indicators on time at 2100 hours on the aiming point—Krupp's works, plumb in the middle of Essen. Three Mosquitoes found their equipment unserviceable; nevertheless the initial marking was sufficiently accurate, and was so well supported by the 22 backers-up that the Main Force attack by 412 aircraft (of which 53 were abortive in one sense or another) bombed on alternates of red and green markers in 38 minutes, two minutes under the allowed time. So well timed and concentrated was the Main Force attack that Pathfinder crews were in danger of being bombed, possibly because a further marking refinement had been introduced, which doubtless helped the laggards, although it produced bunching over the target. This marking was a yellow track indicator, dropped at the point of the final leg, 15 miles short of the target run in mark. 'Yellows' were to become an accepted feature of the Pathfinder kaleidoscope—and to lead to some interesting 5 Group variations on the Bennett aiming point concept, resulting in a considerable rivalry between the two Groups and less than absolute camaraderie in the two distinguished airmen who commanded them.

On the morning of 6 March 1943, however, and in the subsequent days of photographic reconnaissance, Bennett and his colleagues had much to make them confident that the future lay with them. 293 attacking aircraft of the Main Force returned with photographs of the target, and although neither *Oboe* nor later pictures proved anything conclusively, there was little doubt at High Wycombe or on the stations that the 'large and spreading fires', which continued to rage for days, heralded something new. More to the point perhaps, the raid camera analysis showed that 153 aircraft had bombed within three miles of the aiming point; it was not to be expected therefore that Krupps should escape, since 'the heaviest concentration of damage was right in the centre of the town'. With only 14 aircraft lost through enemy action from 442 despatched, a missing rate of just over three per cent, Harris could justifiably say that Bomber Command was ready at last.

But in war, as in normal life, most action and many decisions are a set of competing interests; the raid on a complex of dams in the Ruhr valley on 16–17 May was not directly a reflection of the 'precision' lobby or the 'panacea' mongers, but from the particular heroism with which it was carried out and in the apparent success which attended it has come something of a legend that this was war in the third dimension at its most gallant, resourceful and effective. The dams raid had—and has—something for everybody responsive to the individual's place in total war, who abhors the indiscriminate suffering which that totality implies. That Wing Commander Gibson was a leader, an airman and a brave man beyond compare needs no emendation from me; that his crews were equally brave must also be obvious. But the facts are that 19 of Bomber Command's most experienced crews left Scampton in Yorkshire on 16 May; eight returned; the most important dam, the Sorpe, was undamaged; two others, the Ennepe and the Lister, were not attacked at all; and although the Möhne and Eder dams were severely damaged in circumstances where most airmen would have settled for one run over the target and away, they were repaired within two months, after causing trivial damage to the Ruhr's industries—and providing a note for senior German officials on how post-war dams and reservoirs should be built, sited and seen as elements in an economic infrastructure rather than as mere sources of water or of amenity.

Thus British courage in waging war was met by German brains in controlling its effects; although these tables were to be turned the following year, the dams raid must be recorded as a tragic example of how idea and execution require the element of operational feasibility to form a strategic whole. What is so especially tragic about the raid was that it plays little part in the evolution of techniques for relatively accurate attacks on specially selected targets; there was no agitation for the dams to be attacked; no new intelligence had come to light suggesting their paramount importance and reviving therefore the debates of 1942; the results of the raid only confirmed the inherent operational odds against low-level attack and bore no fruit in terms of techniques used subsequently, although it is true to say that this lesson has still not been grasped in some quarters. No less than five of the 19 aircraft may have been lost because of the basic, and arguably unacceptable, risk—unless unlimited numbers of very skilled, experienced and brave airmen are readily available—of flying a large aircraft fast and low across unfamiliar terrain.

The dams were lightly defended; flak there accounted for only one aircraft, and the whole operation was conducted at such a low height and with such remarkable displays of flying virtuosity that enemy fighters forebore to attack until the survivors set off for home. Finally the overt strategic objective of the operation—to prove the capacity of Dr Barnes Wallis' two-and-a-half-ton aerial mine for destroying point targets of particular robustness—was demonstrated successfully only in the sense that devotion to duty and flying skill saw the weapon dropped precisely as its inventor had intended and with the effects he claimed. But leaving the operation's cost aside, the fact remains that dropping the 'block busters', which largely derived from the aerial mine and which increasingly succeeded the incendiary bomb in late 1944 and 1945, was a task which virtually all crews could do only by the technique of high-level bombing on blindly laid marker. 617, as a squadron, continued to use some of Gibson's techniques, and low-level marking may have owed a little to them. But low-level attacks by Bomber Command remained the province of Mosquitoes—although these made very few—and 'precision' bombing in 5 Group developed as a variant of, not an alternative to, that carried out by 1, 3, 4, 6 and 8 Groups.

It can fairly be said therefore that, because the dams raid fitted no planned or potential pattern of feasible strategy, Harris was right to be tepid about it at the time and to show only recognition of 617 Squadron's sacrifice in his subsequent comments. According to most authoritative sources, Gibson and his crews were told that their raid, in a specially formed and arduously trained squadron, would be a real war-winner; Harris, although happy enough to talk about winning the war by his methods, could only say of it that 'the enemy still had the water from other reservoirs whose dams were unbroken and from wells'. He has also been reported as saying that the whole thing was a propaganda exercise, and indeed it must be said that the atmosphere surrounding the raid lends some support to this criticism. Although, on the night of operation 'Chastise', Gibson's messages to Scampton that the Mohne and Eder had been breached, caused Harris at 5 Group Headquarters to telephone Portal at a Washington dinner party with the news, we must ignore the unprecedented public relations campaign which surrounded the raid and concentrate for a few moments on what 617 Squadron actually did.

This was to carry out certainly one of the most accurate attacks ever delivered against targets difficult to find and more difficult still to bomb. Gibson and his crews spent 2,500 hours—equal to a major raid on the Ruhr by 500 bombers—on training to fly their specially lightened Lancasters on a cross-country course, visually navigating in moonlight, and practising over a reservoir high in the Derbyshire hills an entirely new technique of releasing a mine exactly at 60 feet so that it literally skipped over the water (to escape nets and other defences) struck the dam wall, sank and exploded, knocking the wall over and freeing the waters behind. It was necessary therefore to attack the dams when they were fullest and when, in theory, their contents were about to be most valuable to the industries of the Ruhr, to Kassel and to the agricultural area to the east. It is symptomatic, however, of the haste which surrounded the whole affair that Gibson was snatched from an operational station a bare six weeks before the raid, told to collect two–tour crews, form a squadron and attempt an entirely new operation of war.

Gibson's account loses its habitual flippancy as the task developed and magnified; the mood to which the crews were strung up after their exacting and dangerous training is exactly caught. Rarely indeed can fighting men have been plunged so completely into a task requiring not only cold-blooded courage and skill but a professional approach to a multiplicity of problems which few of them had ever needed or bothered to apply before. It was from intensive discussion among the crews and in the brief non-flying intervals of those spring days that the idea was born of fitting two lights in a Lancaster's belly, whose beams would intersect on the water at exactly 60 feet; it was to air and ground crews that most of the additions, innovations and improvements were due, including direct voice contact by very high frequency radio, maximum-range tracer for the single-gun front and rear turrets—and the technique of 'moonlighting' so that the bombers actually dodged behind trees to confuse flak and fighters as they circled the dams in the two hours during which they strove to put a novel idea into effect by very English and empiric methods.

For the real difficulty lay in the fact that the dams were cradled in the hills—this was especially so with the Eder—and to attack them at 232 miles an hour from 60 feet meant a steep diving approach, an absolutely level run across the reservoir and a fast climb away to avoid hitting the water or being blown up by the mine. It was no wonder that 617 set off from Scampton, having learned the target only that morning, with the crews keyed up; 'most of them wore expressions varying from the "Don't care a damn" to the grim and determined'. But they were tired too; Gibson, who had been in the secret all along, had sat up most the previous night making a copy of the squadron operation order in case he should not return; the 17th, 'a boiling hot day', had been taken up with briefings and last minute flaps.

> Our favourite Yank, F/L McCarthy, caused quite a disturbance. He arrived at his aircraft and after finding she had hydraulic trouble, came dashing back to our only reserve aircraft. When inside he noticed he had no compass card and came rushing back to the flights frantically screaming for one. He had also pulled his parachute by mistake and the white silk was streaming all over the ground, trailing behind him. With perspiration dropping off his face, good old Mac ran back to his aircraft with everyone behind him trying to fix him up with what he wanted. He got off just in time.

At 2128 hours the first aircraft, captained by Flight Lieutenant R. N. G. Barlow took off. The 19 crews, including another American serving in the Royal Air Force, Squadron Leader Young, 13 Australians and two New Zealanders, set off in two main groups and a reserve group, flying low and on a course designed to take them through the Dutch flak belts, or north of the Zuider Zee, the intention being to attack the five dams in two waves, converging south west of Münster after flying north of 'happy valley'. But the 'Sorpe' force of five aircraft lost four of its number on the way to the target, leaving the survivor Flight Lieutenant McCarthy, to attack and return alone. Although the one surviving aircraft of the reserve group also attacked the Sorpe two hours after McCarthy, the main concentration was achieved by Gibson's leading group of nine, which attacked the Mohne and Eder in turn. One of Gibson's group crashed en route, but on arriving over the Mohne after a journey involving constant hazards, he called up the seven surviving aircraft and settled down to a target already lit up by concentrated flak. The dam, as Gibson said, 'looked squat and heavy and unconquerable; it looked grey and solid in the moonlight . . . a structure like a battle-ship was showering out flak all along its length . . . .'

Gibson attacked first and failed to break the dam; the next aircraft was destroyed on its run in; the third, escorted by Gibson in an attempt to divert enemy fire (for once the airgunners had something to fire back at and did so vigorously) got nearer the mark; the fourth, again covered by Gibson, got its mine exactly on the spot, but the dam held; the fifth attack was hard to observe from the spray its predecessors had thrown up, even although between each attempt painful minutes passed while the dam's waters surface seethed and the flak blazed, and it was some time before Gibson could see that the dam had rolled over, and that 'a huge cataract of water was rushing through the breach', with one solitary gun still firing as the flood poured towards the Ruhr, where headlights of 'cars racing for safety . . . changed colour, first to green and then eventually to dark purple' as they were submerged and valley filled with mist. Hastily ordering aircraft six not to attack, Gibson set course for the Eder, supported by Squadron Leader Young and the three aircraft still carrying mines.

By the time the Eder was reached around 0120, there was light in the eastern sky and no time to be lost. Nevertheless, the same meticulous procedure was followed, and the same extraordinary courage displayed. The first attack made a small breach; Squadron Leader Maudsley in the second aircraft, making, like Flight Lieutenant Shannon before him, his third run over an almost impossible target, breached the dam 'but a second later there was a vivid explosion on the parapet of the dam itself which lit up the whole valley for a few seconds. Then no more was seen of the Lancaster.' Maudsley, 'remembered as an Olympian swell at Eton . . . who would always go to the limits of safe endurance trying to make sure of finding and hitting his targets . . .',[8] had been destroyed with his crew by the mine they had dropped. But the Australian Pilot Officer Knight attacked as soon as possible after the spray from Maudsley's explosion had cleared, and it was this final attempt which deeply breached the Eder; though the dam wall held at the top, the waters below spewed out, looking like 'stirred porridge in the moonlight'.

The survivors set course for home; Squadron Leader Young was shot down; Gibson landed with two of the eight who had set out with him; the Sorpe was attacked without success; Flight Sergeant Townsend's crew made a solitary attack on the Ennepe dam, returning over Germany with the other survivor of the reserve group after dawn had broken. Photographic reconnaissance in the course of the next days revealed two empty reservoirs and scenes of flooding and damage. An airfield was under water, as was much of Kassel. For this result 54 members of 617 Squadron had been killed, including both flight commanders (Maudsley and Young); Gibson was awarded the VC, and 32 other aircrew were also decorated.

Such was the strategic air offensive's most famous operation. No one had blundered; the crews would have gone again; maybe the morale shock to Germans was more prolonged than their astonishing recovery from the raid suggested at the time. But even temporary industrial set-back had been bought very dear, and Gibson and his crews, as he records, knew that their attack would not have an appreciable effect on the course of the war. By contrast, the Friedrichshafen raid was a considered attempt to combine the best that 5 and 8 Groups could do against a target which lacked the dramatic quality of the dams, but was arguably of the greater importance. 'On 20–21 June 1943, when the nights were shortest, I laid on an attack on the former Zeppelin works at Friedrichshafen on the shores of Lake Constance, a factory which was producing radar apparatus.'[9] The target's primary importance to Harris was undoubtedly its distance from the United Kingdom, and the warning which an attack on it would—or should—give to those responsible for defending Germany; the warning should show that there were no havens from the striking power of Bomber Command. Indeed, it may be said that, from the war's earliest nights, the Trenchard interpretation of flexibility had been largely seen in terms of how far bombers could reach into Germany, creating alarm and despondency among the German people and ridiculing the notion that the Third Reich was inviolate.

Because some highly specialised types of German industry and manufacturing capacity had since the thirties been located in distant and inaccessible places, it is to confuse the purpose of Harris' long-range strategy to suppose that he saw them as targets for selective attack. When, in late 1943, he began to order attacks on targets lying south and east of Berlin (by which time the German aircraft industry had begun to disperse thence), it was natural for some to assume that Bomber Command was belatedly fulfilling a role in the Pointblank campaign. So it was, but by accident rather than design. These distant targets never received attention comparable to that given to the Ruhr and Berlin; the latter, of course, was distant too, but occupied a unique place in Bomber Command's plan of campaign. When Harris again reverted to area bombing in the autumn of 1944, it was to the final destruction of the Ruhr and Berlin that he devoted most of his energies.

Having made Harris' views plain, it should however be emphasised that to the proponents of selective bombing—specifically the Commander and professionally inclined members of 5 Group—Friedrichshafen was a

target of prime strategic, operational and tactical significance.[10] The factory there made radar equipment for the German night fighter force,
which was a factor likely to be of increasing importance in the struggle for
winning the defensive battle, or, more positively, gaining air superiority;
command of the air was, to Cochrane especially, always the fundamental
first objective for 5 Group. He saw no point in losing his best crews just
because the German defences were allowed to remain inherently superior
to the offensive forces. Friedrichshafen's operational significance was as a
feasible objective in terms of likely loss over target, the outward route
to be followed—and the flight on to North Africa. No regular 'shuttle'
between the United Kingdom and North Africa was implied in this
decision, because senior officers of Bomber Command were as one in
agreeing that airfields in North Africa could not properly service Lancasters—and it was by a carefully chosen force of 56 Lancasters of 5 Group
that Friedrichshafen was to be bombed. Nevertheless, an occasional shuttle
introduced some variation into a pretty monotonous theme and, in this
instance, gives to the well-planned and executed Friedrichshafen raid
something of the clarity of purpose which characterised Cochrane himself.

The raid's tactical significance lay in the plan to see what some of the
most experienced Pathfinder Force and Main Force crews could jointly
achieve with a small force—for mid-1943—and in a strategic context
where it was probable that Harris was not going to allow 1, 3, 4 and 6
Groups to acquire a like independence. If Cochrane and Bennett could
work together on the Friedrichshafen raid, there was no reason why 5
Group should not increasingly (although not regularly) bomb targets
whose intrinsic importance nobody could dispute. In the event, the two
Group commanders had a row—civil, but a row nonetheless—over the
execution of the Friedrichshafen attack. Thereafter, 5 Group began to
form its own Pathfinder Force, a process which delayed many attacks of
the Friedrichshafen type in 1943, but led to some considerable successes
against Overlord targets in 1944. By that time a fair number of targets
requiring specialised and variable treatment were perforce on Harris'
list, but only 3 Group, equipped with the refinement of *Oboe* known as
G–H, enjoyed much 'independence', being committed to daylight operations against cities, leaving 1, 4 and 6 Groups, led by 8, to bomb assorted
targets, mostly at night.

It must therefore remain a matter of speculation whether a Bennett-
Cochrane accord on how aiming points should be marked (initially,
whether 'centred' or 'offset', and subsequently, whether from high or low
level) could have come about, and whether this accord would have led

to a substantial addition to the list of specially selected targets for 5 Group. All that one can say at this distance of time is that it seems unlikely that true understanding between two such opinionated commanders was possible. Although arguments over tactics were real enough, the short point is that Bennett was closer to Harris than Cochrane in believing in city busting and was fervent and vocal in the conviction that his Group's high-altitude and 'centred' marking was accurate for this purpose; criticism from others was rudely rejected, for Bennett was a commander who could not—or at any rate did not—see that there might be two sides to an argument. Bennett, moreover, had shrewdly acquired most of the Mosquitoes being built for Bomber Command, and was rapidly increasing his 'Light Night Striking Force', to a size where he could validly claim that, in conjunction with *Oboe*-Mosquitoes, it was both a superb instrument for deception and diversion, and a power in itself for selective attack should the need arise.[11] That the Light Night Striking Force was to be used mostly in support of Main Force targets, would frequently bomb them on nights when the latter was grounded, and is best remembered for the remarkable achievement of its Mosquitoes in carrying a 4,000-lb. bomb to Berlin only goes to show how closely Bennett allied himself with the Commander-in-Chief.

The narrow tactical point is, however, not without interest, especially since it was Cochrane's theory that, in high-level marking, whether with sky or ground markers, and whether laid visually or blindly, target indicators should be offset, or dropped some distance from the plotted aiming point so that they could be seen more clearly amid the smoke by air bombers, who thereupon made the necessary calculation to place their bombs on the actual target. In the Friedrichshafen raid, Cochrane put his offset marking theories into practice for bombing a target small enough to be rapidly hidden by smoke. He was enabled to do this due to the fact that despite, or perhaps because of, Bennett's habitual aggressiveness, criticism of Pathfinder marking accuracy increased rather than diminished as a minority of Main Force crews became expert at recognising targets and the various decoys lit or laid by the Germans in an endeavour to protect them. The Official History, in the chapter in Volume Two dealing with 'Night Precision Bombing', goes so far as to state:

> ... aiming from higher levels at markers was the stock in trade of the whole of Bomber Command. The development of marking techniques was, therefore, of much wider significance than the development of complex bombing techniques, and because the most efficient markers were so much lighter than the most destructive bombs the operational possibilities of

precision marking were greater than those which existed in the case of precision bombing.

But, the statement continues,

> ... it was the relative inaccuracy of the marking and not the bombing error in aiming at the markers which was the operative factor in delaying the progress of 617 Squadron and, in a less refined degree, in denying to the main force of Bomber Command the ability to hit precision targets, either with consistency or reasonable economy of force.[12]

The reference in this statement to 617 Squadron is only meaningful in the context of the latter's misfortunes after the dams raid and in the gradual discovery of a valid operational role when, in April 1944, Wing Commander Cheshire (as he then was) began low-level marking. The references to the lack of bombing error in aiming at markers is fair, but given that, at best, but 40 per cent of Main Force crews got within the three-mile limit (and, except occasionally, only an insignificant proportion of target indicators fell outside that), it seems unlikely that 'the ability to hit precision targets' would ever have been achieved in the conditions obtaining over Germany from mid-1943 onwards. The tactical issue then in the Friedrichshafen raid was to see how accurately Pathfinders could mark when the preparations were most carefully made, and how accurately good crews could bomb on the marking in question. The 5 Group Lancasters, increased just before the raid to 60 aircraft, had trained assiduously for operation 'Bellicose'. Because a master bomber was to control them over the target (the first time this technique had been employed, apart from the dams raid), some practice (all too brief) was made in communication between aircraft. Four Pathfinder H_2S-equipped Lancasters were to identify the target and aiming point with ground target indicators; thereafter the master bomber was to offset-mark the aiming point for crews, who would be further aided by track markers guiding them on a timed run to the target area. It will be apparent at once, therefore, that one innovation claimed by 5 Group had already been employed by the Pathfinder Force, and in the Hamburg raids of the following months was to figure largely, if not always usefully, in Bennett's tactics.

What happened in fact in the Friedrichshafen raid was that, with the exception of the master bomber's aircraft, forced to return with engine trouble, and another which lost its way to the target and flew straight to Blida in Algeria, the Main Force crossed France in bright moonlight, reached the rendezvous, north-west of Lake Constance and prepared to attack. Wing Commander Gomm, the deputy master bomber, then decided that flak and searchlights were likely to cause heavy casualties unless the Force climbed from 10,000 to 15,000 feet, But, according to 5 Group sources, this change lessened the accuracy of the Pathfinder Lancaster air bombers, whose target indicators fell wide of the aiming point. Gomm therefore intervened, as he was empowered to do, ordered the Main Force to stand by and himself marked the target from low level; critical of the track marking of the Pathfinder crews, Gomm worked out a track for the Main Force to fly to a timed point, where they released their bombs. Aircraft bombed individually, without interference from fighters and relying mainly on the marking and instructions of the deputy master bomber. The absence of fighters can only be explained by the German controller's supposition that this highly visible Force, flying in loose formation, would be intercepted on its way back to England. Not for the first time, however, the simple 'shuttle' tactic fooled the waiting fighters.

The Lancasters flew on, and landed at Blida without loss. Not only that, but subsequent photographic reconnaissance revealed that about half of the main factory buildings had been destroyed or severely damaged, even though only nine per cent of the bombs were on target. Given the vulnerability of the delicate precision instruments in radar equipment to even superficial damage, the raid must therefore be accounted a justification of the Cochrane premise, even if to Harris it was satisfactory for other reasons. With several other successful attacks of this kind already recorded or about to take place, and with a list of targets of comparable importance and feasibility to Friedrichshafen not hard to find, there were some experts engaged in, or observing, Bomber Command operations at this time who expected a significant shift towards meeting the Pointblank and associated objectives. But, as we have seen, this was not to be. Not only had Cochrane and Bennett failed to co-ordinate their crews' skills and tactics (a failure for which 617 was to pay dear in its operations of September and December), not only was Bennett convinced of the superiority of his methods, whether at Friedrichshafen or anywhere else, but the Battle of the Ruhr was about to expand, and it was a question of calling on all Main Force squadrons for an effort over Hamburg of unique destructiveness and quite unprecedented repetition.

Between 24 July and 2 August, therefore, 8 Group was engaged in its busiest period of operations to date, with Mosquitoes making two substantial raids between Main Force attacks, thus giving to Bennett an operational responsibility far greater than his fellow commanders. But it was in all the permutations of track, target area and aiming point marking that for the raid on 24 July the Pathfinder Force came into its own. So severe were the fires after this first raid, that the Main Force had no difficulty in finding the target area for the second and most destructive attack. Thereafter, an attempt was made to shift the aiming point further east, so that fresh residential areas might burn. But Pathfinder marking for third and fourth raids was extremely inaccurate, and this factor, plus the the tendency of Main Force crews to bomb simply on fires, undoubtedly saved this great city from almost total destruction. The struggle between bombs and concrete remained undecided.

In tactical terms, it is surprising that Hamburg did live to fight another day. Although a relatively distant target of this kind obviously increased the likelihood of fighter successes, *Window* took care of that factor until the last raid. Thus not only were the odds for once in favour of the bomber, but Hamburg was, even without the Pathfinder Force, a relatively easy target to locate, and with its distinctive port layout, not an insuperably difficult one to attack. It was an ideal H_2S target (as we have seen already),[13] and for this reason it was natural that Bennett should make a maximum effort, even to the extent of adopting or adapting some of 5 Group's theories and, most important of all, re-marking the target to cut down the 'creep back' caused by crews unable or unwilling to look for the target indicators. Given the volumes of smoke and jets of flame billowing and shooting forth, and in the absence of a master bomber, Pathfinder crews had to shepherd their flocks, providing initially the track and aiming points, and thereafter fresh series of target indicators.

For the track marking in fact, almost greater preparations were made than for the target itself. The 791 Main Force bombers, flying east from the Elbe estuary, were the beneficiaries of yellow markers laid by six H_2S-equipped 8 Group aircraft, supported by 30 backers-up. Showering *Window* well west of the target, the Main Force flew just after midnight towards a city of grounded fighters, baffled flak batteries and aimlessly weaving searchlights, to see red target indicators laid by no fewer than 28 8 Group aircraft, which were to be supported throughout the raid's duration of 48 minutes by 53 backers-up dropping green target indicators: 11 of the latter, listed for remarking, endeavoured to keep the Main Force on target but, as with their H_2S-equipped colleagues 'only a moderate success attended their efforts'; '. . . a marked "creep back" developed and by half past one a carpet of incendiary bombs stretched back for seven miles along the approach to Hamburg'.[14] One clear lesson of the battle had been that H_2S was not really in the same class of consistent 'six-mile radius' accuracy as *Oboe*, and even if the former was intended eventually for widespread distribution to the Main Force, it would solve few of its fundamental bombing problems.

Nevertheless, some of the basic criteria were sufficient to convince Harris that another considerable victory had been won. Due to *Window*, only 12 aircraft failed to return from the first raid; of the 740 crews who arrived over the target area, 725 claimed to have attacked it, and the night camera analysis suggested that no less than 306 got their bombs within three miles of the aiming point. To even the most convinced proponent of area bombing, this statistic means little by itself; it is evidence of 'overkill' and the attraction of fires as target indicators. Only if high explosive had predominated in the second raid and burning Hamburg had been blown up as well, would such duplication of effort have caused a fresh shock in the German mind. As it was, enough of the city's heart and life remained for mass flight to be temporary rather than permanent.[15] After the week of horror, Hamburg was left virtually alone by Bomber Command for the remainder of the war.

Doubtless the missing rate of four per cent for raids three and four, compared with under two and three per cent for raids one and two respectively, had something to do with this relative immunity. But the Battle of Hamburg marks, in a sense, an isolated rather than an absolutely significant stage in the strategic air offensive; repetition had been planned and achieved, to a degree indeed unmatched before and not to be found again for one single city within so short a time for the remainder of the war. Yet Hamburg had survived and while it was suffering devastation no other city was attacked with sufficient weight to indicate the onset of an area offensive covering all western Germany. Hence the following summary of cause and effect must be borne in mind when considering what Bomber Command set out to achieve:

> Speer considers that the gradual build-up of the Allied night air offensive contributed to what he describes as its initial failure. The steady increase in the weight of attacks served as training for the Germans, both as regard to defence methods, ARP and repair organisation. The civilian population also got hardened to the raids in a gradual way. 'Shock effects' were produced by the first 1,000 bomber raid on Cologne, and especially by the series of attacks on Hamburg in summer 1943. After the latter attacks, Speer had voiced the view that if another six big German cities were similarly devastated, he would not be able to maintain armaments production. He changed his view, however, when he saw the speed with which Hamburg industry recovered from the attacks, which came as a surprise to him.[16]

Speer, being wise after the event, is minimising not only what Bomber Command but also the 8th sought to achieve. In fact, although a remarkable industrial salvage job was undertaken in Hamburg (most of the 180,000 tons of shipping sunk in the six main raids of the week in question was subsequently raised), a major blow had been struck at a great port which was also a crucial manufacturing centre. For the rest of the war, Hamburg's traditional function was in abeyance, even although its revival as a city, as a place where people continued to live and have their being, was so remarkable. It had suffered the fate of Coventry and Liverpool, not that of one of the 'cities of the Plain'.

The 8th Air Force attacks on 25 and 26 July were directed at Hamburg's industrial heart, that system of docks and waterways reaching well into the city, which once again has given it such a big place in Germany's economic life. The relative success of these two attacks[17]—judged by shipping destroyed—is, rather surprisingly, given scant praise in the US Strategic Bombing Survey, which concentrates on Hamburg's revival and ignores the accuracy of daylight attacks in conditions where bombardiers had to calculate their aiming point as the centre of the undamaged area, surrounded by smoke and fires. What is more surprising, however, is that no particular inferences seem to have been drawn from the two raids by 8th Air Force Headquarters and the Committee of Operations Analysts. Ports and the industries associated with them and located on the Friesian and Jutland coasts had certainly figured largely in the 8th's missions to date; in 1943, and up to 25 July, 1531 sorties had been flown against Wilhelmshaven, Emden, Bremen, Kiel, Flensburg and Cuxhaven, for the loss of 95 aircraft through enemy action. This was a missing rate of approximately six per cent, which might appear to destroy the notion that ports were less difficult targets than the industrial areas of inland cities. But no less than 42 aircraft had been lost in two raids (of 17 April and 13 June, both on Bremen), where the missing rate was over 15 per cent. For the other 12 missions, the rate stood at four, and from two of them (Flensburg on 19 May and Kiel on 13 June) all aircraft had returned.[18]

No aircraft were lost over shattered Hamburg either (which was not perhaps surprising, but nonetheless welcome), but despite what might validly appear to be a situation where certain ports were relatively accessible, undeniably industrially important and less obviously expensive in terms of the missing rate, only 19 attacks were made on them for the rest of 1943, of which no fewer than seven were on Bremen.[19] No further attacks were made on Hamburg in 1943, although even on a dog-leg track, flown to avoid the Dutch coast, the maximum round trip range was 1,000 miles. This was well beyond fighter escort range, but it was only against Bomber Command at night that German fighters made interceptions well out to sea. The short-range, single-engined day fighter fought predominantly over land, unless he pursued a sinking bomber over water to execute the *coup de grâce*.

One is forced to conclude therefore that the inflexibility which characterised the 8th's operations until disaster struck was displayed in the assumption that Hamburg was finished after a total of eight raids in one week; Harris had declared that 10,000 tons would destroy the city;[20] approximately 9,000 tons had been dropped, and although the 8th's share of this was small and mostly confined to HE, the B.17s and B.24s were thereafter shifted to new targets. And the attack on Marienburg on 9 October doubtless appeared to confirm the optimistic diagnosis by which Spaatz and Eaker had sold the Casablanca Conference on unescorted deep penetration daylight bombing nine months before. After a tricky pregnancy, the air offensive seemed about to produce a lusty baby.[21] Craven and Cate wax enthusiastically over the Marienburg mission, a testament supported by one of those pairs of strike-reconnaissance photographs which do indeed show the nature and the effect of high-altitude bombing—in ideal conditions. The claim is made that:

> the Focke-Wulf plant was almost completely destroyed by high explosive and incendiary bombs dropped with unprecedented accuracy... of the 598 × 500 pound GP bombs dropped over Marienburg, 286 were identified by aerial reconnaissance as having fallen within the factory area. Of these, at least 35 were direct hits on buildings.

The improved accuracy which these figures revealed was particularly gratifying to a force which since operations began 14 months before had been grappling with relatively high—certainly unexpectedly high—crew losses, the demands of the North African campaign and the inevitable mistakes made by new men. Understandably enough, the 8th not only made greater claims for accuracy at all times than Bomber Command, but, less wisely, took finer limits of measurement—feet, not miles. Craven and Cate claim that by October 1943, 53.8 of the 8th's bombs fell within 2,000 feet of the aiming point. The only flaw in giving much value to this claim is that the evidence comes from photographs, not German factory figures. Like most bombing criteria seen only from 'one side of the hill', the figures bear no relation to the enemy's capacity—in 1943—to ignore or quickly to recover from the effect of bombing in dribs and drabs.

Therefore to have virtually destroyed a factory by 35 bombs of this low calibre in an attack where only 96 aircraft actually bombed would have been a remarkable achievement. Even allowing that the mission was highly successful, particularly in that only two aircraft were lost in the 8th's deepest penetration of Germany to date, the danger of drawing the wrong conclusion (that unescorted raids of this range could be operationally feasible) was brutally revealed by the attack on Münster the day after Marienburg. 274 aircraft were despatched, 236 bombed, 30 were lost, a missing rate of 11 per cent. A diversionary force of 39 returned without loss, but on this occasion failed to prevent a substantial victory for the German fighters, employing tactics and weapons which broke up the bombing formations and cut deep into the survivors boring steadily and bravely across the autumn sky.

Not only was a particularly determined attack made on the lowest formation (destruction of the leading elements being thereby reserved for later), but rocket projectiles were lobbed by Fw. 190s and Me. 109s at 1,000–1,700 yards range. Groups of up to 40 aircraft, including Ju. 88s and even Do. 217s and Do. 215s, attacked in echelon, in pairs or singly; shorter range rockets found their mark amid the bomber phalanx; explosive cannon shells shot the lame ducks out of the sky. At least 177 fighters were claimed as destroyed, but the actual figures were 14 destroyed and 9 damaged. The rockets seem to have been particularly hated by the hapless crews, and to have aroused emotions similar to those of the inhabitants of London and its suburbs when, in 1944, they watched the V.1 begin its remorseless descent on their homes.

> These rockets, which travelled slowly enough to be clearly visible, were an especially chilling sight to the American fliers. One of the bomber pilots flying the Schweinfurt mission watched in horror as a rocket arched through his formation, heading straight for a nearby B.17. It hit the fuselage just at the back of the cockpit, tearing open the side of the plane and blowing one wing completely off. The pilot briefly glimpsed the men in the cockpit still sitting at their controls; then they were engulfed in flames.[22]

'Second' Schweinfurt was the mission in which this kind of war reached its peak, an air battle of 'epic proportions' as Craven and Cate call it, in which sustained onslaught for several hours on end by relays of every type of German fighter, even extending to 'several Stuka dive bombers, looking very much out of place at a height of four miles',[23] was directed at two strong forces of 149 and 142 bombers respectively, flying some 30 miles apart. Given the total number of 291 bombers committed to wreaking further damage on this favourite target of the 'selective' analysts, a gap of only 30 miles did not allow much chance for either force to escape from the fighter attacks; a sweep by a mere 29 aircraft was a gesture rather than a diversion, although, as planned and partly executed, one small element of the Schweinfurt forces was routed to the south. But a compromise between concentration and dispersal was probably unavoidable, given that although fighter escort was most carefully planned, it could not separately cover two large forces. Therefore, if all the 323 Fortresses and Liberators originally assigned to the mission had got successfully airborne, the only result would have been still heavier losses. But escort planning was not the nub of the issue; range was. Beyond Aachen and until that area was reached on the return, the bombers were on their own, and on this date the General Staff of the German Air Force decided to make a maximum effort, call in fighters from all over Germany and from Central France, and shatter the Eaker doctrine beyond repair. Not until February 1944 did the 8th seek distant targets in Germany, and never again without escort.

As with so much of the history of the strategic air offensive, it is all too easy to be wise after the event. Unlike the 17 August raid, there was no 'shuttle' plan; one wonders why; the bombers were exposed to the full fury of the German fighters for three solid hours, losing heavily on the way to the target, thus reducing the numbers attacking to 229; the fighting took place in a sky of 'brilliant, sunwashed blue',[24] across which flashed apparently endless arcs of fire, as relays of fighters formed up for the slaughter, then dived for the attack so fast and frequent that the sweating and deafened turret gunners were reduced to the role of the man with an airgun in a fairground, firing in the blind determination to hit something, but rarely doing more than stab the air.

As the fight wore on, the more disciplined gunners, in crews whose members could talk quietly of fighter positions on the interphones amid the thud of shells, held their fire. 'They tracked the fighters carefully, and shortened their bursts, calmly calling off new attacks.'[25] It was essentially a battle of the most primitive kind, not unlike an Indian attack on a stockade or a waggon train, with every man who could handle a gun firing when he got the enemy in his sights; in the B.17 the bombardier and navigator shared three nose guns; the top turret gunner had a pair; the radioman a single gun, as had the waist gunners, 'standing at their open windows in the biting wind . . . ankle deep in empty shell casings before the battle was an hour old'[26]; the ball turret and the tail turret gunners had pairs of guns, swinging round sharply in a concentrated endeavour to catch the fighters as they hurtled past, banked and came in through a blind corner before flipping away out of fleeting sight and range.

By the time Schweinfurt was reached, 28 bombers had gone and 34 had turned for home with mechanical failures or battle damage; they were soft options for any fighters lurking by, who swarmed round these helpless laggards, although one doughty B.17 was flown and fought back to the English Channel on a single engine before it succumbed. The 229 bombers who made it to Schweinfurt took 12 minutes to accomplish their mission, and had stuck together so well, had 'closed up' again and again as the Light Brigade at Balaclava had 'closed in to the centre' on their death ride, that all turned with the surviving lead plane just short of the target to confuse the fighters and see their bombs go down a sky for merciful minutes free of rocket and tracer.

But the journey home was grimmer than the trip out. The tired crews had to face new fighter attacks, from an enemy refreshed with full tanks and ammunition belts. Shooting down another 32 bombers, pursuing them like a merciless swarm over the channel, the luck of the draw had the weather close in as the coast was reached; the waiting escorts could do little to help. All told the 8th lost 65 bombers on the raid; a further 17 were so badly damaged that they were scrapped; 121 more received lesser, repairable damage; 186 fighters were claimed as destroyed, but at most 43 had gone down; 642 of the 8th's aircrew were killed, captured, or wounded. 'Now we have got Schweinfurt', said General Arnold a few days later, speaking to newspaper correspondents. When the outcry back home did not die down after so facile an assertion, Arnold found it necessary to write in a despatch: 'Our attack was the most perfect example in history of accurate distribution of bombs over a target. It was an attack which will not have to be repeated for a very long time, if at all.'

Harris never faced public disquiet, and, like Haig, would probably have ignored it. Arnold, like other American generals, lived in the public limelight, or knew that it could fix on him with unpleasant suddenness and brightness. It was necessary to say Schweinfurt was a success, to ignore the calculations of the target analysts, calling for more attacks as reasonably accurate and destructive as that of 14 October, to ignore the truth, even as Craven and Cate suavely state it: 'The fact was that the 8th had for the time being lost air superiority over Germany.' An unofficial account puts the matter more bluntly: 'The Luftwaffe had won the autumn battle decisively . . . . The 8th had been stopped cold.'[27]

Nor is it true to claim of 14 October, as do Craven and Cate, that 'strategically it was the most important of the 16 raids made during the war on the Schweinfurt plants', unless one interprets 'strategic' as the German response to what might eventually befall if further dispersal and protection of plant was not made. Thanks to the energetic efforts of Philip Kessler, one of Speer's best lieutenants, such moves were made. Kessler, through 1943 and even 1944, records almost with the pride of a collector of bizarre records just how many extra ball-bearings had been produced over given periods, and especially in the last quarter of 1943, when production increased by one-eighth over the third quarter.[28] It is, of course, always possible to say that production would have increased more but for the 17 August and 14 October raids, just as it is proper to point out that between July 1943 and December 1944, an estimated 7,500 fewer German military aircraft than planned were produced as a result of the strategic air offensive.[29] But it is no criticism of the arguments justifying this offensive in any of its aspects to say that Germany did not lose the war through shortage of aircraft or of ball-bearings. What is relevant here is that Spaatz had to find out how the offensive could be prosecuted by means less impossibly expensive than the loss of a third of the 8th Air Force's operational strength in one week's attempt to break through the fighter barrier.

The answer was to be found in the Mustang. But before that escort appeared in its true long-range version, the Wiener-Neustadt raid by the day-old 15th Air Force (to which Eaker was appointed, being replaced in command of the 8th by Major-General Doolittle of Tokyo fame and Mediterranean experience)[30] gave a clear hint of the double threat facing Speer and all others working strenuously to plant out industry in new centres and then protect it by flak concentrations and fighters. Few formations have had a more stimulating start to their career than the 15th Air Force in this raid of 2 November; few World War Two attacks indeed demonstrated, or appeared to demonstrate, so conclusively the freedom to be enjoyed by those who wielded power in the 'third dimension'—*provided* stiff, and at times crippling losses could be accepted in the knowledge that better days lay ahead. What is really so interesting about the raid of 2 November is that despite a missing rate of approximately ten per cent (112 B.17s and B.24s sortied, 11 were lost in combat),[31] there was little doubt in Eaker's mind that attacks from Mediterranean bases on targets in southern Germany and adjoining territory offered a better option and came closer to the Pointblank requirements—now, of course, virtually synonymous with the survival of American strategic air forces in Europe—than the 8th's endeavour to blast its way across the intensely defended centre of the Reich. In 1944 the 8th was to triumph—but increasingly with methods developed by Bomber Command, most notably and frequently in its raids on Berlin; throughout 1944 the 15th continued to attack a wide variety of targets, from aircraft factories to bridges, and its commander had no need to resort to area bombing in order to prove the efficacy of air power.

Although it is true that no attack by the 15th comparable to that on Wiener-Neustadt took place until the following spring, the explanation lies in weather, shortage of radar equipment, the tactical demands of the

Italian campaign—and the success of the attack under review, actually the third on that target, following those of 13 August and 1 October.[32] Although to the veterans of the 8th, these explanations might have seemed facile, the fact is that the recorded German production figures for the Wiener-Neustadt Messerschmitt 109 complex show that production was 218 aircraft in October, 80 in November and 30 in December.[33] In circumstances where the averaged missing rate for the three attacks was seven per cent, where long-range escorts were about to appear, and where it seemed to be likely—and proved to be the case—that the Luftwaffe could not deploy enough aircraft and crews to protect all targets, the raid of 2 November must be accounted an outright victory for offensive air power.

The raid is also interesting in another context, indicated by the above reference to the Italian campaign, and illustrated by two quotations from Craven and Cate in the chapter dealing with the 15th's inception; namely that attacks by 'Mediterranean-based planes should further the advance of our land and sea forces in accordance with plans for the occupation of specific geographical areas',[34] and that the justification of a new strategic air force was that it emphasised the need 'to strike directly at the enemy's capacity to wage war ... by the attainment of air superiority through counter air force operations and the destruction of the enemy's aircraft production'.[35] Contrasting these quotations, and bearing in mind that the 15th by the end of 1943 lost its medium bomber element, which it had inherited from the 12th Air Force,[36] it might be thought that a classic division between strategic and tactical air bombardment had been made, as complete in effect as that made in Bomber Command when 2 Group was removed the preceding May.

Such division was, however, neither the intention nor the effect of Allied air operations in the Mediterranean, where General Eaker and Air Marshal Slessor were as one in directing operations more varied and complex than those mounted by the 8th Air Force and Bomber Command. This study is not concerned with the Mediterranean (and Balkans) theatres as such, but it should be noted that bomber forces were there used as required by the Supreme and Army Commanders, and not in accordance with theories of air power which called for the elimination of major cities or posed the destruction of an enemy's war economy by attacks on his industrial centres. The quotations given above therefore complement each other; they represent no conflicting theories. It may be that in some measure the Allied Air Forces in the Mediterranean were blessed with commanders readier to unite, rather than to argue, than were their compatriots serving under Eisenhower; Tedder's legacy was undoubtedly valuable; certainly Eaker had endured and learned much, and Slessor was a widely experienced commander, with intellectual absorption as well as a rare professional insight into the problems of armies, particularly those as diverse in composition as the forces under the supreme command of General Alexander.

Whatever arguments may range about the importance of the Mediterranean and the Balkans in terms of grand strategy, it cannot be denied that the American 5th and the British 8th armies—together with the latter's Commonwealth comrades and the considerable forces provided by Free France, Poland, Brazil and a post-Badoglio Italy—faced unique difficulties, ranging from vague political objectives to diminished or inadequate logistic facilities, which required a most flexible air effort to ease.[37] That there were few great human conglomerations for the 15th to bomb may also have made for a practical rather than a theoretical approach to the role of air power; that the most vital branch of German industry continued to disperse south and east to join the oil refineries of that area as prime objectives obviously simplified the strategic targeting requirement; that fighter defences—airfields around refineries excepted— rarely approached those of northern and central Germany must not be forgotten.[38] But when all is said and done, a reasonable verdict on these operations is that they contributed *directly* to the defeat of enemy forces; in this sense they should be contrasted with the *contribution* to victory made by the strategic air offensive.

Berlin and Beyond—The German Response

The points so far discussed can be emphasised by examining the first phase of the Battle of Berlin in its operational rather than its political context. We have already seen how there was good cause for Sir Arthur Harris to seek distant targets in the long nights of late autumn and early winter, an objective which neatly answered many critics of his offensive and enabled him to include Berlin as a target whose significance hardly required justification or explanation. We have also had some inkling of what Harris' crews were to endure in the first three months of 1944. What should concern us here is whether greater tactical flexibility could have been introduced into the Berlin battle within the strategic and operational limitations of an area offensive at night executed by a Main Force composed of inexperienced crews. Could the bombing have been more accurate and less costly? Could tactics, in the precise sense of routes, diversions and spoofs, have been more imaginative? Above all, could better use have been made of that versatile aircraft, the Mosquito?

In one sense, the obvious answer to all but the last question is 'yes'; there is no final solution to operational or tactical problems, just as there is no such thing as an ideal strategy. Moreover, the basic factor of slow bombers (relative to fighters) and the causal relationship between blind bombing at night and the destruction of people rather than the tools of war could only have been different if British political and strategic history in the twenties and thirties had been different. It is also relevant to suggest, even if impossible to prove, that the temper of Bomber Command was heroically well suited to sacrifice but less responsive to technical and tactical challenge; even an insistence on the truth that in most cases the most dangerous phase of a raid was the journey back to base seems to have concerned only a minority of squadron and flight commanders and captains; arguably, the truth was self-evident, but if this was so, and was comprehended by so many, it is odd that scant attention seems to have been paid to experimenting with larger crews; by early 1944, despite Bomber Command's operational force hovering around the thousand mark, there were more airmen than the seven-man crew establishment required, and the war ended with many a frustrated pilot and airgunner performing duties whose very tedium had dissuaded them from joining the Army. With crews less concerned to fight fatigue and emotional strain, and with more energy to battle with the resurgent German night fighter force, casualties might have well been lower and a higher proportion of experienced captains and crews might have survived, leading probably to a body of tactical doctrine which could have matched that of 5 Group in innovation and ingenuity.

There is also something approaching a consensus among senior officers that a more flexible and imaginative use could have been made of operational training and Heavy Conversion Units, and that too great a distinction existed between green, or 'freshmen', crews and the small minority of old hands, who had lived to fight another night by learning how to run away. We see here, alas, yet another example of that besetting weakness of British Service practice—good, sometime outstanding standards and performance at the individual and unit level; lack of co-operation, leading to sterility of ideas, at the formation level. It is true that an outstanding personality fighting a war of attrition is a combination that militates against tactical innovation becoming an imperative at all levels, and it may be said that only exceptional commanders and staff officers in Bomber Command were sufficiently aware of this factor to attempt some alleviation of it. If more group commanders and senior air staff officers had expressed a professional zest in the execution of their duties, casualties might well have been lower, even though the fundamentals of Harris' strategy would have remained untouched.

These observations are speculative only in the broadest sense; supporting evidence comes not only from the statements of former aircrew, but from a passage in 'Australia In The War of 1939–45'; *Air War Against Germany and Italy, 1939–43*. Referring to the experiences of Bomber Command's Australian aircrews in the late 1943 raids on Berlin, this history states: 'Many of the comparative failures at this time were due to human errors in navigation or airmanship',[39] a remark which would be obvious or otiose had it not been made in a paragraph describing increasing losses at a time when 'Bomber Command was in the middle of a delayed expansion programme with many new squadrons forming. . . .'[40] This Australian history, like that dealing with the New Zealand contribution to Bomber Command, is normally at pains to minimise difficulties; both histories adopt a tough Antipodean attitude to loss and suffering; many of the most spirited accounts of combat, escape and survival are to be found in their pages.

In conclusion therefore it seems that tactical flexibility to compensate for vulnerable aircraft would only have been possible with a higher standard of operational training and leadership, or what might fairly be called a more professional approach to the business of air war. But it is as fair to argue that a war of attrition precludes the attainment of such standards, whether the Commander-in-Chief and his captains are powerful or passive personalities; even although the most skilful pilots and determined crews did stand a marginally greater chance of survival than the majority, this factor could only have raised the general standard if there had been a breathing space for Bomber Command, during which the newcomers could have been fed into the battle line. No such breathing space could be permitted with the strategy, one largely dictated by political considerations, by which Bomber Command continued to play a major part in the British waging of World War Two in the European theatre.

Thus a vicious circle was made, which affected Main Force crews most seriously, but the Pathfinder Force in like degree. By the turn of the year, Bennett's crews were in the unfortunate position of incurring both criticism and casualties. 8 Group contained a high proportion of Australians and New Zealanders, not unnaturally so in view of Bennett's known and frequently expressed preference for his fellow countrymen and their neighbours. It might be thought that any criticism of the Pathfinder Force might be confined to disgruntled 'Pommies'. Yet it was crews of the Royal Australian Air Force 460 Squadron of 1 Group, flying Lancasters from Breighton in Yorkshire, who reported the inaccuracy of Pathfinder marking during the raid on Berlin of 2–3 December. By the Australians' account, this raid was a 'costly failure',[41] partly due to fickle winds, which blew aircraft off course and scattered the Main Force, and because fog blanketed the target, but also due in part to the Pathfinders' failure in identifying and marking the aiming point.

> It was a very black night for No. 460; it lost five Lancasters, and three more had to struggle home on three engines. Several aircraft from the other Australian squadrons were damaged by gun fire during their return, when use of forecast winds again caused confusion so that they faced not only the defences of Berlin but the defences of the Ruhr during the same flight. The nightly battle of bluff on this occasion prevented clear thinking by some of the Australian navigators, who clearly saw Pathfinder route markers, but as they were so far distant from their own track, they dismissed them as enemy decoys.[42]

We therefore find a situation where Pathfinder route-marking was reasonably accurate, but where a combination of faulty aiming-point marking (another Australian account estimates an error of seven miles, for the Berlin raid of 26–27 November),[43] and mediocre navigation led not only to inaccurate bombing but an overall missing rate of nearly nine per cent. The raid of 2–3 December was in fact the most costly of the pre-Christmas phase, but what should be emphasised is that the Battle of Berlin did become unacceptably costly for 8 Group, and not only for the Main Force in general and the Halifax-equipped squadrons of 4 and 6 Groups in particular. Air Vice-Marshal Bennett has indeed given his opinion that another five raids on Berlin would have seen the end of 8 Group as an operational formation.[44] The Group's early months, following the 1942 experimental phase, had coincided with the advent of the Mosquito, whose losses were negligible; the heyday had been the Battles of the Ruhr and Hamburg, when heavy bombers had been indispensable to 'back up' both the *Oboe*-Mosquitoes and the Main Force, but when nonetheless the Group's losses had remained well below the Bomber Command average.

But by the time that Harris set out on the road to Berlin, Bennett was as keen to seek new outlets for his fertile brain as was Cochrane and Air Commodore Addison, commanding 100 Group. The result was the steady build up of Bennett's Mosquito-equipped Light Night Striking Force, which drained 8 Group of some of its most experienced pilots and navigators, leading inevitably to lowered standards among his Main Force, plus a missing rate which matched that of the other groups and on one occasion rose to no less than 13.5 per cent.[45] The result was that at the precise moment when the German night fighter force and the whole defensive machinery was coming back into the act with a vengeance, when Bomber Command was rapidly expanding and inexperienced crews were fighting their way through winter weather to Berlin and other distant targets, and when the night sky was filled with a whole Brock's benefit of markers which could confuse as well as comfort, the Pathfinder Force was split into two parts of very different experience and skill. The results of that decision were reflected in the casualties for Berlin 1943–44 and the admissions made about the battle by Harris and Bennett in person.

To make this point and to emphasise its effect on the tactical execution of the Battle of Berlin is neither to deny nor to minimise Bennett's contribution to the strategic air offensive. A great navigator, a real leader, a highly professional and thoughtful airman behind his abrasive Australian facade, he rightly saw the Mosquito's potential, and would doubtless have found satisfaction in Speer's expressed conviction that the operations of the Light Night Striking Force produced a quite inordinate degree of damage.[46] But the fact remains nonetheless that Bennett's control of this considerable force of World War Two's most versatile aircraft is a clear example of lack of cohesion at the higher levels of tactical planning, resulting in a use of Bomber Command's Mosquitoes by crews who would have been better employed as guides to the Main Force, or as the spearhead of diversionary raids in strength on targets where the German defences were already engaged. Failure to use the Mosquito in either a true diversionary or a supporting role to the Main Force reflected Bennett's determination to go one better than his fellow group commanders.

There are four factors to be considered here, which taken together do pose the question of whether the Battle of Berlin might not have been fought in a more imaginative way. The supply of Mosquitoes was limited, although less by production *per se* than by the demands of the Royal Air Force in all commands throughout the world; the aircraft could carry, and did, a 4,000-lb bomb to Berlin—a bigger bomb load over a longer range than the B.17 and B.24 was thus carried by a wooden, twin-engined aircraft, designed for the England-Australia air race of 1936, but originally rejected by the Air Ministry because it was '*too* versatile';* if the German

* Author's italics.

defences were not to wreak havoc among the Main Force it was absolutely essential to execute diversionary raids, not rely on mere feints or
the operations of 100 Group; the Main Force, growing in size and committed to operations over Germany's industrial heartland, must remain in
being. On this last factor, there was no disagreement between High
Wycombe and the Air Staff.

We may say therefore on the one hand that in terms of aircraft availability and political-cum-strategic imperatives, it would *not* have been
possible to replace the Main Force with an all-Mosquito force after March
1945, as an Air Ministry appreciation, written in 1947, suggests. Even if
Fighter Command could have been prevailed upon to disgorge some of its
night fighter Mosquito squadrons (which were numerically over strength
and operationally under employed by the winter of 1943–44, other than
those which had been detached to 100 Group and 2nd Tactical Air Force),[47]
and retrain them for bombing operations, the number of aircraft available
when added to a Light Night Striking Force under Command orders
would not have matched the Main Force in the capacity to destroy lives
and property. A most impressive air offensive might well have been
conducted—Bomber Command's Mosquitoes sortied 2,034 times during
the Battle of Berlin[48]—but a campaign of this kind was, as we have seen,
politically unacceptable; moreover it would not have enabled Harris to
wage an 'independent' offensive. It was the very inflexibility of his Main
Force and its alleged unsuitability for operations demanding great accuracy
and co-operation with other elements which partly enabled its Commander to pursue so independent a strategy.[49] A bombing weapon as delicate
and subtle as 300–400 Mosquitoes would, in all probability, have been
coveted and secured by Tedder if not by Spaatz.

On the other hand, it is arguable that Harris, in fighting the Battle of
Berlin, could have made more consistent use of Bennett's Mosquitoes;
the latter had evolved into a powerful and economic weapon of air war,
which logically should have been at the immediate disposal of the Commander-in-Chief and not a subordinate. It must be said here that by
November 1943 it had become apparent to Harris and his staff that split
Main Force raids and not mere diversions by a double-figure element were
essential if the German defences were to dissipate their effort. On 26–27
November, for example, the Main Force set course for Frankfurt, then split,
Halifaxes heading for Stuttgart and Lancasters for Berlin. Despite the
faulty Pathfinder marking for Berlin already referred to, Berlin's size permitted considerable damage (measured by the Harris canon) to be inflicted,
particularly on the suburbs of Tegal and Reinickendorf; because of the

Stuttgart raid, fighter opposition over the city was not at its peak; despite a cloudless night, which lessened the effect of *Window* on flak and searchlight predicting and ranging, the missing rate was just over six per cent.[50]

Thus it is reasonable to argue that a split Main Force operation put the defences in two minds, or at least did so in the period before an arbitrary combination of factors once more tilted the balance. These factors were in the period in question: Hitler being 'very much depressed'[51] about Berlin and determined to recover his standing with Berliners; fewer skilled and experienced German night fighter pilots, yet a mounting confidence among German controllers about the sureness of their assessments.[52] This confidence led them to go banco with the forces at their disposal on any one night, and to feed both single- and radar-controlled twin-engined fighters into the bomber stream, with results which were sometimes catastrophic for and sometimes beneficial to Bomber Command. This was the situation which developed in the first three months of 1944. But in the last two months of 1943, Bomber Command was, at best, feeling its way towards new tactics, and it cannot be said that the maximum degree of help in deceiving the German controllers and dissipating their forces' efforts was given by the available Mosquitoes.   The notion that scattered raids, by Mosquitoes or any other aircraft, deceived these controllers has been disproved by evidence found in Germany after 1945 and analysed by the Intelligence Branch of the Air Ministry.[53] What might however have presented the most serious tactical problems for the controllers would have been combined Mosquito and Main Force raids on the same or adjoining targets, made at different times on the same night and both made in strength.

The notion that German fighters would have ignored the Mosquitoes and concentrated on the 'heavies' rests on the fact that the former were rarely attacked; during the first phase of the Battle of Berlin, and, taking operations over Germany as a whole, of the 2,034 Mosquito sorties flown, ten aircraft failed to return, a missing rate of 0.4 per cent.[54] This happy situation continued throughout the second phase, and substantially for those later months of 1944, when Mosquitoes began, at last, to bomb Berlin seriously, these raids constituting a major campaign in its own right (certainly in the Berliners' opinion), while the Main Force was engaged elsewhere. Nevertheless, it must not be supposed from these figures that German fighters were incapable of engaging the Mosquito; a comparison of performance characteristics shows that this was not so. But a situation where an elusive and very fast bomber, flying at high altitude, operated in relatively small numbers against many scattered targets, and did so when the German fighters could destroy the 'heavies' almost with impunity once contact had been made, obviously allowed the former's crews to enjoy most of the stimulus of night bombing operations with few of the tedium and perils and the horrors of them.

Harris, in his *Memoirs*, goes so far as to admit that towards the end of the first phase of the Battle of Berlin, 'diversionary attacks by Mosquitoes were by now having little effect',[55] which is not surprising when one considers that, although Berlin was all told to receive 6,000 Mosquito sorties before the war ended, the tactics considered adequate for the period in question were to make diversions all over Germany with these aircraft, or to bomb Berlin with the Light Night Striking Force (by December 1943 consisting of four squadrons of 20 aircraft each)[56] when the Main Force left it alone or operated elsewhere. Although by early 1944, the Operations Branch at Bomber Command Headquarters had begun to consider and occasionally to attempt the use of Mosquitoes in a more flexible way and in direct support of the Main Force, this decision was a belated appreciation of the aircraft's value, and one which did little at the time to check the Luftwaffe in its energetic efforts to defend the Reich.

These efforts as 1943 ended were directed predominately at bringing the night bomber offensive to a stop by shooting down bombers en route to *or* returning from the target; although Ludwigshafen was bombed by the 8th Air Force on 30 December with the largest daylight force yet despatched to a single target in Germany (698 aircraft, of which 23 failed to return),[57] the operation is more significant for the fighter escort provided for such a distant target than for the defence actually encountered. The 8th had not yet recovered from 'black week' in terms of conducting a sustained offensive against primary targets; Bomber Command was conducting such an offensive, and, as a result, received the full attentions of the defence. It is the post-*Window* period which, as we have already seen, called on the energies and resourcefulness of the German defences, although it was not until the early months of 1944 that personal rivalries within the Luftwaffe were sufficiently contained for different tactical concepts to be co-ordinated, with results which, aided by especially atrocious weather and the time available for fighter concentration ahead of or over distant targets, proved so costly to Bomber Command.

Here, therefore, it is sufficient to explain that in the post-*Window* period and until early 1944, the single-engined night fighter, operating on the 'wild sow' principle, did pretty effectively plug the radar gap in the German defensive system.[58] Despite Hitler's continued preoccupation with an offensive strategy against Britain, reflected in the V-weapon programme and nuisance raids, the Luftwaffe bomber squadrons stationed in Germany and on the Western Front were virtually non-operational throughout 1943. From these idle squadrons came recruits to fill the depleted ranks of the night fighter squadrons, and especially those flying Me. 109 single-engined aircraft, whose pilots occasionally scored notable successes but were either too green or too indifferent in quality to stay in business for long. The numbers of single-engined fighters deployed in Germany and the Western Front increased from 635 to 870 between January 1943 and January 1944; although this was a numerically larger but proportionately smaller increase than in the twin-engined fighter force (from 410 to 780), and although the single-engined fighter squadron's overall successes, even when operating in co-operation with flak and searchlights, were derisory compared with those achieved by the radar-equipped units, the readiness of the 'wild sows' to seek their prey did undoubtedly keep the Luftwaffe offensive spirit alive at a most threatening period.

As 'distant targets' became the norm of Bomber Command, the chances of bagging the odd bomber obviously increased, although in this context bad weather could not be considered as other than a neutral factor. The route to Berlin allowed for little variation, and even the motley collection of 'highly qualified ex-bomber pilots, pilots in disgrace seeking reinstatement, social failures etc.', posed a serious threat to the new squadrons of Bomber Command. 'Loosely organised and rather like guerilla bands in their attitude to authority', the three Gruppen under the command of Oberst Herrmann, a pilot of renown, were given ample propaganda backing and apparently operated in a lurid atmosphere more akin to that of the 'Blue Max' than Bomber Command's subfusc. 'If fuel runs out and there is no possibility of landing, bale out', ran one rather absurd injunction, on which a British intelligence summary makes the dry comment: ' . . . soon the majority of pilots had more parachute jumps on their records than victories.'

Obviously this was not a state of affairs which could continue indefinitely, and the six new radar systems developed between July and December 1943 by German scientists and technologists is clear evidence that the more sober heads in the Luftwaffe knew full well that the battle for command of the air would be won by brains rather than brawn or bravura. As has been well said, the battle 'afforded a spectacle of the highest scientific ingenuity and tactical skill of two countries engaged in continuous thrust and parry'. But more than awareness of the battle's nature was required, and at deeper understanding of what was at stake had to sustain the contestants than unrelenting determination and a mixture of dare devil and devices. The issue was nothing less than deciding whether Overlord would be mounted. Harris had his views on the necessity of that venture, but, firmly embedded in command, never wavered in the conviction that, if it had to be mounted, his Groups and squadrons would ensure its success, albeit by the execution of a strategy which his critics thought misconceived and none could doubt was most terribly costly.

The Commander-in-Chief's opponents were as well aware of the issues, but enjoyed no comparable security of tenure in their appointments; thus, until Goering's nominee, General Schmid, replaced General Kammhuber in September 1943 as Commander of all night fighter forces, two tactical doctrines existed in uneasy coalition; even when Schmid, by early 1944, was firmly in the saddle, and Kammhuber, an airman in the British view of the greatest skill and of unique experience, had been packed off by Goering to command the Luftwaffe in *Norway*, differences and difficulties remained. General Martini retained, indeed developed, his own relations with other branches of the defensive organisation; but by contrast, an increasing flow of aircraft and the new equipment for them was not matched by a comparable improvement in the numbers and quality of aircrew; although Schmid was sensible and shrewd enough to combine the best of both doctrines once he had entire responsibility for them, the enormous responsibility resting on the controllers could not lessen. Thus although the defenders of the Reich from the assault from the air were to enjoy their greatest successes in the first three months of 1944, and were to match Bomber Command in every weapon brought to bear, the signs were not wanting for those German airmen with the courage to recognise them, that defeat was, one day, to be their portion.

PART IV

The Years of Success
1944–1945

The Issues

1944–45

The Background

It is not proposed in these two final chapters to deal with the issues and operations of the last year of the war in such detail as was found suitable for the earlier phases and particularly for that crucial one between March 1943 and March 1944, which effectively culminated in the triumph of the Mustang and the beginning of the destruction of the German Air Force at its source as well as in the air. Once Overlord had passed from a planning to the mounting stage and once the Mustang had appeared to enable the day and night raids to continue, the issues came down to two of great, if somewhat painful, simplicity, both residing in command and control: the American determination to run the war their way; Harris' determination to run the war his way. As we shall see, the result was a decisive victory for the latter, a result which even caused some deflection of American strategic objections. Although Eisenhower was powerfully supported by Tedder at all times in his insistence that Bomber Command be committed to the support of the land battle, whether the targets lay in Germany or in front of the opposing troops, Harris' strength lay in his ability to defy Portal, the principal channel of communication with High Wycombe.

The American determination to be the prime mover in the campaign to liberate Western Europe from the Nazis was expressed in somewhat different terms from Harris'; it was not so obviously personal, or expressed in the views and statements of one commander; although Spaatz was given great power, he always said that he was happy to serve under Eisenhower[1];

until the strategic stalemate of the summer and autumn—a stalemate originally obscured by the 'breakout' from the Normandy lodgement in mid-July—Spaatz appeared to be reconciled to committing his two strategic air forces to the support of the land battle whenever the Supreme Commander or his subordinates thought necessary. Moreover, although strategic bombing by the 8th Air Force came increasingly to resemble that of Bomber Command, its operations orders and the subsequent reports were written so as to suggest a carefully planned campaign of attrition against selected industrial targets—aircraft, transport, oil.

Nevertheless, the collective American belief was that the final defeat of Nazi Germany was an American show, to be headed by an American, who was to be served by American subordinates. Not only on the ground but in the air the combined resources of the forces under Spaatz's command swamped those finally responsible to Portal. The 8th Air Force alone had well over 2,000 B.17s and B.24s in front-line service by the time of D-Day, while Bomber Command, although immensely more formidable in terms of bombload and sheer destructive power, had not many more than 1,000.[2] The prodigality of American resources in terms of manpower, let alone material, may be measured by the fact that by the autumn of 1944 the 8th Air Force had two complete crews for each aircraft.[3] In view of the high and sustained sortie rate maintained for these aircraft throughout the year, this double crew system was doubtless beneficial, especially as disturbing reports reached Arnold in September that neither morale nor bombing accuracy was all that it might be.[4]

Be that as it may, the sheer size of the American effort convinced American commanders that the direction of affairs should be in their hands. On the whole they had little to complain about: Eisenhower was Supreme Commander; Admiral Ramsay was British, but the naval side of affairs was relatively unimportant, and certainly involved no fundamental strategic decisions; Montgomery's command of the land forces was known to be temporary, and was in the event honoured more in the breach than the observance. In the air, however, an entirely different situation obtained, and it must be said that at no time was any American officer, from Eisenhower downwards, prepared for one moment to accept that Air Marshal Sir Trafford Leigh-Mallory, as Commander of the Allied Expeditionary Air Force, had any say whatsoever in the control or distribution of the American air forces committed either to strategic or tactical objectives.[5] This opposition to British control is mentioned here for one specific reason: its effect was to make Spaatz as independent a commander as Harris; the effect of that independence was to lead him to wage a compaign remarkably similar in *method* and not really so dissimilar in objectives to that waged by the Commander-in-Chief Bomber Command. The record of 8th Air Force operations in the final year of the strategic air offensive makes this quite clear, not least in the reliance on blind-bombing by radar, which produced ' . . . an average circular probable error of about two miles . . . which meant that many of its attacks depended for effectiveness upon drenching an area with bombs'.

For the Germans the issue was survival as, in a different context, it had been for Britain in 1940 and 1942. The narrower issue was whether the defence should be given resources to lessen, if no longer to prevent, the most frightful losses in life and property or whether some new offensive weapons should be produced in order to check the Anglo-American onslaught before its full might was unleashed.

Due largely to Speer's ability to keep Germany functioning as an armaments base and to provide indeed more material than Hitler's crumbling armies could use, his authority advanced in the early and middle months of 1944, and his insistence on increased fighter production for defending German towns and, to some extent, German industry, was conceded. But by September 1944, his battle was virtually lost, because the Anglo-American air offensive against oil targets, although a halting affair when considered at the policy-making level, was in a short space of time sufficiently decisive to wreck most of Speer's plans. The story of the last nine months of the war so far as the defence is concerned is therefore best told as a record of death and devastation. Nevertheless, as has been said earlier, the German Air Force fought on while any fuel and crews were left to get machines into the air.

The German increase in fighter production throughout the first eight months of 1944 was certainly amazing and, coupled with the threat of jet aircraft becoming operational in large numbers, both surprised and depressed the Allied commanders. Spaatz, late in the year, was much given to forebodings; so were his deputies; in January 1945, Major-General Anderson, Spaatz's chief operations officer, reported 'that the strategic air situation was "very sad".'[7] This conclusion was based largely on estimates of a revival of the German Air Force, and in part on the apparent recovery of the German petrochemical and synthetics industries. Although when Anderson spoke Von Runstedt's Ardennes offensive was being effectively countered by Allied ground and air forces, the former's gloom was also in part due to realisation that Germany's oil supplies had been sufficient for this major attack to be launched; the gloom was compounded by the additional fact that attacks by the strategic air forces on Germany's western transport system between September and December had served principally to reveal its strength and resilience.

But General Anderson and his colleagues did Speer and his subordinates too much credit. Although in a sense German industry 'recovered' twice from USAAF attacks on aircraft and oil (attacks to which Bomber Command contributed powerfully but infrequently), this was much more apparent than real. Despite Speer being 'a great genius' at organisation—an estimate of Goering's in which Craven and Cate soberly concur—he could not plug all the holes all the time. Despite 'Big Week' and its aftermath, fighter production rose; but the effect of the strategic air offensive against the German aircraft industry was to destroy some of the best remaining elements in the German Air Force's front line day fighter force; these strategic attacks, coupled with those executed by the Allied Expeditionary Air Force against airfields before, during and after D-Day, ensured that the Pointblank objective was attained, and in time, even although the Combined Bomber Offensive was 'legally concluded' on 1 April in the revealing American phrase without any Allied certainty as to that success.

Essentially the same situation obtained with the petrochemical and synthetics industries and with transport. By extraordinary efforts, and by using slave labour, Speer and his colleague Edmund Geilenberg, succeeded in repairing all these elements in the German war economy each time the strategic air forces had apparently devastated them. Speer said after the war that this seeming recovery could not have taken place if isolated attacks had been replaced by raids repeated until a particular plant was utterly smashed.[8] Given that by April 1945, both Harris and Spaatz recorded that they were 'out' of targets, Speer's point is really only relevant to the accuracy of attacks, not their weight or repetition. But, in retrospect, the point is also somewhat academic: the accumulated effects of the 1944–45 strategic air offensive directed at industrial towns was such as to make any really genuine recovery by Speer impossible after September 1944. That this fact was not known to the Allied high command must partly explain and may partly excuse why the last eight months of the war were devoted to a bombing offensive which was 'strategic' only in name.

On the Allied side the year is without much interest at the operational level, with the exception of interesting improvements in the application of radar, both in respect of greater accuracy even in the area compaign, and, more significantly for the post-war era, a rapid increase in the variety and effectiveness of radio counter-measures. If there is one operational

feature of the last war which can engage our attention today it is the activities carried out by Air Commodore Addison's 100 Group. It has already
been pointed out that the Air Staff was slow to appreciate the importance
of establishing a Group of Bomber Command for the specific purpose of
carrying out radio counter-measures. There are no straightforward
reasons to explain this hesitation, although it may be supposed that shortages of aircraft, of equipment and of suitably qualified and experienced
radar and radio operators were delaying factors. An Air Staff dislike of
seeing yet another formation established under Harris' command may also
have been a factor. The prime one, however, making *for* 100 Group's
establishment was the price of the Battle for Berlin and the realisation late
in 1943 that the German Air Force had recovered from the effects of
Window, and had, moreover, responded by designing and producing
improved marks of AI radar. The main function of 100 Group, therefore,
and its main achievement in 1944 and 1945 was defensive—to fly off its
aircraft ahead of Main Force attacks and to jam German radio traffic and
AI radar by airborne equipment, supplementing those operated from the
south and east coasts of the United Kingdom.

Craven and Cate are wrong in suggesting that radio counter-measures
were mainly carried out by the 8th Air Force[9]; they were primarily a
British responsibility, although the 8th did fly jamming and spoof operations on occasion. The British lead in electronic warfare was, however,
as long as in the design and application, if not necessarily in the production
of radar. It was a variant of H_2S which the 8th Air Force relied on to maintain the momentum of bombing in the last year of the strategic air
offensive. H_2X was a British equipment in all but name; without it is fair
to say that a daylight offensive—albeit conducted on an 'area' principle—
would have been impossible. A sustained offensive required radar to
diminish, if never entirely to ignore, the fact of weather; in 1943 radar
was available in quantity; in 1944 and 1945 bombing through the
'overcast' accounted for well over the half the missions carried out by the
8th Air Force, and a high proportion of those executed by the 15th.

To mention these facts is not in any way to suggest the superiority of
one national effort as against another; it is simply a fact that the nature of
the strategic air offensive, when it became an integrated element in (if
never an integral part of) the Eisenhower campaign, required a high sortie
rate; that in turn required devices to beat the weather—and, somewhat
more than coincidentally, to baffle the German fighters; these factors led,
with like inevitability, to area bombing on the Bomber Command scale.
Having made this clear, it should however be emphasised that the main

contribution of radio and radar *counter*-measures was first to preserve Bomber Command as an operational force, and second to provide a gamut of deceptions, not only in support of that Command, but in support of Allied operations of war as a whole. Arguably, 100 Group's biggest contribution to the success of these operations was on the eve of D-Day, rather than in the months that followed, when a largely spent German Air Force only occasionally presented a serious threat to Bomber Command.[10]

The German Air Force could not match these and other operations. Moreover, as the night and day fighter squadrons, together with other elements of the German armed forces, fell back on the Fatherland, it became difficult to distinguish the fight against the Allies' Strategic Air Forces from the battle for survival as a whole. Flak developed in intensity and effectiveness and indeed, in 1944 and 1945, accounted for more of the bombers engaged on daylight operations than did the fighter force.[11] The latter's power decreasingly reflected its nominal size; no sustained defence became possible after Big Week; thereafter aircrew standards dropped alarmingly; massed attacks on day bomber formations were reserved for isolated occasions, while at night the ground controllers increasingly came to rely on the tactics of feedings the fighters into the bomber stream, rather than concentrating near or over the target.

The only factor which might have redressed the balance would have been a concentration on jet aircraft production. Theoretically, and if Hitler had left his subordinates alone, it would have been possible to have had two or three hundred jets flying operationally by the spring of 1944. The Allies were working on jet aircraft design and production too, but it was not reckoned that anything remotely approaching an operational force would have been available before the following October.[12] Even if it had, the problem would have remained that jet engined escort fighters could only have operated from airfields within, at the most, 100 miles or so from the target to be bombed. It can be seen therefore, that at the end of 1944, when many such targets were at a far greater distance than this from airfields in France and the Low Countries, in default of accurate intelligence about the German jet programme, Spaatz had some cause for disquiet.

On the other hand and in retrospect, it is almost undoubtedly the case that the final issue would have been decided by sheer weight of numbers and quantity of resources, including possibly the use of atomic weapons. Thus we need only note in the context of this history that the virtual non-appearance of jet aircraft justified the Eisenhower and Tedder insistence in attacking oil and transport throughout the middle months of 1944. Here were two factors preventing the war dragging into a seventh year.

But the war did drag into a sixth year, and the essential interest on the Allied side of this period lies in the fact that, while German cities were being pounded to rubble, and as Dresden joined Guernica, Warsaw, Rotterdam, Coventry and Hamburg in a record of devastation which still has power to numb, the air commanders and their superiors were engaged in a protracted and meaningless wrangle of the Humpty Dumpty variety. Although selective and precision bombing of industrial resources remained as the strategic objective of air power, the nature of total war and the fact that American troops were fighting down below, ensured that the 8th Air Force wreaked destruction in Germany on a scale and in a manner not far removed from that of Bomber Command. It is a measure of Harris' domination of the strategic air offensive that Berlin in 1944 and 1945 was bombed by the 8th Air Force as savagely and frequently as by Bomber Command. It may be noted too that, although the destruction of Germany's oil and transport resources was brilliantly executed by the three Strategic Air Forces in combination, the so-called close support given to Eisenhower's troops was largely ineffectual and frequently positively damaging to the Allied cause. Towns were so devastated that troops were impeded rather than helped in their advance; relatively few Allied troops were killed by the bombs of their own side, and both green and battle-weary units became insistent in their demand for air cover; nevertheless the feeling gradually grew, and was forcefully expressed by Tedder towards the end of 1944, that the doctrine of tactical support by heavy bombers was possibly one capable of revision.[13]

Before D-Day

We must now therefore deal in a little detail with how disagreements arose among the Allies and why American strategic objectives became blunted and diverted from their original course. It is a singular, unattractive and significant story for the student of Allied strategy in the European theatre in the closing stages of World War Two. The problem originally arose from a lack of clarity as to who would have effective command of Air Forces before Overlord was mounted. Although Eisenhower had been made Supreme Commander of all forces, sufficient lacunae were left in the directives issued to him to make it relatively easy for his requests to be ignored or disobeyed. It must be said to Harris' credit that he never disguised his detestation of the objectives that were laid down for Bomber Command. By the beginning of 1944 he had come to accept that Overlord was inevitable and that some diversion of his forces in its support was unavoidable[14]; the crippling losses suffered by Bomber Command in February and March also made it imperative that the bombing of Germany should be temporarily halted. In that sense therefore Harris was prepared to accept the 'panacea' of bombing Overlord targets, even though he remained unrepentant about the strategic need for them, and sceptical about the results which could be achieved. But when expressly ordered in March and April to commit his Groups to attacks on French transportation targets, he met his obligations by despatching squadrons of 4 and 6 Groups, supported by 617 Squadron, the latter operating in a low-level role.[15] Paradoxically, the effectiveness of these attacks was such that it seemed as though Harris was hoist with his own petard, and it is probably the case that the prolongation of Bomber Command's overall support of Overlord until August had something to do with the fact that Bomber Command was not quite as blunt an instrument as Harris averred.

The more substantial point, however, is that Harris continued to ignore the significance of the command structure that was being painfully cobbled together as a compromise expression of Anglo-American policy; later when he could no longer afford to ignore it he chose to flout it. As a result, by October 1944 'tragic consequences' ensued, which were resolved by partial capitulation to Harris' beliefs and the effective commitment of the 8th Air Force, although not the 15th, to an area campaign. It can now be said that, if clarity had entered into Anglo-American discussions of command problems rather earlier than the eve of Overlord, the deadlock might have been resolved in a different way—although it remains a matter of debate whether the war would actually have been shortened. But it is worth for a moment returning to the Casablanca Directive in order to understand the perils of ambiguity, and the use that was made of them by commanders either instructed by their governments to put the national interest first, or more than ready to do so. The Casablanca Directive, for example, which referred to the contribution which Bomber Command and the 8th Air Force might make to Overlord, did no more than say, 'You will afford them [i.e. ground forces] all possible support in the manner most effective'.[17]

Some of the effects of so ambiguous a statement have already been discussed in the final passages of Chapter 6, in which it will be seen that,

control so far as it affected operations in the air had to be properly decided. On 22 March 1944 a compromise solution was reached. General Eisenhower's authority was made utterly unequivocal, and in consequence that of his deputy was strengthened; little doubt then remained that it would be successfully asserted, and particularly in respect of the strategic air offensive.[20] We must note that General Spaatz retained *geographically* greater authority than Tedder, and therefore remained effectively outside this new arrangement. But it is the case that for some months all other commanders knew who their masters were and what they had to do. That General Spaatz remained outside the new arrangements and that he should specifically refuse to take orders from Leigh-Mallory was unfortunate[24]; that, temporarily at any rate, Harris should be forced to take orders from the Supreme Commander and his deputy was satisfactory. Or so it appeared at the time.

Although the command problem appeared to have been settled, that of objectives was in fact still in doubt. Eisenhower was primarily concerned with harmonious relations among his subordinates and, apart from promising his troops an aerial umbrella, rarely interfered in the selection of targets or the planning of operations. Tedder's views, on the other, hand were clear and pronounced: due to his long experience in North Africa and the Mediterranean, he was a partisan of using air power as an interdiction weapon, believing that this was not only the most economic and efficient use of both strategic and tactical forces, but one which contributed directly to the success of ground operations. Eisenhower's deputy was, in fact, something of a soldier manqué. Spaatz's views were equally pronounced, being governed by belief in his authority—one which was obviously supported by the Joint Chiefs of Staff, by the control of two air forces, and by a conviction that strategic air power in the classic sense could still be employed against industrial targets. He therefore urged that oil should have priority.[22]

Harris' views were even better known and were notable more for the vigour with which they were expressed than for their originality or relevance to the problems which confronted his colleagues in the other Services. Repeatedly in the early months of 1944 he urged on all who would listen—and many who preferred not to—the inevitability of area bombing and the fundamental contribution it could make to hastening Germany's downfall.[23] When short of a strategic argument he would deploy an operational one; he found that the anxious months of 1942 and late 1943, in which, with every justification, he explained that the strategically desirable was governed by the operationally feasible, came in very handy when seeking to advance his case before the critical and doubtful audience clustered around Eisenhower. When asked to undertake daylight operations he said they were 'absolutely out of the question and could in no circumstances be undertaken'.[24] He said that his aircraft lacked the necessary ceiling, armour and armament; that his crews were untrained for the task, and that radar apparatus, although constantly improving, was not of the type which could enable precision bombing to take place, even in ideal conditions.

For the time being, however, Harris was not in the ascendant. In a directive of 4 March 1944, Portal laid down targets within the French railway complex, whose selection was governed by the Tedder belief in interdiction and endorsed by Portal's temporary determination to show who laid down bombing policy.[25] The six marshalling yards, Trappes, Aulnoye, Le Mans, Amiens-Lougeau, Courtrai and Laon, were duly attacked in a series of raids beginning on 6 March and concluding with an impressive demonstration of precision bombing on the last night of that month. This series of attacks temporarily put Tedder in the ascendant: a demonstration had been given of what Bomber Command could achieve when operating outside its normal pattern, and it was one wholly directed at neutralising the German lines of communication. But there was little real follow-up.

The Official History of the US Army Air Forces shows that the 8th and 9th Air Forces from this time onwards carried out heavy and continuous attacks on every available kind of target, but, although the efforts of Bomber Command as such did become increasingly directed towards the support of the campaign on the ground, the main thrust of Harris' objectives was still directed at Germany. Moreover by the end of March a further complication had arisen. On the 25th, Portal took the chair at a meeting at which were present additionally Eisenhower, Tedder, Spaatz, Harris, Leigh-Mallory, representatives of the War Office, the Joint Intelligence Staff and the Ministry of Economic Warfare. The object of the meeting was to decide whether it would be necessary to continue the interdiction campaign throughout the summer months, or whether oil targets should now receive priority. The issue, ostensibly one of strategic objectives, quickly became one of command and control.[26]

Although the result of the meeting was temporarily to strengthen Tedder's position and to ensure that the Transportation Plan, as it came to be called, should be the priority objective for the Strategic Air Forces, Spaatz took the opportunity to stress that he regarded the destruction of Germany's oil resources as of paramount importance. Like

Harris in a different context, Spaatz was prepared verbally to agree to compromises and to become the recipient of directives ordering his forces to attack certain targets. But in practice the 8th Air Force, and particularly the 15th Air Force, continued to regard the bombing of oil targets as having a greater priority than that of communications. Although on 15 April another meeting at Eisenhower's headquarters appeared to advance Tedder's case (he took the precaution of taking the chair himself),[27] we should note that he had by now two, not one, rivals for authority, and two commanders both possessed of a conviction that their use of Air Forces was more likely to hasten the defeat of Germany than commitment of them to interdiction and tactical targets.

Indeed, the actual directive issued by Tedder on 17 April conceded much of Spaatz's case, while, by implication, it did nothing to rebut that urged by Harris. The directive stated that:

> The overall mission of the Strategic Air Forces remains the progressive destruction and dislocation of the German military, industrial and economic system, and the destruction of vital elements of lines of communication. In the execution of this overall mission the immediate objective is first the destruction of German air combat strength, by the successful prosecution of a combined bomber offensive. The entry on the Continent constitutes the supreme operation for 1944; all possible support must, therefore, be afforded to the Allied Armies by our Air Forces to assist them in establishing themselves in the lodgement area.
>
> The primary objective of the United States Strategic Air Forces is the German Air Force, which is to be attacked by all means available, including attrition in the air and on the ground.[28]

The directive continued by giving to those Air Forces the task of bombing all installations supporting the German Fighter Air Forces. The enemy rail communication systems were given to General Spaatz as a 'secondary objective'. If the weather or tactical conditions precluded precision bombing, General Spaatz was given permission in the directive for blind bombing attacks on Berlin and other important industrial cities, despite the fact that blind bombing on area targets was a denial of the American behest in precision attack. The directive further added that, in the words of the Official History, 'these targets were to be selected with a view to inflicting casualties upon the German bomber and fighter forces, and dislocating the German communications system'.[29] This directive, a masterpiece of fudged objectives and imprecise instructions, made no mention of oil and disposed of the role of Bomber Command thus: 'In view of the tactical difficulties of destroying precise targets by night, RAF Bomber Command will continue to be employed in accordance with their main aim of disorganising German industry.' There were various other supporting paragraphs in the directive, relating to the Admiralty, the Special Operations Executive and the need to neutralise the V-bomb threat.

We can see, therefore, that for every step forward that Tedder, as the proponent of interdiction, took, two steps backwards were taken and genuflexions were made on the altar of area bombing. It is true that from April to August Bomber Command dropped far more bombs on targets in France and the Low Countries than it did on those in Germany.[30] But this effort conceals the fact that all the while Harris was being given implied authority to revert to his original concept of 'wrecking Germany from end to end' whenever he thought fit. It seems to have escaped the attention of those responsible for framing the strategy for defeating Germany in Europe that the Commander-in-Chief, Bomber Command's time scale might differ radically from that of General Eisenhower, but this in fact is what happened. It is now clear, moreover, that, although the contribution of Bomber Command to the success of the landings in Normandy and the lodgement that was thereafter secured should not be minimised, it was not decisive and in many ways was misdirected.

Harris was absolutely right when he said that Bomber Command had limitations; those limitations became apparent when Groups were ordered to attack targets of which they had little knowledge and which could not be bombed with accuracy. But the same point does not apply to the contribution which Bomber Command might have made to a quicker and more effective destruction of German industry. It has been implied throughout this history that there were strict operational limitations on what Bomber Command could achieve, apart from destroying German cities. But it is clear from the achievements of Main Force squadrons in 1944 and 1945 that there was an area between that of wide-scale urban devastation and 'pickle barrel' bombing in which the Command could perform with considerable accuracy. The bombing of oil installations in June furnished in fact an example of what ordinary, average crews were capable of when led to the target by experienced Pathfinders.[31] This situation obtained increasingly after September 1944, and particularly in respect of 5 Group, but it is from this time onwards that Harris once again returned to his original concepts, despite the decreasing casualties its crews suffered. It also marks the period when the Allied Armies became bogged down, and when hopes of a swift victory in Europe, with all its political rewards, were submerged by Anglo-American dissension about objectives and methods.

American Air Power Comes to Fruition

There would be several analysts of American air power as it was deployed and demonstrated over Europe's skies in the last year of the war who would dispute that dissension about objectives and methods was noticeable in the period under review, or, at any rate, that the forces under General Spaatz's command were in any way unsure of where they were going. Craven and Cate draw on every available source for this period in an effort to show that, just as Harris was reasserting the independence of his command, the 8th and 15th Air Forces were being directed anew on to carefully selected industrial targets in Germany. Certainly the record of industrial destruction wrought by these two Air Forces between September 1944 and April 1945 is impressive enough, just as the losses which were suffered are mute testimony to the price which was paid. In their narrative and analysis of the year as a whole, the American historians describe every mission in terms of a particular industrial location; yet despite this attempt to convince the reader that precision bombing in daylight remained a clear objective, other admissions, most notably about radar, reveal that it did not.

Yet, undoubtedly, great strides were made between Big Week and, after giving interdiction and close support to Eisenhower's armies in their march from the Normandy beaches to the Meuse, the offensive which was resumed in September. The important point to grasp in this connection is that although Harris supported Overlord objectives and ground forces reluctantly and Spaatz did so willingly (despite his objections to Tedder's Transportation Plan), the American commander was as much determined to revert to his notion of a 'strategic' offensive at the appropriate moment as was his British compatriot. Indeed, Spaatz planned to resume this offensive with great care, and did so while the fight on the beaches was still raging. Unlike Harris, who confined his contribution to the oil campaign to July and August, with intermittent attacks (predominantly on Ruhr industrial complexes thereafter), Spaatz in mid-1944 saw oil as the only target of true strategic significance; his sustained offensive against oil targets from July to September, executed by both his strategic air forces, is arguably the most important and decisive battle in the strategic air offensive.

That this battle was mounted and maintained just as stalemate was setting in at the higher levels of Anglo-American direction and command, is but one more indication, if perhaps the most revealing, of how 'independent' the strategic air offensive was of 'grand' or Allied strategy as a

whole. It is true that Arnold and the Joint Chiefs of Staff favoured Spaatz's
ideas and supported his plans, even when their execution was costly.[32]
It is equally the case that when the Allied armies halted their advance
(ironically because they too were suffering from shortages of fuel), neither
Eisenhower nor his Staff considered whether Spaatz could break the
impasse. Spaatz had become set on course—selective operations merging
insensibly into an area campaign, denominated as 'beating up Germany's
insides,'[33] and nobody in authority saw fit to deflect him from it.

With these factors in mind, it is possible to indicate how Spaatz
operated from 8 June onwards and how he saw the issues once his forces'
main part in the Transportation Plan had been completed. From his
point of view, he had exercised considerable patience. Although he had
the growing resources of the 15th Air Force to call on whenever he felt
that attacks on oil or aircraft assembly targets were urgently necessary to
follow up the operations of Big Week and the like, he carried out his part
of the bargain over Tedder's strategy; indeed, Craven and Cate claim that
most of the 8th's operations in mid-summer were directed at targets which
were not in the 'strategic' category at all. It might be borne in mind, too,
that a good case could have been made, and by implication was made, for
concentrating the 9th Air Force on transport targets; there were those who
pointed out that using heavy bombers to attack French rail centres would
not only wreak such havoc that Allied logistics would be seriously affected
when the march east began, but that casualties among French civilians
would be very heavy.

This last issue did in fact exercise Churchill and Roosevelt considerably
at one point, and in March Lord Cherwell, of all analysts, was asked by
the Prime Minister and others who opposed such attacks to produce
figures showing the possibly catastrophic effects on French civil life if they
were put into effect. Cherwell, employing his best arithmetic, came up
with a figure of 160,000 casualties which might be caused. It will occasion
those readers who have correctly assessed the priorities which governed
Anglo-American rather than Allied strategy during this period no
surprise, that despite this figure, the Transportation Plan was accepted by
Churchill and Roosevelt. As Eisenhower said on 26 March: 'There is no
other way in which this tremendous air force can help us, during the
preparatory period, to get ashore and stay there.'[34]

Spaatz did not agree, but after his final plea on 5 March that oil should
have priority, got down to the transport task. But, as a further curb to his
growing conviction about oil (itself part of a deeper conviction that 'a
properly conducted strategic air war would eliminate the need for the

invasion by land forces, or at least reduce it to a mere occupational operation'),[35] Spaatz was also persuaded by political factors, namely the need for Anglo-American harmony wherever possible, to commit a relatively high proportion of the 8th Air Force to attacks on flying-bomb on 'Crossbow' targets during the period when he was itching to open an oil campaign in earnest. The 9th Air Force had been reconnoitring such sites since December 1943, and Spaatz must have believed—although he at no time expressly stated—that since most of the operational flying-bomb sites were within comfortable range of that Air Force's medium bombers, the 8th could be spared the task of attacking them. Moreover, American commanders at all levels could not be expected to feel as intensely about the flying-bomb threat to the United Kingdom as their British compatriots. That Air Marshal Leigh-Mallory, for whom most American commanders had a quite unwarranted dislike,[36] was, as Commander-in-Chief Fighter Command, a former prime mover in any plans for the destruction of their sites, only increased the reluctance with which Spaatz accepted this unwelcome chore.

Nevertheless, and despite strong opposition from General Arnold, the 8th was in part diverted to Crossbow sites. Arnold got his staff to argue that 'the Crossbow diversion may well make the difference between success and failure in accomplishing our pre-Overlord objectives.'[37] But, 'by the spring of 1944 a more or less fixed pattern of Crossbow bombing operations emerged. Massive raids by heavy bombers of the 8th Air Force—principally B.17s—were supplemented by almost continual attacks (weather permitting) flown by medium bombers of the 9th and the RAF, by smaller-scale attacks at frequent intervals by heavy bombers from the 8th, and by fighter-bomber attacks.'[38] It must be recorded to the credit of Spaatz, and to the greater credit of the men serving under him that up to 12 June, when phase one of Crossbow operations was suspended, 5,950 sorties had been flown by the VIII Bomber Command, for the loss of 49 aircraft and 462 men, the latter including some of the more skilled navigators and bombardiers. It must also be recorded as an instance of Harris' ability and freedom to pursue his own course, that 'of the 25,150 sorties and 36,200 tons expended during all Crossbow operations prior to D-Day, RAF Bomber Command accounted for only 3,900 sorties and 3,500 tons . . .'.[39]

Not much imagination is required therefore to perceive that when, on 18 June, '15 combat wings of B.17s were despatched against 11 oil installations in north-western Germany',[40] Spaatz most probably felt that *his* strategic air offensive was under way at last. Bomber Command was to be engaged in concentrated, if intermittent, raids against oil targets too

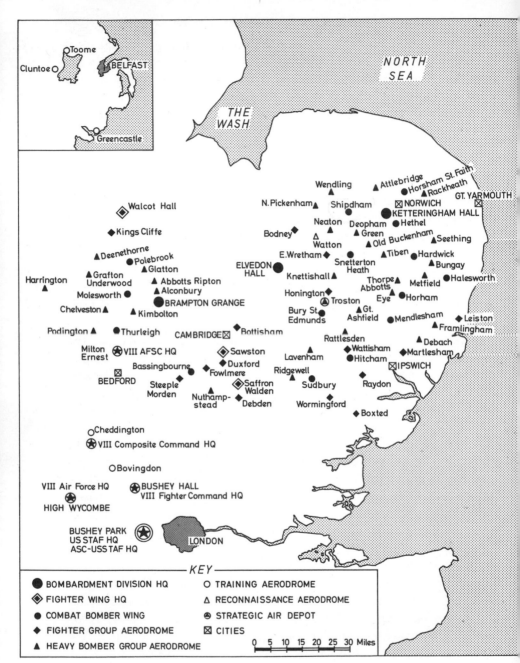

KEY

BOMBARDMENT DIVISION HQ   ○ TRAINING AERODROME

◈ FIGHTER WING HQ   △ RECONNAISSANCE AERODROME

● COMBAT BOMBER WING   ⊛ STRATEGIC AIR DEPOT

◆ FIGHTER GROUP AERODROME   ⊠ CITIES

▲ HEAVY BOMBER GROUP AERODROME

0 5 10 15 20 25 30 Miles

8th Air Force, June 1944

over the next three months, as it was with equal infrequency in the concluding months of the war, but since, unlike Spaatz, Harris regarded such
operations as a diversion from *his* campaign, a record of these raids belongs
more properly to Chapter 10. The 8th and 15th Air Forces, however,
supported by their fighter components—a total force of well over 4,000
aircraft—took oil targets as their main *stated* strategic objective from 18
June onwards.

It is because this battle for oil was such a singular, such an American
example of the belief in selective bombing, that it is accorded a place
here, in the chapter devoted to the issues. We should also note that the
battle for oil targets waged between June and August, and on many occasions thereafter, was not confined to Germany. Rumania, Czechoslovakia
and Austria all possessed targets of prime importance.[41] In this battle the
strategic air offensive was put in new geographical context; for that
reason too it deserves to be narrated and assessed here.

As laid down by Spaatz in his order of 8 June,

> The general arrangement was to assign to the 15th Air Force the crude oil
> refineries around Ploesti, Vienna and Budapest, together with such syn-
> thetic petroleum plants in Silesia, Poland, and the Sudetenland as Brüx,
> Oswiecim, Blechhammer North, Blechhammer South, and Odertal . . . The
> 8th Air Force undertook to destroy synthetic oil plants in central and eastern
> Germany (Pölitz, Zeitz, Magdeburg, Merseburg-Leuna, Ruhland, etc.) and
> crude-oil refineries around Hamburg, Bremen and Hannover.[42]

By and large, this programme was carried out, and, measured in
terms of 'cost-effectiveness', or what Spaatz could afford to lose and still
keep his forces in the line of battle against damage caused which Speer
(by now almost personified as the enemy) could not afford to ignore,
the result was an undoubted success. The momentum was initially slow,
because Crossbow and close support to the ground forces wedged in the
Normandy beachhead continue to be prime commitments. But by the end
of June the tempo of attacks on oil targets increased; it is one of the virtues
of Craven and Cate that they present a continuous narrative, and from it
one is able to see how the 8th and the 15th waded into the still immensely
powerful German petrochemical industry with all the resources and re-
source which they could bring to bear on formidably defended targets.
If the losses of these two Air Forces had matched those suffered during the
same period by Bomber Command it is doubtful whether this crucial
battle would have continued to be fought; losses suffered by day were heavy,
but the edge of the battle was with Spaatz, not Speer, and the former knew
it. Other 'strategic' targets continued to be attacked in July, among them

city centres; Munich was thus bombed on the 11th. But whenever the 8th was stalled or diverted, the 15th took up the fight. By contrast with its earliest period of operations, the cost of the 15th's operations by July was exceedingly high; in July alone it lost 318 heavy bombers.[43] But General Nathan Twining's crews methodically attacked the targets on Spaatz's 8 June list; there were few days that month that the crews of the 8th and the 15th enjoyed any sort of respite.

August saw the tempo increase still more, with Ploesti finally extinguished on 24 July as a strategic target. The 15th then turned its attention to targets in Germany. On the day of the Ploesti shut down—one of the very few occasions in the course of the strategic air offensive when an industrial plant was finally eliminated—the two Strategic Air Forces combined to launch a series of attacks by 1,900 heavy bombers on oil targets all over Germany and occupied Europe. September saw this tempo diminish somewhat, and it is noticeable as one studies operations for this month that a check had been imposed on the battle, due to factors ranging from the demands of the airborne operations in Holland, through aircrew fatigue and logistic problems, to what was almost the last attempts by the German Air Force to respond in strength to this American version of the strategy of aerial attrition. On 11 September, 1,136 heavy bombers of the 8th Air Force attacked seven synthetic oil plants, together with three other targets of major industrial importance; on the 12th, 888 of the 8th's heavies attacked six oil targets; on the 13th, 748 heavies bombed five targets. On these three days the German Air Force put an approximate 400 fighters up to do battle. The missing rate from these three operations was under two per cent. The German losses cannot be calculated accurately, since by this time unit records were not being kept as carefully as formerly. But, at a conservative estimate, probably one-third of the defending force was shot down or damaged. More to the point, jet aircraft put in an appearance but, by all accounts refused combat. Considering that the numerical odds against them were ludicrous, this caution was understandable.[44]

But above all the caution was revealing. The day fighter pilots of the German Air Force never lacked courage, and it may accurately be said of them that they went down fighting. But Spaatz had won his battle; the days of October 1943, when the 8th Air Force had been 'stopped' cold', had been avenged. And it is in this light of a decisive success and a major contribution to victory that one should assess the first phase of the oil campaign, and, in a sense, that fought during and since Big Week. In these eight months USSTAF emerged as a weapon of extraordinary power and resilience, able to withstand the most grievous losses and meet out the most significant punishment. Taken in isolation, only the losses in men and aircraft may seem significant; taken over this eight months period, it is the destruction of Germany's industrial base which should be remembered and evaluated.

Big Week was not in fact such a striking success in root and branch destruction, as the figures for German aircraft production reveal. The overall missing rate on all the 8th's and 15th's operations was six per cent,[45] and although production capacity was lowered by as much as thirty per cent at some aircraft plants,[46] production as a whole was stimulated rather than the reverse by these attacks. We can now see that the reverses were more fundamental than seemed to be the case at the time, but it is only when we come to examine some of the statistics relating to loss of oil resources and production that the full significance of Spaatz's strategy becomes clear. It is, of course, the case that the destruction of the German's war industrial life blood owed much to Bomber Command.[47] But in no sense can the operations be said to form part of the Harris strategy. Only an inkling of these losses could be ascertained at the time, but we now know that 'the amount of petroleum available to Germany declined to 472,000 tons in June, compared to 715,000 tons in May and 927,000 tons in March'.[48] These figures represented about half Germany's output, a success in the strategic air offensive war at a cost which at one time would have been prohibitive. On 20 June, for example, 48 heavies of the 8th Air Force were shot down from a force of 1,361. The actual losses were high; the missing rate was 'only' three per cent.[44]

It was not until the autumn, however, that a really significant assessment could be made of the effects of the offensive against oil targets. The August raids on Ploesti were quickly assessed, because the area was captured shortly afterwards by Russian troops, who allowed American survey parties to examine the plant.[50] This was reckoned, at the most generous estimate to be capable of operating at ten per cent of capacity—surely an indication in at least one instance of the truth of Speer's observation that only repeated attacks on a target eliminated it. The overall missing rate suffered to achieve this objective (bearing in mind that before this sustained onslaught Ploesti, in common with other plants, had been quickly repaired) was seven per cent.[51] Here surely was a 'cost effective' operation of war. By the end of September, as is now known, only about 23 per cent of Germany's fuel supplies available before the Spaatz campaign were being produced.

This proportion was to rise temporarily to approximately 30 per cent by the end of October.[52] This artificial recovery (brought about by the enforced cessation of the offensive due to weather and wastage rather than by the efforts of Speer and Geilenberg) had two by-products: it tempted Hitler into the Ardennes offensive, which finally wrecked the German forces on the western front and reduced virtually to zero the material and supplies on which they depended; but it led Spaatz to press again in the inconclusive Allied discussions of the late autumn and early winter for a resumption of the oil offensive rather than a reversion to the transport campaign.[53] As we have seen, and as the two final sections of this chapter will amplify, both objectives degenerated into an area campaign, governed in part by Spaatz's virtual conversion to the Harris strategy, and much influenced by the 30 January 1945 declaration at the end of the Malta conference that bombing should be directed at 'Berlin, Leipzig, Dresden and associated cities where heavy attack will cause great confusion in civilian evacuation . . . '.[54]

Before turning to this last, and most depressing, period of the entire strategic air offensive, it is as well to make one more comparison between achievement and cost, and to do so moreover in a context which has not much been studied, namely the effect of the Spaatz offensive on the land battle, an effect which may be compared with that of Big Week—and subsequent attacks on the aircraft industry by the three Strategic Air Forces —on the German Air Force in the front line. In this context, and in concluding this section, one cannot do better than cite the following account:

During the summer months of 1944 the 8th Air Force, the 15th Air Force, and RAF Bomber Command had exerted their maximum power against the German enemy. The bomb tonnages dropped by the 8th alone amounted to 36,000 in May, 60,000 in June, 45,000 in July, 49,000 in August, and 40,000 in September. Even though the weather was perversely unseasonable for some weeks after D-Day the 8th's bombers flew on 28 days during June, 27 in July, and 23 in August. The ratio of losses was correspondingly high, notwithstanding the weakened state of the Luftwaffe, because flak was more deadly now and because bombers often went out under conditions that would have been regarded as unflyable a year before. Out of its 2,100 operational heavy bombers, the 8th Air Force lost 280 in June, 324 in July and 318 in August. VIII Fighter Command losses for these months were 242, 153 and 279 out of about 900 fighters that were constantly available for combat units. The 1,100 operational heavy bombers of the 15th Air Force suffered a still higher ratio of losses, considerably exceeding staff planning estimates. After the record loss of 318 heavy bombers in July, General Eaker estimated in August that 30 per cent of the 15th's crews who engaged the enemy were brought down on hostile territory, and MASAF actually lost more men during that month than did the 5th and 8th Armies in their ground fighting. RAF

Bomber Command's losses were comparably high. Air Chief Marshal Harris pointed out that the casualties of his forces exceeded those of the British Second Army for some weeks after the invasion, and Ambassador John G. Winant commented with much feeling on the terrible rate at which RAF operations were consuming Britain's young manhood.

If the human and material costs of the summer's operations was great, so were the achievements. The bombardment of German oil refineries and synthetic petroleum plants, together with the final exclusion of the Germans from any of the resources of Ploesti, brought the enemy's fuel position to the point of catastrophe by September. USSTAF estimated that German oil production in that month was only 32 per cent of the pre-attack level; and later and better evidence placed the percentage at 23, with gasoline production several points lower. For some weeks the decline of oil output had signified more to the Germans than portentous statistics. At the battle of Caen they had been compelled to employ their stranded tanks merely as small forts dug into the ground whose guns they could not traverse for lack of fuel and lubricants. Later in the summer they were abandoning their tanks and motor vehicles all over France, fleeing on foot, rescuing what equipment they could with horses, or surrendering in droves. Training in tank warfare became for the Germans a luxury beyond reach, and even the Luftwaffe reduced its training period to a few insignificant weeks because aviation gasoline could not be spared. The scientifically planned Allied bombings were strangling the German war machine, leaving to the enemy no hope as he desperately rebuilt his damaged plants, save that the autumn and winter might shield his oil production system.[55]

We now know that recovery on this scale did not occur; after September Germany had shot its war industrial bolt and, overall, production steadily declined. Speer's gifts and his colleagues' energies, great as they were, could not stem the Allied tide, shore up the crumbling industries of the Reich or feed those which were starving for lack of raw materials; the latter were either no longer in production or importable, or were cut off from the manufacturer by the effects of Allied strategic bombing in general—dead, dehoused and demoralised workers and shattered cities—and the transport campaign in particular, in which Bomber Command's repeated attacks on the focal points of the north German canal system played a crucial part. But it is also clear from the account just cited that SHAEF Headquarters and other, subordinate or related commands neither accurately assessed the extent of the German collapse, nor had the evidence of their own eyes for it. We must now try and see why it was that the final eight months of the war saw as little imagination and flexibility in the strategic air offensive as in the conduct of operations on the ground.

Strategic Stalemate

Despite what has been written in the preceding section, the period between the directives of March and April and the resumption of the area offensive in early September is somewhat difficult to put in the context of the strategic offensive as a whole, even if we take Bomber Command and USSTAF together. So great were the resources of the 8th and 15th Air Forces that when, on 17 March, General Arnold suggested to General Spaatz that oil targets could be attacked in addition to those already discussed, no difficulty was found in adding them to the list of specifically Overlord targets. Moreover, despite Tedder's objectives and directives, General Eisenhower had, on 19 April, 'by word of mouth,'[56] authorised General Spaatz to initiate a limited offensive against German oil production with the 8th Air Force'. Although the Air Staff was, and not for the first time, inclined to look with favour on oil targets, nothing more positive than inviting Air Marshal Harris to give an appreciation of how and when this might be done was actually undertaken, and that not until the eve of D-Day. The reader will not be surprised to learn that Harris' reply showed a marked lack of enthusiasm for these 'panacea' targets, although it must be recorded that he informed the Air Staff that he had already agreed with Tedder to attack oil plants as part of his 'marginal effort'.[57]

That Harris for once had not utterly repudiated a proposal from higher authority was, however, sufficient to encourage Portal to ask by 4 July what progress was being made.[58] The Director of Bomber Operations who, it should be remembered, was a proponent of 'selective attacks', had to tell him that nothing specific had yet been done and that no directive had yet been issued. What in fact happened was that oil plants at Gelsenkirchen, Sterkrade, Wesseling and Homberg had been attacked, but mostly by Mosquito Forces, and only on two occasions by the Main Force.[57] Although, therefore, this record to date was unimpressive, and was supported by no directive, it encouraged Portal not merely to revive his interest in oil, but appears to have reminded him that the time perhaps had come when he should reassert his authority. The difficulty in so doing was that command was meant to reflect, however vaguely, the achievement of a particular objective and the fact of the matter was that a considerable part of Spaatz's Forces were attacking oil targets while only a 'marginal effort' was being devoted to them by Bomber Command. Arnold and Spaatz had at least two strings to their strategic bow; if Bomber Command had more than one, Harris was not going to reveal the fact; if Portal wished to reassert his authority, which meant in effect giving orders to Harris, it meant that he had to do so by instructing the Commander-in-Chief, Bomber Command to turn a marginal effort into a major one.

The time for reasserting authority in this way certainly appeared to be approaching, and an Air Staff Brief of 21 August suggested that 'serious consideration should be given to according overriding priority to the attack of oil targets by the Allied Strategic Bomber Forces'.[60] Weight was given to this belatedly expressed view by a strategic situation in which the V-bomb menace appeared to be diminishing and where the Russian advance into Roumania, with the consequent loss to the Germans of the oil fields there, made the retention or the destruction of those remaining a matter of supreme importance.[61] As a result of these factors, the Air Ministry suggested to Eisenhower's headquarters on 30 August that 'we are presented with an exceptionally favourable opportunity in the next few weeks of imposing on the enemy a critical situation in his war economy which, if exploited to the full, may prove decisive to our efforts'.[62] But it was at this seemingly propitious moment in affairs, with a clear objective at last expressed for Bomber Command as well as for USSTAF, that Harris was again provided with an opportunity to plan for the resumption of an area offensive.

In the first place, the Air Staff Brief and the Air Ministry Appreciation suggested that Bomber Command should concentrate on oil targets in the Ruhr rather than anywhere else. Harris did not dissent from that proposition; Berlin apart, the Ruhr was his primary objective, exemplifying to the full his view that 'in order to destroy something you have to destroy everything'.[63] Secondly, and more surprisingly, Tedder pondered whether the Battle of Berlin might be renewed.[64] Nowhere can one find any reason for this shift in emphasis by an airman whose fame and success stemmed from his appreciation of the land battle and the contribution which air power could make to its successful resolution. Berlin, although an industrial centre of undoubted importance, was primarily a political target; Tedder knew well enough when he made his suggestion in early September that the basic problem in Allied strategy was to maintain momentum in the land campaign, not to be bogged down, either in the mud of north-west Europe or in the problems of unconditional surrender. It is of course true that Eisenhower's headquarters was to some extent, and unavoidably so, a centre of political warfare; the Supreme Commander had constantly to keep in mind the problems of a stricken as well as a defeated Germany. Although he may not have been privy to Roosevelt's and to Churchill's discussions and fears about what kind of

Europe would emerge from the ashes of war, Eisenhower was fully aware that nothing which he did could be separated from political factors.

Tedder, an articulate airman with many interests outside the narrow path of his profession, was doubtless as well aware as Eisenhower of all the problems involved in unconditional surrender, and it may be that his curious suggestion for reviving the Battle of Berlin sprang from too close an association with political factors, plus possibly a degree of frustration with his inability to command the support of those whom he regarded as his subordinates, whether it was Harris or Montgomery. Be that as it may, the first few weeks of September did mark a surprising—if sluggish—shift in Allied thinking as to the future conduct of the campaign in and over north-west Europe. One of the effects of a move away from activity on the ground to increased slaughter from the air was to be felt only five months later—in the destruction of Dresden, an avowedly political target, which made no contribution to the German war effort, and which had been hitherto unscathed. It is possible that at the time the implications and the after-effects of attacks on the scale of Dresden were not appreciated by the Combined Chiefs of Staff and others who turned with such seeming enthusiasm to the resumption of the air offensive, which was given the grandiloquent code name of 'Thunderclap'.[65] Early in September Eisenhower shifted his headquarters from the United Kingdom to France, but, paradoxically, this move did not presage any acceleration of the war on land, but rather the reverse. In the first week of September British troops were defeated at Arnhem and thereafter the Armies under Eisenhower's command ground to a halt, while the air fleets commanded by Harris and Spaatz started methodically to knock German cities to pieces.

It is an academic question now whether it would have been possible to resume the momentum of the Allied advance if a settled policy could have been made about the function of air power. In the many discussions which have ebbed and flowed since 1944 of how Allied strategy on the ground should have been conducted, little space has been devoted to the part which air power might have played.[66] It is a fact that the winter of 1944–45 was one of the worst for many years, and it would be unkind and unfair to the men who fought on the ground in those vile conditions to stress too much that the Russian forces on the eastern front had equally inclement conditions to content with yet managed to maintain the momentum of the offensive more positively than did those in the west. The truth of the matter most probably is that the Allied ground offensive in September 1944 simply ran out of steam, out of ideas, out of its more effective units and formations, and even to some extent out of material.[67] There was disagreement between Roosevelt and Churchill, let alone their subordinates, not only on how the ground campaign should be fought, but what its overall objectives should be.[68] There is little point, therefore, in suggesting that it could have been resumed earlier than February 1945 if those responsible for framing policy had been of one mind as to air power's contribution. The fact nevertheless remains that they were not of one mind and it follows therefore that airmen who knew what they wanted to do were allowed to go ahead and do it, and in their own way.

There are three main factors to bear in mind when considering the nature and extent of this strategic stalemate: lack of clear objectives; changes in command and control; a revival of the belief that the strategic air offensive had not yet been used to the full in 'city-busting'. Each of these three facts strengthened the hand of air commanders who wished to prosecute an independent strategy; in combination they gave Harris and Spaatz an unprecedented degree of freedom. It is important in this connection to realise that although Harris, despite his supposed loss of influence, was determined to ignore suggestions, flout directives and disobey orders if need be, Spaatz was not far behind him in revealing his true thoughts about the purpose of a strategic air offensive. He had earlier in 1944 expressed Harris' belief that a properly conducted air offensive could reduce the role of ground forces to a mere 'occupational operation'; he was sustained by the success of the oil campaign; he had ample strategic and tactical air forces at his command should he be asked to attack new targets or again support ground operations, and by the end of 1944 he was to demonstrate his willingness and ability to do both by renewed attacks on flying-bomb sites and repeated missions flown by the 8th as well as the 9th Air Force in support of troops fighting in the 'Battle of the Bulge'.

Having said that, however, it must be stressed that, above all, Spaatz was determined to maintain the momentum of the strategic air offensive, and to do so whatever the weather. Now it is a matter of record that the winter of 1944–45 was compounded chiefly of cold, gales, fog and mud. Yet the 8th Air Force and 15th Air Force pressed on, bombing on H_2X— and also employing a variant of *Gee-H*—and hence bombing inaccurately. The targets were enumerated as carefully as ever in terms of industrial significance, and the priority again given in the directives of October and December to transport and fuel gave sufficient coloration to the notion that a selective campaign was once more being waged. And it is true that by the time Spaatz's air crews 'ran out of targets'[69] in April 1945, nothing remained of the German petrochemical industry and not much, in the west, of its transport. It also has to be remembered, however, that, as Allied armies advanced to the borders of Germany, the 9th and 12th Air Forces, together with the 2nd Tactical Air Force wreaked much havoc on the German lines of communication, and gave to 'interdiction' virtually a new meaning in geographical and tactical terms. It is also a fact, and one candidly admitted by Craven and Cate, that 'strategic' attacks on Germany's transport system, particularly the railways, were not by themselves particularly effective.[70]

Spaatz indeed believed that this would be the case, and said so as forcefully at the autumn conferences at which transport was again officially given first priority as he had in the spring when the Transportation Plan was approved.[71] But it was not so much the possible feasibility of this plan to which Spaatz was opposed, as the command and control implications which it carried. The conferences, directives and command arrangements held, issued and made after September 1944 are as confusing to study as those of the spring, but it is at least clear that Spaatz, while remaining nominally under Eisenhower's command, at last freed himself from any sort of allegiance to British commanders. He had been unrelenting in his hostility to Leigh-Mallory, and the winding up of the AEAF headquarters on 15 October was hailed everywhere by American commanders as one of the war's more agreeable victories. Although Spaatz's staff was prepared to reconsider a revived force with AEAF's function, their notions of how it was to be organised and commanded hardly suggest an Anglo-American outlook:

> Its chief *must* be an American with the rank of lieutenant general. The chief of operations *must* be an American with the rank of major general. Signals and plans *should* be headed by US officers with the rank of brigadier general. The chief of intelligence *might* be a Britisher with the rank of air commodore, but the camp commandant *must* be an American in the rank of colonel.[72]

The necessity of the camp commandant being an American is a nice touch, but in all seriousness it must be pointed out that the views expressed in the passage quoted are a revealing indication of the outlooking prevailing in the Anglo-American camp in the weeks of indecision following the advance to the gates of Germany. 'The Americans disliked serving under British officers',[73] and that was that. The effect of this dislike was as much compounded by a determination to prosecute an independent strategy, as it was so frequently eased by good personal relations and imaginative understanding of an ally's problems and the requirements of effective command and control. Harris, immersed in High Wycombe.

44 Before departure: briefing, December 1943

US 8TH AIR FORCE

45 After return: crew of a Fortress, January 1944

46–7 Hamburg oil refineries bombed by 8th Air Force, June 1944

THE SELECTIVE ATTACK, AMERICAN

48   Cologne: something survived

49 Mannheim 1945: the climax of de-housing

50 German city: ordeal by fire

51   Berlin suburbs destroyed by fire and high explosive

52   Hanover 1945: the effect of fire raids

53 Funeral pyre, Dresden, February 1945

could and did ignore these factors, but Spaatz, a frequent visitor to SHAEF Headquarters, and as sharply aware as Arnold of the hierarchy of power, could not. There were moreover late in 1944 two checks on his final assertion of an independent command, both residing in the frayed but still surviving framework of Anglo-American planning for a combined bomber offensive.

The two checks to Spaatz were, as on previous occasions, Portal and Tedder. The former, at his own request and after the Octagon conference in September, had been given joint authority with Arnold to plan for a revised strategic air offensive, and had concocted a scheme whereby his deputy, Sir Norman Bottomley, and Spaatz between them, were to be made responsible for its day-to-day execution.[74] Secondly, although Tedder was to see area bombing replace an interdiction campaign in 1945, he did not in fact press his 'political' strategy over Berlin in the autumn of 1944 (although the thoughts he voiced on Thunderclap were arguably a harbinger of the Yalta strategy of the following January), but succeeded, at a conference on 28 October, in getting transport as second priority to oil in the formal list of strategic objectives.[75]

Thus, at this time, Spaatz seemed hedged about by the British; yet, by February 1945, the Commander USSTAF had side-stepped this curb, much as the actual establishment of his command on 1 January 1944 had partly offset the coming into being of the AEAF.[76] Yet in freeing himself from dependence on Portal and Tedder, Spaatz moved inexorably into the Harris camp. This development is clearly illustrated if we compare the directives issued under Spaatz's and Bottomley's signatures on 28 October 1944 and 12 January 1945 respectively. Again, one must particularise in these tedious and ambiguous matters of command and planning; although the meeting immediately preceding the issue of the 28 October directive had agreed to make oil the first priority for the full resumption of the strategic air offensive, the actual directive led to a programme which gave this place, or at any rate gave it initially, to transport. Following the issue of the directive, the Combined Strategic Target Committee established a group to supervise the transport programme; Germany was divided into nine zones, reflecting the pattern of Germany's transport system.[77]

By a further paradox, the Combined Strategic Targets Committee, which had been established in October to provide guide lines for Bottomley and Spaatz, was not, collectively, especially keen to make transport the priority objective.[78] Nevertheless the last two months of 1944 saw the 8th Air Force committed to attacks on 'marshalling yards and repair facilities at Bielefeld, Cologne, Coblenz, Frankfurt, Hamm, Hamburg,

Ludwigshafen, Minden, Neunkirchen, Oberlahnstein, Rheine and Saarbrücken . . .'.[79]. Bomber Command attacked its habitual targets in the Ruhr, and although transport was given too as the prime objective, the record in the Official History and the Bomber Command *Quarterly Review* rather suggest that this was no more than a convenient gloss on the full resumption of the area campaign. As Dr Frankland records of this period:

> The area offensive was spread far and wide over Germany . . . The greatest effort was made against Duisburg, Essen, Cologne and Düsseldorf. In the case of Duisburg there were four major operations involving the despatch of some 3,119 sorties and the dropping of nearly 13,000 tons of bombs. . . . Essen was also bombed four times and over 11,500 tons of bombs were aimed at it. Cologne was bombed three times and nearly 9,500 tons of bombs were dropped. In a single attack on Düsseldorf involving the despatch of 992 sorties more than 4,400 tons of bombs were dropped. In smaller attacks on Bochum, Gelsenkirchen, Dortmund, Hagen, Witten, Oberhausen, Neuss, Solingen, Münster, Hamm, Duisburg and Leverkusen about another 22,000 tons of bombs were dropped. Thus, *in the last and utterly crushing Battle of the Ruhr between the beginning of October and the end of December 1944,*[*] some 14,254 sorties were despatched, 60,830 tons of bombs were dropped and only 136 bombers failed to return. This was a missing rate of less than one per cent of the despatched sorties.[80]

This account has been given here rather than in Chapter 10 because it perfectly compares with what, in late 1944, USSTAF was still committed to, and what, so far as Portal, Tedder and Bottomley were concerned it remained eminently suited for. We may also note how the 'operationally feasible' had become so much an article of faith with Harris that, although Bomber Command could now roam the skies almost at will, the strategic air offensive had become an exercise in overkill; USSTAF had the lead in aircraft—although by December 1944 Bomber Command had over 1,500 of all types in front line service, including nearly 1,000 Lancasters—but the latter set the record for tonnages and for sheer death and destruction.[81] Of course there were selective attacks in this period, and many operations which showed the tactical versatility of some elements in Bomber Command. But there were no sustained attacks, nor for that matter was there a sustained offensive on the Speer pattern.[82]

If, however, we look at the directive which Spaatz and Bottomley issued on 12 January 1945, it is fairly clear that some shift, and that arguably a regressive one, had occurred in American strategic thought. In words which faithfully repeated those of the Casablanca and Pointblank

---

[*] Author's italics.

directives, that of 12 January stated in effect that 'the overall mission of the strategic air forces remained . . . the progressive destruction and dislocation of the German military, industrial and economic systems . . . .'.[83] In 1943 the 8th Air Force had attempted to interpret that directive in 'selective' and 'precise' terms, and had been 'stopped cold'; in 1944 the attempt had been repeated and had in large part been brilliantly successful, although, overall, a sustained campaign had only been possible by committing all of USSTAF and its fighter support; in 1943 Harris had interpreted the words as a mandate for area bombing, for 'wrecking Germany from end to end'; that great effort had been partly successful, although achieved at 'unacceptable' cost; in 1944, Bomber Command, needing to husband its resources—which were much less in terms of men and machines than USSTAF—had returned to area bombing whenever Harris had been let off the Overlord hook.

The question that must now be asked and answered is: why did Spaatz commence an area campaign after the issue of the 12 January directive? Some of the reasons why he did so have been given or implied; but there were two other reasons, namely the policy pursued by Harris, and the increasingly political nature of the strategic air offensive in the last four months of the war. It is to a consideration of these factors that we must now turn.

The Final Blows and Harris' Last Bow

In the last eight months of the war Bomber Command returned to the area offensive; it did so under Portal's nominal authority, since as we have seen, the Chief of the Air Staff was restored to his position as co-ordinator of the Anglo-American strategic air offensive by arrangements made with the combined Chiefs of Staff in September. Portal therefore was ostensibly in a position where he could, at last, assert his authority. He had at intervals announced himself as a proponent of the bombing of oil targets; he would have been in a distinct minority if he had strongly argued a case for using air power to support the Armies on the ground; Bomber Command had demonstrated, in daylight operations as well as those by night, that relatively accurate attacks could be made on targets which formerly had been excluded by virtue of the fact that they were difficult to find or extremely heavily defended. In August the Chief of Air Staff went so far as to write a careful appreciation of the opportunities then facing the

Allied Strategic Air Forces—but instead of concentrating on industrial targets he expressed the overriding objective in terms which played straight into Harris' hands. After reviewing all the pros and cons, Portal suggested that it might be desirable very soon 'to apply the whole of the strategic bomber efforts to the direct attack on German morale'.[84] Thus, in proposing such an offensive, Portal conceded Harris' case by favouring what was in effect a return to area bombing; through subsequently muddling in the issues of command and control by his 'dual arrangement' he then virtually stopped himself from ordering Sir Arthur Harris to do anything which might conflict with such a strategy. When, therefore, Sir Norman Bottomley sent a new directive to Harris on 25 September, it mattered little what the words themselves said, just as it mattered little what directives the Deputy Chief of the Air Staff might later issue jointly with Spaatz. Harris knew that an area offensive lay at the root of Portal's desire to reassert authority; it may also be said, although there is no direct evidence to support it, that Harris was reasonably sure that nothing he chose to do would meet with more than protest from his superior officer. The directive of 25 September did in fact give oil and transport as priorities in the new offensive,[85] just as that of 28 October did, but this only serves to emphasise the disingenuousness which characterised the orders given to the Commander-in-Chief Bomber Command, not only at this period of the war, but indeed throughout his entire term of command. What in fact happened in the concluding eight months was that Harris employed most of his forces on an area offensive, but used them in such a way that for long after it was extremely difficult for Portal or any other of his superiors to specifically assert that he was operating within any breach or defiance of the 25 September or any other directive.

As we have seen, Bomber Command could put into the air by this time well over 1,000 heavy bombers, supported by the many different aircraft in 100 Group, and led to the target by strong Pathfinder forces. It is simply not true to say that, because area bombing was unavoidable in a strategic air offensive was to be waged at all for the first four years of the war, there was no other method of conducting it in the final year. But this in fact is what happened. Brushing aside all opposition, Harris proceeded on his way. He was assisted in meeting his objectives by the tactical situation on the ground. Although the Allied offensive had come to a halt in early September, the front line ran extremely close to the German frontier at some points; attacks in western Germany, and in particular the final destruction of the Ruhr, could well be construed as a contribution to 'interdicting' the German armies should they attempt to replenish or to achieve more than purely local mobility. In fact the sheer weight of Harris' offensive in this final period had the same effect in this tactical context as his early attacks had in support of troops in the beachhead; after the crossing of the Rhine was secured by the first week of March 1945, advancing Allied troops found their progress impeded by shattered town after shattered town, stark monuments to Trenchard and to his disciple.

Further Air Staff directives continued to be issued in November[86]; frequent reference was made to transport and oil; it made little difference to the plans for the destruction of Magdeburg, Leipzig, Chemnitz, Dresden, Breslau, Posen, Halle, Erfurt, Gotha, Weimar, Eisenach and what remained of Berlin. Harris was able to resist protestations and complaints, whether made by Portal or by the Bishop of Chichester, because he knew that he was the one man sure of his objectives among the many who were divided. There is no doubt, as the Official History is at pains to explain, that Harris' domination over his superior officer sprang from a number of understandable causes; he had been Commander-in-Chief for three years, and had acquired a reputation based on persistence and courage, and on the fact that he was a leader in the fullest sense of the word; by 1945 he was one of the very few senior British officers who seemed able to ignore, let alone to deny, the American predominance in the conduct of grand strategy; above all he did not much mind what people thought or said about him, Churchill always excepted. Portal appears to have been extremely concerned with preserving amity among his colleagues. It was doubtless desirable, indeed a necessary, aim but it made him impotent when dealing with his subordinate.

The issue eventually came to a head, and did so at a time when the American Strategic Air Force had virtually concluded its campaign against oil and transport as such, and when Spaatz was therefore considering an offensive not very different in methods and execution from that being carried out by Bomber Command. That fact alone robbed Portal's protestations of much of their authority because he was unable to show that a more effective campaign than area bombing could be waged. Nevertheless, on 5 November he wrote a letter to Harris which marked the opening shots in a brief but acrid verbal campaign. The purport of the letter was that Harris should concentrate on certain selected targets, or see the war prolonged by several months. Harris replied the next day in terms which, while appearing to concede final authority to the Chief of the Air Staff, had more relevance to the destruction of German cities than to specific industrial targets. Harris quoted chapter and verse to show that targets were chosen with far greater care than the Chief of the

Air Staff cared to think. Relations between the two officers had, however, reached the stage where correspondence only served to exacerbate the situation.

In a letter of 12 December Harris launched one of his more considered attacks on those who wrote appreciations in Whitehall as to the necessity and the efficacy of bombing ball-bearing plants, molybdenum factories and the like. Ten days later Portal replied, expressing great disappointment at Harris' point of view. He added, with a caution which is only explicable in political terms, 'While you hold this view you will be unable to put your heart into the attack on oil'. Having thus thrown away one of his few remaining cards, the Chief of the Air Staff then repeated for the nth time all the arguments as to the feasibility of selective attack with the forces which Harris now had under command. Such arguments, proceeding from a source which only four months earlier had proposed an outright attack on German morale and, indeed, the German Government, merely led Harris to make another outburst, writing to Portal on 28 December in terms which are more those of commander to a subordinate than vice versa. This was the sticking point; the issue was not now one of whether Harris was right or wrong in his appreciation of the operationally possible. In that quarter his experience and his deep understanding of what his crews could accomplish was not likely to be challenged. The issue was not even one governed by the broader strategic objectives; it was one which lay in the field of discipline and obedience, it was therefore one which could be resolved only by a final assertion of authority. But it was precisely this which the Chief of the Air Staff was unable or unwilling to make.

On 3 January 1945 he pleaded with Harris to revise his opinion about selective bombing: 'I should have thought that at least you could have tried harder to destroy Schweinfurt', Portal wrote in tones which suggest despair rather than determination. The letter continued in similar vein, arguing that the general area offensive was a waste of time now that the German air defences had effectively ceased to exist. But it was too late to reason and for reasonable arguments, and on 20 January Portal wrote an official letter to Harris, which illustrates what strength of mind can do when it is backed by conviction that the right policy is being pursued.

I willingly accept your assurance [wrote Portal], that you will continue to do your utmost to ensure the successful execution of the policy laid down. I am very sorry that you do not believe in it, but it is no use my craving for what is evidently unobtainable. We must wait until after the end of the war before we can know for certain who is right. But I sincerely hope that until then you will continue in command of the Force which has done so much in defeating the enemy and has brought such credit and renown to yourself and to the Air Forces.

Pull baker pull devil then was the situation which obtained between Harris and his superior officer; it would be a considerable exaggeration to suggest that Spaatz wished to achieve such independence by exercising comparable disobedience or, indeed by going openly against the main stream of American strategic thought. But whatever he was not, Harris was an exponent of air power in its simplest, its most basic, its most 'independent' form; any commander who sought to execute a strategy which was justified on the grounds that it could achieve results which no other could—and Spaatz's views, so similar to those of Harris, have been quoted in that respect—was bound to be influenced by the latter's achievements. Thus, such a commander, so influenced, was bound also to adopt some of the methods as well as many of the precepts of an area bombing strategy.

The narrative and analysis given in this chapter (and both treatments have been considered necessary for this concluding year of the strategic air offensive) do reveal that Spaatz's Air Forces increasingly came to adopt the area bombing strategy of Bomber Command; the former were as subject to operationally 'bad' weather as the latter, and yet their commanders were as determined as was Harris to mount and execute a sustained, and not, as in 1943, an intermittent offensive. Thus again, in 1944, the methods of blind bombing came to be the rule and not the exception in USSTAF, as, since early 1943, they had been for Bomber Command.

Approximately 80 per cent of all 8th Air Force and 70 per cent of 15th Air Force missions during the last quarter of 1944 were characterised by some employment of blind bombing devices .... Constant study and assessment continued to show the not unanticipated conclusion that radar bombing was far less accurate than visual.... The 8th Air Force had an average circular probable error of about two miles on its blind missions, which meant that many of its attacks depended for effectiveness upon drenching an area with bombs.[87]

Such developments, as indicated by the above statements, may have been unavoidable or inevitable. The important point to grasp is that they took place as elements in the growth of the American bomber offensive. They were an American version of the Harris dictum that the operationally feasible dictates the strategically possible; nevertheless there is one crucial difference, and it aptly emphasises how Eisenhower and his American colleagues came to hope that air power would, against all American doctrine, 'win' the war. Spaatz turned to area bombing after he had achieved command of the air, not before. The same strategy, it may also be remarked, was adopted in 'conventional', and finally in nuclear terms to subdue Japan.

The second factor relevant to this chapter must therefore be examined, namely the increasingly political nature of the strategic air offensive in the during the last four months of the war. This factor, incidentally, goes some way to explaining why Spaatz had no need to seek independence of command and strategy from his superior officers; the Malta doctrine of area bombing gave him the authority he sought. To be sure, the stated American view of this final phase is that only Bomber Command engaged in 'area raids'; by what must charitably be deemed a terminological inexactitude, 'an average circular probable error of about two miles' was somehow considered consonant with a 'significant distinction between morale bombing and radar attacks on transportation targets in urban areas'.[88] It was Arnold who, in February, 1945, wondered whether the distinction was being observed; it was Spaatz who repeated that 'he had not departed from the historic (sic) American policy in Europe, even in the case of Berlin . . .'.[89] This reply was sent on 19 February, a few days after the 8th Air Force had made its final contribution to the destruction of Dresden—the despatch of Mustangs to machine gun the survivors.[90] The reply was sent just over two weeks after the Berlin daylight raid of 3 February, when 'civilian casualties were exceedingly high, the number of fatalities perhaps reaching 25,000 . . .'.[91]

Yet it would be as little right to indict Spaatz for borrowing the area strategy as to charge Harris for perfecting it or Peirse with initiating it. These commanders are their own best judges of whether they did right or not. It is far more to the purpose of this history to show that the confusion of Anglo-American aims which characterised these concluding months of the war made, at the last, a round-the-clock area offensive against what was left of Germany's cities almost inevitable; inevitable, that is, given the doctrine of unconditional surrender, the frustration of seeing Eisenhower's armies grind to a halt late in 1944—and the new menace of a Red Army sweeping across half Europe. In connection with this last point it needed only be said—since this work is but marginally concerned with what used to be called 'grand strategy'—that one justification for the last area bombing campaign of the war is wide of the mark politically and strategically.

Dresden and similar cities were not bombed in order to assist Russian troops in their westwards advance; whatever the cause, the Soviet Union had *not* co-operated with the United States and United Kingdom over strategy in fighting a beleagured or policy in ruling a defeated Germany; a relatively minor example—the failure of 'Frantic'—showed that this was so long before the Yalta conference.[92] By the time of that conference Churchill certainly and Roosevelt possibly had come to view Stalin as a less than absolute ally, to put it mildly.[93] Secondly, and on the narrowly strategic point, the bombing of Dresden, Leipzig, Munich and other cities did not sever rail communications with the east; after the Dresden raids, which were the most concentrated and, in technical and tactical terms, about the most carefully planned operations of the entire war, the marshalling yards and railway stations remained virtually undamaged.[94]

Spaatz concluded USSTAF's career with an area bombing campaign because no more original idea occurred to him; the campaign was approved by higher authority because no more original ideas were circulating there either. General George Marshall's views, or with respect, hunches, do illustrate this sad truth. By widespread consent, Marshall was one of the few British or American senior officers in World War Two who consistently put the cause above the country, the aim above the arm of the Service to which he belonged. He was also regarded as wise, moderate and, so far as one of an alliance's military leaders can be in an atmosphere of 'unconditional surrender', magnanimous. Yet it was Marshall who,

> on a visit to the European theater—in October 1944—had taken the initiative in formulating plans to bring about the defeat of Germany by 1 January 1945. The chief of staff in discussions with air leaders made it clear that he was not satisfied that full pressure had been put in the right places, and he suggested that long-range objectives of strategic bombardment be abandoned for an all-out effort to force an early victory.[95]

It was Marshall who, in January 1945, sanctioned the area offensive, too late to force 'an early victory', now we can see, too crude an instrument of strategy to force a 'victory' at all. But if Marshall, soldier-statesman par excellence of the Grand Alliance, could think of no better way, is it to be wondered that his subordinates adopted the strategy he assigned to them?

The Battle
1944–45

The Operational Triumph of Bomber Command

The opening paragraphs of the chapter devoted to the issues which engaged the Allies in the final year of the war indicated that the operational aspects contained little of striking interest or innovation, with the exception of the steady growth in the effectiveness of radio counter-measures. It seems necessary, however, to narrate how Bomber Command took advantage of its growing size and lethality to practise certain variations on well-tried tactics and gave 1, 3 and 4 Groups opportunities to mount and execute operations which had hitherto virtually been the prerogative of 5 and 8 Groups. It should be stressed that such operations (primarily flown by day in 1944) relying on *GH* radar, were made possible almost entirely by the crumbling of Germany's defences, occurring first with the day fighter forces in the summer of 1944, followed by the sudden and drastic decline in the quality of the night fighter defence after the Autumn.

No apologies are made for introducing this final chapter with the summary on page 290.[1] Few passages of text can show better how Bomber Command in 1944 finally triumphed over operational adversity and deployed all its many skills against a stricken yet far from defeated enemy. Much is unavoidably masked in this summary of bombing techniques, but four aspects of the operational story may perhaps be noted here to give that summary a fuller weight and meaning:

   1. The growing strength and versatility of the Mosquito.

2. The growing immunity from night fighters over the target.
3. The increasing accuracy of both day and night attacks.
4. The growing importance of radar, both as a direct aid to bomber crews and as a crucial element in the effectiveness of counter-measures.

In all major operations of the final year one or other of these elements was present, and usually all four of them. They do not represent the sum of material or technical achievement—the final re-equipping of the Main Force squadrons with Lancasters and Mark III Halifaxes and the introduction of 22,000-lb. bombs are at least as significant—but they do more positively suggest than any other factor the emergence of Bomber Command as a force with freedom to operate and wreak destruction almost at will. Heavy losses were still suffered on occasion, and the months of May and June 1944 in particular show that the German night fighter was not yet a spent force. On the night of 3 May attacks on a variety of targets in France and the Low Countries resulted in missing rates with between 11.3 and 13.5 per cent.[2] During attacks in June on four of the oil targets earlier discussed, missing rates of nearly 30 per cent were encountered.[3] Such figures do validate much of Air Marshal Harris' assertion that Bomber Command was a force only suitable for area attack; the weakness of his case was that it implied that his command would never find itself in a situation, either through its growing strength or through the increasing weakness of the enemy, where it could be employed without unacceptable loss on carefully selected targets directly related to Germany's power to continue fighting.

None of the achievements of the final year would, however, have been possible without the defeat of the German fighter force by the US 8th and 15th Air Forces, and little of the confidence and thoroughness with which Bomber Command set about its final nine months' assault on German cities would have been possible either if Harris' crews had not been granted something of a breathing space by the diversion of attacks from targets in Germany to those specifically related to Overlord. The overall missing rate was five per cent in February 1944; three per cent in March; two per cent in April; less than three per cent in May; approximately two per cent in June; two per cent in July; 1.2 per cent in August; two per cent in September.[4] These figures tell their own story, and should be set against the heavy losses mentioned above, indicating that even at this late stage of the war there were isolated and incidental operational factors which could not easily be assessed and were indeed a deterrent to making long term appreciations.

BOMBING TECHNIQUES 1944–45

Oboe Sky Marking (Musical Wanganui)
Blind *Oboe* sky marking—Main Force normally approaches in the same direction as *Oboe* run in and bombs sky markers at 165 m.p.h. with zero wind velocity on bombsight.

Oboe Ground Marking (Musical Paramatta)
Blind *Oboe* ground marking backed up as necessary with Target Indicators of different colour. Main Force aims preferably at *Oboe* Target Indicators.

Controlled Oboe
Oboe Target Indicators are assessed by Master Bomber who instructs Main Force by Radio Telephone and sometimes backs up best *Oboe* markers with further Target Indicators of distinctive colour.

8 Group Visual
Similar to controlled *Oboe* (though may be used beyond *Oboe* range with H_2S or eyesight). Master Bomber visually assesses *Oboe* markers and re-marks visually.

H_2S Ground Marking (H_2S Paramatta)
Similar to *Oboe* ground marking but, because H_2S is less accurate, more initial markers are put down and backers up aim at mean point of impact. Main Force aim at this backing up and not at the H_2S marking.

H_2S Sky Marking (H_2S Wanganui)
Similar to *Oboe* sky marking.

H_2S Newhaven
A form of 8 Group visual. Starts in same way as H_2S *Paramatta* but flares are also dropped. Pathfinder Force visual markers then mark aiming point visually.

Musical Newhaven
Same as H_2S Newhaven but with initial proximity marking by *Oboe*.

5 Group Visual
Flares and proximity marking followed by visual dive marking with the offset modification.

Oboe Formation (Daylight)
Aircraft fly in formation. Leading aircraft bombs on *Oboe* indication and re-maining aircraft bomb on signal from leader. The only visibility requirement is for the pilots to be able to see each other's aircraft.

G-H Formation (Daylight)
Similar to *Oboe* formation but with *G-H*.

Bearing this proviso in mind, we should nevertheless note that the average missing rate for the final nine months was one per cent; thus for nine months out of 57 Bomber Command did enjoy that freedom of the third dimension which the theorists of air power and the proponents of Royal Air Force independence had sworn was the airmen's by right. In fact that freedom was won at bitter cost, and the airmen of Bomber Command who roamed the skies almost at will in those nine months, dropping 397,593[5] tons of bombs and bringing German cities and industry to final and utter collapse, were reaping the rewards of a freedom really won on the seemingly hopeless nights of 1941 and 1942 and during the American battles above Schweinfurt and Regensburg in the late summer of 1943.

Great as were the improvements in accuracy in Bomber Command it must also be said that these were due primarily to lack of opposition over Overlord targets before September and virtual absence of an effective defence anywhere in Europe thereafter. In this context, the courage of the crews which bombed Gelsenkirchen, Sterkrade, Wesseling and Buer in June must be recorded, because in order to strike these oil targets so accurately by the employment of techniques which the Pathfinders and other elements had developed by this time, it was necessary to breach one of the cardinal tactical rules; airmen stayed within the target area until the master bomber was fully satisfied that the object of the exercise was achieved.

After September the picture altered dramatically; the German Air Force began to run out of fuel; the early warning radar stations, on which Schmid, his staff and ground controllers depended, were overrun and captured; mobile radar stations increased the effective range of equipment borne aloft; above all, radio counter-measures came triumphantly into their own. However, the period between March and July is, in one sense, of greater interest regarding the last-named factor. In this period the German night fighter force was still a formidable threat to Bomber Command. It may be thought that the air staff had been slow not to establish 100 Group until November 1943, as a force separately trained and equipped to capitalise on the achievements of British scientists and fortified by many months of electronic blow and counter-blow with a clever and resourceful enemy. Once, however, the Group was in operation, the results were such as to add a further protective shield to Bomber Command. Specifically, 100 Group was largely able to neutralise if never entirely to silence the tactics of the German controllers during the period in question, tactics which clearly reflect the operational truth that each solution virtually creates a fresh problem.

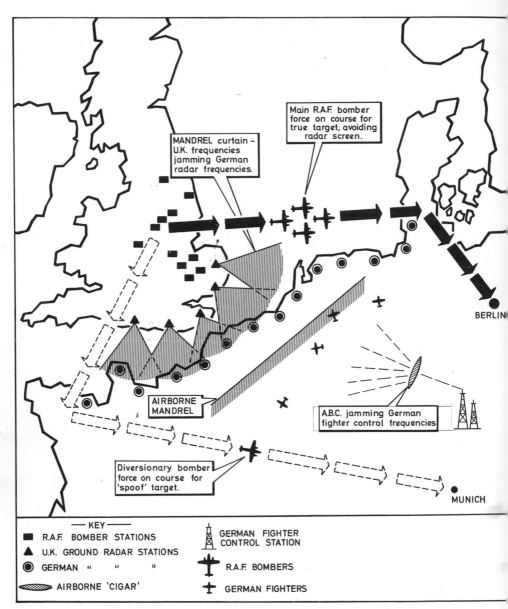

MANDREL curtain –
U.K. frequencies
jamming German
radar frequencies.

Main R.A.F. bomber
force on course for
true target, avoiding
radar screen.

BERLIN

AIRBORNE
MANDREL

A.B.C. jamming German
fighter control frequencies

Diversionary bomber
force on course for
'spoof' target.

MUNICH

—— KEY ——
■ R.A.F. BOMBER STATIONS
▲ U.K. GROUND RADAR STATIONS
◎ GERMAN   "   "   "
▱ AIRBORNE 'CIGAR'

GERMAN FIGHTER
CONTROL STATION

✈ R.A.F. BOMBERS

✛ GERMAN FIGHTERS

Night Bomber Operations, 1944–45

This is a greatly simplified 'picture' of how Bomber Command outwitted the
German defences once 100 Group was fully operational in 1944. No specific raid
is here reconstructed; in any event, night operations maps for the last year of the
strategic air offensive would have shown a much more complex raid and deception pattern, including minelaying, Mosquito and operational training sorties.

By early 1944 the bomber stream had become an element in a major raid which seemed almost immutable; nevertheless after the Nuremburg raid on 31 March, this stream took its place in the limbo of discarded tactics[6]; when analysed, that costly operation showed that the German controllers had accepted the impossibility of predicting by probability or hunch what the principal target was likely to be, and had begun to practice a new type of defensive attrition, namely attacks along the entire length of the bomber stream rather than over the target itself. Two events saved Bomber Command from a further bout of heavy casualties at this point. Firstly, the diversion to Overlord targets, which, with some exceptions were either lightly defended, or if in Germany, were so scattered as to require attacking not by one stream but by several, thus presenting the German controllers with a new set of different choices. Secondly, jamming and spoofing by 100 Group began to present problems to a defence already wilting under hammer blows and its own divided councils.[7]

Essentially therefore we have two developments to narrate in the final year; on the one hand is Bomber Command's increasing versatility, in operations by day as well as by night, a versatility with regard to Overlord and its aftermath made possible both by the decreasing effectiveness of the German Air Force and the growing confidence of Main Force groups that they too could employ pathfinding and other techniques. On the other hand there are the achievements of 100 Group. There are six main stages in the operational record as such: the attacks on French railway targets, principally executed by the more experienced squadrons of 1 and 4 Groups; the night attacks on German targets, executed by all Main Force groups, but increasingly employing aiming and marking techniques developed by 5 Group; attacks on oil targets; daylight attacks on Overlord targets; area daylight attacks on German targets; the resumption of the night offensive against Germany, in effect if not always in intention an onslaught against 'new' cities and those already heavily damaged.

The accuracy of the attacks on railway targets was due to a series of developments in marking and aiming techniques, which owed much to 5 Group in general and 617 Squadron in particular. It will be remembered that this famous squadron had sought a variety of roles after its attack on the dams in May 1943. Not until early 1944, and the acquisition of Mosquito aircraft for marking purposes did the squadron again really get into its stride, and it might not have done that had it not been that Wing Commander Cheshire (as he then was) had become convinced that low-level marking was essential if really accurate attacks were to be achieved other than on very special occasions, and then quite likely with the loss of most of the force.[8] Wing Commander Cheshire believed that visual marking from as low as 1,000 feet would enable Main Force crews to bomb with sufficient accuracy for the designated strategic purpose, provided the whole operation was controlled by radio telephone in the master bomber's aircraft—the nub of the entire tactical concept was that throughout the bombing the master controller should be able to *see* with the naked eye his own marking, should be able to communicate at all times with the Main Force, and that aircraft flown by specially experienced crews should be able to back the master bomber up, both by releasing additional target markers and by relaying directions to the Main Force as to how they should 'off set' their bombing pattern.

5 Group had developed the concept of 'off set' marking and bombing over a period of years; the tactics summarised above were, in a sense, culmination of those tried and proved effective in several very specialised raids. What is remarkable about the raids of March and April 1944 is that Main Force crews were able to achieve a high degree of accuracy with such little experience of bombing in this highly sophisticated way. It is true that earlier attacks, mostly flown by the Halifaxes of 4 and 6 Group, had accustomed them to bombing relatively precise targets on markers laid blindly by the *Oboe* Mosquitoes of the Pathfinder Force. However, although that force by early 1944 had achieved a very considerable degree of expertise in marking area targets, neither Air Vice-Marshal Bennett's crews nor those of the Main Force had much experience against those of the small and unknown variety.

It is unfortunately the case that some of the disagreements about objectives which characterised the strategic air offensive at the level of high command were exacerbated by arguments about methods within Bomber Command itself. The low-level tactics adopted by Wing Commander Cheshire were not approved by Air Vice-Marshal Bennett, and he was not slow to point out that although success might occasionally attend these efforts, there could be no certainty that area bombing on the very large scale which had become possible would be more successful by this more sophisticated technique. Bennett argued that the Main Force squadrons, however relatively skilful they became, would always have to bomb on sky or ground markers dropped from a high altitude by Pathfinder squadrons, and 'backed-up' by reinforcing aircraft, not only on the way to the target but at regular intervals over it.

For a time, controversy over which was the most effective and economical method of marking targets in Germany was put in abeyance; the summer months of 1944 were predominantly those in which Bomber

Command concentrated its attention on targets in France and the Low Countries. Radar bombing by day was practised by 3 Group, supported by the Pathfinder forces; short-range targets were bombed at night and the Pathfinders were active in marking them; but the numbers of aircraft despatched to these targets was relatively small, and the targets themselves were so scattered and widespread that accurate marking with the forces available was as little possible as strictly accurate bombing. As with so much else concerning Bomber Command during the strategic air offensive, the main thrust of activity and innovation was directed towards improving the destructive capacity of the Main Force squadrons, and it was towards assisting in the attainment of this objective that the Pathfinder Force was originally constituted and remained in being. Wing Commander Cheshire's innovations were certainly important, and made for some extraordinarily accurate bombing on occasion. The destruction of the Dortmund-Ems and Bielefeld canals, and the sinking of *Tirpitz* are cases in point.[9] It is a fact however that Cheshire's tactics were only grafted on to those employed by the Main Force; towards the end of the war, high-level and low-level marking were employed on the same raids; again, Dresden, in so many ways the culmination of the strategic air offensive, saw this blend of tactics employed to the full.

Climax and Overkill

By August 1944 Bomber Command was approaching the peak of its operational performance. More than 1,000 aircraft with crews were in regular front-line service; the Main Force groups, while still committed in intention if not always in practice to area bombing of German towns, had shown themselves capable of occasional variations on this theme; many kinds of marking were available, and despite the disagreements between Bennett and Cheshire—or more precisely between Bennett and Cochrane—could be used together or separately as occasion demanded. More important perhaps than all these, however, was the enormous flexibility of the Mosquito, whether employed on individual sorties, as part of Bennett's 'Light Night Striking Force', or forming part of Air Commodore Addison's 100 Group.[10] If there was a weakness in Bomber Command, with all its variety of aircraft, equipments and tactics, it lay in the standards of the crews themselves. There was no lack of courage, as ever; there was no lack of skill among individual crew members, and in some instances, particularly where crews survived as a unit throughout most of a tour, operational standards were possibly higher than at any stage during the war. For example, the standards of accuracy reached by some air bombers during daylight operations in support of ground forces (operations, incidentally, invariably encountering heavy flak however trivial the fighter attacks) were far in advance of anything achieved at earlier stages of the war.[11]

But the pressures on the training machine were very heavy, so heavy indeed that large numbers of aircrew who had completed their final training found themselves 'surplus to requirements' because the rapid expansion of 1942 and 1943 had not been absorbed by the operational squadrons. By the summer of 1944 the heavy losses of the preceding winter had been made good; by this time the missing rate, with occasional exceptions was rapidly decreasing, and the demand for replacements naturally diminished also. The last months of the war saw many a young man kick his heels, ready to go into action but not required to do so. When committed to operations, lack of opposition did little to improve his skill or demand new discipline.[12]

It is indeed odd to read the accounts of the operations flown by Bomber Command in the concluding stages of the war. After over four years of frustration and loss, crews bombed almost with impunity. Naturally enough, there were challenges and disappointments, but the record on the whole is one of almost unrelieved success. The daylight operations carried out by 3 Group had shown what a Main Force formation, which for long had been denied a particular role, could do when provided with different targets and new equipments. Possibly because of this factor, the Group Commander, Air Vice-Marshal Harrison, urged Harris in October to allow his Group to be employed on the daylight bombing of German targets.[13] It may be said here that the Commander-in-Chief required little urging, since he had already decided that area bombing of German towns was to be resumed as quickly as possible once Eisenhower's armies had virtually gone into winter quarters, and he saw no reason to doubt that, despite his earlier forebodings, this revived campaign could be waged by day as well as by night. This new version of a round-the-clock offensive began on 18 October, when 128 Lancasters of 3 Group attacked Bonn. Why this totally unimportant town should be singled out for devastation must remain a mystery, but devastated it was none the less; it may not have been so treated on the scale Bomber Command as a whole was now able to wreak whenever it chose, but it was bombed sufficiently heavily to demonstrate the effectiveness of the daylight assault.

While further day attacks on Germany were being contemplated, night operations were resumed with unabated force. A curtain-raiser to this resumption of the area offensive had in fact taken place in late July, when widespread attacks were made on several German cities, while for ten days the oil offensive into the Ruhr was resumed. By now, the Lancaster was habitually armed with a 4,000-lb. bomb, and was thus an infinitely more lethal weapon system than the Halifax, the Fortress or the Liberator. Thus the potential for destruction of what might be called 'semi-precise' targets was enormous, given the size of the front line force and paucity of the opposition it had to meet. August, however, was the month in which the return to Germany in the old form properly took place. Twelve major night attacks on German cities were made in that month— and 12 in September. The record, as set out below, is the most absolute indication which can be given that the area offensive had been resumed in full, but with the fundamental differences that it was now one which could be conducted with trifling loss, enabling Harris to pick and choose his targets, and to range as far and as widely as he chose.[14]

	Target	Despatched		Missing	
Aug.					
12–13	Brunswick	379	(0)*	27	(0)
	Rüsselsheim	297	(10)	20	(0)
16–17	Kiel	348	(9)	5	(0)
	Stettin	461	(0)	5	(0)
18–19	Bremen	289	(7)	1	(0)
	Sterkrade	234	(14)	2	(0)
25–26	Rüsselsheim	412	(0)	15	(0)
	Darmstadt	196	(6)	7	(0)
26–27	Kiel	382	(10)	17	(0)
	Königsberg	174	(0)	4	(0)
29–30	Königsberg	189	(0)	15	(0)
	Stettin	403	(1)	23	(0)
Sept.					
9–10	München-Gladbach	137	(24)*	0	
11–12	Darmstadt	240	(14)	12	(0)
12–13	Frankfurt	387	(9)	17	(0)
	Stuttgart	217	(13)	4	(0)
15–16	Kiel	490	(7)	6	(0)
18–19	Bremerhaven	213	(7)	2	(1)
19–20	München-Gladbach	237	(10)	5	(1)
23–24	Neuss	549	(17)	7	(0)
	Münster (Canal)	141	(5)	14	(0)
	Münster (A/F)	113	(5+1)†	1	(0)
26–27	Karlsruhe	237	(11)	2	(0)
27–28	Kaiserslautern	227	(10)	2	(1)

* Mosquito figures in brackets.   † One Lightning.

As has been said earlier, most of this record of destruction and loss is explained by the collapse of the German fighter defences; the immediate operational reasons for that collapse have also been given. But something further must now be said of the contribution made by 100 Group, because it was the jamming not only of early warning and airborne radar, but of the German controllers which made such opposition as was put up a thing of shreds and patches. The *Mandrel* jamming device had been in use for some considerable time when the Main Force resumed the area offensive, but the large numbers of aircraft now available to Air Commodore Addison and the refinements in technique which had proceeded in parallel with the expansion of his Group, meant that he could not play an integral part in the tactics devised at Bomber Command headquarters and adopted or adapted by Groups, stations and squadrons. The map on page 292 shows in outline how 100 Group was able to screen the operations of the main force by blanketing, jamming or spoofing communications between German ground controllers and fighters. The benefits of size (by the period in question 100 Group was composed of over 200 aircraft), and the variety of equipments available not only enabled radio counter-measures to be mounted when major raids were in progress, but allowed Addison to virtually stage his own operations on nights when the bulk of Bomber Command was grounded. As the Official History puts it: 'on nights when no operations of consequence were despatched the *Mandrel* screen was flown and other symptoms of Bomber Command getting airborne were simulated. A special *Window* dropping force then emerged from behind the screen and for the benefit of German radar, faked the approach of a bomber concentration. Thus, on several occasions, German night fighters were drawn into the air to oppose attacks which did not exist and, incidentally, to consume petrol which would be ill afforded.'[15]

The development of diversionary tactics by Main Force squadrons was comparably effective. It will be recalled that the 8th Air Force had from the outset practised tactics of diversion, even when the total numbers of aircraft despatched was small and the opposition likely to be encountered negligible. Bomber Command however, under Harris' leadership, had preferred to put most of its eggs in one basket; a tactic which may partly account for the latter's repeated insistence that he, of all commanders, put his forces at greater risk every time he mounted a major operation.[16]

By October and November 1944 however the horn of plenty was such that, in effect, two Main Force attacks could be mounted on any one night. Yet again, despite the availability of aircraft and the relative frequency with which diversions were flown, the latter were essentially subsidiary to the set-piece attack, which Harris had perfected; as increasing numbers of Mosquitoes came into service they were employed to divert and to harass; for the Main Force whenever possible was reserved for the overwhelming blow. When such a blow was combined with a high degree of operational experience and skill the results to the town attacked were almost certain to be catastrophic. On 29 August, for example, Königsberg was attacked by 175 Lancasters from 5 Group. Königsberg was a distant target, which had rarely been bombed. A *Mandrel* screen concealed 5 Group's objective until well into Germany, but after 100 Group aircraft had dispersed there was still a considerable distance to travel before the target was reached. As a result German defences were able to plot the 5 Group forces and also to provide strong opposition over Königsberg itself. Visibility was poor over the target and the attack was late in starting.

In earlier months this combination of opposing factors would almost certainly have resulted in the destruction of a large part of the attacking forces. But on this occasion not only was it estimated that 134,000 people had been rendered homeless and another 61,000 had had their houses damaged, but, more significantly, only four bombers were destroyed.[17] What this meant in practice was that, if he chose, Harris could mount several raids of this intensity on any night in the month; he could make good his belief that Germany could be wrecked from end to end. The only enemy which still stood in his path was the weather, but this too in 1944 and 1945 was far less of a bogey than it had been in earlier years. Radar brought crews home as well as sent them on their way; illuminated flare path techniques were developed to beat fog, much less cloud.

It is not for nothing therefore that the Official History states that 'operations between October 1944 and May 1945 were the climax of the strategic air offensive. The Bomber Command part in them represented the realisation of most of the hopes and ambitions which had inspired the British Air Staff for a quarter of a century.' This statement is borne out by the record: 163,000 tons of bombs were dropped in the last three months of 1944, compared with 40,000 tons during this period in 1943 and 8,000 in the same period of 1942. '53 per cent of this tonnage was accounted for by area attacks on large industrial cities. 14 per cent of it was aimed at oil targets, 15 per cent at railways and canals and 13 per cent at targets such as enemy troops and fortifications which were directly associated with the land battle. The remaining 5 per cent was devoted to naval and other objectives.'[18]

Sixteen towns in the Ruhr were bombed and bombed repeatedly; distant targets in south and south-west Germany were added to the list of slaughter —11 towns in this area were bombed. Not only was the offensive crushing in size and severity, it brought new terrors, new forms of suffering. Many German cities were ruined shells by this time, gutted by the fire-raising attacks of previous months. In order to ensure that not a stone was left upon a stone, high-explosive bombs superseded incendiaries.[19]

Thus relatively new targets or targets rarely bombed were struck with a force and destruction which even the great holocausts of 1943 had failed to achieve. Ulm, Stuttgart, Karlsruhe, Heilbronn, Freiburg, Ludwigs-hafen, Saarbrücken, Nuremberg, Munich, Bonn, Coblenz, Brunswick, Osnabrück and Giessen went down before the bomber. Here is the list of destruction, wreaked at a time when directives from the higher echelons of the Grand Alliance suggested a carefully composed aerial attack on targets of great importance. Naturally oil plants were attacked in this area offensive, because German industry had become so 'synthetic' by this time that few major towns did not contain a plant of some kind devoted to the manufacture of a substitute for crude petroleum.[21]

The only three raids which can arguably be called selective in this period were those against Castrop Rauxol on 4 November, Leuna on 6 December and Politz on 21 December.[22] It will be recalled that, in the distant days of 1941, Air Marshal Peirse had asked his Group Commanders to suggest oil targets; Leuna and Politz had appeared on a list which reflected aspiration rather than policy. But now such distant targets could be chosen and bombed at will. Both operations indeed are interesting today because of the technical expertise displayed by the Pathfinders, rather than for any strategic factor. Emphasis is added to this comment by noting that the first attack was wholly a Main Force affair, a demonstration, if demonstration be required by this time, that Harris had denied the credibility of his own rank and file in asserting that they were incapable of anything other than area bombing.

Thus by the beginning of 1945 all Germany lay open to Bomber Command. 'The question in 1945 was no longer what could be destroyed but what ought to be destroyed.' The question was answered in an unsurprising way:

> ... between the beginning of the year and 8 May, Bomber Command dropped over 180,000 tons of bombs, which amounted to nearly a fifth of the aggregate for the whole war ... in this part of the offensive there were 36 major operations against 39 different towns, all of which were carried out in January, February and March. The smallest of these attacks was that

made against Gelsenkirchen on the night of 22 January when 152 bombers were despatched. The largest was a daylight attack on 12 March when 1,107 aircraft carrying about 5,000 tons of bombs were despatched to Dortmund, but undoubtedly the most destructive was the operation carried out in two waves against Dresden on the night of 13 February when some 805 bombers were despatched.[23]

Thus although in this final period there were some brilliant achievements at the level of selective and precision bombing, the overwhelming fact with which this part of the history is concluded is that Bomber Command at its operational peak was also at its peak of destruction over a wide and inevitably indiscriminate area. The reader must judge whether this was unavoidable or inevitable; it is also a matter of speculation whether the final damage and loss to German industry could have been achieved more economically. Whether or not Bomber Command should have been brought more firmly within the ambit of Portal's or Eisenhower's control is likewise a matter for conjecture and the partisan view. But this much can be asserted: the bombing of Dresden on the nights of 13 and 15 February and 2 March 1945 expressed to a stupefying degree the use of an instrument of major war for purposes more elemental than even those who forged it could have dreamt. It is not proposed here to recapitulate the bombing of Dresden; that has been done by abler pens than mine, and Herr Hochhuth has recently added dramatic prose to more sober accounts. Only for the record will it be said that Dresden was selected for no reason which anyone who fought in the strategic air offensive can justify; it was bombed without any regard to such trivial targets of military importance as it did possess, and its destruction achieved the rare distinction of having no open partisans at all. In every sense, Dresden exemplifies the dangers of carrying an idea to its logical conclusion, a fact well exemplified in words which may serve not only as the epitaph of a city which an older generation knew, but, perhaps, on total war, *circa* 1945:

Early in the morning we came to a large city through which ran a broad river. It was Dresden on the Elbe. A great moon, emerging from behind clouds, brought eighteenth-century buildings into stark relief and cast pink shadows on rococo walls. Then, entering a wider street, it became clear that this was not a city, only the ghost of a city. Dresden was dead, these walls were its bare bones. Only the facades were there; behind, as in a film set, was rubble. Three days before an enormous force of bombers had passed this way: Dresden had been gutted 30,000 Dresdeners killed.

The Operational Triumph of the United States Army Air Force

The bombing of Dresden on the night of 13 February was followed by a daylight attack by the 8th Air Forces on the 14th. Craven and Cate are, for once, more disingenuous than the official British historians in describing the daylight attacks as directed against 'railway centres'.[25] The fact of the matter is that Dresden was comparatively unimportant as a railway centre, and the argument that it was crucial in providing logistic support to the armies opposing Russian forces is not borne out by the situation which actually existed in 1945. In any event, as we have seen, the main railway stations in Dresden were hardly damaged during one of the few occasions that the British and American Air Forces destroyed a town between them. The American contribution was relatively small by comparison with that of Bomber Command—a mere 771 tons were dropped on 15 February. The significance of the attack, however, lies less in the weight of bombs dropped than in the objectives which governed its selection.

Although the commanders of the 8th and 15th Air Forces remained as much wedded to the doctrine of selective and precision bombing in 1944 and 1945 as they had been in 1942 and 1943, and were indeed well able to put it into effect, the march of events was such that area bombing became at least as important in the daylight offensive as anything which could be related to a particular strategic objective. A partial explanation for this paradoxical shift in policy has already been given, but at the operational level the change appears to have been caused by factors which were not at all governed by politics. The answer to the mystery of why towns like Dresden were attacked now appears to be twofold: General Spaatz disposed of two Air Forces, and this combination provided him with a spectrum of choice which no air commander before or since has been given. The 8th Air Force consisted solely of heavy bombers, but the 15th Air Force had until December 1943 a powerful immediate bombardment element, and even after that date its commander, General Twining, was able to call on the 12th Air Force as occasion required. The same point was true for General Eaker and his relations with General Vandenburg, commanding the 9th Air Force. Together these four air forces comprised some 4,000 aircraft, operating from the United Kingdom and Italy and, after D-Day, from northern France as well. The four air forces were also fused into some form of entity, if not an entirely homogeneous one, by the authority vested in General Spaatz and by the clear view he held as to the targets which should be bombed.

On the other hand (and here we come to the second factor), there was a limit to target selection on the Spaatz premise. It should first of all be remembered that the decisive victory of Big Week was followed by renewed attacks on German aircraft factories; this was an offensive in which the 15th Air Force was at least as significant an instrument as the 8th, because it could strike at factories in the south and east and thus negative much of the attempt at dispersal made belatedly by Speer and his colleagues. By the middle of 1944 German aircraft production had been damaged, although not irretrievably by these attacks. But the attack on the oil targets was irretrievably damaging; the record of the 8th and 15th Air Forces in this respect is impressive indeed, and, taken together with their effect on the German fighter force and on fighter production *especially in respect of new types*, the attack ensured that by the autumn of 1944 the Pointblank and Overlord objectives had been attained.

Thus by the end of the year the oil campaign had virtually come to a close and, although that against transport continued to be executed until the closing months of the war, it inevitably became of decreasing importance once the full effects of the destruction of oil supplies was felt by German industry, let alone the Armed Forces. Hence, in that sense, the United States Army Air Forces ran out of targets; this is not to say that there were no targets left to attack, nor is this the place to revive the argument that closer co-ordination between ground and air forces would have ensured a continued advance by Eisenhower's armies in the winter months; such an advance might well have been achieved by a second round of close support bombing, not confined to the 2nd Tactical, 9th and 12th Air Forces. Operations of this nature were being carried out in Italy, but the campaign had dwindled through the despatch of ground forces for 'Anvil', the invasion of southern France; it seems to be a quirk of strategy that co-operation between ground and air forces flourishes when resources are scarce or even reduced rather than when they are abundant.

Doubtless there is a case for saying that the 8th and 15th Air Forces could have combined with the armies in a new offensive, but the fact remains that they did not. Yet air power is a branch of strategy where dogma prevails, and the notion that operations in the air might be suspended or curtailed did not appeal to commanders of air forces who saw many German targets still lying unscathed. As a result, the 8th Air Force conducted its final six months' operations on lines marked out by Bomber Command in earlier years. Cities were pounded into destruction by day as well as by night.

It is certainly true that the cumulative effect of this daylight area offensive was to destroy any chance which Speer might have had of withstanding the blows of Bomber Command. The relative accuracy of the 8th Air Force and of Bomber Command is hard to measure, and the nearest one can get to it is to say that both bombed with extreme accuracy on some occasions. But, apart from the fact that really accurate bombing cannot be carried out repeatedly, the pattern of the 8th Air Force's bombing in the closing stages of the war was such as to preclude single industries being selected for destruction. Increasingly in the last months attention was turned towards the Ruhr, or what was left of it.[26] Whatever the arguments about area and selective bombing, it is surely undeniable that this conglomerate of towns can never be and could never have been separated into sectors suitable for isolated attack on particular industries, while other sectors were defined on the Cherwell scale. Harris had grasped this point much earlier than any of his confreres and his argument that the Ruhr was the great target for destruction and fatally weakened Germany was based on his understanding of its overall importance, not on the significance of individual industries.

When the 8th Air Force therefore turned its attention to the Ruhr, leaving to the 15th attacks on otherwise distant targets, the American concept of strategic bombing became drastically modified in effect, if not in function or precept. When to these attacks on the Ruhr we add the mounting attacks on Berlin, it must be admitted that the shift in the operational pattern had become very considerable. Thus the war for the United States Army Air Forces in Europe ended with a singular paradox unresolved, indeed compounded by the emergence of Air Marshal Harris as the successful proponent and exponent of mass destruction. A force designed as a precision instrument had become one expressing the concept of total war. This change had not been intentional and the fact of a change taking place would certainly be denied by most senior American officers who held high command in these concluding months. But the record is against them. It is a record of industrial destruction, wrought during the course of an area offensive; it is not a record of industrial destruction as seen in the determination to bomb Schweinfurt or Regensburg or aircraft factories or oil installations or transport centres. As with most other aspects of the strategic air offensive, it is probably the case that this change was inevitable, certainly once strategic objectives became superseded by those derived from the doctrine of unconditional surrender. Perhaps all one can say is that nothing more aptly illustrates the near-impossibility of returning to strategic first principles once the pressure of events and changes in purely increasingly political circumstances have blunted or distorted them.

The Defeat of the German Air Force

One of the most telling accounts of the bombing of Dresden was given by a pilot of a German fighter squadron station nearby. Due to failures in communication, his squadron was forced to wait on the airfield while the city burned.[27] This chapter therefore concludes with an account of what that final defeat of the German Air force really meant.[28]

The German defences by February 1945 had indeed been reduced to impotence. Although large numbers of aircraft remained in service, and although the march of the invading armies perforce concentrated the bulk of them in Germany itself, no defensive capacity could long survive the double blow of attacks on aircraft factories and on oil. Of the two, the attack on oil was the most damaging, because the drastic cut in fuel supplies to the Air Force which Speer insisted on from September onwards means that training standards deteriorated sharply through the limitation of flying time which was also imposed.

Yet for some months preceding and during the final year, the German Air Force remained formidable in numbers and quality. Until the heavy attacks on oil targets began, the fuel situation actually improved; indeed, at the beginning of 1944 reserves were higher than at any time since the summer of 1941. Training in 1943 had also improved, following General Leutnant Kriepe's appointment in June 1943. More crews were available at the beginning of 1944 than at the same time a year earlier. Most significant of all, given the enormous stress at last being placed on German industry, new and improved types of aircraft came into service. The Fw. 190, in its latest version, became the principal single engine fighter. The Me. 410 and the Me. 219 also now appeared as twin-engine fighters. Two factors, however, combined to retard this research and procurement programme from achieving significant dimensions. In the first place, and by Hitler's orders, a new bomber programme was instituted, centred on the Ju. 188; this decision of Hitler's cut deeply into the resources available for fighter production. Secondly, no firm decision was reached about jet aircraft. Although in the last stages the Me. 262 came into service, production having begun in March 1944, too few appeared to significantly affect the course of operations. Only 59 had been built by July.

In fact, Hitler's notions of reviving a bomber offensive affected the jet aircraft programme as well as that centred on propeller driven types. He not only ordered the Me. 262 to be developed as a bomber, despite the violent opposition of Galland and other senior officers; he encouraged the development and production of other jet types, including the He. 162 and the He. 163. These aircraft, like the other jets, show the considerable fertility of ideas which flourished in Germany even in those dark days. Unfortunately, fertility at source was not matched by an output of types or an allocation of functions which bore the slightest relevance to what was required. If any of the types mentioned had been produced in quantity there is little doubt that they would have destroyed many hundreds of British and American bombers; there were no fighter aircraft in the Royal or the United States Air Forces which could match the jets in performance, and although the latter's range was necessarily short, this became of decreasing importance as the ring closed round the Reich.

There remain, however, two other equally fundamental aspects. The first is the effectiveness of the Anglo-American attack on the German air-craft industry. Once the Mustang had appeared the whole situation com-pletely changed. As has been well said, 'the long-range escort fighter at a stroke capsized German air defence strategy, for the Luftwaffe planning staff had been lulled into a false sense of security during the winter of 1943-1944 on the assurance of the Research and Development Branch that such an aircraft was a technical impossibility. . . . Its appearance at the shortest notice in large numbers meant that the German defensive commitment had overnight been modified beyond all expectations. . . . The weight and accuracy of the February assault on the aircraft industry brought a new and forceful resolution of the meaning of allied air power and the extent of the threat to German war as a whole. In these February attacks alone 23 air-frame and three engine factories were hit and the weight of bombs was only slightly less than in the whole of the previous bombing of aircraft plants.'[29]

It is true that Speer took the most vigorous means to combat this threat, and succeeded in raising production by nearly 25 per cent until September. As a matter of fact, the number of aircraft produced in September 1944 was nearly twice as high as in the previous December. But the increase by itself was of little importance, since the initial destruction was quickly followed by the far more damaging attacks on the German oil industry. Moreover, although production did increase by this impressive percentage, it did so not only because of Speer's unusual gifts, but because of his decision in the propeller driven field to concentrate on existing types rather than on prototypes of improved aircraft. As we have seen, the existing types of reasonably formidable aircraft were by a straight comparison as good as, if not better, in all-round performance characteristics than anything which the Allies could produce at the time. But for the desperate situation in which Germany was now finding itself, no one expedient could be more than a short-term answer to a particular problem. For Speer to have increased aircraft production by 25 per cent in a year in which German cities were suffering as never before is a remarkable achievement, and negatives many of the claims made by the more sanguine intelligence officers at General Eisenhower's headquarters and elsewhere that the Combined Bomber Offensive was primarily effective in terms of industry damaged.

But what was required was not just more aircraft but radically new aircraft, with well-trained crews to fly them and plenty of fuel for them. Loss of fuel supplies wrecked Speer's chances of making the kind of recovery which might have given his master a breathing space, even if it could not have avoided defeat. It was not only in terms of procurement, however, that the German defences suffered; command and control suffered also and in two senses. Schmid did not command the same degree of respect which Kammhuber did, and his relations with his subordinates became increasingly strained. In the more literal sense of 'control', the German defences suffered from the increasingly effective jamming carried out by 100 Group of Bomber Command, an operation executed so successfully and relentlessly that most German controllers appeared to have become nervous wrecks by the time the war ended. Moreover, although 'wild sow' tactics were reverted to when no others were possible, the main defensive objective was still to concentrate large numbers of fighters whenever possible against a bomber stream; as we have seen, such tactics could be very successful, and striking successes were caused as late as 16 March 1945. On that occasion, Nuremberg, rarely a 'lucky' city for Bomber Command, was attacked by 293 aircraft. From 1 Group alone, 24 aircraft were lost. Yet concentration tactics called for highly trained fighter crews. Clearly AI identification diminished in importance, as controllers sought to direct concentrated forces on the stream; in one sense concentration as such diminished in importance too, given the numbers of bombers being committed to operations in 1944 and 1945. But what was of prime importance to a well-organised defence built round the ground controllers was well trained air crews, responsive to their orders at all times. It was bad enough that such orders could be jammed or spoofed by the enemy; it was far worse when mangled orders reached untrained and inexperienced crews.

A partial recovery took place in early December, although it was not one indicated by any striking successes against bombing forces. But there had been a pause in the American attacks on oil targets, and from a mere 18,000 tons of aircraft fuel being produced in October, output rose to 39,000 tons in November. But this was a short-lived recovery indeed.

> The final phase of the Allied bombing offensive began in the middle of December when, with an improvement in weather conditions, operations could once more be resumed against those installations now back in production. This renewal of the offensive opened with a remarkable series of consistent operations by the US 15th Air Force directed at the immobilisation of the Silesian synthetic plants and also of the one at Brux; these were accompanied by heavy RAF night bombing attacks, carried out with great accuracy and success, of Politz, Leuna and Brux, while the US 8th Air Force continued its operations by day. With these developments the final outcome of the Allied offensive was no longer in doubt. By March, the remaining stocks of fuel were almost exhausted and at the beginning of April practically the whole industry was immobilised, while during the month most of its constituent units were rapidly overrun by the Allied ground forces. With the whole German war machine on the point of collapse so that repair and disposal schemes could no longer be implemented, the task of dislocating the German oil resources had been completed and the remnants of the German Luftwaffe were grounded with empty tanks while unable to play any part in the closing stages of the German collapse.[30]

What did this collapse really mean? It meant impotence; it meant that fighter crews were forced to sit idly by and watch Bomber Command destroy their cities by night. Among all the many tragedies of the Dresden raid this sense of utter helplessness by the defence must be included, because it marks the final turning of the tide in the long battle between Bomber Command and the elaborate defensive system established by Kammhuber and his successors. It is for this reason that on account of the Dresden raid in which this aspect is stressed forms the last passages of this narrative of the strategic air offensive; the account, in establishing the belated triumph of Bomber Command, is the requiem of the German Air Force. Yet though the Dresden raid of 13–14 February 1945 marked the final defeat of the German Air Force and the final triumph of Bomber Command, it was not an operation which Harris and his staff embarked on with enthusiasm. There were political factors; there were operational problems. Above all, there was the fact that relations between the commanders of 5 and 8 Groups had never been smooth; 3 Group had developed largely as a day bomber force since the preceding autumn; the other Main Force Groups had also turned to tactical innovations of their own since command of the air had been won; hence it must be remarked that the Dresden raid's interest does lie in its being the clearest example of Bomber Command operating together as one mighty force. At the same time, it is also possible to argue, and it has been argued, that such a double blow on a major target—and a 'distant' one at that, bearing in mind that Bomber Command was still operating wholly from the United Kingdom—could only have been mounted at this stage of the war, and that even then it was attended with considerable risk.

Although the German defences had lost their early warning systems along with much else as France and the Low Countries were liberated, there was the simple physical fact that what was left of the German Air Force had a diminishing area to defend. This fact—of an inexorable enemy advance into the homeland—doubtless helped to demoralise some German fighter pilots and crews, but it may have stiffened the resolve of others to go down fighting and to take as many British and American bomber crews with them as possible. Such factors may be considered as 'variables' rather than 'constants' now; at the time they were all part of the assessment which Harris and his staff had to make about Dresden, a virgin target, 40 miles from the advancing Russian armies, for which no up to date target maps even existed. Bomber Command was tired too; Dresden was a long way off; it was small comfort to the specialist crews briefed for the raid, and carrying in their aircraft the latest radio, radar and electronic equipment, that if they were forced to land it should be anywhere but in 'Russian' territory; all this was not very friendly. Moreover, this February night of 1945 was not necessarily going to be meteorologically more friendly than those of any other winter war year.

Hence the plan of a double blow on Dresden, or two Main Force raids on the same target over the same night of the 13–14 February, separated by only three hours *and* supported by a major diversionary raid plus a number of spoofs, not only reflected tactical innovations but also safety measures; these measures were still considered necessary, after all but two years of an area offensive planned and executed in Harris' terms, and nine months or so after Bomber Command had been provided with command of the air by courtesy of the Mustang. The double blow was designed to deceive the German Air Force into rising to meet the first challenge, the lesser of the two, and then to remain grounded—through having exhausted its night's ration of fuel—while the second and major blow was struck unchecked.

What happened in fact—and it is just here that we measure the full extent of the defeat of the German Air Force and the defensive system for the Reich with which it spent its last, declining years—is that the night fighter squadrons remained grounded throughout the raids; the guns did not fire; the searchlights were mere probes; the elaborate systems of civil defence—even in sheltered Dresden these existed—helpless against a tempered and pitilessly wielded weapon of war; only the discipline and extraordinary resilience of the German people prevented a total collapse of law and order when the last machine gunning Mustang had passed on. The weather turned out in Harris' favour; thick cloud en route to the target added to the controller's fundamental difficulty of assessing where a relatively small force (the first 'blow') was going and what Harris was going to do with the bulk of his command that night; light cloud over the target did nothing to hinder the marking and target indicating processes. The sheer variety of choice available to Harris, not the tactics of deception as such, were his most potent weapons in the Dresden raid. 100 Group participated, but as part of the second blow, a tremendous, and immensely complex force of over 700 aircraft, representing every single technique of marking, illuminating, re-marking, 'backing up', 'centring', together with voice link between master bombers, aircraft and base, plus the full array of radio counter-measures. Against this kind of force, there was, in February, no effective defence.

The other tactical feature which must be noted is that 5 and 8 Groups did co-operate very successfully over marking and indicating at all stages, and both could claim an equal and yet a complementary share in the night's work. The pattern of these operations repeated pretty faithfully the varying degrees of experience and expertise which the crews of 8 Group and the specialist crews of 5 Group had acquired. 8 Group crews first marked the target blindly by H_2S; 5 Group crews registered on this marking, visually indicated the aiming points by indicators of a special brilliance, then, via the master bomber and his deputy, controlled the first force of some 300 Lancasters; 8 Group crews then re-marked the target for the second force, and continued to do so throughout the night, until indeed Dresden was simply an ascending and ever spreading cloud of fire.

The third tactical feature of the raid is the sheer extent of the diversions planned and executed. The complexities and, in a sense, the originality of the double blow were in themselves remarkably confusing to the defence, but one major diversionary raid was also carried out between the two Dresden blows, together with four spoof attacks. An oil refinery near Böhlen—a town sufficiently close to Dresden to provide further problems for the ground controllers—was bombed by a force of 320 Halifaxes from 4 and 6 Groups; Bennett's Light Night Striking Force was at last justified in the eyes of the Commander-in-Chief and other Group commanders by attacking Dortmund, Bonn, Nuremberg and Magdeburg. Attacks, real and spoof on these four widely spaced towns, were intended to bring about the final collapse of the German control system in a welter of indecision. In the event, as we have seen, such refinements were hardly necessary. By the time the first force reached Dresden, the system had collapsed, to the extent indeed that the controller at Döberlitz (near Berlin), headquarters of the 1st Night Fighter Division, and responsible for the Dresden area among others, thought that the Mosquito target indicating by Air Vice-Marshal Constantine's 5 Group crews was in fact the Main Force attack going in.

The fourth tactical element, was a feature, not an innovation, but it is the one which should most powerfully remind us of how little in essence the area offensive changed its fundamental character through all the years of war. Dresden was an unbombed city, and it was an old city; like Lübeck, like Rostock, like Hamburg, it would burn. So the fire storm was once more resorted to; once again the incendiary pattern produced first the furnace of fire, then a hurricane of fire. But a new touch was added. Formerly, German city dwellers died by fire or by high explosive, rarely from both together. The citizens of Dresden suffered the double blow.

Summing Up

The purpose of this summing up of the strategic air offensive is simple: it is to examine what seem to be the five principal factors relating to it, and to do so with particular reference to the last year. The five factors are: control of operations must be concentrated; intelligence of enemy strength (however 'strength' is defined) must be reliable and up to date—more so than is required for ground operations; the collapse or even the deterioration of enemy civilian morale should not be included as an objective; command of the air is more than the capacity to continue operations; 'precision bombing' is a term of art only, making for false optimism and inaccurate estimates of the ratio of force to target. The factors are examined here in relation to what happened, rather than what should or might have happened. The Introduction deals largely with the 'iffy' questions. The achievements of Bomber Command and its American compatriots have also been set down in that part of this history.

The first three years, for all three contestants, was essentially a period of preparation, whether it was consciously seen by commanders and combatants in these terms or not: it has been said before, but is worth saying again here, that not the least of Harris' gifts as a Commander-in-Chief was the ability consciously to measure out time, to distinguish between operations that had to be flown because they were an act of faith and those that could be mounted and executed as an act of war. That Harris combined this fairly unusual gift with a less agreeable, although arguably as necessary, talent for propaganda is interesting only insofar as it reminds us that he was, as C-in-C Bomber Command, a more complex individual than he chose to be thought at the time or as he has been usually regarded since. However, it ought to be said too in his favour that he first spoke up for Bomber Command when there was no assurance that it was going to be properly equipped for a real strategic task, whatever that might be, when indeed there was a likelihood that it would continue to be regarded by higher authority as having a role to perform primarily in propaganda terms.

The fourth year of the war—or, more strictly, that period lying between the middle of the fourth and the fifth—showed the offensive under way and the defence alerted to the dangers posed by a combined bomber offensive. This year is by a long stretch the most interesting, although not the most instructive, of the five-and-a-half, because the contestants were pretty evenly matched, while the classic difference between defeating an enemy's forces and destroying his resources was put to the test.

The 8th Air Force failed to defeat the German Air Force until the last moment, and then only in terms which showed the 'self-defending formation' thesis to have been wrong from the first; that discovery also adds to the interest of this year, because the narrow margin by which a decisive defeat was won and command of the air secured further emphasis that air bombardment was as much a matter of nip and tuck as any territorial campaign, and that all the grand theories of the strategic air offensive were just theories.

Bomber Command, however, had failed to win its particular campaign by the time of Overlord, and that failure raised more fundamental issues—although, paradoxically less for Harris than for Spaatz—as the war entered its sixth year. By September 1944 the greater paradox existed that, although the German Air Force had been virtually extinguished as an element in enemy forces, the German industry which, in part, it had fought to defend, was going strongly enough for much pessimism to seep into the Anglo-American camp. USSTAF had defeated the German Air Force in the air, and had destroyed enough of it on the ground to make Overlord a feasible operation of war; but, no more than Bomber Command through its strategy of dehousing, demoralising and destroying the German industrial worker was USSTAF *known* to have succeeded in imposing a significant check on industrial output as a whole. We now know that the bombing of what, for simplicity, may be called oil targets did immediately alarm those few men in Germany who kept their heads and their wits; above all was this true of Speer, who may not have been a 'great genius' but was, in his war time roles, possessed of extraordinary energy and not less extraordinary honesty about the real state of the German war economy, both in its good and bad aspects.

Spaatz must be praised for having urged that the destruction of oil targets would strike directly at that economy: his belief was partly based on the inherited conviction that a selective attack on industrial targets was one prime function of a strategic air offensive, partly in the belief that USSTAF was an instrument of war singularly apt for that task. But the mood of pessimism just referred to, which was so widespread at various Anglo-American political and military headquarters between late September 1944 and the failure of the airborne operations in Holland, and early March 1945 when the ground offensive was effectively resumed, was strong enough to release all those notions of 'winning' the war by an all-out aerial blow, a thunderclap or holocaust from the skies. In form Thunderclap never took place, and its cut down version, Clarion, was partly characterised by resort to the machine-gunning of German civilians.[1] This practice had become habitual among the Allied Air Forces since June 1944; that the trick was first taught by the German Air Force is quite irrelevant and is, in point of fact, not true. It is mentioned here to indicate that the strategic air offensive, fought for so long and with so much heroism by all contestants, above all by the bomber crews, concluded with Dresden and indiscriminate revenge on the lines of an old frontier war.

So much for the background. Now for the five factors. *Control of operations must be concentrated.* This was largely but by no means wholly achieved in any of the three Strategic Air Forces on the Allied side; nor was it achieved in the German Air Force. All four Air Forces were operated efficiently enough, often extremely efficiently, in the purely technical sense; all four were subject, naturally and properly, to political direction. But the role of none was fully or intelligently understood by higher, let alone the highest, authority. Hitler's interference with the German Air Force should be dealt with first in this connection, since it represents in the most extreme form the effect of the 'inspired' strategic amateur on the whole body, not merely the operations of a branch of the armed forces. The German Air Force had been the most ingeniously secret of Hitler's pre-war weapons; when the disguises were stripped away and it stood revealed as large, modern, formidable, the Spanish Civil War gave sufficient opportunity to gain battle experience, test theories and improve aircraft. The commanders and indeed much of the staff and senior ranks of the German Air Force were, by widespread consent in all camps, able, imaginative and above all moderate in their beliefs as to air power's role and contribution to the overall national strategy of war. In Germany the theories of Douhet and the precepts of Trenchard neither flourished nor languished nor were stillborn. From the outset it was understood that the primary role of the German Air Force was to support the ground forces;

an 'independent' strategy, possibly involving bombing cities, remained subordinate to the political imperatives of conquest or the military objectives of occupation.

Yet Hitler destroyed that sensible and limited theory of war. The failure of the German Air Force in the Battle of Britain led to what, in effect, if not wholly in intention, was an indiscriminate campaign of city bombing. Apart from legitimising Bomber Command's area offensive, the Blitz blunted the edge of what had been a considerable instrument for selective industrial bombing; a little more patience by Hitler, and the Blitz might have won him his war. The general staff and senior commanders of the German Air Force had the wit to see that retaliation lay in store for the German people: due largely to the insight of Kammhuber, and to that particular energy which marks the German nation in arms, retribution was long in coming. Yet Hitler interfered again in removing much of Kammhuber's defensive effort, and then proceeded to wreck the German Air Force's chance of matching the strategic air offensive by his fundamental indifference to the development of jet aircraft. It may be said that hindsight is being employed pretty freely at this point; indeed it is, since this is an unavoidable element in the historian's task. The observations on jet aircraft are made, however, to record rather than to assess. The *Luftwaffe War Diaries* show that Hitler was not alone in failing or refusing to see the significance of jet aircraft; but they show particularly that it was Hitler's own notion of using these aircraft in an offensive role which finally destroyed any chance that enough might be built as day and night fighters to meet the strategic air offensive on level terms.

The attitude of the Supreme Anglo-American Command and the national elements within it to the air forces led by Harris and Spaatz was very different to Hitler's; but there were two interesting similarities. Neither Roosevelt nor Churchill not their senior strategic advisers, namely the Combined Chiefs of Staff, really understood the scientific and technical aspects of air power, nor appreciated that the strategic air offensive was also subject to the same laws of war as that governing naval, amphibious and ground operations. The scientific advisers played a role comparable to court magicians, wizards or astrologers; if their advice was objective, dispassionate, independent or critical, they were removed. Secondly, senior airmen simply did not cut much ice; in the case of the Royal Air Force as a whole, the new Service was widely regarded at policy-making levels in Whitehall as a parvenu. Arnold, by his own account, never knew whether he was above or below the salt; in the estimation of others it did not much matter where this able, industrious and

co-operative airman sat. The same thing happened to the few senior
German Air Force officers on the OKW.[2]

Portal occupied a somewhat different position, partly by virtue of the
fact that, through more than a semantic difference, a Chief of the Air
Staff is not the same thing as the Chief of Staff of an Army Air Force. But
Portal was an airman of singular political understanding. He knew perfectly well how to assess the curious wartime atmosphere of Whitehall;
he knew that the popular and public affection for the Royal Air Force was
not felt or widely shared at the level where the cash, the resources, the
men and the strategic tasks were provided; above all Portal knew that
Bomber Command was a blunt instrument and that, even when provided
with improved material, it would remain a blunt instrument, a bludgeon
to destroy the German people, not a rapier to pierce the vital organs of
German industry. Whether Harris appreciated Portal's understanding of
Bomber Command's weaknesses is doubtful; he was too much wrapped
up in his own worries to believe that others might have them too. But
it is worth noting that, although Portal allowed Harris to make bombing policy, not merely to execute it, both knew, if not in unison, that
Bomber Command was not the flexible instrument of war some propa-
gandists made it out to be. In 1943, when Bomber Command fought on
alone, and made its great contribution to victory, the Portal-Harris
relationship made sense; in 1944, when command of the air had been won
and the direction of the European war had passed into American hands,
it did not.

The really striking difference between the German and Anglo-American
views of air power however resides in a paradox: Hitler interfered in a
service which had no inflated ideas of its own importance; Roosevelt
and Churchill virtually ignored services who, in varying degrees, had been
nurtured in the belief that air power could make a decisive contribution
to victory. Few things are more revealing to a student of the strategic air
offensive than the fact that the leaders of the Grand Alliance accorded it no
place in grand strategy. 'The strategic air offensive at no time enjoyed official recognition in US war plans except as a preliminary to the invasion of
Western Europe or a programme undertaken in support of that invasion',
say Craven and Cate in their summing up of the entire campaign[3]:
'... on this subject [the strategic air offensive] there is surprisingly little
in Sir Winston Churchill's *War Memoirs*',[4] adds Dr Frankland. The offensive, planned with such care, fought with such courage at such terrible
cost, fraught with so much terror and compact of so much sheer devastation, was thus, in grand strategic terms, a supporting operation. Whether

this order of priorities was right is difficult to say; perhaps all that one can say is that it allowed strong-minded airmen greater freedom of action than many of their naval and military brethren: control of operations was not concentrated at the political level because the operations were considered as relatively, not absolutely important. The crucial exception to this factor was Pointblank: before Big Week the factor just summarised obtained; after Big Week it did so again.

Intelligence of enemy strength must be reliable and up to date—more so than is required for ground operations. Both sides knew a great deal about each other; neither knew much about each other's resources, or rather the industrial strengths and weaknesses of their respective countries. Both official histories and various accounts of the German Air Force deal in great detail with 'intelligence', that difficult activity. The central point, however, is that industrial intelligence is a sufficiently different activity from the military variety for the closest liaison between officials and officers to be required. This nowhere happened. Harris, not content with openly regarding industrial intelligence officials in the Ministry of Economic Warfare as incompetent time-wasters, had little liaison with targeting committees and their associated bodies. Spaatz, Eaker and other American officers, less hidebound in this respect (and perhaps better able than Harris to appreciate the civilian's contribution to war), paid more attention to targeting committees and the like, in respect of both intelligence and options for attack. But then the American contribution to the strategic air offensive was, overtly, the destruction of selected portions of German industry. The German Air Force knew a good deal about British industry, but conducted a strategic air offensive too briefly to benefit from the information.

There are really two elements to consider here—finding things out and evaluating what is discovered. Now it is a matter of fact, although one not hitherto much discussed, that it was extremely difficult to find out what was going on in Germany once war began; put another way, British spies in Germany and spies employed by Britain there were few and far between, and those available were not trained in industrial intelligence.[5] The American State Department relied on information from British sources, or the reports made by United States Embassy in Berlin and consulates in Germany between the outbreak of war and Pearl Harbor, plus some perceptive analyses of German industry made by American businessmen and journalists in that time. Once America had declared war on Germany, some use was also made of the comparative method, whereby an analysis was made of what might happen to a major American industrial complex in a raid of a given weight; the conclusions were then, as it were, transferred to what was considered a comparable German complex; the alternative process was also practised.[6] This comparative method was ingenious but, in the event, not much help. It is mentioned here as one indication that expedients may be ever so ingenious, but they are only a partial substitute for the real thing.

Having said this, there is no doubt that, as the years went by, a large if rarely tightly organized Anglo-American effort did make for the acquisition of quite a lot of information. The trouble was to decide what to do with it, how to evaluate it, how to process it so that higher authority would quickly grasp its significance. The greatest achievement in this direction was undoubtedly in photographic intelligence, in both reconnaissance and interpretation. Here indeed was an Anglo-American collaboration that was cordial and effective. The USAAF came to provide an increasing number of photographic reconnaissance squadrons, but the Central Interpretation Unit at Medmenham, close to Bomber Command and 8th Air Force headquarters, served throughout the war as the key organisation for all with a legitimate need.

The Unit was important and successful because it dealt with original observation, not with assumptions. It is an interesting speculation whether it would have been possible to photograph German industry as a whole, and draw certain conclusions from that; the conclusions might well have been depressing in revealing what a tremendous objective 'the progressive destruction and dislocation of the German military, industrial and economic systems' really was. It must always be remembered that until well into 1944 those systems were supported and if necessary replenished by similar if lesser systems throughout most of Europe. The strategic air offensive was in reality intended industrially to destroy the richest, the most highly developed region in the entire world. This was an impossible task, considered in retrospect, and it may be said, if somewhat cynically, that, if its magnitude had been evaluated with true objectivity and on the basis of up to date information, it might never have been undertaken. Even when, in 1944, USSTAF begin to strike at vital targets in occupied Eastern Europe, the objective did not become attainable in more than partial terms.

Intelligence from some parts of occupied Europe was, however, consistently higher than from Germany itself, from which it was consistently sparse and poor. The reason for this difference is that, despite a lack of British or British-recruited agents in these countries before 1939, there was no lack of patriotic, brave and intelligent resistance workers after 1940.[7]

From this gallant band came high-quality intelligence: it may be said without fear of contradiction that the marking of the Kammhuber Line and the proper evaluation of the 'ski sites' would not have been possible without accurate intelligence from sources in the occupied states of Western Europe. But even these gallant patriots could not provide Bomber Command or the 8th Air Force with a dossier on the full industrial potential of their countries. Even if they had there were, as we have seen, considerations to inhibit a consistent attack on this potential. The bombing of the French railway system before Overlord may be argued as an exception, but it is a fact that Germany's war effort would have been greatly hampered by an earlier offensive against Western Europe's industry.

But finally, even the best intelligence would have only confirmed what some analysis and staff officers involved in the strategic air offensive suspected, namely that the war economy of Germany and its slave states was not in any way stretched. Setting aside the considerable contributions from neutral Spain and Sweden, and, in the earlier years, from Japan, Hitler's empire coasted along very happily for nearly four years, while Bomber Command crews, later joined by those of the 8th Air Force, suffered steadily increasing casualties.[8] This situation changed with dramatic speed between February and October 1944—one factor above all which makes it extremely difficult to assess the offensive's contribution to Allied victory—but there is no blinking the fact that the equally dramatic diplomatic and military victories which Hitler won between 1936 and 1940 did produce a situation which negatived most of the Douhet doctrine.

Civilian morale should not be included as an objective. The other part of the Douhet doctrine is that given a kind of strategic measurement by Trenchard in his assertion of the 'morale' factor: this part of the doctrine might well have been openly asserted as the primary aim of the strategic air offensive if the size as well as the hardness of the industrial nut had been appreciated *or* if Hitler had planned or launched indiscriminate aerial attacks on the British people from the outbreak of war. In the event, a combination of ignorance about German industry, plus fear of what Hitler might do, led to a situation where an area offensive was prosecuted once the phoney war ended. But it was not openly stated that the object of the exercise was to make the German people crack. Nobody, not even Cherwell, was prepared to do sums showing how many Germans would have to be killed before that point would be reached.

The moral issue is not being discussed here. All that is being discussed is the fact that 'the German people remained calmer, more stoical and much more determined than anticipated'.[9] It may be argued that misconceptions about these tough non-combatants flourished in the earlier rather than the later period of the war. That was so; in 1944 nobody spoke of the German morale as 'rotten'; equally, nobody supposed that they were not 'war-weary'—who was not? But it should be remembered that the panacea of an overwhelming blow at the German people was advanced in 1944 and practised rather consciously in 1945. Among Harris' invisible assets which remained with him throughout his term as Commander-in-Chief was the undeclared conviction of many of his overt critics that he was right. Churchill and the British Foreign Office came openly to doubt all that Harris advocated in the fire and sword line, but this parting of the ways came somewhat late in the day—after the Dresden raid.

Nevertheless, and still keeping clear of the moral issue, it is hard to blame the Allied High Command for its collective belief that there was a ratio between the number of German cities destroyed and the length of the war. The British people, if privately asked, might well have returned a dusty answer to the proposition that they could 'take it'—indefinitely. There was also a fairly widespread belief that the ordinary German loathed Hitler and all his works, and that he would turn and rend the dictator once the cities of the Reich became funeral pyres. Exactly how this rending process was to begin or be carried on was rarely discussed. The supposition was natural perhaps but, again, it was based on assumption rather than analysis. All of Cherwell's calculations, wide of the mark though they were, deliberately distorted though they have been, were not more fallacious than the belief that the German people would crack, either through hatred of Hitler's war or through fear of the Allies' revenge.

Arguably morale in total war is a question of national characteristics and national social and political systems. There is a school of thought on this subject which admits the toughness of the Germans under the bombing but declares that only fear of the Gestapo kept the ordinary civilian from caving in.[10] Apart from dodging the admittedly difficult question of how the civilian element of a nation at war does, as it were, surrender, the Gestapo theory is as little supported by evidence as most others on how Hitler kept his people fighting. There is no evidence to show that the average German opposed Hitler or disliked the thought of what was widely regarded as paying off old scores. The Gestapo made no impact on the lives of the ordinary German; its greatest impact, and then in a round-about, paradoxical sort of way, was after major raids; Goebbels, with typical cunning, gave Gestapo and other 'special' forces para-military and civil defence tasks. It has to be stated for the record that these tasks were carried out with efficiency and, if the word may be allowed in this context, humanity.[11]

Command of the air is more than the capacity to continue operating; 'precision bombing' is a term of art, making for false optimism and inaccurate estimates of the ratio of force to target. These two final factors are summed up together because they are those which most closely affected the narrowly strategic and tactical aspects of the strategic air offensive, whether conducted on the premise that something should be hit or the principle that some things should be hit.

'Command of the air' is not exactly the easiest principle of strategy to discuss, partly because it is not easy to define. We may perhaps say that in broad terms such command enables contestant A to prosecute a chosen strategy without having constantly to revise his calculations in the light of contestant B's capacity to destroy forces over random periods or recover more quickly than assumed or estimated from the effects of an offensive. Command of the air is thus not just a matter of tactical or technological superiority or advantages, such as the ability to destroy interceptors or beat radar or ignore anti-aircraft fire. The pith of this command is to be able to say: 'We will do such and such *within a predetermined time scale*. If we fail it will be due to our errors—low crew standards, faulty bomb sights or whatever.'

Comparably, the terms 'area bombing', 'precision bombing' and 'selective bombing' are misleading, because they imply absolutes. There is certainly such a thing as area bombing, and it is possible to define it as the lowest common denominator or factor of accuracy of a given force; Bomber Command's radius factor in 1940 was approximately five miles, in 1944 about three; the 8th Air Force's radius factor in 1944 was approximately two. On the other hand, precision bombing is an arbitrary standard which *some* crews in certain conditions *occasionally* achieve. When laid down as not only desirable but possible—as was done for the 8th Air Force in 1942 and 1943—precision bombing becomes an aspiration or an assertion, not an objective or an achievement.

Selective bombing likewise requires clarification; or, rather, the notion that the phrase indicates a process whereby a target or group of targets is chosen for some particular reason needs strengthening by adding the Speer criterion—namely that there is no point in making this distinction between targets in general and particular targets unless the latter are bombed until a strategic or tactical success has been unequivocally gained. It was occasionally possible to gain such a success in city busting—Lübeck and Rostock in 1942, Hamburg in 1943 and Dresden in 1945 may be cited as examples. It was very rarely possible to gain such a success in 'precise' or 'selective' terms, *except at prohibitive cost*, whether the attack was made once or repeatedly. Thus we are brought back to the equally fundamental question: what does command of the air really mean?

It must be a comprehensive strategic and tactical advantage, even if it is held for a limited time and over a limited area. Bomber Command did not have it at any time *before* the defeat of the German Air Force by USSTAF; it is that fact which makes the courage of the Command's air-crews so remarkable; it also accounts for much of what Harris said and did. Before March 1944 Bomber Command was unable to afford to isolate a target or series of targets and go to work on it with the results known to both sides (and affecting within a reasonable time the overall strategic position) and the missing rate going down and not up. What Sir Ralph Cochrane has called 'the curve of success' was constantly dragged down by the curve of unacceptable loss, and by such factors as weather, German civilian courage, the sheer size and strength of German industry, and its increasing dispersal into obscure or distant areas. Isolated events like the Eindhoven raid of December 1942, the Dams raid and many of the subsequent operations of 617 Squadron, emphasise this fact as much as do the Ruhr, Berlin and distant target battles of 1943 and 1944.

The 8th Air Force, and later the 15th, did achieve command of the air, and did so in time to gain what was arguably the strategic air offensive's most important and decisive contribution to Allied victory—a sky clear of enemy aircraft for Eisenhower's mix of green and stale soldiers to secure their Normandy lodgement. But the cost of winning this command was terribly high in terms of sheer human loss and suffering; only a country rich in young men unwearied in war and backed by industries capable of turning out B.17s and B.24s like cans of beans could have kept its air forces in the line of battle or returned them so quickly to the fray after the savage losses and outright defeats of the autumn of 1943. Even then, it must be said, the humble drop tank saved the day. Really it was a 'damn'd nice thing'. If the Mustang had not appeared as a very long range escort—*and* the German jet had been produced in numbers—those green and stale troops of Eisenhower's might have had some rude shocks. If Crossbow had failed—who knows?

On the other hand, the tide of war was flowing so strongly in the Allies' favour by the summer of 1944 that it is also possible to argue that even command of the air—which indirectly affected both the V-bomb and jet programmes—was a useful rather than a vital element in Allied strategy. The difficulty of arguing this point resides partly in the difficulty of determining how psychologically important it really was for the Normandy landings to be unaffected by the German Air Force. It is certainly possible to say that Eisenhower was too insistent on this point, and that his pledge of an air umbrella was to have some unfortunate consequences. There is also the Allied Expeditionary Air Force to be taken into consideration. This force, in size and strength, was certainly capable of dealing with the German Air Force in the West and carrying out a tactical offensive role as well.

What is perhaps more relevant in this summing up is that once USSTAF had won command of the air it was able to commence a programme of genuinely selective bombing—the destruction of oil targets. Again, it must be emphasised that the phrase 'strategic air offensive' is meaningless unless it is taken to mean an offensive directed at targets throughout Europe; it was USSTAF's capacity to bomb round the European map which made it eventually, a selective instrument of war. Yet the selective campaign directed on oil targets took place against a background in which USSTAF as a whole and in the final year of the war came to adopt many of the precepts urged by Harris and to adapt to many of the methods relied on by his crews. Even the oil campaign, intelligently planned and bravely executed as it was, can in no sense be described as a sustained example of precision bombing.

Thus we are left with one clear reminder of a painful truth: the laws of war applied as much to the strategic air offensive waged over Europe's skies through five-and-a-half bitter years as they did to the sailors and soldiers on distant seas or in the mud and sand below. Occasionally the airman may have felt himself living and fighting in a new dimension, just as the air force commander may have sometimes felt he enjoyed a freedom of manoeuvre denied to admirals and generals. But the airman died and the air force commander was defeated and stalemated unless the laws were kept. When they were kept, success came; until they could be kept, hope was kept alive by courage only. The strategic air offensive is above all, and for all, a tale of courage; for far too long, that priceless virtue was all the Allies had. They were fortunate, and we in the West are fortunate, that in this respect the men of Bomber Command and the United States Army Air Force never failed.

Appendix 1   Code Names

ABC   *Airborne Cigar;* Airborne transmitter which jammed the German fighter control frequencies.

AI   Airborne Interception; night fighter radar equipment.

Album Leaf   Improved kind of *Oboe.*

Aspirin   Jammer to counter the German *Knickebein* navigational aid.

Benjamin   Jammer to counter the German *Y-Gerät* bombing aid.

Bernhard   German ground-to-air communication system.

Boozer   Radar receiver fitted to RAF bombers.

Bromide   Jammer to counter the German *X-Gerät* bombing aid.

Chain Home   British early warning radar.

Cigar   See ABC.

Circus operations   Fighter-escorted daylight bombing attacks against short-range targets with the aim of bringing the enemy air force to battle.

Clarion   The American plan to disrupt German communications and morale by widespread bombing attacks.

Corona   Counterfeit orders to German fighters.

Cossac   Collective title for Anglo-American staff groups which planned Overlord before General Eisenhower's appointment as Supreme Commander.

Crossbow   The attack on V-weapon launching sites.

Domino   Jammer to counter the German *X-Gerät* bombing aid.

Düppel   German name for metal foil dropped to confuse radar.

Eureka   Ground radio transmitter for guiding bombers to their target.

Flak   *Fliegerabwehrkanonen;* anti-aircraft gun.

Freya   German early warning radar.

Gee   Radar aid to navigation and target identification.

G-H   Blind bombing radar device.

Giant Wuerzburg   German fighter control radar.

Grand Slam   22,000-lb. penetrating (earthquake) bomb.

Himmelbett   German system of controlled night fighting.

H₂S   British bombing aid.

H₂X   American version of *H₂S.*

Knickebein   German navigational aid.

Lichtenstein   German night fighter radar.

Mandrel   Radio swamping of the German early warning system.

Meacon   Device to mask the radiations from German radio beacons.

Monica   Radar fitted in rear of Bomber Command aircraft to provide some 'early warning' of night fighters.

Musical Paramatta   Method of ground marking a target by coloured target indicators dropped blindly on *Oboe*.

Musical Wanganui   Method of sky marking a target by coloured markers dropped blindly on *Oboe*.

Naxos   German radar device enabling fighters to home on H_2S transmissions of bombers.

Newhaven   Method of ground marking a target by flares or target indicators dropped blindly on H_2S followed by visual identification.

Oboe   Blind bombing radar device.

Octagon   The second Quebec Conference, September 1944.

Overlord   The Allied invasion of France in 1944.

Pointblank   The directive for the Combined Bomber Offensive, June 1943.

Quadrant   The first Quebec Conference, August, 1943.

Sea Lion   German plan for the invasion of England.

Sextant   The Cairo Conference, November–December 1943.

SN-*2*   German night fighter radar.

Tallboy   12,000-lb. penetrating (earthquake) bomb.

Tame Sow   German tactics, designed to bring night fighters in contact with bombers moving to and from target, using co-ordinated groups.

Tinsel   Scheme for broadcasting engine noises on the German fighter control frequencies.

Thunderclap   Plan to deliver a sudden, catastrophic blow by bombing Berlin and other cities with a view to bringing about German surrender.

Torch   Allied invasion of French North Africa in 1942.

Trident   The third Washington Conference, May 1943.

Wassermann   German early warning radar.

Wild Sow   German tactics to engage bombers over the target by individual fighters.

Window   Tinfoil strips designed to confuse German radar.

Wuerzburg   German radar used to direct A.A. guns, searchlights and, for a short time, night fighters.

X-Gerät   German bombing aid.

Y-control   A method of controlling night fighters using modified *Y-Gerät* equipment.

Y-Gerät   German bombing aid.

Appendix 2   Selected Documents

1 Bombing Directive No. 22

14 February 1942. Air Vice-Marshal N. H. Bottomley (Deputy Chief of the Air Staff) to Air Marshal J. E. A. Baldwin (Acting Air Officer Commanding-in-Chief, Bomber Command)

Sir,

I am directed to refer to Air Ministry letter dated 4.2.42,* and to say that, in order to enable you to make your offensive fully effective on the introduction of TR 1335† equipment on operations, it has been decided that the principle of conservation of your forces, laid down in Air Ministry letter dated 13.11.41, should be modified. You are accordingly authorised to employ your effort without restriction, until further notice, in accordance with the following directions. Clearly this does not warrant pressing your attacks if weather conditions are unfavourable or if your aircraft are likely to be exposed to extreme hazards.

2. In the opinion of the Air Staff, the introduction of TR.1335 will confer upon your forces the ability to concentrate their effort to an extent which has not hitherto been possible under the operational conditions with which you are faced. It is accordingly considered that the introduction of this equipment on operations should be regarded as a revolutionary advance in bombing technique which, during the period of its effective life as a target-finding device, will enable results to be obtained of a much more effective nature.

3. The period in which this device can be used as an aid to target location and blind bombing will be governed by the ability of the enemy to develop counter-measures when the secret of its nature and operations has been disclosed. Much will depend on the security measures observed in its employment and the care taken by air crews to ensure the destruction of the apparatus and to avoid mentioning or discussing it in the event of their aircraft being forced down over enemy territory. It is unlikely, however, that under the best possible conditions this period will exceed six months from the date of its introduction. It is accordingly of first importance to exploit the advantages it confers to the full. The maximum effort possible having due regard to weather and other hazards should be exerted throughout the period it is thus available, and particularly in the first few weeks of your operations.

4. In addition to the foregoing primary factor, a resumption of your offensive at full effort is considered desirable for the following reasons:

(i) This is the time of year to get the best effect from concentrated incendiary attacks.

(ii) It would enhearten and support the Russians if we were to resume our offensive on a heavy scale, while they were maintaining so effectively their own counter-offensive against the German armies.

(iii) The co-incidence of our offensive with the Russian successes would further depress the enemy morale, which is known already to have been affected by the German armies' reverses on the Eastern Front.

5. In accordance with these principles and conditions, a review has been made of the directions given to you in Air Ministry letter dated 9.7.41, and it has been decided that the primary object of your operations should now be focussed on the morale of the enemy

---

* Not printed.
† i.e. *Gee.*

civil population and in particular, of the industrial workers. With this aim in view, a list of selected area targets (taking account of the anticipated range of the TR.1335 equipment) is attached in Annex 'A' to this letter. An additional list of targets beyond this range, which can be attacked when conditions are particularly favourable and when a correct assumption of the accuracy and powers of concentration obtainable with the equipment has been made, are also included in Annex 'A'.

6. You will note that Berlin has been included amongst the latter targets. In this case, your operations should be of a harassing nature, the object being to maintain the fear of attack over the city and to impose A.R.P. measures. The scale of effort and tactics employed should be designed to incur the minimum casualties and for that reason they should be undertaken at high altitude even if this entails carrying reduced bombloads. Apart from these particular operations against Berlin, the cardinal principle which should govern your employment of TR.1335 from the outset, should be the complete concentration on one target until the effort estimated to be required for its destruction has been achieved. Estimates of the scales of attack required are given in Annex 'C'.

7. Essen is the most important of the selected primary targets, and by attacking it first, the maximum benefit should be derived from the element of surprise. I am to suggest, therefore, that this should be selected as your initial target for TR.1335 operations, to be followed by attacks against the remaining priority areas listed in Annex 'A'.

8. When experience in the employment of TR.1335 has proved that, under favourable conditions, effective attacks on precise targets are possible, I am to request that you will consider the practicability of attacking first, the precise targets within TR.1335 range and, later, those beyond this range listed in Annex 'B'.

9. During the estimated effective life of TR.1335 as a target-finding and blind bombing device, it will not be possible to equip more than a relatively small proportion of your force. It is, therefore, of the first importance that tactical methods to assist the remainder of the force to achieve concentration, both when the target is capable of being illuminated and under blind bombing conditions, should be studied, developed and applied to the maximum possible extent. In this connection I am to remind you of the principles and scales of attack with incendiary weapons laid down in Air Ministry letter dated 25.10.41.*

10. Apart from your primary offensive on the above lines, I am to say that the following additional commitments will still have to be met from time to time:

(i) Attacks on factories in France are to be undertaken as notified to you in Air Ministry letter dated 5.2.42.* If a favourable opportunity for the initial attack on the Renault plant has not occurred before you begin operations with the TR.1335 equipment, attacks on the French factories are to be carried out only when weather conditions are particularly favourable and at the same time are unsuitable for the concentrated bombing of targets in Germany within this Directive.

(ii) The operations of No. 2 Group are to continue to be governed by the directions in Air Ministry letter dated 25.11.41* bearing in mind the commitment for army air support as stated in para 7 of that letter.

(iii) Periodical support for the operations planned by the Adviser of Combined Operations will be required in accordance with the directions issued to you in Air Ministry letter dated 21 December 1941.*

11. Finally, I am to say that, although every effort will be made to confine your operations to your primary offensive, you should recognise that it will on occasions be necessary to call upon you for diversionary attacks on objectives, the destruction of which

* Not printed.

is of immediate importance in the light of the current strategical situation. In particular, important naval units and the submarine building yards and bases may have to be attacked periodically, especially when this can be done without missing good opportunities of bombing your primary targets.

(Sgd.) N. H. BOTTOMLEY

ANNEXE 'A'
TO AIR MINISTRY LETTER DATED 14.2.42
PRIMARY INDUSTRIAL AREAS
(Within TR.1335 range—350 miles from Mildenhall)
Central (Ruhr) area,
    Essen (Transportation and heavy industries)
    Duisberg (Transportation and heavy industries)
    Düsseldorf (Transportation and general industries)
    Cologne (Transportation and general industries)

ALTERNATIVE INDUSTRIAL AREAS
(Within T.R.1335 range—350 miles from Mildenhall)
Northern (coastal) area,
    Bremen (Naval dockyards)
    Wilhelmshaven (Naval dockyards)
    Emden (Naval dockyards)

ALTERNATIVE INDUSTRIAL AREAS
(Involving deeper penetration beyond TR.1335 range)
Northern
    Hamburg (Naval and general shipbuilding)
    Kiel (Naval dockyards)
    Lübeck (Baltic port) (Industrial and armament centre)
    Rostock (Heinkel factories)
Central
    Berlin (General industries)
    Kassel (Locomotive industry)
    Hanover (Rubber manufacture)
Southern
    Frankfurt (Chemical and general engineering)
    Mannheim (Transportation, chemical and general engineering)
    Schweinfurt (Ball bearings)
    Stuttgart (General, electrical and precision engineering)

ANNEXE 'B'
TO AIR MINISTRY LETTER DATED 14.2.42
PRECISE TARGETS

Within TR.1335 Range
Operational

Number	Detail	Remarks
G S 162	Chemische Werk, Hüls	Producing approximately 20% of
	Synthetic rubber	Germany's total rubber supply.

G O 1236   Quadrath (Fortuna)   Production capacity 250,000 kw.
            Power Station

G O 1237   Goldenberg Werk, Koln   Largest steam power plant in Europe.
            (Knapsack)   Production capacity 500,000 kw.
            Power Station

G O 1428   Brauweiler (Koln)   Outdoor transformer and switching
            Switching and Transformer   station controlling 1,500,000 kw.
            Station   of plant output. Controls the flow
                                           of power from South into Ruhr-
                                           Rhineland.

G O 1128   Gersteinwerk (Stockum)   150,000 kw. Steam Station.
            Power and Switching   Also controls flow power from
            Station   East in Ruhr-Rhineland.

G Q 1509   Gelsenberg-Benzin A.G.   Annual output 390,000 tons fuel.
            Gelsenkirchen (Nordstern)
            Synthetic oil

G Q 1537   Hydrierwerke Scholven   Annual output approximately
            Gelsenkirchen A.G. (Buer)   300,000 tons fuel.

G Q 1510   Union Rheinische Braun-   Annual output 240,000 tons fuel.
            kohln Wesserling

Outside TR.1335 Range

G S 153   Bunawerke Schopau (Merse-   Produces approximately 30%
            burg)   Germany's total rubber supply.
            Synthetic Rubber

G Z 2805   V.D.M. Frankfurt Heddern-   Leading German airscrew manu-
            heim   facturers and aircraft components.

G B 3280   Robert Bosch—Stuttgart-   Most important factory in Germany
            Fuerbach   making dynamos, injection pumps
                                           and magnetos.

G Q 1515   I.G. Farben Leunawerke   Annual output 480,000 tons fuel and
            (Merseburg)   large capacity fixation of nitrogen.
            Synthetic Oil

ANNEXE 'C'

TO AIR MINISTRY LETTER DATED 14.2.42

ESTIMATED WEIGHT OF ATTACK FOR DECISIVE DAMAGE

1	2	3	4	5	6 Wt. of attack required on a basis of 7 tons per sq. mile and 50% efficiency	7 Wt. of attack required on a basis of 1 ton per 800 pop. and 50% efficiency
Selected Area	Size of total area (sq. miles)	Size of built-up area (sq. miles)	Size of central vulnerable area (sq. miles)	Pop. of total area		
A. Essen	70	25	9	650,000	1,000 tons	1,600 tons
B. Duisberg	55	16	3	440,000	800 tons	1,100 tons
C. Düsseldorf	62	18	3	500,000	850 tons	1,200 tons
D. Cologne	100	30	5	750,000	1,400 tons	1,800 tons

2 The Pointblank Offensive

The Combined Bomber Offensive from the United Kingdom (Pointblank) *as approved by the Combined Chiefs of Staff, 14 May 1943*

1. THE MISSION

(a) The mission of the United States and British bomber forces, as prescribed by the Combined Chiefs of Staff at Casablanca, is as follows:

To conduct a joint United States-British air offensive to accomplish the progressive destruction and dislocation of the German military, industrial and economic system, and the undermining of the morale of the German people to a point where their capacity for armed resistance is fatally weakened. This is construed as meaning so weakened as to permit initiation of final combined operations on the Continent.

2. THE PRINCIPAL OBJECTIVES

(a) A thorough study of those elements of the German military, industrial and economic system, which appeared to be profitable as bombing objectives, was made by a group of Operations Analysts consisting of eminent United States experts. The report of the Operations Analysis concludes that:

The destruction and continued neutralisation of some sixty (60) targets would gravely impair and might paralyse the western Axis war effort. There are several combinations of targets from among the industries studied which might achieve this result.

(b) Examination of this report shows complete agreement by United States and British experts. From the systems proposed by the Operations Analysts, six systems, comprising *seventy-six (76) precision targets*, have been selected. These targets are located within the tactical radius of action of the two air forces, and their destruction is directed against the three major elements of the German Military machine: its submarine fleet, its air force, and its ground forces, and certain industries vital to their support.

The six systems are:

Submarine construction yards and bases.

German aircraft industry.

Ball bearings.

Oil.

Synthetic rubber and tires.

Military transport vehicles.

Concentration of effort against these systems will have the following effect. The percent of destruction is as indicated by the Operations Analysts:

(1) *Submarine construction yards and bases.* Destruction of the submarine building yards selected will reduce present submarine construction by eighty-nine percent (89%). Attack of submarine bases will affect the submarine effort at sea. If it is found that successful results can be achieved, these attacks should continue whenever conditions are favourable for as long and as often as is necessary.

(2) *German aircraft industry.* Depletion of the German air force will fatally weaken German capacity to resist our air and surface operations. Complete domination of the air is essential for our ultimate decisive effort. Destruction of forty-three percent (43%) of the German fighter capacity and sixty-five percent (65%) of the German bomber capacity is provided for in this plan, and will produce the effect required.

(3) *Ball bearings.* The critical condition of the ball-bearing industry in Germany is startling. The concentration of that industry renders it outstandingly vulnerable to air attack. Seventy-six percent (76%) of the ball bearing production can be

eliminated by destruction of the targets selected. This will have immediate and critical repercussions on the production of tanks, airplanes, artillery, diesel engines—in fact, upon nearly all the special weapons of modern war.

(4) *Oil.* The quantities of petroleum and synthetic oil products now available to the German is barely adequate to supply the life-blood which is vital to the German war machine. The oil situation is made more critical by failure of the Germans to secure and retain the Russian supplies. If the Ploesti refineries, which process thirty-five percent (35%) of current refined oil products available to the Axis, are destroyed, and the synthetic oil plants in Germany which process an additional thirteen percent (13%) are also destroyed, the resulting disruption will have a disastrous effect upon the supply of finished oil products available to the Axis.

(5) *Synthetic rubber and tires.* These products are vital to all phases of German Military strength on land and in the air. Provision is made for destruction of fifty percent (50%) of the synthetic rubber capacity and nearly all of the tire production. This destruction will have a crippling effect.

(6) *Military transport vehicles.* Seven (7) plants produce a large proportion of the military transport and armored vehicles. The precise proportion is unknown. Loss of these plants will strike directly at the German Military strength. *The cumulative effect of the destruction of the targets comprising the systems just listed will fatally weaken the capacity of the German people for armed resistance.*

(d) The selection of these objectives is confirmed by the fact that the systems about which the Germans are most sensitive, and about which they have concentrated their defenses, such as balloons, camouflage, anti-aircraft, searchlights, decoys and smoke, are:

Aircraft factories.

Submarine construction yards.

Ball-bearings.

Oil.

3. INTERMEDIATE OBJECTIVE

(a) The Germans, recognising the vulnerability of their vital industries, are rapidly increasing the strength of their fighter defenses. The German fighter strength in western Europe is being augmented. *If the growth of the German fighter strength is not arrested quickly, it may become literally impossible to carry out the destruction planned and thus to create the conditions necessary for ultimate decisive action by our combined forces on the Continent.*

(b) Hence the successful prosecution of the air offensive against the principal objectives is dependent upon a prior (or simultaneous) offensive against the German fighter strength.

(c) To carry out the Eighth Air Force's part of this combined bomber offensive it will be necessary to attack precision targets deep in German territory in daylight. The principal obstacle to this is the growing strength of the German air force. The growth of this fighter force has become so pronounced as to warrant a brief review of this development (Chart A).*

(d) The upper curve shows what has been happening to the German air force in the past nine months. The bomber strength has been sharply reduced from 1,760 bombers to 1,450 in operational units. The fighters, on the other hand, increased from 1,690 to 1,710. They suffered a reduction in strength, doubtless caused by the intense operations in Russia and the Mediterranean as well as on the Western Front, but those losses have been made good at the expense of the bombers. That same trend is reflected in the lower curve, which shows production was maintained fairly constantly for about five months and

* Not printed.

then increased, so that fighter production has risen from 720 to 810 per month. Over a longer period of time, from the entrance of the United States into the war until the present time, the trend has been ever more pronounced. German fighter strength has increased by forty-four percent (44%) in that period in spite of the heavy losses. This chart shows the margin of production over average monthly wastage in German fighters. Of course, the monthly wastage has not been constant over the past seven months, as shown on the chart, but the average for that period has been fairly accurately determined at 655 fighters per month. The production rate of last February showed 810 fighters per month. The average increase in production over the six-month period depicted indicates a monthly surplus of production over average wastage of 108 airplanes. If this trend simply continues in its present ratio, it is well within the capacity of the Germans to produce enough fighter airplanes over and above wastage to provide a strength of 3,000 fighters by this time next year. (See Chart B.*) This is, of course, a capability and not necessarily a German intention, although current German development points very strongly in that direction. The increase in fighter strength is not reflected in this curve covering the past eight months; however, during that period the Germans converted a great many fighter-type airplanes into fighter bombers and fighter reconnaissance airplanes. The wastage rate was very high in those units and that probably accounts for the temporary decline in German fighter strength; however, in the last three months it has shown a sharp uprise.

(e) The disposition of German fighters is also significant (see Chart C).* The top line shows the number of fighters on the Western Front. Since we entered the war that strength has nearly doubled. It has risen from 420 to 830. This, in spite of the heavy drains on the Russian and Mediterranean fronts. When we entered the war only thirty-six percent (36%) of German fighters were concentrated on the Western Front; to-day, fifty percent (50%) of all fighters available to the German air force are concentrated in opposition to our principal bombing effort from the United Kingdom. The German fighter force is taking a toll of our forces both by day and by night, not only in terms of combat losses, but more especially in terms of reduced tactical effectiveness. If the German fighters are materially increased in number it is quite conceivable that they could make our daylight bombing unprofitable, and perhaps our night bombing, too. On the other hand, if the German fighter force is partially neutralised our effectiveness will be vastly improved.

(f) For this reason German fighter strength must be considered as an *Intermediate* objective second to none in priority.

4. INTEGRATED RAF–UNITED STATES ARMY AIR FORCES' OFFENSIVE

(a) The combined efforts of the entire United States and British bomber forces can produce the results required to achieve the mission prescribed for this theater. Fortunately the capabilities of the two forces are entirely complementary.

(b) The tremendous and ever-increasing striking power of the RAF bombing is designed to so destroy German material facilities as to undermine the willingness and ability of the German worker to continue the war. Because of this, there is great flexibility of the RAF to direct its material destruction against those objectives which are closely related to the United States bombing effort which is directed toward the destruction of specific essential industrial targets. It is considered that the most effective results from strategic bombing will be obtained by directing the combined day and night effort of the United States and British bomber forces to all-out attacks against targets which are mutually complementary in undermining a limited number of selected objective

* Not printed.

systems. All-out attacks imply precision bombing of related targets by day and night where tactical conditions permit, and area bombing by night against the cities associated with these targets. The timing of the related day and night attacks will be determined by tactical considerations.

(c) This plan does not attempt to prescribe the major effect of the RAF Bomber Command. It simply recognises the fact that when precision targets are bombed by the Eighth Air Force in daylight, the efforts should be complemented and completed by RAF bombing attacks against the surrounding industrial area at night. Fortunately the industrial areas to be attacked are in most cases identical with the industrial areas which the British Bomber Command has selected for mass destruction anyway. They include Hamburg, Bremen, Hanover, Berlin, Leipzig, Wilhelmshaven, Bremerhaven, Cologne, Stuttgart, and many other principal cities. They also, of course, include smaller towns whose principal significance is coupled with the precision targets prescribed for the Eighth Air Force.

5. GENERAL PLAN OF OPERATIONS

(a) It would be highly desirable to initiate precision bombing attacks against German fighter assembly and engine factories immediately. However, our present force of day bombers is too small to make the deeper penetrations necessary to reach the majority of these factories. Considering the number of German fighters which can be concentrated laterally to meet our bombers on penetration, and again on withdrawal, it is felt that 300 heavy bombers is the minimum operating force necessary to make deep penetrations.

(b) The general tactical plan of operations with this minimum force involves the following general conception: a holding attack intended to attract German fighters to a particular area and prevent their massing against the main attacking force. For this purpose 50 heavy bombers with fighter escort are required. Second, a main striking force to penetrate through the fighter defenses and carry out the destruction of targets in Germany and return. Two hundred bombers is considered the minimum requirement to provide self-protection and at the same time carry out worthwhile destruction. Third, the covering force to attack still another area and attract fighters in order to divert them from the main force on withdrawal. Again, 50 bombers with fighter escort is the minimum force to carry out such a function.

(c) In order to establish a yardstick to be used in the determination of the number of bombers required to destroy the objectives desired, the following procedure was employed:

Twelve successful missions were conducted in January, February and March. Approximately 100 bombers were dispatched on each. It was found that sufficient bombs fell within a circle of 1,000-foot radius centered about the aiming point to cause the desired destruction. For each prospective target the number of 1,000-foot radius circles necessary to cover it has been calculated. The yardstick, as determined by experience, is, therefore, the number of 1,000-foot radius circles of destruction, each requiring 100 bombers.

(d) The plan of operations is divided into four phases (see Chart E).* The depth of penetration, the number of targets available and the capacity of the bombing forces increases successively with each phase.

(e) Seventy-six precision targets have been selected for Eighth Air Force bombing operations. Having selected these 76 targets the questions arise: Can they be effectively

* Not printed.

destroyed, and, if so, how many bombers will be required? As to the first question, operational experience answers yes.

6. EFFECTIVENESS OF EIGHTH AIR FORCE

(a) The operations of the United States Army Air Force in daylight bombing of defended objectives in German-occupied Europe have been sufficient to establish a criterion of precision daylight bombing effectiveness; the operations of the RAF Bomber Command leave no room for doubt of the ability of that force to devastate industrial areas.

(b) The daylight operations of the Eighth Air Force from the 3rd January, 1943, to the 6th April, 1943, definitely establish the fact that it is possible to conduct precision-pattern bombing operations against selected precision targets from altitudes of 20,000 to 30,000 feet in the face of anti-aircraft artillery and fighter defenses.

(c) Of 20 missions dispatched by the United States Eighth Air Force in that period, 12 have been highly effective. These 12 daylight missions have been directed against a variety of targets, including:

> Submarine bases
> Locomotive shops
> Power houses
> Marshalling yards
> Shipbuilding yards
> Motor vehicle and armament works
> Airplane engine factories

The average number of aircraft dispatched against these targets has been 86. The destructive effect has, in every case, been highly satisfactory. From this experience it may be definitely accepted that 100 bombers dispatched on each successful mission will provide entirely satisfactory destructive effect of that part of the target area within 1,000 feet of the aiming point; and that two-thirds of the missions dispatched each month will be successful to this extent.

7. FORCES REQUIRED

(a) *Heavy bombers*

(1) In computing the force required, a yardstick of 100 bombers dispatched per target area of 1,000 feet about each aiming point has been accepted as a reasonable product of actual experience to date. Each target has been evaluated in terms of these 'Target Units,' or the number of 1,000-foot radius circles in which this destructive effect must be produced.

(2) Experience in the European Theater to date indicates that at least 800 airplanes must be in the theater to dispatch 300 bombers on operations. Hence, until the level of United States bomber strength in this theater reaches approximately 800, it will not be feasible to sustain a precision bombing offensive against the German fighter factories. It is estimated that we will be able to accommodate and train a force of this capacity by July of this year. In the interim every effort should be made to reduce the German fighter force by attack of those fighter factories which can be reached, and by combat under favourable conditions. The repair depots and airdromes are included for the purpose of giving commanders the necessary tactical latitude. Concurrently, operations can be conducted against submarine installations within reach and against other targets contributing directly to the principal objectives which are within covering range of our own fighters, or which do not require deep penetration. Some operations will have to be conducted to provide the neces-

sary training for the incoming forces; such operations must be conducted against objectives within the listed categories.

(3) During the next phase, from July to October, in which it is estimated that we will be able to penetrate to a limit of 400 miles, a determined effort must be made to break down the German fighter strength by every means at our disposal, concentrating primarily upon fighter aircraft factories. During this time interim an additional increment of 248 bombers are required, so that the strength in the theater by October should be approximately 1,192. This would provide a striking force of 450 bombers at the end of this period. The average striking force during this period would be 400.

(4) During the third phase the German fighter force must be kept depleted, and the other sources of German strength must also be undermined. During this phase our bombing offensive forces must be adequate to perform all their major tasks.

(5) From October to January an additional increment of 554 bombers are required, bringing the total to 1,746. This should provide an operational striking force of 655 bombers at the end of that time. The average striking force during this period will be 550 bombers.

(6) During the last phase—early 1944—the entire force should be used to sustain the effect already produced and to pave the way for a combined operations on the Continent. This will require a force of 2,702 heavy bombers.

(7) It will be observed that the charts of the actual location of the targets to be attacked in each phase show the joint bombing effort of each phase. It will be noted that, in the first phase (see Map 1),* operations are limited to relatively shallow penetration. They include submarine bases along the coast, submarine construction yards, and the Fock-Wulf airplane factory at Bremen. Actually, of course, these operations have all been undertaken with the small forces available and in the case of the submarine yards at Vegesack and the Focke-Wulf plant at Bremen, a long step has already been taken towards completion of the plan. There are two other systems of operations calling for deep penetrations shown in this phase. One of them calls for an attack against oil installations in the Ruhr. This operation is entirely contingent upon an earlier attack from the Mediterranean area against the oil refineries at Ploesti in Rumania. Such an attack is under consideration now, and if it is carried out we will be forced to operate against the Ruhr refineries in order to exploit the advantage achieved in Rumania. The other attack calls for a very deep penetration at Schweinfurt. This operation might be undertaken as a surprise attack in view of the tremendous advantages accrued from a successful destruction of these plants; however, it would be most unwise to attempt it until we are perfectly sure we have enough force to destroy the objective in a single operation. Any attempt to repeat such an attack will meet with very bitter opposition. In the second phase (see Map 2),* the plan calls for a concentration of effort against the German fighter assembly and fighter aircraft factories as well as attacks against airdromes and repair facilities. It is anticipated that approximately 75% of the striking force will be applied to this end during this phase. The other 25% is directed against submarine construction yards. In the third phase (see Map 3)* an all-out attack against all the principal objectives is provided as well as repeat operations to continue neutralisation of installations which have been destroyed and which can be repaired. During the fourth phase (see Map 4),* these operations are continued and allowances made for concentration of attacks against installations

* Not printed.

more directly associated with a cross-channel operation such as rail transportation, arsenals, Military installations, &c.

(8) The determination of the number of aircraft required in each phase has been based strictly upon past experience. As to the rate of operations, the Eighth Air Force has averaged six per month over the past six months. In the past three months, it has actually carried out twelve highly successful operations out of a total of twenty. This plan is based on a total of twelve successful operations in each three-month phase and recognises the probability that the other six will for one reason or another be less satisfactory. Experience has shown that about 3/8ths of the total number of airplanes in the theater can be dispatched on operational missions at any one time. This makes allowances for the airplanes in depot reserve, those in depot repair, and those being ferried and modified. There is every reason to believe that our forces will be more effective in the future than these figures indicate. In order to be as realistic as possible, however, the plan has been based in each case upon actual past experience.

(9) Chart E* tabulates all the targets for contemplated destruction by the United States and British bomber forces to carry out the mission. The precision targets for attacks by the United States Bomber Command are shown as small symbols. The cities and towns in or near those precision targets and which constitute the complementary targets of the RAF are shown as in circles. The German fighters are at present deployed in four main concentrations positioned well forward toward the coast. In general, the day fighters are in four lots of approximately 100 each in the general areas of north-west coastal Germany, Holland and Belgium, the channel coast of France and western France in the vicinity of the submarine pens. These fighters are capable of concentrating laterally from bases at least 200 miles away, so that forces of 300 fighters might be employed against our main efforts if we penetrated directly towards the Ruhr without distracting or diverting part of them.

(10) Chart D* is illustrative of the effect of this plan of operations upon the intermediate objective, German fighter strength. This chart must be considered as pictorial rather than precise. The top line shows the increase in German fighter strength. That is a German capability if they choose to follow it. If German production is not interrupted and if German wastage is not increased, it is possible for Germany to have in operation 3,000 fighters by next April. The broken line shows the effect of our operations upon that German fighter strength. In the first phase we do not expect to accomplish a great deal because our forces will not have been built up to decisive proportions. In the second phase, our attacks against German fighter factory and engine factories and the increased attrition should cause the levelling off of the German fighter strength. In the third phase the full effect of the attacks against German fighter production should make themselves felt so that German fighter strength should fall off rapidly in this phase. In the fourth phase that German fighter strength should decline at a precipitant rate. This second line has been computed in the following manner: The decrease in German fighter strength is the result of two factors. One is the attacks against German fighter factories, the other the accelerated rate of combat wastage caused by our increased bomber forces. This wastage rate has been computed in an extremely conservative manner. It is realised that past claims of enemy aircraft shot down may seem high, although our evaluation of them is very careful; nevertheless, in order to avoid any charge of unwarranted optimism combat claims have been arbitrarily divided by four, the

* Not printed.

resulting decrease in German fighter strength dependent upon expected combat wastage is at a rate only one quarter as great as our present combat claims. Even under these very conservative assumptions it is apparent that the German fighter strength will have passed its limit by the end of the second phase, and its powers of resistance should decline very rapidly thereafter.

(b) *Medium bombers*

It will be noted that no United States medium bombardment aircraft have been specifically included in the computation of force required above. That does not mean that medium bombardment is not necessary to implement this plan. Supplementary attacks against all strategic targets within range of medium bombers are anticipated as necessary adjuncts to the heavy bomber attacks. In addition, medium bombardment is required in order to conduct repeated attacks against German fighter airdromes, to aid the passage of the heavy bombers until the attacks against the German aircraft industry make themselves felt. Medium bombardment will be necessary to support combined operations in early 1944. The crews must be operationally trained in this theater by that date.

(c) *Fighters*

At all times there is a need for an extensive United States fighter force both to protect the bombers and to assist in the reduction of the German fighter strength. Prior to the initiation of operations on the Continent, this fighter strength must be at a maximum, and must be fully trained for operations in this theater.

Note. This plan deals entirely with the requirements for the strategic bombing force, except for its use in the 4th Phase on missions which will render most effective support to surface operations on the Continent, which may begin in early 1944. In order to supplement this force in providing the close support required for the surface operations, steps must be taken early to create and train a tactical force in this theater. This force must include light bomber, reconnaissance, fighter, and troop carrier elements.

8. CONCLUSIONS

(a) *Recapitulation of United States bomber forces required:*

	Heavy	Medium
1st Phase	944	200 Bombers required by June 30, 1943.
2nd Phase	1,192	400 Bombers required by September 30, 1943.
3rd Phase	1,746	600 Bombers required by December 31, 1943.
4th Phase	2,702	800 Bombers required by March 31, 1944.

(b) If the forces required as set forth above are made available on the dates indicated, it will be possible to carry out the mission prescribed in the Casablanca Conference. If those forces are not made available, then that mission is not attainable by mid-1944.

(c) Depletion of the German fighter strength must be accomplished first. Failure to neutralise that force will jeopardise the prosecution of the war toward a favourable decision in this theater.

(d) The following bombing objectives should be destroyed under the provisions of the general directive issued at the Casablanca Conference:

(1) *Intermediate objectives:*
German fighter strength.

(2) *Primary objectives:*
German Submarine yards and bases.
The remainder of the German aircraft industry.

Ball bearings.*

Oil.* (Contingent upon attacks against Ploesti from the Mediterranean.)

(3) *Secondary objectives in order of priority:*

Synthetic rubber and tires.

Military motor transport vehicles.

(e) The following statement of principle, expressed by the Operations Analysts, is concurred in:

> In view of the ability of adequate and properly utilised air power to impair the industrial source of the enemy's Military strength, only the most vital considerations should be permitted to delay or divert the application of an adequate air striking force to this task.

3 The Harris Memorandum

Note by Air Marshal Sir Arthur Harris for the Prime Minister and War Cabinet, and prepared at the request of the Prime Minister, on the Role and Work of Bomber Command, 28th June 1942

1. Those who advocate the breaking-up of Bomber Command for the purpose of adding strength to Coastal and Army Co-operation Commands and overseas requirements are like the amateur politician who imagines that the millennium will arrive through the simple process of dividing available cash equally between all. Ignorance of what is available for distribution is such that he does not realise that the outcome would be to give every individual £50 once at the cost of wrecking the entire industrial organisation and income of the country. Similarly, if the Medium and Heavy Bomber Operational Squadrons of Bomber Command were distributed between the many claimants for favour on the one hand, none of these claimants would receive anything more than a mere morsel towards the satisfaction of their alleged requirements. On the other hand, our only offensive weapon against Germany would be destroyed. One cannot win wars by defending oneself. The defensive use of offensive weapons must therefore be reduced to the irreducible minimum necessary to survival.

2. There is surprising ignorance about the effective strength of Bomber Command. On an average, it is able to produce about 30 operational medium and heavy night bomber squadrons and six light bomber squadrons, the latter with no reserves of aircraft behind them. The first-line strength of the operational squadrons of Bomber Command represents no more than 11 per cent of the total operational first-line strength of the Royal Air Force and Fleet Air Arm, and well over half of the effort of this 11 per cent is directed against Naval and Military targets. (See Appendix 'A'.)†

3. People often point to the vast training organisation behind Bomber Command. It is truly and necessarily great. What such people fail to realise, however, is that the Bomber Command training organisation provides the whole requirements for reinforcing all the bomber forces overseas and much else besides. At present, for instance, it provides 148 pilots per month for overseas bomber squadrons, including 95 complete crews. In the past this quota has at times been even higher. In addition to this monthly output for overseas requirements, Bomber Command has trained, equipped, and then given away or lent to Coastal and Overseas Commands and other claimants, 24 squadrons in the last year. It also provides the crews of two squadrons employed on special SOE and SIS

---

* A successful initial attack on the key element of either of those systems would demand the immediate concentration of effort on the remaining elements of that system to exploit the initial success.

† Not printed.

duties, and crews to man a great number of experimental and special training Units, which work for all Commands, at home and overseas. Finally, it is required from time to time to find from 300 to 400 operational aircraft in order to make up the 1,000 or so required to carry out specially heavy attacks against objectives of major importance.

4. Another common error is to suppose that the effort of the Command is devoted to the bombing of targets in Germany remote from and chosen without reference to the general military and naval situation. Nothing could be further from the truth. Approximately 50 per cent of the total operational effort of Bomber Command during the twelve months April 1941–March 1942 was directly employed against the enemy's sea power. (For details see Appendix 'B'.)* During the last three months the proportion has been well over 50 per cent. All the remaining efforts of Bomber Command have great direct effect on the Naval and Land war situations as a whole.

5. For all practical purposes the squadrons of Bomber Command have done almost all the air-sea mining throughout the War. They have laid some 2,000 odd mines from the beginning of the War to December 1941, which accounted for one known enemy ship per 26·2 mines (it can be reasonably assumed that at least one unknown ship was sunk or damaged for every known one). The Command has enormously increased its mining efforts since the beginning of March this year. It is now laying mines at the rate of over a thousand a month, and already the reports on sinkings are greatly increased over anything previously achieved. Amongst particular mining successes can be counted the closing of the Kiel Canal to heavy enemy ships for some four months and the damaging and sinking of several of the highly specialised Baltic train ferries and ice-breaker ferries on which the enemy is peculiarly dependent. Also, the sinking by mining and bombing, according to the evidence from German wreck charts, of something over 300 enemy-employed ships, and damage to a large number more. The mining of both *Scharnhorst* and *Gneisenau*, and also other enemy war vessels and troop transports, some of which are known to have resulted in great loss of life, must also be taken into account.

6. The story of the *Scharnhorst* and the *Gneisenau* is perhaps an outstanding incident of the vast effect of the small Bomber Command force on the Naval war. These two ships, on their one and only raid into the Atlantic, did appalling damage to our shipping, sinking no fewer than 19 vessels, totalling 150,000 tons. They returned to Brest to refuel and turn round prior to repeated forays, but since that date, over fifteen months ago, and almost entirely due to the efforts of Bomber Command, they have never been able to sink another British or Allied ship. They have only just been able to escape and stagger home, both of them striking air-laid mines on their return journey. Since their arrival in Kiel for repair, *Scharnhorst* is known to have been further hit and heavily damaged. *Gneisenau* has been so heavily hit and damaged by bombs that she has been taken away to Gdynia and largely dismantled. There are circumstantial reports that it has been decided to abandon repair on her. *Prinz Eugen* was also hit at Brest by Bomber Command. The direct result of the damage to these important ships is that *throughout the war the German Fleet has never been able to operate as an entity, with all that that implies.* It was directly due to the immobilisation of *Scharnhorst* and *Gneisenau* that *Bismarck* essayed her lone raid in the Atlantic and to that fact can be largely credited her subsequent destruction. To Bomber Command, therefore, can also largely be credited the fact that *Tirpitz* in her turn is now a lone wolf.

7. Additional and direct effects on the war efficiency of the German Fleet arising from the efforts of Bomber Command are as follows:

* Not printed.

(i) The main enemy Naval base at Kiel has been repeatedly and very heavily damaged by bomber attacks. A large number of workshops have been destroyed and the dockyard workers' quarters have received vast damage, with all that that implies in regard to delay in Naval supply and repair work.

(ii) Amongst other instances the depot ship *Monte Olivia* was bombed and burnt out, with reported heavy loss of life to submarine ratings and some of *Gneisenau's* crew who were living on board.

(iii) There is no doubt that the morale of enemy Naval personnel, who largely come from the German coastal ports, has been seriously affected by the heavy damage, and the raid-fear inflicted on these ports and their populace.

8. The six light bomber squadrons of Bomber Command are responsible for the close support of the Army in the event of invasion, or in the event of the Army proceeding overseas. They provide the bait for Fighter Command without which the fighter sweeps would be ineffective, because the enemy often refuses battle unless bombers are present. They also provided the detachments at Malta which so successfully attacked the enemy's lines of communication. They are known to have sunk some 51,000 tons of enemy shipping on that supply line. By direct bomber attack in European waters, these light bomber squadrons have sunk some 250,000 tons, seriously damaged 287,000 tons and damaged a further 380,000 tons.

9. The effects on the enemy's submarine activities have been equally important. It is known that repeated interference with submarine crew training resulted from our mine laying in the Baltic and the Bight. It is known that, from time to time, considerable damage has been done to submarine building yards at Hamburg, Kiel, Rostock, Emden and other ports. Heavy damage has been done to the three main submarine Diesel engine factories at Augsburg, Deutz, and the Germania yards at Kiel. Damage has also been done to one of the two main submarine accumulator factories. In addition, the widespread damage done to German industry by Bomber Command, perhaps especially in Cologne, must have profoundly affected the submarine campaign. It is known that, at the submarine building yard at Le Trait, three submarines under construction were reported destroyed and between 150 and 200 workmen employed on them were killed.

10. It can also be safely assumed that damage has been inflicted on submarines operating from the French West Coast ports. Although the actual cause of loss of a submarine which does not return can seldom be determined, the known losses inflicted on German shipping remove any shadow of doubt that some losses, possibly considerable losses, have been inflicted on the enemy submarine fleet by Bomber Command's minelaying. (For details see Appendix 'C'.)*

11. By smashing up the invasion ports and the invasion barges and shipping concentrations, there is little doubt that Bomber Command had impressed upon the enemy the difficulties, if not the impossibility, of invasion. Indeed history may yet show that invasion was prevented by the Command. It certainly can be if it is attempted in future.

12. The known results of the bombing raids on Germany show that they cause vast destruction and vast embarrassment to the enemy. It would not be possible in a note to detail a tithe of the known immense damage occasioned in Germany. Whilst it takes approximately some 7,000 hours of flying to destroy one submarine at sea, that was approximately the amount of flying necessary to destroy one-third of Cologne, the third largest city in Germany, in one night, a town of vast industrial import. 250 of its factories were damaged or destroyed. This must have gravely embarrassed the enemy war effort in every direction. The towns of Rostock, Lübeck, Emden and Cologne have all been

* Not printed.

destroyed to or beyond the point where they can be counted as a liability rather than an asset to the enemy. The very heavy damage to the Heinkel Aircraft Factory at Rostock is known to have gravely affected the Heinkel output, and is reported to have had the most serious effect on the enemy's air war on all fronts, and also at sea. The Focke Wulf works at Bremen have also been very seriously damaged.

13. The destruction of the Renault Factory might be counted as an astounding achievement of Bomber Command. Achieved in a few hours with practically no loss it is clearly a major victory against the enemy's land forces such as no other of our forces has yet achieved. Through the loss of this factory and the Matford works at Poissy, the enemy is known, according to the Ministry of Economic Warfare, to have been permanently deprived of the armoured fighting vehicles and transport equipment sufficient for the formation and maintenance of 10/11 motorised divisions.* The important enemy aircraft factories at Gennevilliers and Salmsons have been destroyed. The Goodrich rubber factory, and the Thomson Houston and Ericsson Electrical gear factory have also been destroyed, and 16 neighbouring factories damaged, some 'on a tremendous scale'. (Interpretation Report.)

14. One of Germany's most pressing problems is to maintain her system of internal transport. The German Transport Minister recently stated that, unless the problem of improving the transport facilities inside Germany were solved, Germany's victory would be imperilled. He said that in the western and north-western regions of Germany, where frequent bombing raids had taken place, the transport service was carried out under extremely difficult conditions. An additional strain is thrown upon the railways by the diversion of traffic caused by sea-mining, while the bombing of ports and industrial towns has been shown to do much incidental damage to the transport services. It is known that the internal transport system has recently been put under the control of the German Minister responsible for armaments production and that very high priorities, which must interfere with other production, have been given to locomotive and wagon construction, and repair. Concomitant with this declaration by the Reich Minister, Bomber Command virtually destroyed the important rolling-stock works at Cologne and severely damaged another such works at Bremen.

15. To the negative, but very worthwhile, credit of Bomber Command can be counted the strain upon the enemy of maintaining an enormous and ever-increasing mine-sweeping effort, and also the establishment and maintenance of the largest anti-aircraft and ARP organisation in the world. Some three-quarters of a million personnel are employed on anti-aircraft duties in Germany. If one adds to that the ARP services, the damage and repair organisation and the manufacture of guns and their anti-aircraft ammunition, and also the mine-sweeping and mined ship repairing organisation, there is little doubt that the very existence of Bomber Command costs the enemy the whole-time services of at least three million able-bodied personnel. In addition, Bomber Command forces the enemy to maintain a large and rapidly increasing force of night fighters, which now amounts to some 300 aircraft. Many of these are Ju. 88's, a type which, if released, could be used effectively for the attack of our shipping. There is no doubt that, if the Bomber policy was to be abandoned, the release of this vast man-power for other essential work would be of the greatest value to Germany. The release of the twin-engine fighter bombers and the anti-aircraft guns for service on the eastern front and in the Mediterranean would have a powerful and perhaps even a decisive effect on those campaigns.

* More than our Libyan operations have destroyed in the whole course of the war, almost as much as we lost at Dunkirk.

16. The purely defensive use of air power is grossly wasteful. The Naval employment of aircraft consists of picking at the fringes of enemy power, of waiting for opportunities that may never occur, and indeed probably never will occur, of looking for needles in a haystack. They attempt to sever each capillary vein, one by one, when they could, with much less effort, cut the artery. Bomber Command attacks the sources of all Naval power, rather than the fringes of the one type of enemy Naval operation which obviously menaces us—the submarine. An outstanding example of waste of air effort is the taking away from Bomber Command of all the Hampden aircraft for conversion to torpedo bombers for the defence of this country. These squadrons have, for more than two years, exercised continuous and direct pressure on Germany. Since allocation to Coastal Command they have done practically nothing. It is within the bounds of possibility that they will never get an opportunity to achieve anything. The enemy is not such a fool as to flaunt valuable ships within reach of shore-based aircraft otherwise than when compelled by circumstances to do so, and then only on his own terms as to weather and fighter cover.

17. To sum up, Bomber Command provides our only offensive action yet pressed home directly against Germany. All our other efforts are defensive in their nature, and are not intended to do more, and can never do more, than enable us to exist in the face of the enemy. Bomber Command provides the only means of bringing assistance to Russia in time. The only means of physically weakening and nervously exhausting Germany to an extent which will make subsequent invasion a possible proposition, and is therefore the only force which can, in fact, hurt our enemy in the present or in the future secure our victory. It is the only type of force which we shall ever be able to bring directly against Japan.

18. Finally, it is apparent that an extraordinary lack of sense of proportion affects outside appreciation of the meaning, extent and results of Bomber Command's operations. What shouts of victory would arise if a Commando wrecked the entire Renault factory in a night, with a loss of seven men! What credible assumptions of an early end to the war would follow upon the destruction of a third of Cologne in an hour and a half by some swift moving mechanised force which, with but 200 casualties, withdrew and was ready to repeat the operation 24 hours later! What acclaim would greet the virtual destruction of Rostock and the Heinkel main and subsidiary factories by a Naval bombardment! All this, and far more, has been achieved by Bomber Command; yet there are many who still avert their gaze, pass by on the other side, and question whether the 30 squadrons of night bombers make any worth-while contribution to the war.

Bibliography

This bibliography is in no sense inclusive, being confined to the principal available sources of information and guidance. The nature of the Public Records Acts precluded examination of all but a small amount of material in the British Ministry of Defence Air Historical Branch. The British and American official histories of the Strategic Air Offensive do, however, cite original sources wherever possible. Moreover, log books and target maps used by aircrew have been made available. It has also been possible to obtain access to official or semi-official material which is not subject to the limitations of the Public Records Acts.

Primary Material

Bomber Command *Quarterly Review*
Bombers' Baedeker
Dickens Report on German Night Defences
Galland, Adolf, *Birth, Life and Death of the German Day Fighter Arm*
History of German Night Fighting
Police Presidents' Reports of attacks on German cities
Rise and Fall of the German Air Force, 1933–45
Bomber Command Squadron Operational Record Books
Strategic Air War Against Germany, 1939–45: Report of British Bombing Survey Unit
United States Strategic Bombing Survey: Papers on the German War Economy

Secondary Material

Air Ministry, *Bomber Command Continues*, HMSO, 1942
    Operational Research in the RAF, HMSO, 1963
Arnold, General H. H., *Global Mission*, Hutchinson, 1951
Barker, Ralph, *Strike Hard, Strike Sure*, Chatto & Windus, 1963
Batty, Peter, *The House of Krupp*, Secker & Warburg, 1966
Bekker, Cajus, *The Luftwaffe War Diaries* (translated from the German and edited by Frank Ziegler), Macdonald, 1967
Belfield, Eversley & Essame, H., *The Battle for Normandy*, Batsford, 1965
Bennett, Air Vice-Marshal D. C. T., *Pathfinder*, Muller, 1958
Birkenhead, The Earl of, *The Prof in Two Worlds*, Collins, 1961
Blackett, P. M. S., *Studies of War*, Oliver & Boyd, 1962
Boyle, Andrew, *Trenchard*, Collins, 1962
Bryant, Arthur, *The Turn of The Tide*, Collins, 1957
    Triumph in The West, Collins, 1959
Butler, J. R. M., (Ed.), *Grand Strategy*, Vol. II, History of the Second World War, HMSO, 1957
    Grand Strategy, Vol. III, Part II, History of the Second World War, HMSO, 1964
Churchill, Winston S., *Second World War*, Vols I–VI, Cassell, 1948–54

Clark, Ronald W., *Battle for Britain*, Harrap, 1965
  Tizard, Methuen, 1965
Collier, Basil, *The Defence of the United Kingdom*, History of the Second World War, (Ed. J. R. M. Butler), HMSO, 1957
Craven, W. E. & Cate, J. L., *The Army Air Forces in World War II*, Vols. I, II & III, University of Chicago Press, 1948, 1949 and 1951
Davis, Kenneth S., *The American Experience of War, 1939–45*, Secker & Warburg, 1967
Divine, David, *The Broken Wing*, Hutchinson, 1966
Douhet, Giulio, *The Command of the Air* (Tr. Dino Ferrari). Reprinted by Permission of Coward-McCann, Inc., New York, 1942
Ehrman, John, *Grand Strategy*, Vols. V & VI, History of the Second World War (Ed. J. R. M. Butler), HMSO, 1956
Ellis, L. F., *Victory in the West*, Vol. I, History of the Second World War (Ed. Sir James Butler), HMSO, 1962
Frankland, Noble, *The Bombing Offensive Against Germany*, Faber & Faber, 1965
Gibson, Wing Commander Guy, *Enemy Coast Ahead*, Michael Joseph, 1946
Greenfield, R. R. (Ed.), *Command Decisions*, Harcourt Brace, 1959
Gwyer, J. M. A., *Grand Strategy*, Vol. III, Part I, History of the Second World War (Ed. J. R. M. Butler), HMSO, 1964
Harris, Marshal of the RAF, Sir Arthur, *Bomber Offensive*, Collins, 1947
Herington, John, *Air War Against Germany and Italy, 1939–43*, Australia in the War of 1939–45. Air, Vol. III, Canberra, Australian War Memorial, 1954
Hibbert, Christopher, *The Battle of Arnhem*, Batsford, 1962
Howard, Michael (Ed.), *The Theory and Practice of War*, Cassell, 1965
Irving, David, *The Destruction of Dresden*, Kimber, 1963
  The Mare's Nest, Kimber, 1964
Ismay, General Lord, *The Memoirs of Lord Ismay*, 1960
Jackson, Maj.-Gen. W. G. F., *The Battle for Italy*, Batsford, 1967
Jasper, Ronald, *George Bell, Bishop of Chichester*, Oxford, 1967
Johnson, E. A., *Defence By Committee: The British Committee of Imperial Defence, 1885–1959*, Oxford, 1960
Jones, H. A., *The War in the Air*, Oxford, 1937
Lawrence, W. J., *No. 5 Bomber Group, RAF*, Faber & Faber, 1951
Liddell Hart, B. H., *Memoirs*, Cassell, 1965
Macmillan, Harold, *The Blast of War*, Macmillan, 1967
Playfair, Major-General I. S. O., *The Mediterranean and Middle East*, Vols. I–III, History of the Second World War (Ed. Sir James Butler), HMSO 1960–67
Price, Alfred, *Instruments of Darkness*, Kimber, 1967
Quester, George H., *Deterrence Before Hiroshima: The Airpower Background of Modern Strategy*, Wiley, 1966
Richards, Denis, *Royal Air Force 1939–45*, HMSO, 1953
Roskill, Captain S. W., *The War at Sea*, Vols. I & II, History of the Second World War (Ed. J. R. M. Butler), HMSO, 1954 and 1956
  The Strategy of Sea Power, Collins, 1962
Ross, Squadron Leader J. M. S., *Royal New Zealand Air Force*, War History Branch, Department of Internal Affairs, Wellington, New Zealand, 1955
Rumpf, Hans, *The Bombing of Germany* (tr. Edward Fitzgerald), Muller, 1963
Saundby, Air Marshal Sir Robert, *Air Bombardment—The story of its Development*, Chatto & Windus, 1961
Saward, Group Captain Dudley, *The Bomber's Eye*, Cassell, 1959
Sears, S. W. and McFarland, M. W., *Air War Against Hitler's Germany*, Harper & Row, 1964
Shirer, William L., *The Rise and Fall of the Third Reich*, Secker & Warburg, 1962

Slessor, Marshal of the RAF, Sir John, *The Central Blue*, Cassell, 1956
Snow, C. P., *Science and Government*, Oxford University Press, 1961
  A Postscript to Science and Government, Oxford University Press, 1962
Smith, Constance Babington, *Evidence in Camera*, Chatto & Windus, 1958
Taylor, A. J. P., *The Origins of the Second World War*, Hamish Hamilton, 1961
Taylor, Telford, *The Breaking Wave*, Weidenfeld and Nicolson, 1967
Tedder, Marshal of the RAF, Lord, *With Prejudice*, Cassell, 1966
Thompson, Wing Commander H. L., *New Zealanders with the Royal Air Force*, Volumes I and II,
  War History Branch, Department of Internal Affairs, Wellington, New Zealand, 1953 and 1956
Webster, Sir Charles, and Frankland Noble, *The Strategic Air Offensive Against Germany, 1939–45*,
  Vols. I–IV, History of the Second World War, (Ed. Sir James Butler), HMSO, 1961
Wheeler-Bennett, John W., *The Nemesis of Power*, Macmillan, 1953
Woodward, Sir Llewellyn, *British Foreign Policy in the Second World War*, History of the Second
  World War (Ed. Sir James Butler), HMSO, 1962

References

The reader is referred to the bibliography for details of the authorities and sources cited below. The three authorities, respectively British, American and (in subject matter) German most frequently cited are: *The Strategic Air Offensive Against Germany; The United States Army Air Forces in World War Two; The Rise and Fall of the German Air Force*. These authorities are cited as: *SAO*; CC; *R & F*.

Preface (pages 1–6)

1. *SAO*, Vol. I.
2. CC, Vol. I, p. 591.
3. *Poems*, 1933. The phrase was quoted frequently in 1940 at the time of the Battle of Britain.

Introduction (pages 7–30)

1. *SAO*, Vol. 1, p. 315.
2. Frankland, *Bombing Offensive Against Germany*, p. 33.
3. Frankland, *op. cit.*, p. 17.
4. Frankland, *op. cit.*, p. 35.
5. Frankland, *op. cit.*, p. 39.
6. Boyle, *Trenchard*, p. 241.
7. A statement corroborated by others who have been interviewed, not only in relation to Staff College instruction but to Cranwell also.
8. See Liddell Hart, *Memoirs*, Vol. I, *passim*.
9. Harris, *Bomber Offensive*, p. 53.
10. Garnett (Ed.), *Letters of T. E. Lawrence*.
11. See especially Slessor, *Central Blue* and Trenchard, *With Prejudice*, for accounts of the development of this policy.
12. *SAO*, Vol. IV, pp. 72–6.
13. CC, Vol. I, p. 68.
14. In 1966 and 1967 the *RUSI Journal* published many contributions by soldiers and airmen on land-air co-operation. With very few exceptions, comments by soldiers were critical of the RAF, and *vice versa*.
15. Frankland, *op. cit.*, p. 46.
16. Frankland, *op. cit.*, p. 40.
17. House of Commons debate 270, Col. 632. The portentous note struck in Baldwin's speech did nothing to encourage clear thinking.
18. Harris makes it plain in his account of the strategic air offensive that he regarded close relations with Churchill as a necessary ingredient for success.
19. 'Such ideas . . . were aberrations inspired by excessive optimism or excessive depression.' *SAO*, Vol. I, p. 10.
20. See p. 306 on Mustang's effect.
21. By comparison with these achievements, the 'Dams' raid of 16 May 1943, and other well publicised operations, were of little strategic importance, however gallantly executed.
22. *SAO*, Vol. I, p. 310.
23. See also Chapters 6 and 9, *passim*.
24. See also *SAO*, Vol. II, p. 193.
25. Spaatz did, however, insist on being strategically independent of British control: see p. 260 *et seq.*
26. General Arnold's subordinate position in the American Service hierarchy is made plain in Craven and Cate and other accounts.
27. CC, Vol. I, p. 51.
28. CC, Vol. I, p. 38.
29. CC, Vol. I, p. 44.
30. CC, Vol. I, p. 36.
31. Possibly the clearest example of this strategic doctrine is reflected in the strength, deployment—and cost—of British ground and air forces in the Gulf. By far the biggest element in the sums allocated for this area was spent on airfields and equipment to operate the new types of American aircraft which the RAF still hopes to receive into service over the next three years. Of the 6,000-odd Service personnel stationed in the Gulf, nearly 2,000 are RAF.

Chapter 1 (pages 33–57)

1. *SAO*, Vol. I, pp. 34–51.
2. There appears to have been no notion of a 'strategic air offensive' in the mind of the German High Command, any more than there was in 1939, or, in terms of one independent of a land campaign preceded by an amphibious assault, in 1940.
3. CC, Vol. I, Part I, *passim*.
4. Yet it was Churchill who was 'vigorous in economy' as Chancellor of the Exchequer

from 1924 to 1929, and specifically over the Services Votes. *SAO*, Vol. I, p. 57.

5. *SAO*, Vol. I, p. 54.

6. *R & F*, p. 1.

7. *R & F*, p. 3.

8. Writing in a foreword to Fredette, *The First Battle of Britain*.

9. Slessor, *Central Blue*.

10. See also *R & F*, Part I.

11. *R & F*, p. 3.

12. Divine, *Broken Wing*, p. 163.

13. Divine, *Broken Wing*, pp. 161–2.

14. Divine, *op. cit.*, p. 190

15. Information from interviews.

16. Information from interviews.

17. Cf. *The Special Relationship: an Anglo-American Myth, in a Century of Conflict 1850–1950*, Essays for A. J. P. Taylor.

18. The 'Principal Targets' map, accompanying the US Air War Plans Department appreciation of 11 September 1941, showed the UK as a base for 52 groups of bombardment and pursuit aircraft. *CC*, Vol. I, facing p. 152.

19. See also Greenfield, *Command Decisions*, *passim*.

20. Greenfield, *Command Decisions*, p. 11.

21. Richards, *Royal Air Force, 1939–45*, Vol. I, p. 21.

22. See also Collier, *Defence of the United Kingdom, passim*.

23. Collier, *Defence of the United Kingdom*, and Pile, *Ack-Ack, passim*.

24. Richards, *Royal Air Force, 1939–45*, Vol. I, p. 8.

25. Howard (ed.) *Theory and Practice of War*: Essays Presented to Captain B. H. Liddell Hart, p. 194.

26. Slessor, *Central Blue*, p. 183; *SAO*, Vol. I, pp. 72 and 136.

27. *SAO*, Vol. I, p. 57.

28. *SAO*, Vol. I, p. 54.

29. *SAO*, Vol. IV, pp. 62–70, gives the minutes of this meeting.

30. *SAO*, Vol. IV, pp. 76–83.

31. Divine, *Broken Wing*, p. 208. See also Scott, *Vickers*, for an extended account of this incident.

32. General Galland, in captivity, supplied details of how Lufthansa was used as a Luftwaffe training establishment.

33. Shirer, *Rise and Fall of the Third Reich*, p. 282.

34. Shirer, *passim*.

35. *SAO*, Vol. I, pp. 95–6, 100, 112, 115, 120, 124.

36. These were 13 main plans, drafted in October 1937, together with several subordinate and alternative plans. All concentrated on strategic targets in the military, not the 'morale' sense. *SAO*, Vol. I, p. 94 *et seq.*

37. Slessor, *Central Blue*, p. 221. See also generally Ch. IX, Bomber Policy—the Czech Crisis—Anglo French—Staff Conversations.

38. Shirer, *Rise and Fall of the Third Reich*, p. 590. There are many other references in Shirer to the improbability of an air offensive against Britain as a priority strategic offensive. There is also the more material fact that the German Air Force did not possess a heavy bomber element. *R & F, passim*.

39. *R & F*, p. 7.

40. *R & F*, p. 11.

41. *R & F*, p. 11.

42. *CC*, Vol. I, p. 65.

43. *CC*, Vol. I, p. 65.

44. See 'Germany First: The Basic Concept of Allied Strategy in World War II in Greenfield, *Command Decisions*.

45. Greenfield, *Command Decisions*.

46. Greenfield, *op. cit.*

47. *CC*, Vol. I, p. 150.

48. Arnold, *Global Mission*, p. 111.

49. Arnold, *op. cit.*, p. 102.

50. *CC*, Vol. l, pp. 49–71.

51. *CC*, Vol. I, pp. 49–71.

52. Greenfield, *Command Decisions*, p. 15.

Chapter 2 (pages 58–78)

1. Clark, *Tizard*, p. 116 *et seq.*, gives an admirable account of the events and the atmosphere of this period.

2. See *passim SAO*, Vol. I; Collier, *Defence of the United Kingdom;* Roskill, *War at Sea*, Vol. I.

3. Divine, *Broken Wing*, p. 187.

4. Divine *op. cit.*, pp. 195–6.

5. Divine, *op. cit.*, p. 211.

6. Barker, *Strike Hard, Strike Sure*, p. 57.

7. *SAO*, Vol. I, pp. 76–7.

8. *SAO*, Vol. IV, pp. 99–102.

9. *SAO*, Vol. I, p. 118.

10. *SAO*, Vol. I, p. 118.

11. Slessor, *Central Blue*, p. 206.

12. Harris, *Bomber Command*, p. 35.

13. See also Slessor, *Central Blue, passim.*

14. See also Divine, *Broken Wing, passim.*

15. Divine, *Broken Wing,* p. 198.

16. Slessor, *Central Blue,* pp. 175-6.

17. Harris, *Bomber Command,* p. 144.

18. Information from interviews.

19. *SAO,* Vol. I, p. 113.

20. *SAO,* Vol. I, p. 100.

21. Information from interviews.

22. *SAO,* Vol. I, p. 112 fn.

23. Clark, *Tizard,* p. 162.

24. Clark, *Tizard.*

25. See Blackett, *Studies of War, passim.*

26. *Operational Research in the Royal Air Force,* pp. 43-4.

27. Clark, *Tizard,* p. 189.

28. Eddleston (Ed.), *Correspondence from Sir Isaac Newton to Roger Cotes.*

29. Clark, *op. cit.,* p. 190.

30. Clark, *op. cit.,* p. 190.

31. Clark, *op. cit.,* p. 190.

32. Information from interviews.

33. *SAO,* Vol. I, pp. 107-10.

34. Richards, *Royal Air Force, 1939-45,* Vol. I, p. 73.

35. Adam Smith, *John Buchan,* p. 460.

36. Richards, *op. cit.,* p. 73.

37. Richards, *op. cit.,* p. 74.

38. Several sources for the eve of war period convey the twin—and seemingly contradictory—emotions of apprehension about German power and relief that the issue was to be put to the test. See especially Slessor, *Central Blue;* Ismay, *Memoirs.*

39. See *passim:* Taylor, *Origins of the Second World War;* Shirer, *Rise and Fall of the Third Reich.*

40. Taylor, *Origins of the Second World War.*

41. Shirer, *Rise and Fall of the Third Reich,* p. 590.

42. *R & F,* p. 42.

43. *R & F,* p. 18.

44. *Strategic Air War Against Germany, 1939-1945.*

45. *R & F,* p. 45.

46. *R & F,* p. 45.

47. Gibson, *Enemy Coast Ahead,* p. 31.

Chapter 3 (pages 81-102)

1. After analysing German air defence, the authors of AWPD/1 came to the conclusion 'that by employing large numbers of aircraft with high speed, good defensive fire power and high altitude, it is feasible to make deep penetrations into Germany in daylight'. This was predicated upon the belief that US bombers, initially B.17s and B.24s, and subsequently B.29s and B.32s, could beat off attacks from fighters currently deployed by the GAF'. CC, Vol. I, p. 600. But the succeeding passage introduces a note of ambiguity: 'To cope with improved German models in the future, the AAF should begin immediately development of an escort plane with speed somewhat superior to that of heavy bombers, with equal range, great firepower, and heavy armor.' But such a programme was not put in hand, doubtless due in part to the apparent success enjoyed by the Eighth Air Force in 1942 and early 1943. When the GAF struck hard, in the late summer of 1943, the Eighth was left unescorted for all but short-range operations.

2. The British Official History of the strategic air offensive examines internal Air Staff arguments and disputes in some detail; not so Craven and Cate.

3. It is unfortunately the case that Bomber Command was not well served by propaganda during the strategic air offensive. HMSO published several highly coloured accounts of operations in the early part of the war: the *Bomber Command Quarterly Review,* although technically a classified publication, was in part a vehicle for Harris' views; between 1943 and 1945 John Strachey, then serving at the Air Ministry, broadcast frequently on the BBC, arguing the supremacy of air power to an audience which had no means of measuring the value of what he was saying.

4. It must be remembered here that the role of Bomber Command in 'grand strategy' is given but passing reference in the British History of the Second World War devoted to the Supreme Command; nor is there much to be found in Churchill's History or the accounts by Alanbrooke, Ismay and others who moved between Whitehall and Washington.

5. See Harris, Ismay, Slessor and other authorities. See also *SAO,* Vol. I, *passim.*

6. *SAO,* Vol. I, p. 368 fn.

7. *SAO,* Vol. I, p. 144.

8. *SAO,* Vol. I, p. 144.

9. See Chapter 9, *passim.*

10. It is a curious and unfortunate fact that that

those in the Air Ministry who advocated 'selective' bombing spent little or no time seeking closer co-operation with like minded Americans; and *vice versa*. Tedder was an exception to this unfortunate insularity of outlook, but his *control* over strategic air operations in 1944 was tenuous, to say the least.

11. Like all others prosecuting the war, Churchill was inconsistent, and not least about the strategic air offensive. In September 1940, he declared that 'only the Air Force could win the War'. In October 1941, he pointed out: 'One has to do the best one can, but he is an unwise man who thinks there is any *certain* method of winning this war, or indeed any other between equals in strength. The only plan is to persevere.' In 1942 he observed with 'sorrow and alarm' that Bomber Command was not expanding as quickly as he and Harris desired, and backed the latter strongly over the '1000 Plan'. See *SAO*, Vol. I, *passim*.

12. Richards, *Royal Air Force, 1939–45*, p. 406; Divine, *Broken Wing*, p. 213.

13. Slessor, *Central Blue*, pp. 238–9.

14. A partial exception to this policy was Eisenhower's temporary control of all Allied Air Forces committed to Overlord. But Churchill remained opposed to any integrated Strategic Air Force.

15. See Part III.

16. See p. 101.

17. Lord Snow's *Science and Government*, in which these comparisons were made, is a highly partisan account of the Cherwell-Tizard controversy. Much of what Lord Snow avers was effectively rebutted by Professor R. V. Jones in his article in the *Oxford Magazine* of 9 May 1963, entitled *Lord Cherwell's Judgement in World War II*. See also Clark, *Tizard*; and Birkenhead, *The Prof in Two Worlds*. Lord Birkenhead's biography is as partisan as Lord Snow's Lectures; historians should be grateful to Mr Clark and Professor Jones for their objectivity over issues which were more important than temperamental discord between a greatly gifted scientist and a great public servant.

18. *SAO*, Vol. I, *passim*; Snow, *op. cit.*; Roskill, *War at Sea*, Vols 1 and 2; much information from interviews and correspondence. Captain Roskill and Sir John Slessor have earned the gratitude of historians by their fair

and careful appraisals of requirements and priorities during this period, especially in the correspondence columns of *The Times*.

19. *SAO*, Vol. I, p. 167.

20. Harris, *Bomber Offensive*, p. 137.

21. *SAO*, Vol. I, pp. 257, 310; see also Tedder, *With Prejudice*, p. 253.

22. *SAO*, Vol. I, p. 282.

23. *SAO*, Vol. I, pp. 422–3.

24. See for example *Bomber Command Continues* published by the Air Ministry in 1942; the series of broadcasts by John Strachey between March 1943 and May 1945 had a comparable purpose.

25. Squadron Operational Record Books are especially revealing on this aspect of operations.

26. *SAO*, Vol. I, pp. 347–8.

27. See p. 107 *et seq.* for a fuller consideration of this report.

28. But the secrets of High Wycombe were jealously guarded and little liaison permitted with, for example, the Ministry of Economic Warfare.

29. *SAO*, Vol. I, pp. 348, 463–5.

30. Information from interviews.

31. *SAO*, Vol. I, p. 135.

32. *SAO*, Vol. I, p. 135.

33. The Squadron Operational Record Books for 2 Group in 1940 show a sortie rate, let alone a missing rate, which would have been quite 'unacceptable' if the circumstances had been less desperate—and the aircraft more heavily crewed or of greater credibility.

34. *SAO*, Vol. I, p. 309.

35. These figures are calculated from the Night Raid tables in *SAO*, Vol. I, pp. 431–3.

36. *SAO*, Vol. IV, pp. 431–3.

37. Harris, *Bomber Offensive, passim*.

38. Including one by a member of the Cabinet Office and another by a High Court Judge!

39. Clark, pp. 309–13. Tizard did criticise Cherwell's obsession with area bombing at night and he personally believed that a more economic use of Bomber Command was *first* to assist in defeating the U-boat. But a strategic air offensive was not otherwise objectionable, provided it was not conducted at crippling cost to Bomber Command.

40. Mr Clark makes it clear that one reason for Tizard's decline was his failure to appreciate the significance of German radar for bombing

purposes, and that he made so uncharacteristic a mistake largely because he believed Cherwell was intriguing against him.

41. See Slessor, *Central Blue*, pp. 412 *et seq.*, on the psychological effect of the 30 May Cologne raid, especially in the United States, where sympathy for British defeats was mingled with some apprehension about their effects. See also Bryant, *Turn of the Tide*, p. 392. Many of those interviewed have also emphasised that the dark days of 1942 were infinitely more depressing than the 'siege year'—1940. Bomber Command, nevertheless, was in the fight, and, from Whitehall as well as East Anglia, was *seen* to be in the fight.

42. *SAO*, Vol. I, p. 378.
43. *SAO*, Vol. I, p. 366.
44. See Chapter 6.
45. Harris, *Bomber Offensive*, p. 101.
46. See also p. 339.
47. See p. 340.
48. *SAO*, Vol. I, p. 173.
49. *SAO*, Vol. I, p. 182.
50. *SAO*, Vol. I, pp. 342-3.
51. *SAO*, Vol. I, p. 343.
52. Butler, *Grand Strategy*, Vol. III, Part II p. 528.
53. Harris, *Bomber Offensive*, pp. 105-7.
54. *SAO*, Vol. I, pp. 411, 415.
55. Information from interviews.
56. *SAO*, Vol. I, p. 149.
57. *SAO*, Vol. I, p. 153.
58. *SAO*, Vol. I, p. 159.
59. *SAO*, Vol. I, p. 159.
60. *SAO*, Vol. I, p. 165.
61. *SAO*, Vol. I, p. 332.
62. *SAO*, Vol. I, p. 334.
63. Butler, *Grand Strategy*, Vol. III, Part II, p. 510. This figures should be treated with caution; it represents what extra aircraft Bomber Command might have had; it does not represent net loss of squadrons.
64. Slessor, *Central Blue*, pp. 358, 404-13.
65. Most of the scientists interviewed stressed that they were expected by serving officers to confine their contribution to the analysis of real and simulated events involving equipments; advice on the effect of those equipments on the course of operations, let alone the concept of them, was unwelcome. The scientists in question may be biased, but the continuing national debate on the 'brain drain' suggests that British

scientists are still expected by their employers to stick to a narrow and literal interpretation of their tasks. That science and strategy have a causal, and not a casual relationship was not, on the whole, grasped in Whitehall during World War Two.

66. *SAO*, Vol. I, p. 368.

Chapter 4 (pages 103-27)

1. As with analyses of Bomber Command sorties, missing rates etc., figures for the 8th Air Force are taken from official statistics. CC, Vol. II, pp. 841-52, summarises every operation flown by the 8th from the UK between 17 August 1942 and 31 December 1954. For later periods, analyses are based on figures given in the text.

2. *SAO*, Vol IV, pp. 434-6.
3. CC, Vol. II, p. 220.
4. Shirer, *Rise and Fall of Third Reich;* Rumf, *Bombing of Germany, passim.*
5. Dickens Report, *passim*; information from interviews.
6. *R & F*, pp. 273-87.
7. The USAAF was so convinced of the supreme value of this bombsight that, for security reasons, it was removed from the B.17s which were flown by Bomber Command in 1941. CC, Vol. I, p. 601. The Norden bombsight *was* very accurate in ideal conditions.
8. *SAO*, Vol. I, pp. 356-7.
9. *SAO*, Vol. I, p. 185.
10. *SAO*, Vol. I, p. 186.
11. Herington, *Air War Against Germany and Italy 1939-43: Australia in the War of 1939-45,* Ch. 13—'Fighter Command in 1942,' is one of the few accounts of this period which concedes that this force was under employed.
12. *SAO*, Vol. I, pp. 215 *et seq.*
13. The German JU. 87 dive bomber.
14. Plus information from interviews.
15. Information from interviews. A balance had constantly to be struck between the good effect on aircrew morale of any equipment which eased their navigational and target identification problems, and the fact that indiscriminate use of it aided the enemy.
16. A radar system known as *Naxos* was devised early in 1943, which enabled German night fighters to home on emissions from the H_2S radar. At about the same time, some Bomber Command aircraft were equipped

with *Morica*, a tail warning radar. See Price, *Instruments of Darkness*, pp. 139 *et seq.*

17. Information from interviews.

18. Information from an interview. An implied reference to this loss to Bomber Command is also made in Harris, *Bomber Offensive*, pp. 65–6. Aircraft in 1 Group were eventually armed with this weapon. Harris, *op. cit.*, p. 163.

19. Information from interviews.

20. *SAO*, Vol. IV, pp. 434–6.

21. Squadron Operational Books; information from interviews.

22. See the *Daily Mail*, 5 September 1939.

23. Dickens Report *passim*; given the relative inactivity of the German night fighter force until mid-1943, this supposition was not unreasonable. But it should be noted that, between July 1942 and May 1945, it has been estimated that, in night operations, 2,278 bombers were destroyed by fighters, compared with 1,345 by flak. *SAO*, Vol. IV, p. 439.

24. *SAO*, Vol. III.

25. Operational Record Books of 9, 51 and 83 Squadrons.

26. As footnote 25.

27. Operational Record Books of 82 and 105 Squadrons.

28. Operational Record Book of 82 Squadron.

29. Harris, *Bomber Offensive*, p. 42.

30. *SAO*, Vol. I, p. 176.

31. The figures given on p. 76 of *R. & F* are for 1940 and are of 2,790 of all operational types, including aircraft in units stationed in Norway, but available for operations against the United Kingdom. Although severe losses were suffered in the day and night raids of 1940 and early 1941, this force was the biggest single element of the German Air Force available for operations at the time. See also Taylor, *The Breaking Wave*, p. 321.

32. *SAO*, Vol. I.

33. *SAO*, Vol. I, p. 241.

34. *SAO*, Vol. I, p. 241.

35. *SAO*, Vol. IV, pp. 431–6.

36. Information from interviews. In the Main Force groups expectation of life was reckoned at three months; Clark, *Tizard*, p. 308.

37. Barker, *Strike Hard, Strike Sure*, p. 77.

38. The Boston, Mosquito and Ventura entered squadron service in 1942.

39. *SAO*, Vol. I, p. 438.

40. Collier, *Defence of the United Kingdom*, p. 274.

41. *SAO*, Vol. I, *passim*; Lawrence, *No. 5 Bomber Group*; information from interviews.

42. *SAO*, Vol. I, p. 439. The proportion is greatly exaggerated; moreover the factory staffs were 'going slow' in order to hinder the German war effort; information from interviews.

43. *SAO*, Vol. IV, p. 242.

44. Coastal Command was not placed under Admiralty *command*; Slessor, *Central Blue*, pp. 482–4.

45. *The Alanbrooke Diaries* are particularly revealing on this aspect of the Supreme Command.

46. *SAO*, Vol. IV, p. 241.

47. Harris, *Bomber Offensive*, pp. 38, 39, 69, 138–40.

48. See *The Times* of 17 November 1967; information from interviews. Of all aircraft devoted or diverted to the Battle of the Atlantic, sailors appear to have felt that the Liberator was the most effective.

49. Slessor, *Central Blue*, pp. 469–70.

50. Sonar is a refinement of the Royal Navy's World War Two 'Asdic', a device for locating submarines by transmitting radio waves which reflect back from any large, submerged object.

51. Roskill, *War At Sea*, Vol. I, p. 350.

52. Roskill, *op. cit.*, Vol. II, p. 95.

53. Roskill, *op. cit.*, Vol. II, p. 205.

54. Roskill, *op. cit.*, Vol. II, p. 205 fn.

55. Information from interviews.

56. *SAO*, Vol. I, p. 343.

57. Harris, *Bomber Offensive*, *passim*.

58. Lawrence, *No. 5 Bomber Group*, pp. 138–43.

59. CC, Vol. II, pp. 641–52.

60. See ante.

61. CC, Vol. I, p. 655.

62. CC, Vol. II, p. 213.

63. See ante.

64. CC, Vol. I, pp. 608–9.

65. See p. 52 and notes to Chapter 3.

66. Herington, *Australia in the War of 1939–45; Air War Against Germany and Italy, 1939–43*, pp. 336–55.

67. CC, Vol. II, p. 209 *et seq.*

68. See pp. 318–19 for a comparison of intelligence from different sources.

69. CC, Vol. II, p. 322.

Chapter 5 (pages 128–52)

1. *SAO*, Vol. IV, pp. 431–6, 455–6.

2. *SAO*, Vol. I, p. 407: the Report of the Cologne Police President on the raid does not give damage in tons, but by domestic and industrial units. By this account, 3,330 houses were destroyed and 9,510 were damaged; 36 'factories and industrial installations' were destroyed.

3. It is sometimes forgotten that the German people and the German economy were not placed on a war footing equivalent to the United Kingdom, let alone the Soviet Union until 1944.

4. Information from interviews.

5. *SAO*, Vol. I, p. 189.

6. *SAO*, Vol. I, p. 201.

7. See also *SAO*, Vol. I, pp. 112–14.

8. Information from interviews.

9. *SAO*, Vol. I, p. 207.

10. *SAO*, Vol. I, p. 205 fn.

11. *SAO*, Vol. I, p. 205 fn.

12. *SAO*, Vol. I, p. 208.

13. *SAO*, Vol. IV, p. 26.

14. Information from interviews.

15. That no British bomber would ever appear over Germany.

16. *SAO*, Vol. I, p. 209 fn.

17. Squadron Operational Record Books contain some pretty caustic references to Pathfinders' faulty navigation and marking. See, for example, p. 242.

18. *SAO*, Vol. I, p. 215.

19. *SAO*, Vol. I, p. 226.

20. *SAO*, Vol. I, p. 225.

21. Harris, *Bomber Offensive*, p. 43.

22. Gibson, *Enemy Coast Ahead*, pp. 119–20. Gibson quotes Shirer's Berlin Diary to the effect that ' . . . from what I saw of the bombings myself and from what I have been told by German airmen, I think it is highly improbable that the German Army would ever be able to assemble in the ports of Boulogne, Calais, Dunkirk, Ostend or on the beaches, enough barges or ships to launch an invasion in the force that would be necessary.'

23. See *passim*: Taylor, *Breaking Wave*; Fleming, *Operation Sea Lion*. The Significance of Bomber Command's achievement should not be minimised because it was deterrent rather than destructive.

24. Berlin was first bombed on 25 August 1940; *SAO*, Vol. I, p. 152. The attack was retaliatory, as was that on Mannheim on 16 December, thus emphasising that it is impossible to determine who 'started' area bombing. The more material point is that the German bomber force had the capacity to bomb with relative accuracy; Bomber Command had not.

25. Squadron Operational Record Books; information from interviews.

26. See above, fn. 18.

27. See Chapter 3, fn. 38.

28. *SAO*, Vol. I, pp. 218–19, 224–5. The Official History suggests that crew reports were inaccurate; my reading of Operational Record Books is that crews were remarkably honest; information from interviews suggests that reports were doctored to make them palatable for propaganda purposes. Only by reading *all* Squadron ORBs and *all* station and Group summaries (and a blanket of secrecy is still cast over the latter) would a definitive conclusion be possible.

29. A favourite phrase in Air Ministry propaganda.

30. *SAO*, Vol. I, p. 231.

31. *SAO*, Vol. I, p. 178.

31. *SAO*, Vol. I, p. 178.

32. *SAO*, Vol. I, p. 230.

33. *SAO*, Vol. I, pp. 230–1.

34. *SAO*, Vol. I, p. 231.

35. *SAO*, Vol. I, *passim*.

36. *SAO*, Vol. I, *passim*.

37. *SAO*, Vol. I, *passim*.

38. Lawrence, *No. 5 Bomber Group, passim*.

39. Several senior serving and retired officers made this point. But the 'other side of the hill' tells a different story. The first three years of the strategic air offensive helped British morale; only the last two years of it affected the German *outlook*, and then only incidentally.

40. *SAO*, Vol. I, p. 179. The sole value of the Butt Report was that it made photographic evidence the conclusive element in arguments about accuracy. Unfortunately, one effect of this criterion for assessment was to elevate photographic evidence beyond its deserts. See also p. 318.

41. *SAO*, Vol. I, p. 179; the Report is, ominously, not mentioned in Churchill's own

History of World War II, although his reaction to it arguably marks the moment when he made a distinction between the strategic air offensive being politically necessary and it being strategically significant.

42. The German Air Force collectively reacted to the strategic air offensive in a professsional and flexible way; the Hitler 'apparatus' wavered between ignoring and exaggerating it. See pp. 314-15.

43. Harris, *Bomber Offensive*, p. 73.

44. *SAO*, Vol. II, p. 3 gives a figure of more than '170 operational Lancasters'; the order of battle is 178.

45. Between July 1942 and May 1945 it has been estimated that no less than 2,072 bombers were lost from 'unknown causes'; *SAO*, Vol. IV, p. 439.

46. *R & F*, pp. 185-201. See also *The History of German Night Fighting, passim.*

47. *R & F*, Part II—'The German Air Force on the Offensive, 1939-1942.' See also p. 205, summarising the situation at the beginning of 1943.

48. *History of German Night Fighting*, p. 5.

49. Price, *Instruments of Darkness*, pp. 20-1.

50. Price, *op. cit.*, pp. 31 *et seq.*

51. See *passim*: Collier, *Defence of the United Kingdom*; Gibson, *Enemy Coast Ahead*.

52. *R & F*, p. 106.

53. *History of German Night Fighting*, pp. 5, 6.

54. Information from interviews; the mounting loss of experienced crews in this period had much the same effect on morale as in 1943-44; see p. 200.

55. Although initially only by flak units.

56. The full directive is reproduced in Appendix 2.

57. Hitler's refusal to listen to professional strategic or tactical advice became more pronounced as the balance tilted from offensive operations to defence of the 'New Order's' frontiers and then of the Reich itself. Hitler's contempt for the OKW and Service hierarchy in general has been shown by Mr A. J. P. Taylor and Sir John Wheeler-Bennett to be reasonable enough in the case of men like Keitel and Worlimont. The senior ranks of the German Air Force, despite or perhaps because of Goering, seem to have been well supplied with officers who understood the defensive requirement very well. See *R & F, passim.*

58. All references on pp. 145 are taken from the Official History.

59. Saward, *Bomber's Eye*, p. 195.

60. Price, *Instruments of Darkness*, pp. 104-5.

61. Information from interviews; it is an interesting point that the names of Kammhuber and Martini will not be found in the Official History or Harris' Bomber Offensive; so far as I have been able to discover scientific staffs assisting Bomber Command in this crucial radar battle were not interviewed in connection with the Official History: I am very conscious of the inadequacy of treatment in my pages. The enquiring reader will find that the stories and studies by Price and Saward fill many gaps; in extenuation it may finally be said that some scientists are still subject to security restraints of the most rigorous kind.

62. This may be considered a partisan assertion; it is not mine, but that of a senior officer closely engaged in radio counter-measures; his view is, moreover, corroborated by much circumstantial evidence.

Chapter 6 (pages 155-95)

1. Note too that '. . . I was always willing to join the United States in a direct assault across the Channel [but] I was not convinced that this was the only way of winning the war . . . The fearful price we had to pay in human life and blood for the great offensives of the First World War was graven in my mind.' *The Second World War*, Vol. V, p. 514.

2. *R & F*, p. 208. General Galland's views are elaborated in a British Air Ministry intelligence report, AD1 (k) 373/1945.

3. *R & F*, pp. 219-21.

4. *R & F*, p. 206.

5. *R & F*, p. 208.

6. The Casablanca Conference is well documented. Slessor's *Central Blue* and Tedder's *With Prejudice* are among the less inhibited accounts; Arnold's *Global Mission* is uninformative—possibly because of an unexpressed American conviction that the strategic air offensive was a straightforward affair of General Spaatz and the Norden bombsight.

7. CC, Vol. II, p. 236.

8. Harris, *Bomber Offensive*, p. 137.

9 See also Appendix 2, p. 331 *et seq.*

10. *SAO*, Vol. II, p. 5 and *passim.*

11. See Chapter 9, *passim*.

12. This defect may be remedied when Professor Michael Howard's contribution to *Grand Strategy*, Vol. IV, in the History of the Second World War, is published.

13. Tedder, *With Prejudice*, p. 389.

14. Ismay, *Memoirs, passim*, is illuminating on the very natural fears of another Somme.

15. *SAO*, Vol. II, p. 92.

16. Harris, *Bomber Offensive, passim*.

17. March 1943, when Bomber Command's offensive began by the Harris criterion, saw 10,591 tons of bombs dropped, compared with 2,675 in March 1942; *SAO*, Vol. IV, p. 456.

18. Tedder, *With Prejudice*, pp. 256–7.

19. See pp. 22, 58.

20. CC, Vol. II, p. 843.

21. Harris, *Bomber Offensive*, pp. 144–5.

22. *SAO*, Vol. IV, p. 445.

23. See also *SAO*, Vol. IV, pp. 371–8.

24. Batty, *House of Krupp*.

25. Batty, *op. cit.*, p. 195.

26. Batty, *op. cit.*, p. 195.

27. This striking phrase occurs in one of the many aircrew log books examined.

28. The Official History (from which the quotations are drawn), *Bomber Command Quarterly Review* and the *Strategic Air War Against Germany, 1939–45* have all been used to check this assessment.

29. *Bomber Command Quarterly Review*, April–June 1942.

30. *SAO*, Vol. II, p. 158. See also Irving, *Mare's Nest* and Babington Smith, *Evidence in Camera*, for a full analysis of the effectiveness of Bomber Command attacks on flying bomb sight. Paradoxically Craven and Cate devote more attention to this destructive offensive (as important as the 1940 attacks on invasion ports) than do Webster and Frankland.

31. Irving, *Mare's Nest, passim*.

32. CC, Vol. II, pp. 841–52.

33. CC, Vol. II, pp. 841–52.

34. CC, Vol. II, pp. 841–52.

35. Not so, in fact.

36. CC, Vol. II, p. 229.

37. CC, Vol. II, p. 335.

38. CC, Vol. II, p. 655.

39. *R & F*, p. 270.

40. *R & F*, p. 274.

41. These figures, like others, quoted in the text, are based on those of sorties and losses given in the narrative parts of the Official History, supplemented by the statistical analyses in Vol. IV.

42. Price, *Instruments of Darkness*, p. 120.

43. Price, *op. cit.*, p. 120.

44. Professor Jones, when Deputy Director of Scientific Intelligence, regarded Martini as one of the most capable officers in the German Air Force. This opinion appears to have been widely shared.

45. *History of German Night Fighting*, pp. 7–12.

46. *R & F*, p. 277.

47. *History of German Night Fighting*, pp. 12–18.

48. Bennett, *Pathfinder*, pp. 197 *et seq.*, reveals that from mid-1943 onwards 8 Group losses began to increase steadily, Mosquito Squadrons excepted.

49. Information from interviews.

50. *History of German Night Fighting, passim*.

51. Price, *Instruments of Darkness*, p. 192.

52. Information from interviews.

53. CC, Vol. II, p. 10.

54. CC, Vol. II, p. 482.

55. CC, Vol. II, pp. 566–7.

56. CC, Vol. II, p. 232.

57. Sears and McFarland, *Air War Against Hitler's Germany*, p. 65.

58. CC, Vol. II, p. 263.

59. CC, Vol. II, p. 689.

60. CC, Vol. II, pp. 841–52.

61. CC, Vol. II, *passim*, pp. 841–52.

62. See Chapter 10.

63. CC, Vol. II, pp. 841–52.

64. CC, Vol. II, p. 371.

65. *SAO*, Vol. II, CC, Vol. II, *passim*.

66. CC, Vol. II, pp. 634–5.

67. See Appendix 2.

68. *SAO*, Vol. II, p. 57.

69. It was not until 28 March 1945 that these notions hardened into the Churchill view that: 'It seems to me that the moment has come when the question of bombing of German cities simply for the sake of increasing the terror, *though under other pretexts*, should be reviewed. Otherwise we shall come into control of an utterly ruined land. The Foreign Secretary has spoken to me on this subject, and I feel the need for more precise concentration upon military objectives . . . .' The Official History comments sharply that 'This was, perhaps, among the

least felicitous of the Prime Minister's long series of war-time minutes.' One can see why; a case of the pot and the kettle, even although 'under other pretexts' has been italicised in this footnote only. But Churchill's point was not invalid because he made it. One may note, incidentally, that Woodward's *British Foreign Policy in the Second World War* (a semi-official publication) ignores the whole issue.

70. *SAO*, Vol. II, p. 57.

71. CC, Vol. II, p. 277.

72. Ehrman, *Grand Strategy*, Vol. I, p. 206.

73. Arnold, *Global Mission*; CC, Vol. II, *passim*.

74. Ehrman, *Grand Strategy*, Vol. V, p. 204.

75. This criterion was adopted by the Research and Experiments Department of the British Ministry of Home Security and by *Bomber Command Quarterly Review*.

76. Information from interviews.

77. *SAO*, Vol. II, p. 9.

78. *Bomber Command Quarterly Review*, October–December 1943 and January–March 1944.

79. *Bomber's Baedeker*.

80. See Chapter 10, *passim*.

81. *Bomber Command Quarterly Review*, October–December 1943.

82. For a summary of the British Survey see *Strategic Air War Against Germany, 1939–45*.

83. *SAO*, Vol. II, p. 195.

84. The overall missing rate was nine per cent.

85. *R & F*, p. 283.

86. See pp. 288 *et seq*.

87. *SAO*, Vol. II, p. 48 and fn.

88. See also *SAO*, Vol. III, pp. 78–80.

89. *SAO*, Vol. II, p. 43.

90. *SAO*, Vol. II, p. 44 fn.

91. *SAO*, Vol. II, p. 51.

92. *SAO*, Vol. II, p. 51.

93. *SAO*, Vol. II, p. 51.

94. Information from interviews.

95. *SAO*, Vol. II, p. 9.

96. *SAO*, Vols. II, III *passim*.

97. *SAO*. Vol. II, p. 46.

98. *SAO*, Vol. II, p. 35.

99. CC, Vol. II, pp. 841–52.

100. *SAO*, Vol. II, p. 47.

101. *SAO*, Vols. II and IV, and *Bomber Command Quarterly Review* provided the basis for these figures.

102. Rumf, *Bombing of Germany*.

103. *Strategic Air War Against Germany, 1939–45* contains a summary of BBSU Reports.

104. *SAO*, Vol. II, pp. 287–8.

105. *SAO*, Vol. IV, pp. 371–8.

106. This assessment is drawn from figures published in *Strategic Air War Against Germany, 1939–45*.

107. A figure which is implicitly contested in *R & F, passim*.

108. By 1945 incendiaries had served their turn; see p. 300.

Chapter 7 (pages 196–215)

1. Much of the information in this chapter is from interviews with former aircrew.

2. CC, Vol. II, p. 322; Pathfinder led missions became habitual however, in 1944.

3. *History of German Night Fighting*, p. 9.

4. CC, Vol. II, pp. ix–x.

5. *SAO*, Vol. IV, pp. 440–4.

6. Sears & McFarland, *Air War Against Hitler's Germany*, p. 121.

7. But see Yeates, *Winged Victory*, concluding passages, *contra*.

8. Ketton Cremer, *A Norfolk Gallery*, p. 95.

9. It was perhaps this visual link with the embattled British civilians below which gave the RAF a special place in their attentions.

10. Irving, *Destruction of Dresden*, p. 131.

11. See also Barker, *Strike Hard, Strike Sure*.

12. See Barker, *op. cit.*

13. *SAO*, Vol. II, pp. 3–4.

14. CC, Vol. II, p. 343.

15. CC, Vol. II, pp. 564–72.

16. Information from interviews.

17. Information from an interview.

18. For security reasons, Main Force Groups were given little information on 100 Group operations.

19. Price, *Instruments of Darkness*, p. 165.

20. Irving, *Destruction of Dresden*, p. 113.

21. In other words: Pathfinders would ground mark with red target indicators on 'blind' *Oboe* information; the indicators would be dropped four minutes before the Main Force; green ground markers would be further identification; three minutes allowed for this particular crew to make its bombing run. And as to the Chemnitz raid: Marking by H_2S identification, supported if necessary by sky marking from *Oboe* information; bombing

instructions to be received from Master Bomber; aiming point a red target indicator within green indicators; *alternatively* the centre of green indicators; bombing height 15,000 feet; course (over target) almost due north.

Chapter 8 (pages 216–48)

1. See *SAO*, Vols. II–IV, *passim*.
2. CC, Vol. II, p. 719.
3. CC, Vol. II, p. 720.
4. The 8th did not return to Schweinfurt for four months, when heavy attacks again became possible—and were certainly necessary; see also CC, Vol. II, p. 704.
5. CC, Vol. II, pp. 348–69.
6. It should be remembered that 'cost effectiveness' is the sum of many factors; the 15th Air Force had the capacity to lose eleven aircraft on 2 November without affecting its ability to continue operating, even although this loss was, statistically, the equivalent of a missing rate of approximately ten per cent.
7. Much of the information on pp. 218–24 is derived from interviews; the quotation on p. 223 is from Gibson, *Enemy Coast Ahead*.
8. Slessor, *Central Blue*, p. 376.
9. Harris, *Bomber Offensive*, p. 165.
10. ' . . . the largest producer in Germany of mechanical parts for radar equipment'—Lawrence, *No. 5 Bomber Group*, p. 139. This is hyperbole, but Friedrichshafen was extremely important for the production of night fighter radar, and from that aspect alone was a priority target.
11. Bennett, *Pathfinder*, *passim*.
12. *SAO*, Vol. II, pp. 186–7.
13. This percentage is calculated from the figures given in *Strategic Air War Against Germany, 1939–45*.
14. *SAO*, Vol. II, pp. 151–2.
15. Rumf, *Bombing of Germany*, pp. 77–91.
16. *SAO*, Vol. IV, pp. 371–18.
17. CC, Vol. II, pp. 841–52.
18. CC, Vol. II, pp. 841–52.
19. CC, Vol. II, pp. 841–52.
20. Rumf, *Bombing of Germany*, p. 78.
21. CC, Vol. II, p. 697.
22. Sears and McFarland, *Air War Against Hitler's Germany*, pp. 91–2.
23. Sears and McFarland, *op. cit.*, p. 85.
24. Sears and McFarland, *op. cit.*, p. 85.

25. Sears and McFarland, *op. cit.*, p. 86.
26. Sears and McFarland, *op. cit.*, p. 86.
27. Sears and McFarland, *op. cit.*, p. 95.
28. *SAO*, Vol. II, pp. 273–5.
29. *R & F*, pp. 205–6.
30. CC, Vol. II, pp. 749–50.
31. CC, Vol. II, p. 582.
32. CC, Vol. II, p. 729.
33. CC, Vol. II, p. 582.
34. A concept originating in May 1943. CC, Vol. II, pp. 418–19.
35. CC, Vol. II, p. 582.
36. CC, Vol. II, pp. 566–7.
37. Slessor was Eaker's Deputy from January 1944, as well as being Commander Royal Air Force Mediterranean and Middle East; *Central Blue*, pp. 557–90.
38. *R & F*, pp. 249–70.
39. Herington, *Australia in the War of 1939–45; Air War Against Germany and Italy, 1939–43*, pp. 635–6.
40. The RAAF element in Bomber Command, as distinct from its members serving in RAF squadrons, provided between five and ten per cent of the operational force during the most critical winter months of 1943–44; Herington, *op. cit.*, pp. 636–7.
41. Herington, *op. cit.*, pp. 639–40.
42. Herington, *op. cit.*, pp. 639–40.
43. Herington, *op. cit.*, p. 639.
44. Information from interview; in published account, Bennett states: ' . . . at one stage I thought that the backbone of the Pathfinder Force was really broken' (*Pathfinder*, p. 209). It must be pointed out that the true measure of 8 Group's contribution to the 1943–44 battles, particularly over Berlin, is that virtually every major operation was flown above a dense cloud layer—yet heavy area damage was caused; *SAO*, Vol. II, p. 194 fn. But elsewhere, the official historians argue that Berlin operations were strategically insignificant, and tactically, an outright defeat; *SAO*, Vol. II, pp. 190–6.
45. Information from interviews.
46. *SAO*, Vol. IV, pp. 171–8.
47. See also Harris, *Bomber Offensive*, p. 189.
48. *SAO*, Vol. II, p. 199.
49. See, for example, p. 258.
50. Herington, *op. cit.*, p. 639.
51. Rumf, *The Bombing of Germany*.
52. *History of German Night Fighting*, p. 30.

53. *History of German Night Fighting*, p. 17.

54. *SAO*, Vol. II, p. 199.

55. Harris, *Bomber Offensive*, p. 190.

56. Bennett, *Pathfinder*, p. 283.

57. CC, Vol. II, pp. 841–52.

58. Much of the information on pp. 246–7 is derived from the *R & F* and the *History of German Night Fighting*, *passim*.

Chapter 9 (pages 251–87)

1. Eisenhower apparently expected Spaatz to be his Overlord deputy for air operations, and found the presence of Leigh-Mallory—and possibly Tedder—baffling; CC, Vol. III, p. 7.

2. CC, Vol. II, p. 280; *SAO*, Vol. III, p. 3.

3. CC, Vol. III, p. 306.

4. CC, Vol. III, p. 306.

5. CC, Vol. III, p. 6 and *passim*.

6. CC, Vol. III, p. 723.

7. CC, Vol. III, p. 717.

8. See *SAO*, Vol. IV, pp. 171–8.

9. Information from interviews.

10. Price, *Instruments of Darkness*, pp. 199–211. Radar was employed in two operations, which were variants on classic deception tactics, namely: the pretence of a Main Force through the clever deployment of a minor one, and a feint away from the real objective in order to allow the main force to attack it.

11. CC, Vol. III, *passim*.

12. See Bekker, *Luftwaffe War Diaries*, pp. 322–9. This study appeared in English in 1967, too late for much investigation here of the jet programme.

13. CC, Vol. III, p. 655; Tedder was a persistent critic of the idea that soldiers could get airmen to fight their battles for them; *With Prejudice*, pp. 559 *et seq.*

14. *SAO*, Vol. III, p. 12.

15. *SAO*, Vol. III, pp. 151, 153; Operational Record Book of 617 Squadron; information from interviews.

16. *SAO*, Vol. III, p. 75; the phrase occurs in a section entitled 'The reward of dissension, November 1944–January 1945'.

17. See Appendix 2.

18. See especially Tedder, *With Prejudice* and Ehrman, *Grand Strategy*, Vol. V, *passim*.

19. *SAO*, Vol. III, p. 17.

20. *SAO*, Vol. III, p. 19–21; CC, Vol. III, pp. 80–1.

21. *SAO*, Vol. III, p. 21; but it must also be pointed out that the Joint Chiefs of Staff in appointing Spaatz as Commander, USTAF had placed him in an invidious position; Ehrman, *Grand Strategy*, Vol. V, p. 292.

22. CC, Vol. III, *passim*.

23. *SAO*, Vol. III, *passim*; US commanders *appear* not to have listened to Harris in the early months of 1944, although they respected his leadership and convictions; but they increasingly came to copy him—see p. 282; see also Tedder, *With Prejudice*, pp. 504 *et seq.* for the view that Harris' views were always shared by Spaatz.

24. *SAO*, Vol. III, p. 25.

25. *SAO*, Vol. III, p. 27.

26. *SAO*, Vol. III, p. 32; CC, Vol. III, p. 80. In contrast to the approach habitually adopted, the British Official History deals with this meeting primarily in terms of the issues —area bombing, the Transportation Plan, tactical interdiction or oil targets—while Craven and Cate concentrate on the command problem.

27. *SAO*, Vol. III, p. 35.

28. *SAO*, Vol. IV, pp. 167–70.

29. *SAO*, Vol. III, pp. 35–7. It is stated therein that 'Sir Arthur Tedder was now constitutionally in a position to issue a bombing directive to General Spaatz and Sir Arthur Harris' and, on 17 April, did so; the copy sent to Spaatz was, however, signed by the American Lieutenant General Walter Bedell Smith, Eisenhower's Chief of Staff; the copy sent to Harris was signed by Air Vice-Marshal J. M. Robb, Deputy Chief of Staff (Air) at the Air Ministry; *SAO*, Vol. IV, p. 170.

30. *Bomber Command Quarterly Reviews*, April–June and July–September 1944.

31. Of the attack on Gelsenkirchen on 12 June 'it was estimated that its output, which had amounted to 33,000 tons of oil in May 1944, would amount to nothing in July'; *SAO*, Vol. III, p. 49. There was certainly a marked reduction in overall output in July; *SAO*, Vol. IV, p. 516, drawing on post-war surveys.

32. See CC, Vol. III, *passim*.

33. But see CC, Vol. III, p. 733.

34. CC, Vol. III, pp. 78–9.

35. See also CC, Vol. III, pp. 76–7.

36. See CC, Vol. III, *ad nauseam*.

37. CC, Vol. III, p. 103. The American case for attacking the Crossbow sites by fighter-

bombers and, in support, medium bombers, was based on a major evaluation of alternative methods, including high altitude bombing, at Eglinfield, USA; CC, Vol. III, pp. 98–102. The whole issue is another example of Anglo-American disagreements: US commanders had a good case, and their being overruled certainly rankled with them.

38. CC, Vol. III, p. 104.

38. CC, Vol. III, p. 105 fn.

40. CC, Vol. III, p. 284.

41. CC, Vol. III, pp. 280–2.

42. CC, Vol. III, p. 281.

43. CC, Vol. III, p. 290.

44. See also CC, Vol. III, p. 286.

45. CC, Vol. III, p. 43.

46. But of equal and probably greater significance was the loss of men and aircraft in combat; CC, Vol. III, pp. 46–7; post-war figures indicate that day fighter losses were around 400 in February, of which the majority are likely to have been over Germany. Probably the most objective observation would be that 'Big Week' convinced the Allied commanders by demonstration rather than proof that the German day fighter force would not menace the success of Overlord.

47. But until the final months of the war, when the Ruhr ceased to function because its communications had been destroyed, Bomber Command could claim no outright victories. Other than for this period only Bomber Command's *contribution* to victory is subject to proof.

48. CC, Vol. III, p. 286.

49. Missing rate figures are informative in various ways, but it should be remembered that they are essentially arbitrary; they take no account, for example, of the brutal fact that the loss of ten experienced crews was worse than 20 green ones.

50. CC, Vol. III, pp. 297–8.

51. CC, Vol. III, p. 298.

52. CC, Vol. III, p. 643. The narrative and analysis of the Autumn oil campaign on this and other pages—and in the Strategic Air Offensive—show that by April 1945, German production of petroleum and associated products—predominantly from synthetics—was down to between five and six per cent of its peak output.

53. CC, Vol. III, pp. 640–6.

54. The Combined Chiefs of Staff met in Malta on 30 January 1945, just before the Malta Conference.

55. CC, Vol. III, pp. 302–4.

56. *SAO*, Vol. III, p. 46; on p. 33, Spaatz's 'resistence' to Tedder's Transportation Plan is stressed, as his 'persistent and obstinant advocacy of the oil plan'. *Per contra*, 'General Eisenhower, who leaned heavily on Spaatz in air matters, granted verbal permission on 19 April for the bombing of German oil targets . . .'; CC, Vol. III, p. 175.

57. *SAO*, Vol. III, p. 47.

58. *SAO*, Vol. III, p. 48.

59. *SAO*, Vol. III, p. 49.

60. *SAO*, Vol. III, p. 50.

61. The V-2 menace was, in reality, by no means over; it should be remembered that one of Harris' 'secret weapons' was the argument that indiscriminate rocket attacks on the British population might require defence by even more devastating attacks on German cities.

62. *SAO*, Vol. III, p. 51.

63. Harris, *Bomber Offensive*, pp. 77–81 and *passim*.

64. *SAO*, Vol. III, pp. 52 *et seq*. Tedder's own views remained *basically* unchanged; his priorities were communications and tactical air support, despite his criticisms of ground forces in their assumption of an air umbrella; *With Prejudice*. But in the Autumn of 1944 Tedder was nearly as indecisive about what the next steps should be as his colleagues.

65. The British Air Staff favoured Thunderclap; the Joint Chiefs of Staff, overtly, did not; *SAO*, Vol. III, pp. 98–100; CC, Vol. III, p. 639.

66. CC, Vol. II; *SAO*, Vol. III; Ehrman, *Grand Strategy*, Vol. VI; Greenfield (ed.), *Command Decisions*; Churchill, *Second World War*, Vol. VI; and many lesser authorities, *passim*.

67. CC, Vol. III, pp. 547–92, deals extensively with the logistic problems facing the Tactical Air Forces.

68. See authorities cited in footnote 66.

69. CC, Vol. III, p. 753.

70. CC, Vol. III, pp. 734–5.

71. CC, Vol. III, p. 650.

72. CC, Vol. III, p. 622.

73. CC, Vol. III, p. 83.

74. CC, Vol. III, p. 640; *SAO*, Vol. III, p. 59.

75. Tedder prepared for this and related conferences with characteristic care; *With Prejudice*, pp. 611–15.

76. See p. 185.

77. CC, Vol. III, p. 654.

78. CC, Vol. III, p. 654.

79. CC, Vol. III, p. 654.

80. *SAO*, Vol. III, p. 184.

81. *SAO*, Vol. IV, pp. 416–27, 456–7.

82. The following figures from CC, Vol. III, pp. 793–8 of tonnages dropped throughout the strategic air offensive are revealing: aircraft industry: Bomber Command 29,000; 8th/15th Air Forces 61,671; oil industry (1944–45 only); Bomber Command 90,000; 8th/15th 130,000. The figures are broadly, but not precisely accurate.

83. CC, Vol. III, p. 721.

84. *SAO*, Vol. III, pp. 52–4.

85. *SAO*, Vol. III, p. 63.

86. *SAO*, Vol. III, p. 73. The quotations in the text pages dealing with the Portal-Harris controversy are all drawn from *SAO*, Vol. II, pp. 76–94.

87. CC, Vol. III, Parts 1, 2, 5.

88. CC, Vol. III, p. 727.

89. CC, Vol. III, p. 727.

90. Irving, *Destruction of Dresden*, pp. 151–2.

91. CC, Vol. III, p. 726.

92. 'Frantic' was the code name for a planned series of operations by the 15th Air Force from bases in Russia. The object of these operations was ostensibly to assist the Soviet forces advancing into Germany. Russian co-operation was initially poor, later fair, subsequently nil. This, at any rate, was the American belief; CC, Vol. III, pp. 308–19.

93. The Russian view is, alas for historians in the West, either unobtainable or too subjective for analysis. We should also note, however, that the British and American Official Histories of the Strategic Air Offensive are ambiguous on whether Thunderclap was even ostensibly designed to break German morale or assist the Soviet forces.

94. Irving, *Destruction of Dresden*, pp. 141–2, 172–6, 178, 215. The railways were not in fact included in the sectors marked out for bombing; Irving, *op. cit.*, p. 120. Irving's account is based on primary official sources.

95. CC, Vol. III, p. 649.

Chapter 10 (pages 288–311)

1. The summary in *SAO*, Vol. III, p. 122.

2. *SAO*, Col. III, p. 137.

3. *SAO*, Vol. III, p. 138.

4. *SAO*, Vol. III, *passim*.

5. *SAO*, Vol. IV, pp. 456–7.

6. 'Streaming' still took place; the complexities of feint and deception suggests that the stream alone was no safeguard.

7. Price, *Instruments of Darkness, passim*; information from interviews. It will be appreciated that all information on radio counter-measures is not only unattributable, but had frequently to be given in outline rather than detail.

8. *SAO*, Vol. III, pp. 153–4 *et seq.*; information from interviews; Bennett, *Pathfinder, passim*.

9. *SAO*, Vol. III, pp. 7, 181–3, 188–9, 190–6, 199, 203–5. It must, however, be pointed out that none of these selective attacks was successful by itself. With the exception of the Tirpitz operations, all were rather widely separated in time. None encountered serious opposition from enemy fighters.

10. But the number of Mosquito *night fighter* squadrons available to Bomber Command was still governed by the number supposedly required for Air Defence Great Britain; *SAO*, Vol. III, p. 149 and fn. Arguably the ADGB task in relation to the V-1 increased the extreme reluctance to part with aircraft for offensive purposes; Collier, *Defence of the United Kingdom, passim*.

11. A good example of accurate bombing despite intense flak was the reduction of the Walcheren Fortress in October 1944; *SAO*, Vol. III, p. 196 and information from interviews.

12. Information from interviews.

13. *SAO*, Vol. III, p. 172.

14. *SAO*, Vol. III, p. 177.

15. *SAO*, Vol. III, p. 178.

16. Harris, *Bomber Offensive*, pp. 72–3.

17. *SAO*, Vol. III, pp. 179–80.

18. *SAO*, Vol. III, p. 184.

19. *SAO*, Vol. III, p. 185.

20. *SAO*, Vol. III, *passim*.

21. The *oil* industry *per se* obviously could not disperse as extensively as the aircraft industry; *SAO*, Vol. III, p. 231. But if we take the *synthetics* and *chemical* industries the point is valid.

22. There were 27 attacks on 15 oil plants by Bomber Command in October–December 1944. Only one plant was attacked more than twice, namely Homberg-Meerbeck, which was attacked six times, and in fairly close succession. But the heaviest concentration was 497 aircraft over Leuna on 6–7 December. The average raid strength was in the region of 200 aircraft. Total losses were 57 aircraft; *SAO*, Vol. III, p. 186 and fn.

23. *SAO*, Vol. III, p. 184.

24. Alexander and Romilly, *Privileged Nightmare*, pp. 167–8.

25. It is claimed, at CC, Vol. III, p. 731, that Dresden was destroyed as a communications centre. This is one of those cases which occur in both official histories where post bombing and post war evaluations are considered separately, or the latter conveniently ignored.

26. CC, Vol. III, *passim*.

27. Irving, *Destruction of Dresden*, pp. 144–5.

28. Most of the information given in pp. 305–11, drawn from the final chapters of *R & F*, is corroborated by Bekker, *Luftwaffe War Diaries*.

29. *R & F*, p. 306.

30. *R & F*, p. 352.

31. For a full description of every aspect of the Bomber Command and 8th Air Forces raids and their aftermath see Irving, *Destruction of Dresden*.

Summing Up (pages 312–23)

1. Information from interviews.

2. *R & F*, pp. 401–22.

3. CC, Vol. III, p. 804.

4. *SAO*, Vol. III, p. 284.

5. Information from interviews.

6. CC, Vol. II, pp. 349–65.

7. Information from interviews; see also Foot, *SOE in France*, *passim*.

8. It should also be remembered that Speer could call on the Todt slave labour organisation when the German people went on a war economy in 1944.

9. *SAO*, Vol. III, p. 288.

10. This view appears to have been widely held at Bomber Command Headquarters; information from interviews.

11. Information from interviews: Irving, *Destruction of Dresden*; Rumf, *Bombing of Germany*; Police Presidents' Reports, *passim*.

Index

Index

Note: Where possible, ranks are given as held at the time or in 1945.